TRANSLATION AND SURVIVAL

TRANSLATION AND SURVIVAL

The Greek Bible of the Ancient Jewish Diaspora

TESSA RAJAK

OXFORD
UNIVERSITY PRESS

Great Clarendon Street, Oxford OX2 6DP

Oxford University Press is a department of the University of Oxford.
It furthers the University's objective of excellence in research, scholarship,
and education by publishing worldwide in

Oxford New York

Auckland Cape Town Dar es Salaam Hong Kong Karachi
Kuala Lumpur Madrid Melbourne Mexico City Nairobi
New Delhi Shanghai Taipei Toronto

With offices in

Argentina Austria Brazil Chile Czech Republic France Greece
Guatemala Hungary Italy Japan Poland Portugal Singapore
South Korea Switzerland Thailand Turkey Ukraine Vietnam

Oxford is a registered trade mark of Oxford University Press
in the UK and in certain other countries

Published in the United States
by Oxford University Press Inc., New York

© Tessa Rajak 2009

The moral rights of the author have been asserted
Database right Oxford University Press (maker)

First published 2009

All rights reserved. No part of this publication may be reproduced,
stored in a retrieval system, or transmitted, in any form or by any means,
without the prior permission in writing of Oxford University Press,
or as expressly permitted by law, or under terms agreed with the appropriate
reprographics rights organization. Enquiries concerning reproduction
outside the scope of the above should be sent to the Rights Department,
Oxford University Press, at the address above

You must not circulate this book in any other binding or cover
and you must impose the same condition on any acquirer

British Library Cataloguing in Publication Data
Data available

Library of Congress Cataloging in Publication Data
Data available

Typeset by SPI Publisher Services, Pondicherry, India
Printed in Great Britain
on acid-free paper by the
MPG Books Group, Bodmin and King's Lynn

ISBN 978-0-19-955867-4

Preface

The origins of this book lie in six Grinfield lectures on the Septuagint given at Oxford University in 1995–6. The lectures were entitled 'The Septuagint as a Social and Cultural Artefact'. Grinfield lecturers in recent years have presented an admirably wide variety of approaches to a subject which has sometimes been at risk of becoming arcane. The lecturer in this case (or so I presumed) was chosen in the expectation of bringing together two fields obviously connected but rarely brought together in practice: the study of Hellenistic Judaism, flourishing since the last decades of the twentieth century as perhaps never before, and the study of the Greek Bible itself, in all its intricacies, now also beginning to enjoy a period of creative vigour. The Jewish translations were to be the focus, rather than the Christian Septuagint collection into which they were later gathered. More broadly, a union of several specialist academic disciplines was called for—classics, Judaic studies, and biblical studies (with an admixture of patristics). It transpired that something comparable had been previously attempted within the Grinfield framework, by a distinguished classical historian, and that was in 1979–80 when Arnaldo Momigliano gave the lectures (which, like most Grinfield Lectures, were never published, except in part under other rubrics). He had asked himself, I learnt (through his literary executor Anne Marie Meyer), 'in what sense a lecturer on the Septuagint might lecture without talking about it' and then had taken as his subject 'the nature and limits of Jewish Hellenism or Hellenistic Judaism'. While in no way aspiring to rival Momigliano's authority, scholarship, or wit, I none the less, perhaps rashly and foolishly, sought to take that extra step and to see how one might connect those two areas. I have been delving into the Septuagint ever since.

Given the topic, the audience for my lectures was by no means composed wholly of specialist biblical scholars. I was able to learn much from a range of questions and comments. The text of the lectures has expanded greatly and they have become almost unrecognizable. In almost every way, a huge amount has changed between lectures and book. In the present book, Chapters 4, 5, 6, and 9 had precursors of one kind or another in the lectures. But in thinking about the purpose of my original exercise, and its targeted audience, I have continued on the same path as before, with an ever-increasing sense that the Greek Bible is an important enough part of our cultural past to deserve a presentation to an audience somewhat broader than its usual one.

The crude arguments put forward in the Grinfields have now been greatly refined. One central preoccupation has been much developed, and that is expressed in the subtitle of the book: how we might connect the early history and the character of this vast corpus of translations and texts with the Greek-speaking Jewish world which produced it. Of course, the translations were by no means dissociated from Jerusalem and the land of Israel, as emerges already from the tradition that they originated with translators whom the High Priest himself selected; and some of the translations may even have their origin in the Land of Israel. But the enterprise as a whole is in a real sense the product of a diaspora—the original 'diaspora' indeed, where that word originated. They were the foundations of life for a highly text-centred ethnic and religious minority, in Alexandria but also in the cities of the Eastern Mediterranean, subjected to the impact of powerful imperial cultures, those of Greece and Rome, and of a dominant, 'colonial' language—Hellenistic Greek, the common language, or 'koine'. Yet, for the most part, either the books have been studied apart from their users or the users without their primary books. And users beyond Palestine and Alexandria have simply dropped out of the picture.

The timespan of this study is long, since the translations were a 'work in progress' for nearly four centuries, from perhaps the middle of the third century BCE to probably the mid-second century CE. Towards the end, a new player enters the scene, the early Christian movement, growing out of Judaism itself and therefore in possession of the same body of literature in Greek, which turned the Greek Bible into the Septuagint, a collection made by Christians for Christians.

A thread woven through the chapters is the theme of cultural adaptation in diaspora Jewry. In the Septuagint, we can observe the evolution of Judaism itself in relation to the dominant culture and to successive imperial powers. These developments emerge in the origins and nature of the entire enterprise; in the language of the Septuagint; in the content of the corpus as a whole, especially when the additional material of the 'Apocrypha' and various kinds of small, apparently deliberate, changes to the Hebrew original are taken into account; and, last but not least, in the uses to which the texts were put. It became clear, as I followed this thread, that this largely successful adaptation was achieved more by quiet subversion of norms and of impositions than by forms of collaboration. Scholars studying Hellenistic Jewish communities in the cities of the Greek East concluded some thirty years ago that, far from being the isolated, inward-looking entities of earlier stereotype and caricature, these Jews (and Judaizers), though they had their difficulties, could function as members of the cities in which they lived. From there, some have moved on, correctly I believe, to an even newer appreciation of the potential limits of integration and of the cost of preserving a communal identity. Thus, instead of focusing on these Jews exclusively as practitioners of accommodation, we are now better placed to consider the methods available to them for expressing resistance, subversion or at least reserve. Theory, too, has made a difference to the questions we can ask and the hypothetical answers we give, and I have derived useful models from recent writing on bilingualism and translation theory; on book cultures and textuality; on ethnic strategies and hybridity; and on the weapons and hidden transcripts of the weak.

To understand the Greek Bible's role in the diaspora of the Second Temple period and its aftermath, we need also to grasp what was happening to the Hebrew Bible in those crucial years, and to view the two together. The Bible is not, however, approached here by the more familiar routes of the history of textual traditions or of exegesis. While a premise behind my exploration is indeed that the long survival of canonical texts depends upon the capacity of their users continually to find new readings and new meanings, the approach I have taken is not, on the whole, to dig deeply into the mechanisms of the exegetical process.

At the same time, readers may be disappointed by the number of historical problems that a historian has not managed to solve. Translations, especially those that remain close to their source, are extremely resistant to yielding up the secrets of their origins. These ancient versions were produced anonymously. They do not give away dates or geographical affiliations readily, if at all. Such obstacles became increasingly apparent to me at the time of writing of the Grinfield lectures. I have been fortunate in the extreme to have been able to work in recent years on the more technical aspects of the contextualization of the Septuagint corpus with colleagues in a funded group project. We have been exploring how far it is possible to make legitimate claims about embedding the translations in specific times and places. Here the historical development of the corpus is presumed to be understood only in the most general lines. I have avoided relying on old assumptions, whose foundations we have revealed to be extremely shaky, but I have not been able, given the time of writing, to anticipate new results.

Even if, however, this book does not fully reflect our final conclusions, it could not have been written without the numerous discussions, and the ongoing research of the Arts and Humanities Research Council (AHRC) Parkes 'Greek Bible in the Graeco-Roman World' Project, between 2000 and 2006. I owe an unquantifiable debt to the inspiration of Sarah Pearce, Jenny Dines, and James Aitken (the project's Research Fellow). I suspect they will disagree with some of my ideas, especially on the historicity of the *Letter of Aristeas*, and even perhaps on the very existence over the period in question of an entity which we are entitled to call 'the Jewish diaspora'. But they know that without our work together this book would have looked very different indeed and it would undoubtedly have been much the poorer.

My appreciation goes also to the AHRC and to two successive Directors of the AHRC Parkes Centre for the Study of Jewish/Non-Jewish Relations at the University of Southampton within which the Project operated—first David Cesarani and latterly Tony Kushner, who made the work of the Project possible.

I extend warm thanks to the Grinfield Lectures Committee and to the Faculty of Theology, Oxford University for the honour of the invitation which first took me into the Septuagint and for organizing the lectures. Outside that faculty, Sebastian Brock and Martin Goodman were instrumental in the arrangements and were great sources of support. So too were the Principal and Fellows of Somerville College, who eased the burden of writing and delivery with their ready provision of accommodation and the hospitality of the Senior Common Room.

The University of Reading has tolerated periods of leave which my colleagues in the Classics Department have endured, and the University's Research Endowment Trust Fund has made significant financial contributions to the Greek Bible Project and has also assisted with the support of my own leave. The British Academy has granted conference and travel funding which has contributed to work on the book. I owe a very great debt to Fergus Millar, who most generously read the entire manuscript at a late stage, with incredible speed and care.

Most of this expanded study was written in three exceptionally congenial environments. At the Institute for Advanced Studies in the Hebrew University, Jerusalem, I was a member of a productive and agreeable research group on Hellenistic Judaism and Christian Hellenism whose discussions have played a significant part in my thinking. I thank the organizers of the group, Daniel Schwartz and David Satran, its other participants, and the Director and staff of the Institute. As a Member of the Institute for Advanced Study in Princeton, I brought the book to an advanced stage. I thank the Director and staff there too, as well as the Faculty of the School of Historical Study, and especially Glen Bowersock; they all saw to the provision of a stimulating but wonderfully non-intrusive intellectual environment. In Princeton I also benefited from the excellent facilities of the Speer Library in the Princeton Theological Seminary, and I thank Jim Charlesworth, Ross Wagner, and the Librarian for granting me the privilege of a visiting scholar's study. At Princeton University, Peter Schäfer, Martha Himmelfarb, John Gager, and Elaine Pagels in the Religions Department, and Froma Zeitlin as Director of the Program in Judaic Studies and in Classics, were forthcoming with their friendship and interest, and with practical help too. Kevin Osterloh lent skilled assistance with editing. Finally, during my time as Horace W. Goldsmith Visiting Professor in the Program in Judaic Studies at Yale, the combined impact of my excellent students, my learned colleagues, and the unique resources of the Yale University Library almost led me to rewrite the entire book. I thank in particular the Chair of the Program, Ivan Marcus, the Judaica Librarian, Nanette Stahl, and the Chair of Classics, Christina Kraus. My participation in the postgraduate seminar on biblical interpretation run by Steven

Fraade (of the Program) and John Collins (of the Divinity School) transformed my view of what interpretation is. Steven kindly read and commented on Chapter 4, while drafts of Chapters 1 and 2 were checked by Joshua Burns. Chris Stroup was an able and most willing assistant in IT matters.

Other debts too have been incurred. Erich Gruen's constant support and enthusiasm have meant much. I gladly mention colleagues in the Ancient History Department at Macquarie University, Sydney, and my hosts there, Alanna Nobbs, Sam Lieu, and Edwin Judge; responsive audiences at universities in Australia, the US, Canada, Israel, Germany, and Russia as well as in the UK; my co-chair and colleagues in the Hellenistic Judaism section of the Society of Biblical Literature; and collaborators and advisers of the AHRC Greek Bible Project. I am grateful for the devoted work on the manuscript and bibliography of Michal Molcho, who copy-edited the whole text a second time and is responsible for the index. She also taught me how to use Endnote. My thanks go to the perceptive readers who reviewed the book for the Oxford University Press, and to Hilary O'Shea, Dorothy McCarthy, Kathleen Fearn, and Tessa Eaton at the Press.

Chapter 3 is a revised and expanded version of a chapter originally written for the first volume of the *Cambridge History of Christianity* (2005) and I thank the editors, Margaret Mitchell and Frances Young, and the Syndics of the Cambridge University Press for permission to use it.

My husband, Harry, has gladly and generously travelled all the way with me: I could not have managed without him, but I dare say he would have preferred not to have the book so long in tow. My children, Saul and Dinah, and their partners, have been deeply supportive and always surprisingly interested. My granddaughter, Eve, managed to win the race and appear first. This book is dedicated to the memory of my parents, Sam and Sonia Goldsmith: they would have been delighted to read it but would probably have wondered why it could not have been more concise.

TR
London, July 2008

Contents

Abbreviations	xiv
Introduction	1
From Greek Bible to Septuagint	14
The True Text?	16
The Hebrew Hinterland: Torah and Beyond	20
1. The *Letter of Aristeas* between History and Myth	**24**
Ancient Translation Precedents	24
Interpreting the Tradition	28
The *Aristeas* Narrative	30
Evolution of the Story	34
Fact or Fiction? The Search for Historicity	38
The Bible in the Shrine of Serapis?	43
Reading *Aristeas* as Historical Myth	47
The 'Meaning' of the Story	51
Other Memories of the Early Ptolemies	55
2. Going Greek: Culture and Power in Ptolemaic Alexandria	**64**
Imperialism and Culture	67
Describing the Jews	72
The School of Aristotle and the Jews	74
The Monarch and Judaea	79
Graeco–Egyptians and the Jewish Narrative	82
A Law Code?	84
Jewish Needs and Choices	86
Recipients of Patronage	88
3. The Jewish Diaspora in Graeco-Roman Antiquity	**92**
Diaspora	92
Ideology	100
Diaspora Locations and Populations	102
Jewish Identity	106
Religious Practice in the Diaspora	107

	The Jewish Community	112
	Interaction with Non-Jews	114
	The Ruling Power	119
	Conflict	120
4.	Staying Jewish: Language and Identity in the Greek Bible	125
	Understanding Septuagint Language	127
	Translation Precedents and the 'Dragoman'	136
	A Sacred Text	139
	The Interlinear Theory: Knowledge of Hebrew	143
	Language and Cultural Resistance	152
	Vocabulary and History	162
	Function and Evolution	172
5.	Representing and Subverting Power	176
	Talking about Kings	177
	Wisdom at Court	181
	The Vocabulary of Divine Rulership	185
	The King's Anger	191
	Toppling Idols	193
	Literature and Subversion	204
6.	The Uses of Scripture in Hellenistic Judaism	210
	Preliminaries: Canon and Canonicity	212
	The Hellenistic–Jewish Tradition	216
	The Greek Bible and Jewish Literary Production	222
	Text and Users: Scripture in Action	227
7.	Parallels and Models	239
	The Parallel with Homer	239
	A Comparative Approach to Jewish Biblical Cultures	243
	Situating Hellenistic Judaism	249
	Philo and Josephus	251
	The Biblical Culture of Hellenistic Judaism	255
8.	The Bible among Greeks and Romans	258
	Ptolemy's Legacy	259
	The Exodus Controversies	262
	Further Echoes: Alexandria and Egypt	264

The Roman Milieu	267
The World of Magic	270
Conclusion	276
9. The Septuagint between Jews and Christians	278
The Abandonment Theory	288
Aquila of Pontus	290
Competing Texts	294
Reinterpreting the Evidence	296
Jewish Attitudes to Translation in the Second Century	303
Bibliography	314
Index	367

Abbreviations

AJ	*Jewish Antiquities*
ANRW	W. Haase and H. Temporini (eds.), *Aufstieg und Niedergang der Romischen Welt* (Berlin, 1974–)
B	Babylonian Talmud
Bauer	W. Bauer, W. Arndt, and F. W. Danker (eds.), *A Greek–English Lexicon of the New Testament and other Early Christian Literature* (3rd edn., Chicago, 2000)
BGS	G. Dorival, M. Harl, and O. Munnich (eds.), *La Bible grecque des septante: du judaïsme hellénistique au christianisme ancien* (Paris, 1988)
Bible d'Alex.	*La Bible d'Alexandrie* (Paris, 1986–)
BJ	*Jewish War*
CA	*Contra Apionem*
CAH^2	*Cambridge Ancient History*, 12 vols. (2nd edn., Cambridge, 1924–39)
CCSG	*Corpus Christianorum*
CCSL	*Corpus Christianorum Series Latina*
CIJ	J.-B. Frey (ed.), *Corpus Inscriptionum Iudaicarum*, repr. with a prolegomenon by B. Lischitz (New York, 1975)
CJZC	G. Lüderitz, with J. M. Reynolds (eds.), *Corpus Jüdischer Zeugnisse aus der Cyrenaika* (Wiesbaden, 1983)
CPJ	V. Tcherikover, A. Fuks, and M. Stern, with D. M. Lewis (eds.), *Corpus Papyrorum Judaicarum*, 3 vols. (Jerusalem and Cambridge, Mass., 1957)
DJD	*Discoveries in the Judaean Desert* (Oxford, 1955–)
DNB	*Dictionary of National Biography*
EncJud	*Encyclopaedia Judaica*, 16 vols. (Jerusalem, 1971)
GCS	*Die Griechischen Christliche Schriftsteller der Ersten Jahrhunderts*
Holladay	*Fragments from Hellenistic Jewish Authors*, ed. Carl Holladay, 4 vols. (Chico, Calif., 1983–96)
HR	*A Concordance to the Septuagint and the Other Greek Versions of the Old Testament: (Including the Apocryphal Books)*, ed. E. Hatch and H. Redpath (Oxford, 1897)

Abbreviations

IJO i	*Inscriptiones Judaicae Orientis* i. *Eastern Europe*, Texts and Studies in Ancient Judaism, 101, ed. D. Noy, A. Panayotov, and H. Bloedhorn (Tübingen, 2004)
IJO ii	*Inscriptiones Judaicae Orientis* ii. *Kleinasien*, Texts and Studies in Ancient Judaism, 101, ed. W. Ameling (Tübingen, 2004)
IJO iii	*Inscriptiones Judaicae Orientis* iii. *Syria and Cyprus*, Texts and Studies in Ancient Judaism, 101, ed. D. Noy, A. Panayotov, and H. Bloedhorn (Tübingen, 2004)
J	Jerusalem Talmud
JIGRE	*Jewish Inscriptions of Graeco-Roman Egypt, with an Index of the Jewish Inscriptions of Egypt and Cyrenaica*, ed. W. Horbury and D. Noy (Cambridge, 1992)
JIWE	*Jewish Inscriptions of Western Europe*, ed. D. Noy, 2 vols. (Cambridge, 1993)
JSHRZ	*Jüdischen Schriften aus hellenistisch-römischer Zeit*
LEH	*A Greek–English Lexicon of the Septuagint*, ed. J. Lust, E. Eynikel, and K. Hauspie, (rev. edn., Stuttgart, 2003)
LSJ	*A Greek-English Lexicon*, ed. H. G. Liddell and R. Scott (9th edn., rev. and augmented by H. Stuart Jones, with R. Mackenzie, Oxford, 1996)
LXX	Septuagint
M	Mishnah
MT	Masoretic Text
Muraoka	*A Greek–English Lexicon of the Septuagint*, ed. T. Muraoka (Louvain, 2002)
NETS	*A New English Translation of the Septuagint*, ed. A. Pietersma and B. G. Wright (New York and Oxford, 2007)
OGIS	*Orientis Graeci Inscriptiones Selectae*, ed. W. Dittenberger (Leipzig, 1903–15)
Charlesworth	*The Old Testament Pseudepigrapha*, ed. J. H. Charlesworth, 2 vols. (Garden City, NY, 1983)
PG	*Patrologia Graeca*, ed. J.-P. Migne
PL	*Patrologia Latina*, ed. J.-P. Migne
PSI	*Papyri greci e latini*. Papiri della Società Italiana per la Ricerca dei Papiri (Florence, 1912–79)
Schürer	*The History of the Jewish People in the Age of Jesus Christ (175 BC-AD 135)*, ed. E. Schürer; A New English Edition, rev. and ed. F. Millar, G. Vermes, M. Black, and M. Goodman, 3 vols. (Edinburgh, 1974–87)
Stern	*Greek and Latin Authors on Jews and Judaism*, ed. M. Stern, 3 vols. (Jerusalem, 1974–84)

T	Tosefta
TDNT	*Theological Dictionary of the New Testament* (Grand Rapids, Mich., 1964–74)
TWNT	*Theologisches Wörterbuch zum Neuen Testament*, ed. G. Kittel and G. Friedrich, 11 vols. (Stuttgart: W. Kohlhammer, 1932–79)

NOTE ON TRANSLITERATIONS

Transliterations of both Hebrew and Greek follow a simple, mainly phonetical system. In the case of biblical Hebrew, modern pronunciation is followed.

Introduction

> The translators sit and recycle it all to another
> recycling plan that has no end, and the spirit of God
> hovers above with the whirring wing-blades of a giant fan
> whipping the air, the words whipped over and over like foam.
>
> The translators flee their burning cubicles
> Run out into the streets crying 'Help!'
> And make their way to other, calmer conferences.
>
> Yehuda Amichai (translated by Chana Bloch and Chana Kronfeld)

The Septuagint was the first major translation in western culture. The conversion of the Hebrew Bible into Greek was a new departure for which new tools had to be forged. The size of the initial project alone, the rendering of the first five books of the Bible, the 'books of Moses', made it a very large enterprise already at an early stage of its creation, and the rest of the biblical books, the other three-quarters of the Bible, were to follow. The significance of this achievement was far-reaching: without a Greek Bible, European history would have been entirely different—no western Jewish diaspora and no Christianity.

This book, then, is a book about a book, or rather about a translated book and its impact; about its ancient creators, and its early users and receivers, all of them Jewish speakers of Greek; about its meaning to them; and about how it moulded their lives and their relationships with the world in which they lived. We shall soon discover, however, that nothing is straightforward about this seemingly simple statement. Even the name 'Septuagint', a Christian coinage, is a misnomer, as we shall see. The translation is in reality a massive collection of translations, and a collection which had vague and variable limits in the Christian period.[1] We do not know who the translators were, although it is wholly clear that they were scholarly Jews who knew both Greek and Hebrew well, and that they were quite numerous, spread over time and probably over place too. We do not know their dates, not even for sure when the work really began, though there is a lively and persistent ancient tradition that it was initiated by one of the greatest of the Ptolemies. Would that we could know how the translators toiled, whether in teams or entirely individually, and how they were supported and rewarded.

The principles, assumptions, and purposes of the Septuagint translations are also often a matter of conjecture, for they are not transparent to us. Physical remains of the Greek Bible translations from pre-Christian days are rare in the extreme: the very earliest, of the second century BCE, are just minute scraps of papyrus or leather, impressive in their survival and in their closeness to the date of the translation itself. A handful of slightly later texts, from the late first century BCE, or the first century CE, offer interesting textual variants suggestive of scribal revision and therefore of Jewish care, already then, for the exact matching of Greek to Hebrew.[2] Among these, the Deuteronomy fragments of Papyrus Fouad 266 also contain an intriguing form of the tetragrammaton (Divine Name) as ΠΙΠΙ, inserted awkwardly into the text, which gives us perhaps an inkling of the scribes' sense of God and suggesting that here there is continuity with the later Jewish tendency to avoid expressing the Name.[3] The first biblical manuscripts of any length, in the Chester Beatty collection, are thought to be Christian and of the third century.

There is nowhere near enough from which to reconstruct the history of the material text of the Septuagint as a Jewish document. We have some idea, but not nearly enough, about what was done with the texts: Sabbath readings are perfectly well attested, but beyond that it is mostly guesswork. Parallels are hard to come by. Translations in the ancient world, while fulfilling many of the same social functions as in the modern world, naturally operated in very different circumstances and with different traditions behind them.

---

[1] This is explained below, p. 21.
[2] On all of these, see below, pp. 15–20.
[3] On P. Fouad 266, see Dunand 1966; Aly and Koenen 1980.

And last but not least these are translations of a very special type of texts. The Hebrew original texts were holy books, and the translation was supremely important, in some sense also holy for its users. But the connotations of holiness and sanctity changed through time, and we cannot assume that these are just the same for those who cared for the books then as in later Judaism.

The original core constituency for the translations was Greek-speaking Jews (including converts and perhaps also sympathizers with Judaism) inhabiting, mainly, the Greek cities of the eastern Mediterranean. That itself is a most elusive world, often not well documented. It is true that the making of the Greek translation of the Hebrew Scriptures is commonly associated with Alexandria, the city which epitomizes Hellenistic Judaism for us, and the translation indeed began there: its foundation myth, the legend of Aristeas, presents itself as quintessentially Alexandrian, fixed in the topography of the city. But the stage for our story is far larger, extending wherever Jews engaged with the Greek language. Some of the translated books beyond the Torah (the five books of Moses that make up the Pentateuch) may not have emanated from Alexandria at all and may be presumed to have been translated by scholars in other centres, perhaps Syria or one of the cities of Asia Minor. This was, in short, the Bible of the Jewish diaspora over half a millennium at least, and in some areas much longer than that. And yet the history of that diaspora is told without them. We are fortunate if the Greek Bible receives a passing mention there; usually, it is an invisible presence. Here, it will occupy centre stage.

For all that, there is much to be said about the significance of the translation in its own time and about its role over a very long period. We can look at what was written about and around it. We can devise different techniques for assessing the engagement of the translators with the worlds to which they belonged. We can look inside and consider how, through their interpretations of delicate or controversial matters, the translations might express the way translators and readers perceived their situation in the world and defined themselves. We can think about their choice of translation language: even where their grasp of the original Hebrew was partial, that in itself tells us something about them. And we can assess how later Christianization has distorted interpretation of the evidence.

Peter Fraser has reminded us that the Septuagint translation of the Jewish Torah 'forms a larger bulk of Alexandrian Greek literature than any other single item'.[4] Moreover, the translation language—sometimes so perplexing—in which the Septuagint is couched, embodies more of the common post-classical Greek language, the koine, than perhaps any other body of texts.[5] That the first great translation of the West was made at all owes as much to the particular role of Greek as the dominant language in the world of its making as to the particular role of the Bible among the people who used it. The simple fact is that the Septuagint is part and parcel of the history of Greek culture, if within that culture we allow their proper place to the minority groups that shared in it. The standpoint might be that proposed by Bowman and Woolf. Commenting upon 'the privileged role accorded, in general histories and syllabuses, to Greeks and Romans, as opposed to Etruscans, Carthaginians, Egyptians, Semites and others', they say that 'an authoritative critique and genealogy of the notion of a classical world, along the lines of Edward Said's *Orientalism*, is still awaited'.[6] Or, again, we might cite Fergus Millar's more recent words on 'redrawing the map':

In a 'Western' culture based on a (very partial) fusion of Judaeo-Christian and Classical traditions, it is puzzling to reflect on how very few students of Greek will have been offered the chance to read a private letter on papyrus or an honorific decree put up by a Greek city—or the Septuagint, or the New Testament or Josephus or Eusebius.[7]

The Greek Bible translations are not quite what they seem. What began, when the translation started on its long road, as an unusually creative product of a period of cultural flowering at the dawn of Hellenistic civilization, and as the foundation text for a new Jewish diaspora, has ended up as the Septuagint, a part of Christianity. This cultural artefact moved far from its original habitat. That this is what happened is a part, a major part, of the story of Christianity's emergence, and its very laborious parting from Judaism. From one

---

[4] Fraser 1972: 687 ff.
[5] See now Lee 1983 and Evans 2001.
[6] Bowman and Woolf 1994: 14 (Introduction).
[7] Millar 2006: 506.

point of view, it is a story of appropriation and eventual loss. Along with the Septuagint, Hellenistic Judaism, a remarkable hybrid culture, was itself in part subsumed and absorbed into the Christian church. The existence of that culture was what made possible the spread and growth of the Church. But its transference allowed the recipients conveniently to sideline, to by-pass and sometimes even to forget the Church's original Jewishness and its intimate connection with Judaism. The Septuagint is thus a collection with a contested history.

The result of the Greek Bible's divorce from its primary users and generators has been its existence in a kind of vacuum, as a disembodied text. The great textual scholar of the New Testament, Eberhard Nestle, felt able boldly to state that about the Septuagint's 'pre-Christian times, we know next to nothing'. Restoring this great work to its position means, first of all, putting it back into the Jewish and the Greek worlds which produced it. The quest is to understand how for many centuries these translations enabled and governed Jewish life in the Graeco-Roman world. It was another great German scholar, Martin Hengel, who wrote: 'the Septuagint represents anything but a unity. Rather, it stems from ... turbulent history, and represents the most important self-witness to Greek-speaking Judaism'.[8]

The Septuagint has a very marginal, if not invisible, place in contemporary culture, sharing, indeed, the fortunes of the Bible in modern secular societies, but suffering the same fate writ large. Despite its size, and its continuing significance to orthodox churches, the Septuagint corpus has a minor role even inside Christianity. For Protestant readers a few well-known narratives, which did not become canonical but which, in Greek, are part of the Christian Septuagint corpus, such as the stories of Tobit, Judith, Susanna, and Bel and the Dragon, are familiar as part of the Apocrypha.[9] On the scholarly plane, the Greek Bible figures as the indispensable source of the New Testament. For specialists, the Septuagint has been a vast repository of textual data, giving access to a text of scripture earlier than anything known until the

---

[8] Hengel 2002: p. xii.
[9] Below, pp. 16, 21.

discovery of the Qumran fragments. There have been a few champions of Septuagint as a whole.[10] But the Septuagint translation could never have the seminal literary role that the King James version has had in England or Martin Luther's Bible in Protestant Germany or the translations of Moses Mendelssohn or Martin Buber for German Jewry in the modern age. The language of the Septuagint translation is a brilliant creation which served its purposes wonderfully well—social, religious, and ideological. To the reader of today it has its appeal, but it is characterized by a somewhat ungainly deployment of the common Greek, the koine, of the post-classical era. The density and reverberation of the original Hebrew is echoed, but in fainter form, by the essentially word-for-word translation technique.

In Jewish tradition, the role of the translations was inadequately acknowledged, and often not at all, for a variety of reasons. The chief among them was the promotion of the Hebrew language, and therefore of scripture in Hebrew, as markers of national identity, both by Judaean nationalists—coinage and documents in Hebrew were associated with both the major revolts against Roman rule—and, later, by the Rabbis of Palestine. Moreover, the Rabbis, who came to dominate the record, did not write history for its own sake—what they did not need to know they allowed to lapse into oblivion. Early Christian appropriation of the translations was another factor, which cannot be entirely ignored in interpreting the Jewish reaction; but neither should it be over-estimated.[11] Finally, the Septuagint has suffered, in the Jewish milieu, from the symbolic and pejorative associations surrounding the notion of an essentialized 'Hellenism'. Whatever it has meant in the academy, this problematic concept has been viewed popularly and in traditionalist circles not just as a symptom but as a source of assimilation, epitomizing abandonment of the inherited tradition, the equivalent of whoring after strange gods.[12] Propaganda directed against the Greek translation emerged in the late rabbinic period, as we shall see, leading by a gradual but inexorable process to all but the most tenuous recollections of the translation's Jewish past.

[10] On a Victorian champion, Edward Grinfield, see pp. 286–7.
[11] As we shall discover in Chap. 9.
[12] For 'Hellenism' as metaphor and 'other' in Jewish culture, see Shavit 1997; Rajak 2000e.

The Greek Bible had served, however, as a bridge for Jews to the Greek cultural mainland, even if it was a bridge which most often carried one-way traffic. The existence of a Bible in Greek made possible the remarkable flowering of the diaspora in the Graeco-Roman Mediterranean. These were the communities which determined the pattern of Jewish life outside Palestine for centuries, developing the synagogue as an institution, and modelling prototypes of relations with the ruling power, with the dominant culture, and with the peoples with whom they mixed. Foreign rule was the condition of life in Palestine too, for a large part of the period, and, there too, Greek cities stood, some of them with Jewish minorities. But for the Greek Bible, the diaspora, from the early Hellenistic period to the late Roman, constitutes the heartland. It is to its people that the Greek Bible in the first instance belongs and to this setting that I propose to restore it.

This great act of intellectual bridge-building on the part of Greek-speaking Jews served both to connect and to separate. By virtue of their close adherence to their source language, Hebrew—their high degree of 'literalism'—the translated books did not, on the whole, read as though they were making a bid to be part of elite Greek literature. Yet the translation technique was far more than a life raft, a makeshift access device to scripture for a world without Hebrew. We shall discover that in fact, and paradoxically, the Greek Bible, through its chosen linguistic vehicle, promoted continuing and close contact with the Hebrew language, rather than the reverse. Ownership of their holy scriptures in Greek could help to position the Jewish minority advantageously in relation to the Greek and Roman cultural imperialisms under which they fell; but it also enabled this minority to have things two ways, both to play and not to play the game, both to take account of the prevailing power-structure, engaging in a degree of measured acculturation, and at the same time, quietly, but most persistently, to assert their underlying independence. An important thread in the present study, informed no doubt by a post-colonial consciousness, and in keeping with recent interpretation of the social role of translation, is how the Septuagint worked to achieve accommodation for a colonized group, how the nature and uses of the translation enabled them to define their own hybrid identity, and to retain control over their essential values in relation to the powers-that-be. This recipe for cultural survival, and even a degree of sly subversion, are inherent in the text-centred Jewish culture of the Graeco-Roman diaspora. This means that approaches to the Bible (in Hebrew) and its interpretation fostered by Jews in other contexts will be relevant to my study.

Those who have written about the Greek Bible have tended to overlook the Jewish side of the equation altogether. They have often relied upon a rather static understanding of the Judaism of the period. Old ideas about the sects of Second Temple Judaism (especially the Pharisees), about the meaning of the 'dispersion', the 'legalistic' character of the Torah, the closure of the canon and the early fixity of the text, about Jewish 'literalism' and the diminished position of the Hebrew language, still underpin theorizing about the Septuagint. But our picture of this period is now quite transformed, and still developing. In particular, the Jewish diaspora has in the past quarter century or so been revisited, intensively researched, and dramatically reassessed.

One element of progress is that 'Judaism' and 'Hellenism' are no longer quite so regularly pitted against each other as those automatic polar opposites which could unite only through the birth of the Church. Furthermore, Jewish communities in the Greek cities of the diaspora have proved to be very different from their stereotypic portrait. They were not inward-looking fenced-off entities, closed to the outside world, standing rigid in their not-so-splendid isolation as they refused to join the great Hellenistic enterprise. It is possible to think about them and their communities in social and cultural terms, not simply as carriers of a 'faith'. *Ioudaios*, the standard designation of a Jew in Greek writing and in inscriptions, incorporates a bundle of attributes, refering to ethnicity (membership of a people with real or fictive genealogical links) and to geography ('originating from' or 'belonging to Judea') as well as to membership of a religious group (worshipping the God who resided, or had resided, in the Jerusalem Temple).[13] The *ioudaioi* of the diaspora were rather good at the arts of social accommodation and of cultural survival, and the Septuagint was their main instrument.[14]

---

[13] See now the effective arguments of D. Schwartz 2007 against Mason's position that *ioudaioi* in ancient Greek means only 'men from Judaea'.

[14] My conception of cultural survival is close to that of Weitzman 2005 and we are concerned with similar modes of behaviour–absorption, resistance, finding friends–in short, the behaviour of the weak. But it is striking that even his study leaves the Bible out, focusing instead on the sometimes subliminal influence of the Temple cult.

These sea changes in our understanding allow us to position the Septuagint afresh. The interpretation offered here of the Greek Bible translations as a mechanism for cultural survival in the face of powerful forces is, I should stress, by no means a way of letting the old caricature of isolation and misanthropy in again through the back door. On the contrary, this insight facilitates the rewriting of a history which, remarkably often, and in a surprising number of ways, still tends to be presented as a Christian narrative—or at any rate as one influenced by inbuilt Christian perspectives.

My starting-point in Chapter 1 is the familiar one of the tradition of the seventy-two (later seventy) translators sent to Alexandria by the High Priest in Jerusalem by Ptolemy II Philadelphus. The story has it that he commissioned the translation for the great Alexandrian library. At first sight it seems surprising to open a historical study with what has often been dismissed as a pure legend; and it is perhaps even more surprising to initiate this presentation of the Greek Bible as an expression of diasporic cultural resistance with an exploration of the role of one of the ancient world's most illustrious and autocratic patrons. Yet a memory so persistent deserves a cultural historian's attention, and we shall discover that here, as often, memory and myth are intertwined and tradition is not wholly to be dismissed. We shall also discover, by means of a careful reading of the narrative of the Septuagint's charter text, the *Letter of Aristeas*, with its inseparable mixture of fact and fiction, and then through comparison of this with lingering memories of Ptolemy in Greek literature, that a fair degree of ambivalence towards the royal benefactor lurks within it.

In Chapter 2, the claim that the King commissioned the translation is found to be quite credible when set against the background of his ambitious cultural imperialism. In the early days of Alexandria, the legacy of Alexander the Great kept alive curiosity about other cultures. Aristotelians amassed and catalogued information, and the Jews and Judaism were within their purview. For the King, too, Judaea and the Jews were a part of his empire which demanded attention. As for the Jews of Alexandria, they tied themselves into the Ptolemaic project at an early date, and they showed striking prescience in their ready adaptation to Alexandria's dynamic recreation of the heritage of Athens by their immediate acceptance of the Bible translation. This represents a prompt recognition of the indispensability of operating in the colonial language, the common Greek (koine) of the age. But the community also appreciated the value of standing back from that project and not forgetting Jerusalem.

This dual approach to the dominant power and to the prevailing cultural norms became the hallmark of the Jewish diaspora through the Graeco-Roman era. In Chapter 3, I seek to portray that diaspora on the basis of the primary evidence for its evolution, picking out the landmarks in its eventful history and stressing the continuity of its social, cultural, and religious structures, above all, the synagogue. The emphasis falls on the articulation of the Jewish community with the broader environment, expressed—sometimes in one and the same time or place—by a high level of individual and group integration into city life. We have evidence of interest shown by highly placed non-Jewish benefactors and sympathizers in the local synagogue. But at the same time there were repeated, sometimes widespread, manifestations of tension and even violence. That experience is both the background and the shaping influence for the Greek Bible which reflects the conflicts of life under an imperial power in a polytheistic world—uncertainty and dependence on the one hand, confidence and self-sufficiency on the other.

The technique of adaptation to the colonial language is the topic of Chapter 4, which depicts and accounts in social terms for the very particular Greek of the Bible translation and is the largest in the book. In Alexandria it was desirable to be Greek, not Egyptian. The koine was shaped by the translators in such a way as to make it possible both to 'go Greek' and to 'stay Jewish'. Their labours were made public in synagogue readings, but their work must also have been conceived with the needs of educators and students in mind. Their seemingly artless and 'literal' translation technique, oriented more towards the source than the target language (in the terms used by translation theorists), made a connection for readers, and above all for hearers, with the traditional language of the Jewish *ethnos*, biblical Hebrew. We can see how many of the distinctive linguistic features of the translations achieved this end. Their auditory impact turns out to play an important part in this. The durability of the translation language is one measure of its effectiveness, for, with limited variation and development, it continued in operation through successive waves of translation activity. It was also deployed in original works that were written by Jews during the Hellenistic and Roman periods, some of which were, so it turned out, subsumed into the Christian Septuagint (as will be explained below). Semantic innovation, the coinage of new words and expressions or of new meanings for familiar words, is a hallmark of the Septuagint language, the very term 'diaspora' being one of them. This vocabulary, far from being a mere series of solutions to challenges of translation, represents the translators' intensely creative way of melding and contemporizing their different thought worlds. My emphasis in this chapter, and elsewhere too, falls less on Hebrew's formidable status as a holy tongue (an idea which was not fully to find its time until the rabbinic era) and more on its symbolic role as a cultural reference point, a source of unity and a preserver of tradition.

Continual reinterpretation, adaptation, and addition of the biblical text allowed it to be a repertoire for all seasons; and translation is also a form of interpretation. Chapter 5 shows how translations of late biblical texts, especially Daniel, and newer parabiblical texts, like the story of Bel and the great snake (also about Daniel), or the Epistle of Jeremiah, or the Wisdom of Solomon, could have worked as responses to external political authority, often markedly subversive. Twists and subtle modifications intensified themes that were already prominent in places in the Hebrew Bible, and only occasionally can a Hebrew original different from the Masoretic (standard) text be suspected as lying behind the changes. The denunciation of 'idols' and 'idol worship' had new force and point when linked with the vanity of rulers in a period in which manifestations of the imperial cult impinged on everyone. Representations of tyrannical rage brought together motifs taken from Greek political philosophy with those of oriental wisdom literature, all within the framework of a sharp contrast with the justified anger of the God of Israel. In the Hebrew Bible, a rich and distinctive vocabulary was deployed specifically for divine rage, ensuring that it was kept on a different plane from the human variety; this could not be replicated in Greek, but awareness of the distinction remained. For royal rage, translators who were evidently well-versed in the Greek philosophers incorporated themes and motifs from familiar Greek representations of tyrants which spoke vividly to the experience of subjects of the Hellenistic monarchs.

In Chapter 6, I explore the role of the Bible among the people of the Greek-speaking diaspora in broad terms, asking how the centrality of their Bible text functioned in their lives and how far it made the Jews different from other groups. I explain why 'centrality', rather than 'canonicity', is the term I have chosen to use, discussing along the way recent ideas about the development of the biblical canon in this period, in Hebrew as well as Greek. The common text creates a unity across place and time, even if differently read in different milieux. The possession of a text produced continuity and it made a unit of the Greek-speaking Jewish diaspora, with implications for the future. Arguably, scripture was in this more important than the sensibility of Temple and homeland, since it was scripture that defined and established that very sensibility. Jewish culture was built upon the Greek Bible, as the collection was added to and the style was recycled in free compositions. The texts had multifarious uses, serving, as for Jews through the ages, as familiar friends rather than bearers of a remote sanctity. Pressing the evidence makes it possible to speculate a little about the impact of the Bible on the lives of individuals, but we can say far less than we would like.

In Chapter 7, the biblical culture of Hellenistic Judaism is further explored through the comparative use of different models of text-based communities. A comparison is commonly drawn between the role of the Bible for the Jews and the position of the Homeric poems among all the Greeks. This turns out to be more helpful in highlighting the differences between the two rather than the similarities. Comparisons and contrasts within different Jewish cultures take us deeper into the matter, and for this purpose I invoke two other, very different, worlds of Second Temple Judaism and I assess in some detail the role of the Bible within them. One of these two other worlds is that of the Qumran sect who (in the common opinion) gathered the Dead Sea Scrolls and wrote some of them, operating in the Semitic languages of Hebrew and Aramaic; while the other, reasonably deemed a Jewish environment for this purpose, is the mainly Greek-speaking world of the writers of the New Testament and their readers. Both of these represent a type of community of users that might be called 'Bible-soaked', who immersed themselves in biblical literature (or their preferred parts of it); the documents they have left show how their constant rereading and reinterpretation of those texts was expected to pervade every aspect of their existence. But the lives of the majority of Greek-speaking diaspora Jews were not like this. Bible-centred as they were, they perhaps lived *by* but not *through* Torah. The Greek Bible was an incalculable resource for them. Yet looking as they did in more than one direction, it was important that it could operate as a bridge between their Jewish lives and their immediate surroundings. This was manifestly true for Philo and Josephus, two illustrious if unique individuals, whose closeness to scripture is manifest and whose writings give us access to something of that hybrid thought world.

Although traffic on the bridge was usually one-way, we find in Chapter 8 interesting evidence for sporadic movement in the opposite direction. At Alexandria, the first flush of Ptolemaic interest in the Jewish Law (*nomos*) died away quite quickly. It is perhaps surprising that we can detect any echoes of the Greek Bible at all in what survives of Hellenistic Greek literature. But knowledge and appreciation in philosophical and professional circles surfaces at a later moment, gathering strength in the Roman period. For all social classes, there was another kind of meeting ground in the realm of magic, where biblical quotations in Greek and biblical terminology, above all the Divine Name, were freely used by practitioners and were evidently welcomed by their clients, as we can see from recipes, spells, and curse formulae. These were handed down through the generations, and they survive for us in papyri from late antiquity. Whatever scenario is conjured up to explain the production and use of such material, some response to Jewish scripture on the part of non-Jews has to be implied. They at least knew what it was, and had a sense of what it sounded like; probably quite a lot more than that.

Such forms of contact assisted in the rapid scripturalization of Gentile Christianity which sets the stage for Chapter 9. The new religion was grafted onto Judaism, and Christians defined themselves as the 'new Israel', heirs to the covenant with Abraham and to the 'Old Testament'. For most Christians, that meant the Greek translation of the Hebrew Bible, on which the entire edifice of Christian discourse was built. The Jews themselves could be deemed obsolescent. The Christian narrative, dominating scholarship until recently, has it that at this point the Jews were goaded into discarding the old translations, which they felt unable to share, replacing them with the even more 'literal' version of Aquila which could be triumphantly wielded in Christian–Jewish polemic. The abandonment theory can be easily dismantled and the evidence points rather to a growth of Jewish interest during the second century CE in a multiplicity of Greek versions, including their own 'old Greek'. By facilitating new translations, which are by no means a token of lack of interest in the old one, diaspora Jews more than ever expressed their culture through creative biblical translation. And they expressed their religion through their Greek Torah, just as they had been doing for centuries. The Christian appropriation of their heritage was a gradual and untidy process. Once our own narrative is de-Christianized, developments in Judaism can be understood in their own terms.

The Septuagint emerges at the end of my study as a member of a larger world of Jewish-Greek biblical translations. They in turn have the Hebrew Bible firmly behind them. The Greek versions are but part of the broader history of the emergence of Jewish scripture. In the rest of this introduction, I offer basic orientation in the immense complexities of the biblical corpus during its formative period. A range of terms and concepts has already appeared in my discussion and their full meaning is not easy to grasp. Sometimes, indeed, this is because they are in their nature imprecise. It will be useful, too, to understand how many questions remain unsettled about the formation of the biblical canon.

FROM GREEK BIBLE TO SEPTUAGINT

The term 'Septuagint' does not appear in the title of this book, and that is no accident. It is in fact an inappropriate description for the Jewish Bible in Greek. The problem is that 'Septuagint' is a term which evolved in the usage of the early Church and refers to the corpus created there as we find it in the great biblical codices of the fourth century CE.[15] It is precisely these layers of reception that we shall need to strip away, at any rate until the last chapter of this book. But even were we to resolve to stick with the name, as one of

---

[15] The evolution of this corpus is the subject of the studies appearing in English as Hengel 2002.

convenience, we would soon find that the ambiguities and complications of its usage outweighed that convenience.

At first sight, it might seem to be perfectly obvious what the 'Septuagint' is. It is the great product of Alexandrian Jewry, whose partly legendary creation story is enshrined in that remarkable piece of Alexandrian prose, the *Letter of Aristeas*. Once we begin to look further, however, we find that 'Septuagint' means several things.[16] 'Septuagint' indeed may refer to the Torah, the Pentateuch, as translated in Alexandria, probably in the late third century BCE, that is to say, the term refers to this Torah in the form in which it was originally produced, whatever that was. But what was it? First, most scholars now accept the view associated with Paul de Lagarde, that one single, original version ('Urtext') of the entire Pentateuch came out of Alexandria as the starting-point out of which all subsequent texts developed and which is in principle, to a greater or lesser extent, recoverable.[17] But there can be no certainty, and the challenging thesis of Paul Kahle, that more than one version existed from the very beginning, is showing signs of a revival in modified forms. Second, *Aristeas* is unequivocal that the Law was translated from gold-lettered Hebrew scrolls for the great new library of Ptolemy II Philadelphus by the seventy-two scholars from Jerusalem. He more likely meant the entire Torah, but the Greek formulation does not exclude the possibility that only a legal core was covered in the first instalment.[18] Third, while *Aristeas* speaks of the Law, the church fathers soon took to attaching the Aristeas story to the Bible in its entirety and subsuming the whole entity under the rubric of the Septuagint. This is what Augustine was referring to when he wrote: 'the custom has now become prevalent of calling their [the Alexandrian translators'] translation the Septuagint' (*City of God*,18.42). Jerome tried to correct this habit, telling his Christian readers, quite rightly, that 'Aristeas, Josephus and the whole Jewish school' say nothing about translation of the books outside the Torah.[19] Jerome

---

[16] The issues are disentangled in the various introductions to the Septuagint; but see esp. Dines 2004: 1–24 for a brief, authoritative, and clear analysis.
[17] See Dines 2004: 60 on the two positions.
[18] See further below, pp. 90–1.
[19] Jerome, *Quaest. Hebr. in Gen.*, prologue and *in Ezech.*, 2.5.12.

was not heeded, however, and the label continued to be current in a second sense, as the term for the entire translation. That then turned into a way of describing the Christian Greek canon, or indeed various different canons. The limits of the Septuagint, in this wide understanding, were not clearly defined. Included are the additions to some canonical books as well as the rest of the Apocrypha and usually a few further works. The early church, as witnessed by the great fourth- and fifth-century uncial manuscripts of the Greek Bible, included under the name 'Septuagint' various apocryphal or (in the Catholic Church's conception) Deuterocanonical books, selected somewhat arbitrarily from the heritage of Hellenistic Judaism. The very fact that the Septuagint as an entity is considered and studied, rather than just the translated Bible, attests to the ineradicable imprint of the early Church. The content of the corpus varies today between denominations. But in any event it is the Septuagint corpus, as it now exists in one or other of these forms, that dominates the scene. So deeply has this development stamped the history of the collection that it will often prove impossible altogether to avoid the Christianized term, imprecise and anachronistic though it may be.

THE TRUE TEXT?

The textual transmission of the Septuagint has been an immensely involved process. The Septuagint text, as it has reached us through the manuscripts, has received layer upon layer of alteration. This is apparently already true even of the three famous fourth- to fifth-century Christian uncial codices: Alexandrinus, Vaticanus, and Sinaiticus. An active revision process in the second century CE by scholars ascribed to a Jewish milieu and known as 'the Three', followed by Origen's grand, six-column collations in the Hexapla, had already made the 'old Greek' invisible (even if Origen's purpose had been to salvage it).[20] Further recension in late antique Antioch,

---

[20] For more on Origen's work, see pp. 291 and 295–6.

ascribed to Lucian the Presbyter, left perhaps an even more significant mark on the text.

The texts that have come down to us reflect not only additional accumulated errors, but also conscious revisions and divergent traditions. The process of revision has been much studied, and it is widely accepted that there was active reworking of part or all of the translation from an early stage, often with a view to getting back closer to the Hebrew. The phenomenon is even visible within the Jewish pentateuchal fragments in Greek, on papyrus or leather, that have been found in Qumran, elsewhere in the Judaean desert, or in Egypt, amounting to a total of sixteen that can with certainty be identified. The two very earliest of these are thought to go back to the first half of the second century BCE and very little of textual interest can be discerned in them;[21] but by the first century BCE, signs of textual revision are evident in some remarkable extracts from an unknown Egyptian provenance (the 112 small fragments of P. Fouad Inv. 266 from Deuteronomy). In one case, the celebrated Minor Prophets scroll from Nahal Hever, this correction, which brings the Greek closer to the Hebrew, albeit sporadic, has been of immense significance to scholars.[22]

For John Wevers 'the textual history of the LXX is part and parcel of the LXX'.[23] Emanuel Tov envisages, rather, such extensive cor-

---

[21] The two apparent earliest fragments are Rylands papyrus gr 458 of Deut. 23: 8 from Egypt and, from Qumran cave 4, 4Q122 = 4QLXXDeut of Deut. 11: 4. The fragments of P. Fouad 266b and cDeut. and P. Fouad 266a Gen. are the only other known Jewish papyri datable prior to the Common Era. The earliest material is surveyed and analysed in Kraft 2003. Kraft's list of 'possibly Jewish' fragments from Egypt which appear to date from between c.1 CE and c.400 CE runs to some fifteen items (including one ostrakon) out of a total of some 120 known fragments. But the customary criteria for distinguishing Jewish from Christian scribal practices are challenged by Kraft. Hurtado 2006 accepts the demarcation established by Roberts (see Roberts and Skeat 1983)—principally, Jewish scroll v. Christian codex and Jewish tetragrammaton v. Christian abbreviated 'nomina sacra'. See also Gamble 1995. For the Greek Qumran fragments, see Tov 2003.

[22] The eight P. Fouad 266a Genesis fragments do not reveal any of this. There are also signs of textual revision on the first-century BCE leather scroll 4Q121 = 4QLXXNum. For the Minor Prophets Scroll, 8HVXIIgr, see below, pp. 225 and 301 n. 75. On material aspects of the text, see Kraft 2003.

[23] Wevers 1990: p. xviii.

ruption and alteration in the very early stages of transmission, when the translation resided in separate scrolls that: 'as a result of these corrections, so far as one can tell there were no two identical or nearly identical scrolls in existence for any book of the Septuagint'. His 'rather anarchistic' conclusion was that for 'data... created, not in the course of textual transmission, but at an earlier stage, namely that of the literary growth of the books... it is questionable whether textual evaluation has any application'.[24] However, Tov also believes that the extent of ongoing correction and revision was such that 'by the second and third century CE a recognizable unity had come about in the textual tradition of the LXX'.[25]

The inherent problems are much greater than those presented by most other texts, just because we are dealing with what is understood, one way or another, as Holy Scripture. This means that it was copied many more times and was much more in use than any standard classical manuscripts. Accuracy mattered more and therefore the text was also revised more—which could make things worse with the damage done by Origen's Hexapla. And still today that is a motivating force underlying at least some of the work done on the text of the Septuagint—to recover, tiny step by tiny step, the first Bible. Textual scholars use the term old Greek for the earliest stage of text that we can get to. Of course, this is still not precisely the original translators' work. A goal, more or less explicit, of so much modern scholarship has been the simple yet at the same time highly ambitious one of recreating the words of the original translation, the old Greek; and in fact it is not hard to find programmatic statements asserting that this is or should be the true purpose of all Septuagint study. So Albert Pietersma speaks of 'what would seem to be of necessity the fundamental and methodologically primary aim of Septuagint research, namely the recovery of the O[ld] G[reek] text'. And Sydney Jellicoe in similar vein decreed that the point of it all was 'the recovery of the Greek text as it left the hand of the translators'.[26] It is no exaggeration to say that Septuagint research

---

[24] Tov 1997: 261–3.
[25] Tov 1999: 1; cf. Bickerman 1950.
[26] Pietersma 1985; Jellicoe 1974, Prolegomona.

until recently was understood as essentially textual criticism—understandably, for there is work there for many lifetimes.

There are further complications: the text of the Hebrew Bible was pluriform through the crucial period. The discovery of the Dead Sea Scrolls revealed substantial deviation in the case of some books, with major consequences for scholarship. So we cannot be sure what Hebrew was originally translated. And we cannot know exactly what Hebrew was available to any revisers or re-translators. But we must assume that the Hebrew also continued to be in constant interaction with the Greek. Masoretic-type texts emerge early, but the Masoretic Text which is in standard use by Jews today dates back only to the sixth century CE.[27] Thus, an even more intricate task within the domain of textual criticism is the exploitation of the Greek as a route to our understanding of the development of the Hebrew text. The Qumran material has of course transformed what was a somewhat desultory activity into an all-absorbing investigation. It was interesting to find a distinct reserve over these purely textual goals evinced in a review by James Barr of a Lexicon to Aquila's Greek translation, back in 1967.[28]

And so, because of the complexity of its relationship with a range of Hebrew precursors, because of the sheer number of recensions which the Greek text underwent, and because of our lack of grip on the scope and purpose of these, the textual history is one of mind-bending difficulty. Naturally, then, the Septuagint has been a hunting ground for textual critics, and at times in the past it was virtually abandoned by scholars with other kinds of interests, to remain the exclusive preserve of the textual critics—probably without too much regret.

This then is truly daunting material. For anyone dealing with the Septuagint, the complications can be crippling. Indeed they have

---

[27] The standard work on text criticism of the Hebrew Bible is Tov 1997.

[28] Barr 1967 reviewing Reider-Turner's lexicon to Aquila's translation (1966). Barr identifies Turner's main aim as isolating, via Aquila, the effects of Origen's Hexapla on the Greek text, in order to achieve a purer Greek text—and thus to get to an earlier Hebrew text. He casts doubt upon whether much of this can ever be achieved by such means and he reminds us that Aquila's translation was important for itself, as a milestone in the history of translation techniques, of the Greek language and of Jewish Bible interpretation.

paralysed many. They are enough in themselves to make the Septuagint unapproachable, and to have rendered it so little known outside specialist circles. I venture to suggest that there is a great deal we can take out of the text without worrying about textual obstacles. In many places there are no variants. Broad tranches of wording stay constant across textual diversity. Another point on which I lean is that at any one place and time people had their own conception of the original work of the Alexandrian translators, whether or not they could be sure that the text in front of them was that text; and that conception is eminently worth discussing. Since the translation is just that, a translation, questions of faithfulness to the original inevitably arise. Since it is the translation of a holy book, the questions arise in an acute form. Because scholarship has to labour so hard to recover 'the text as it left the hands of the translators', and the Hebrew behind that, the text's immutability is itself an object of primary concern, as it already was in the early Church. Suffice it to say that here I do not foreground the issues which have dominated, at a guess, 90 per cent of Septuagint scholarship for the past century-and-a-half, and that have deterred even the more adventurous from entering wholeheartedly into other important and interesting questions.[29] One needs to be aware of the instability of the text and to understand how to handle it. But I contend that it is possible to write about the history of the translations without engaging in continual text-critical study—and without waiting another hundred and fifty years.

THE HEBREW HINTERLAND: TORAH AND BEYOND

The Septuagint has important differences from the Hebrew Bible. There is a substantially different ordering of the books. There are book titles for the books of the Bible—we owe many of the familiar

---

[29] Like all generalizations, this one of course is not entirely fair: as early examples of work which sought to advance our understanding of questions of wider significance by relating the Septuagint translations, however hypothetically, to Jewish practice, I would single out Thackeray 1923.

English names, Genesis, Exodus, Leviticus, and so forth, to the Septuagint (though it should be noted that Alexandrian Jewish writing preferred the name *Exagogē* for Exodus).[30] Even more strikingly, there are extra books and there are additions to some translated books. What we describe as the Septuagint was put together in the early Church. The idea was once accepted that our Septuagint corpus represents a selection of Greek books, wider than the Hebrew Bible, already constructed by Alexandrian Jews into their own particular canon, out of which grew the Septuagint of the church; but the evidence is lacking.[31] Rather, a lack of definition about the precise constitution of the Hebrew collection, beyond the Torah, was shared by all branches of Judaism until well into the rabbinic period. The Greek-speaking Jewish world participates in the same process of development. In other words, not only is there no one thing which is 'Septuagint'; at the stage which concerns us, it is also not clear that there is such a thing as 'Bible', if we mean a defined, clearly delimited corpus—which is what the word 'Bible' implies. A 'canon' may have been forming, but was not yet formed in our period. Indeed, from the Jewish angle, there is no distinction between those books which are part of the (Christian) Apocrypha, and all the rest of Jewish–Hellenistic literature.[32]

We can at any rate hang onto the certainty that all Jews distinguished the Torah from the rest. True, the definition of Torah, too, can be elusive, referring to the ten commandments as a minimum (the core revelation from Sinai); or else including the Levitical laws as well; or perhaps the Pentateuch from the twelfth chapter of the book of Exodus onwards. At its most extensive, Torah for the Rabbis can comprise the entire written Torah together with the open-ended collection of oral commentary upon it, that is to say, Torah with interpretation. Seth Schwartz expresses this from the perspective of a modern theorist: '"Torah" was a set of negotiations between an

---

[30] Perhaps, as N. Cohen 1997 suggests, this was because of the strong theatrical associations of the word *exodos*.

[31] The Alexandrian canon theory was disproved by Sundberg 1964 to near universal satisfaction. See Barr 1983: 56. Barton 1986: 27–34 summarizes and endorses Sundberg. Detailed summary in *BGS*: 112–18.

[32] On which see Goodman 2001 and 'The Apocrypha and Pseudepigrapha' in Collins 2002: 55–61.

authoritative but opaque text and various sets of traditional but not fully authorized practice'.[33] But most often it is simply and obviously the five books of Moses.

In Greek, Torah vocabulary yields to a significant semantic shift. There are new connotations. But the reference continues the same. The five books stand out as a unit. Thus, for example, these books are the principal object of Philo's copious biblical exegesis. The Hebrew Torah, whose root meaning is 'teaching' or 'instruction'—commonly, in the Wisdom literature, of a father of his son or wise teacher of a disciple[34]—is generally rendered by the Greek *nomos*, with its cognates, whose root meaning is 'law' or 'custom'. This becomes the standard Jewish–Greek rendering.[35] There is no doubt that the word can operate from an early stage as a kind of calque of the word 'Torah', taking into Greek and to Greek readers much of the associative range of the Hebrew. So, while *nomos* means 'law', about seven-eighths of the Septuagint instances of the Greek word translate not Hebrew legal words such as *mitzvah*, *hoq*, or *mishpat*, as one might have expected, but Torah.[36] This amounts to as many as 250 to 300 appearances, above all in the Psalms and the prophetic books.[37] Interestingly, however, *nomos* is not used by the Genesis translator(s).[38] What has happened is that the semantic range of the term *nomos* expands, through frequency of Greek–Jewish use, rather

---

[33] S. Schwartz 2001: 68.
[34] e.g. Prov. 6: 20–3; 7: 1–4; 13: 14.
[35] On *nomos*, cf. Chap. 4, p. 165. Schechter 1909 provided the classic expression of the gap between these two semantic fields in the two languages. Note the sensitive discussion, written from a twentieth-century Jewish–Christian perspective, in Ellison 1983. Other occasional renderings of Torah in LXX are *logos*, *exēgoria*, *biblion*, *diagraphē*, *diathēkē*, *taxis* (once each), *entolē* (4), *prostagma* (3), *thesmos* (2, of parental teaching), *nomothesmos* (once), *nomima* (6), *deuteronomion* (2, for *mishneh hatorah*). Cf. Schröder 1996: 21–5.
[36] On the other hand, the relatively fixed translation of *mitzvah* is *entolē* and it is revealing that in two Jewish epitaphs from the city of Rome, *CIJ*, i, 203 and 205 (from between the second and fourth centuries CE) the deceased is described as *philentolos*, a lover of the commandments.
[37] There was no doubt, as Dodd points out, that the Septuagint translators knew perfectly well the Hebrew meaning of Torah. That they understood the semantic shift is clear from their rendering of the root *yod*, *reh*, *heh* and the *hiphil*, *horah*, by *didaskein*, *deloun*, *deiknunai*, *sumbibazein*, *anangelein*. Dodd 1935: 30–3.
[38] Genesis has *ta nomima*, once, for Torah: see Harl and Alexandre 1986: introduction: 54. *Nomos* does appear in the Exodus translation however.

than that of 'Torah' shrinking to 'law' alone. There is arguably some room for such growth in the semantic range of the Greek word.[39] The expanded use remains fixed in the usage of Greek–Jewish writers through the centuries. The more focused term *nomothesia*, 'legislation', appears in later texts, and is liked by Philo. The cognates of the Greek *nomos* include words like *nomima*—practices, customs—terms which again allow room for Jewish–Greek writers to build upon the original concept.[40] But behind all such developments lies the Mosaic code, as set forth in the five books, while the language of *nomos*, that catchword of Hellenistic Judaism, encapsulates in miniature the great task of preserving and adapting the code through the endless process of translation, re-translation, and active engagement.

[39] A recent tendency has been either to widen the scope of the Greek *nomos* or to suggest that the sense of 'divine law' was always a possible meaning of the Hebrew Torah, even if it encompassed more than law: see Segal 1987: 131–45 and Richardson and Westerholm 1991; but the gap remains.

[40] This is in fact is an interesting half-way house, because it is characteristically the word used in Greek ethnographic accounts. For example, see Bar-Kochva 1996.

1

The *Letter of Aristeas* between History and Myth

ANCIENT TRANSLATION PRECEDENTS

The first Greek Bible translation was a major step in a new direction, and yet it was not altogether a novelty. In the successive great empires of the ancient Near East, predecessors of the Hellenistic kingdoms, translation had been a regular occurrence. In the third millennium BCE Mesopotamia was already the archetypal land of languages-in-contact, where a more ancient Sumerian stream came together with younger Semitic streams. William Hallo draws a striking connection across the millennia when he writes that 'it is not for nothing that modern examples of linguistic and cultural symbiosis have appealed to Mesopotamian precedent—as when Franz Rosenzweig entitles his essays on German Jewry (too optimistically as it turned out) "Zweistromland [two-rivers land]"'.[1] In ancient Mesopotamia, lexical lists assisted a class of professional translators; they were called in Sumerian *eme-bal*, literally 'language-turners', a term startlingly similar to what would much later be the basic Greek term for translation. Later, during the second millennium BCE, at a time when Sumerian survived only as a language of learning, bilingual texts—rather than freestanding translations—were a product of scholarship on a large scale. In the first millennium BCE, translation activity continued apace in Assyria and Babylonia, often

---

[1] Hallo 1996: 155. In a comparable way, the cultural confluence they discovered in Hellenistic Judaism spoke with great immediacy to German-Jewish scholars and intellectuals.

characterized by 'slavish fidelity' and a preference for an interlinear format.² In the biblical book of Ezra (4: 7), the author who has transmitted the remarkable communications from and to the King concerning the Jews' rebuilding of Jerusalem attests by implication to Jewish contact with a multiplicity of official languages. He sees fit to point out that the accusations about the Jews that were sent, with permission, to Artaxerxes, were 'written in Aramaic and read out [*meturgam*] in Aramaic'.

Translation in the ancient Near East also transcended immediate official needs. One well-loved and very long-lasting work of creative literature that was disseminated in different language versions during the first half of the second millennium BCE was the old Sumerian epic of Gilgamesh. This was translated into Akkadian, and what is regarded as a 'standard version', written on twelve Akkadian tablets, emerged in the second half of that millennium.³

The ancient Near East supplies a meaningful background, yet no real precedents for a translation by Jews of their Torah arising out of Ptolemaic Egypt. Greek experience of the translation process was altogether more limited. Indeed, the principal Mediterranean parallel comes from the milieu of the Romans, who were hit in the mid-third century BCE by a major wave of Greek culture. At Rome, the ex-slave Livius Andronicus translated the Odyssey into Latin, intriguingly at more or less the same time as the Septuagint translation was, according to our tradition, commissioned at Alexandria by Ptolemy II.

By contrast, the bilingual or even trilingual texts of Hellenistic Egypt, where Egyptian, or demotic and Greek are found together, were produced for practical purposes. In Ptolemaic private agreements, we sometimes find each side certifying in their own language, thus bringing languages together while stopping short of actual translation. But, as in the earlier empires, so Macedonian rule in Egypt required that public documents be properly understood, whether they be legal, financial, religious, or honorific. In many

---

² See Hallo 1996 for a general introduction to the rich history of translation in ancient Mesopotamia.

³ For an authoritative study of the Babylonian Gilgamesh epic, with its many ramifications, see George 2003.

cases, the two main language versions are markedly different. The Memphis decree of 196 BCE known as the Rosetta Stone, whose discovery in 1799 opened the door to the decipherment of hieroglyphics by Champollion, is the most famous of a small number of trilingual Ptolemaic inscriptions. It is a decree issued by a council of priests of Upper and Lower Egypt on the first anniversary of the boy-king Ptolemy V's coronation, inscribed on black basalt first in Greek, and then in a translation into Egyptian that is expressed in both hieroglyphic and demotic scripts. Earlier well-known examples, in the same mix of languages and scripts, are the Canopus decree (of 238 BCE), an extended set of resolutions by Egyptian priests honouring Ptolemy III; and the so-called Pithom stele (217 BCE), in which the priests assembled at Memphis accord to Ptolemy IV the full Pharaonic titulature in both Greek and Egyptian versions.[4] Such documents paraded the juxtaposition of the different traditions and interests of rulers and ruled, and they enabled Greek to work as an effective language for an essentially alien regime.

There are allusions in papyri to interpreters involved in various official activities which could have been either written or oral. A mere eight or nine such cases have been found that relate to Ptolemaic Egypt in its entirety, most of them from the Zenon archive, that unique dossier of some 2,000 documents belonging to a high royal official of the mid-third century BCE. But they are clearly the tip of an iceberg: for the most part, the labours of the behind-the-scenes translators simply did not rate mention.[5]

But even were we to recover the lost interpreters, we would undoubtedly find that the Torah translation would have made them sit up. For it is doubtful whether any other large-scale translation enterprises apart from the Septuagint were undertaken in Ptolemaic Alexandria. Pliny the Elder's statement that the scholar and biographer Hermippus of Smyrna, an associate of Callimachus, made available to Alexandrians the content of two million lines of verse

---

[4] *OGIS* 90; 56; *CCG* 22–183. English translations: Bagnall and Derow 2004, nos. 164 and 165. Peremans 1985 reviews the field and has a full conspectus of the translated texts then known. On the cultural significance of the first two texts, see also in Bingen 2007: 262–6.

[5] Wright 2002: 16; Evans 2007.

by the magus Zoroaster, who had lived 6,000 years before Plato is, to say the least, problematic. Nothing further was ever heard of this, and whatever this artefact was, it was scarcely a word-for-word translation.[6] The translation of the Hebrew Pentateuch into Greek was a cultural innovation. And while not quite on the scale of the supposed Zoroaster version, it was still an enormously ambitious project.

It is a fanciful but pleasing idea that inspiration could have come from the West, percolating somehow from Rome. But the question for us to ask is not about influences, but rather about what more immediate realities gave rise to the Septuagint. The search for solutions might take different routes, and by the end of this book we will have explored quite a number of them. It would be perverse not to begin with the very rich ancient account. Users of the translation had indeed their own very clear answer to the question in the form of a narrative which was composed within a few generations of the beginning of the translation, and which continued to satisfy many generations. King Ptolemy II of Egypt, it was believed, ordered the translation to be made for his library, in which he aspired to collect 'all the books in the world'. When told about the unique phenomenon of the Jewish Torah he rose to the challenge. The story's primary surviving form is an independent Greek prose narrative generally known nowadays as the '*Letter of Aristeas*' (in earlier scholarly discourse often *Pseudo-Aristeas*).

The main purpose of this chapter is to focus closely on that tradition, looking at different approaches to its historicity and reflecting on the nature of historical myth. The fact–fiction dichotomy, we shall find, is not always helpful. In Chapter 3, the quest continues and I shall go on to look at ways in which the *Letter* embodies the concerns of the early Ptolemies and the culture they fostered in Alexandria. The Jews had a particular role to play in the making of that culture.

---

[6] On Zoroaster at Alexandria, Pliny *Naturalis Historia* 30.2.3–44; Fraser 1972: 330 and 436, n.745; Bickerman 1976: 198–200; Canfora 1989: 24.

INTERPRETING THE TRADITION

From the outset, it will be apparent that none of the versions we have of the translation story could possibly be entirely true.[7] But might the story still contain within it some part of what happened? Modern research has sometimes become so uneasy with *Aristeas* as an account of the origins of the Septuagint as to advocate a clean break: better, it is suggested, to treat this text as a pleasant piece of Hellenistic–Jewish prose and to detach it altogether from the endeavour of historical reconstruction. However, to decouple the traditions entirely from the texts to which they have been so firmly attached, as such hard-headed Septuagint scholars have advocated, has seemed to others, including myself, to be a rash and extreme move. Echoes of history reverberate in the myth. They are too valuable to jettison, and I shall seek to open up a route to a sensitive reading which allows them to work for us. It is not an insignificant matter that the story derives from the very same Jewish society for which the translations were made. It embodies that society's memories, however hazy. It must share in the thinking which drove the enterprise in the beginning. Side-stepping the fact-fiction dichotomy and approaching the story as historical myth, open to comparison with other reflections of the same period, will also expose some less-noticed elements embedded in the narrative.

We often find that texts of special significance for a society are somehow accompanied by a graphic account of the origins of those texts. Foundational law codes acquire extra authority in this way, and a claim to a place in the heart of the people. In particular, laws of supposedly divine origin gain validity from a narrative of the events surrounding their revelation, endorsed often by the designation of an exact location as well as by tangible interactions between the sacred

---

[7] N. Collins 2000, however, bases her study on an initial assumption of the complete historicity of the *Letter*. From this assumption she draws out what seems to be a circular argument, that the project as described in *Aristeas* would only make sense as a royal enterprise and that therefore its depiction of the King's role must be deemed wholly historical.

and the secular spheres. In relation to the early history of Rome, the historian Livy (1.20) tells us that the second king, Numa Pompilius, supposed founder of the Roman religion, concluded that he needed just such a tale to inspire his simple subjects with fear of the gods. He therefore told them that the nymph Egeria had been meeting with him at night and instructing him on the establishment of rites and priests. The Hebrew Torah of Moses was itself generously supplied with backing: the great Mosaic encounter recounted in the narratives of Exodus 19–30, with its climax at Sinai, is alluded to or amplified when the laws are revisited in each of the other four books of the Pentateuch.[8] Indeed the entire narrative from creation onwards might be seen as preparation for the giving of the Law. Rashi, the leading medieval commentator, observed on Genesis 1: 1 that the Torah, being the law book of Israel, should really have begun with what was the first commandment, 'this month shall be unto you the first of the month' (Exod. 12: 1); he asked why instead it opens with 'in the beginning'. He answered that it was necessary first to demonstrate how God had created everything: he could therefore dispose of it at will, giving Israel the title to the land of Israel.[9]

It is not unexpected, then, that when the *nomos* (law), as the Hebrew Torah is commonly called in Greek,[10] became the central document of Greek-speaking Jewry, an account of the origins of the translation travelled with it on its journey. Indeed, it is not out of place to observe that the tradition endured in Jewish historical memory better than did its hefty and unwieldy subject, the translation itself. The power of the story is thus evident. That of course does not in itself tell us anything about its reliability, a question to which a more subtle approach is needed.

---

[8] On the supreme importance of the Sinai narrative, cf. Sawyer 1999: 96–7.

[9] Rashi's interpretation draws on the words of the Psalmist,'he declared to the people the strength of his works in order that he might give them the heritage of the nations', as well as on Genesis Rabbah 1.2. Brague (2007: 62) reflects on the setting for divine laws.

[10] On the Torah–*nomos* equivalence, see below, p. 165.

THE *ARISTEAS* NARRATIVE

The *Letter of Aristeas* explains how King Ptolemy II of Egypt (280–246 BCE) learns from the head of his library, Demetrius of Phaleron, of the existence of a holy book, the Jewish Law (we are not told what this contained nor exactly how extensive it was). On being told that this is a text written in a strange script, he sends two emissaries, the narrator himself and a man named Andreas, to the most learned High Priest of the Jews in Judaea to obtain for transcription a more correct version of that text than anything available in Alexandria. This will be an addition to the royal library, now set fair to achieve half a million books, where the King aspires to house, with no expense spared, 'all the books in the known world' (a resonant phrase which tends to get repeated verbatim in the modern literature connected with the Alexandrian library). As a token of goodwill, the King, at Aristeas' request and at huge expense to himself, decrees the release of the more than 100,000 prisoners of war from Judaea. Polite letters are exchanged between various parties and the monarch which give an official air to this part of the proceedings. Extravagant gifts, lavishly described, are hand-crafted and presented to the High Priest; and with the holy scrolls, the seventy-two selected (and named) translators are brought back. Wonderfully well received, the translators are wined and dined for a week by the King and their table talk occupies much of the *Letter*. Eventually, they set to work on their task in an allocated workspace on an island which remains unnamed in the text but which is evidently the island of Pharos, location of the famous lighthouse. Enjoying the pure air and the sea breezes, and labouring in perfect harmony with one another, the translators accomplish the task expeditiously and successfully. They present the outcome to their patron and then to the Jews of Alexandria, to great acclaim.

The author referred to his first person narrative at its opening in simple terms as 'something recounted', in Greek a *diēgēsis* (1.1). In Mantua during the 1570s, Azariah de' Rossi, the Jewish rediscoverer and translator of *Aristeas* into Hebrew (from a Latin version), devised for the book the delightful patriotic title 'Splendour of the

Elders'.[11] In early modern scholarship, our author came to be known, prosaically and perhaps a trifle pejoratively, as 'Pseudo-Aristeas', the implication being that he was an unknown person pretending to be a man called Aristeas, also unknown. The more straightforward 'Letter of Aristeas' is a perfectly good name. Moreover, even if some ancient writers used other terms, such as *suntagma* (a 'construction') or *biblion*, the designation as a letter has a respectable pedigree in a fourth-century CE manuscript,[12] and objections on the grounds of inaccuracy are surely misplaced. For while the text of the *Letter* bears few of the marks of epistolary form, in spite of brief attention at beginning and end to a named addressee, a glance at the great variation to be found among the many surviving Greek literary epistles should dispel such concerns. The best-known work of ancient literary criticism, the so-called *On Style* (*peri hermēneias*), takes the trouble to insist that true letters should not turn into treatises in letter form, as those addressed to kings are particularly prone to do: it is interesting that this work was traditionally ascribed precisely to none other than Demetrius of Phaleron, as was a separate guide on 'Epistolary Types' (*tupoi epistolikoi*).[13] In addition to all this, Jews writing in Greek, as Adolf Deissmann pointed out, seem to have been particularly keen on literary epistolography.[14] We may thus feel quite comfortable with the designation as letter. We do need, however, to remember that Aristeas, the purported Greek courtier of Ptolemy II, in fact fills a double role, both as the book's author and as one of its

---

[11] For Azariah de' Rossi's naming of the *Letter*, see Weinberg 2001: 33.

[12] As observed by P. Alexander 1984: 580. Honigman (2003: 1) supports her preference for 'the Book of Aristeas' (*B.Ar*) with the precedent of Josephus (*AJ*12.100), who speaks of *to Aristaiou biblion*. The description *suntagma* appears in Epiphanius, *de mens et pond* 9. Eusebius (*Praep. Ev.* 9.38) spoke of the *Letter* as 'Concerning the Translation of the Jewish Law'. The first appearance of our name appears to be in the so-called Paris Q manuscript, which combines part of *Aristeas* with other material. Other manuscripts have the superscription 'Aristeas to Philocrates', on which see Jellicoe 1968: 30. Deissmann's distinction in modern parlance between 'letter' (private) and 'epistle' (public), endorsed by Jellicoe, scarcely corresponds to contemporary English usage.

[13] For a range of epistolary examples, see the study of Rosenmeyer 2001. For Pseudo-Demetrius on epistolography, see Klauck 2006: 183–96.

[14] Deissmann 1903: 41.

main participants: context can make it clear which we are discussing at any point.

The story, then, displays a king's enthusiastic advancement of a Jewish enterprise, and his additional magnanimity in liberating by decree from forced settlement or enslavement, all Jewish former war captives and slaves in his kingdom, and sending them home with compensation. Ptolemy shrugs this off as a trifle. His acknowledgement of the God of the Jews, whom he learns to be the same as Zeus, and veneration for his worshippers and for his Law, emerge as the basis of his action, and he shows particular esteem for the High Priest, for the priestly hierarchy, and for the Jewish sages-cum-translators. All these are assigned significant roles by the author.[15] Other participants in the *Aristeas* narrative, animate or inanimate, are the land of Judaea, the city—though it remains curiously unnamed—with the Temple in the middle of it, and the two courtier-emissaries. The collectivity of the Jews of Alexandria (*to plēthos* in Greek) appear only when convoked by Demetrius at the end of the *Letter* to hear the translation read out and to request that their leaders—who are not given names—receive a copy of the new text.[16]

However, the foremost participant—the single most visible human individual in the entire narrative—is not the High Priest, nor yet any other Jewish personality from Judaea or from Alexandria, but King Ptolemy Philadelphus himself. Admittedly, the monarch is a little slow to make his appearance. The ostensible purpose of the narration, explained at its opening, is for Aristeas to tell Philocrates, his brother—or just conceivably a friend described as 'brother'[17]—recently arrived in Egypt, about his recent participation in the embassy. But Demetrius of Phaleron soon comes in, without introduction. He is said to have been given a huge sum of money for disbursement when he was put in charge of the royal library (an institution designated as entirely personal to the King), and he is heading up the great book collection project. He sets the scene ably

---

[15] Weinberg 2001: 33, n.1 suggests that de' Rossi, by naming them in the title of the work, made the seventy-two elders the leading protagonists of the story.

[16] More precisely, but somewhat obscurely, *Aristeas* 310 describes those leaders as 'the priests and the elders of the translators and people from the *politeuma* (the administrative body?) and the leaders of the people'.

[17] *Aristeas* 1.5.

for Ptolemy when, in reply to a question, he offers his master a new idea.

We go on to see Ptolemy in a succession of different guises: commanding author of the far-reaching decree cited verbatim in the text, about the liberation of the Jewish prisoners of war; connoisseur, in his commissioning and choice of elaborate artworks to present to the High Priest; pious benefactor, as the donor of new furniture for the Temple; magnificent host at the seven banquets where the translators teach him at length about the morality of statecraft; friendly facilitator; keen interrogator of others in the pursuit of wisdom and knowledge; solemn venerator of a single divinity; and ultimately as the man who can claim credit for the achievement of an unparalleled and enduring accomplishment, the translation of a text in which every word is holy. Every morning, the translators check in to pay their respects to the King before getting down to work.

Overall, the portrayal of the King is positive: even his Jewish instructors take pains to heap praises upon him. Approximately a third of Aristeas' book is taken up with the table-talk of the banquets. No doubt a measure of flattery was part of the author's purpose. At the same time, just a hint of reserve is detectable towards the monarch's high-handedness, as we shall discover. Our narrator displays a shrewd awareness of the undertones.

If the primary setting is the Ptolemaic court, which is evoked in some detail and with some awareness of its Graeco–Egyptian protocol, the author focuses also on communicating by various means a picture of key aspects of Judaism. This stands out in his memorable, highly schematized description of Judaea, the city and the Temple (down to the installations for washing away sacrificial blood), in place of what might rather have been expected, a detailed description of the palace and city of Alexandria. A full treatment is provided of a theme well established in Jewish literature, the High Priest's garb and accoutrements with their mysterious symbolism. Another focus is on the beliefs of the Jews, presented in the High Priest's account of the Jewish conception of the Divine Unity. He gives a rather lengthy symbolic justification of selected Jewish practices, including the use of *tefillin* (phylacteries) and the affixing of *mezuzot* (amulets) to doorposts. He offers careful, quite elaborate and not unsophisticated interpretations of the food laws (128–70): permitted animals have cloven hoofs because this represents separation (from impurity) and they chew the cud because this represents memory (of life); forbidden animals such as mice and weasels have characteristics which evoke evil aspects of man. Finally, we have the banquets with the insights of the participants into the bearing of God's supremacy and Jewish ethics on a monarch's conduct.

The compilation is evidently the carefully contrived literary production of one individual, an apparently Jewish author (of unknown identity) who has blended together a rich variety of ingredients, showing special artistry in his meticulous descriptions of objects and buildings. All this was encapsulated by Aristeas in a highly wrought text composed in assured and accomplished Greek. His vocabulary is marked by a rich use of synonyms and a liking for rare words.[18] His narrative technique, with the participant narrator reporting in the first person on all that transpires, as though from his own observation, is self-conscious and artful.

EVOLUTION OF THE STORY

It is highly likely that the author of the Letter built on the existing understanding of how the Torah translation came to be done; but whether any written accounts preceded his book will never be known.[19] The date of composition need not be particularly far from whatever events gave rise to it—anthropologists hold that mythologized tradition takes no more than three generations to form—but the clues are scant. A mid-second-century date looks likely on literary grounds. Somewhere around the time of Aristeas, a philosophically inclined Jewish writer, Aristobulus, probably an intellectual of some importance at Alexandria, also described the involvement of Philadelphus in the translation and mentioned

---

[18] For a close engagement with the language of the *Letter*, see the studies and word lists in Meecham 1935.

[19] Honigman 2003: 91 and 101 regards it as possible that 'echoes of a pre-existing oral tradition are embedded in the Letter'.

Demetrius of Phaleron, perhaps independently of Aristeas.[20] We do not know which of them wrote first.[21]

What is clear is that the tradition on how the translation came about gained, and then maintained, a vigorous life. The story is to be found in Philo (*Life of Moses*, 2.26–44), in Josephus, in rabbinic literature, and in many early Christian writers.[22] Philo talks of an annual feast and gathering (*heortē kai panēguris*). Held on the lighthouse island of Pharos, where 'the light of the translation first shone out'. This shows that the part of Aristeas' story relating to the location of the translators' labours was accepted as history by Alexandrian Jews in subsequent centuries. He seems to write as one familiar with the festival, describing graphically how celebrants took to tents on the beach, reclining and dining in the open. Though he concludes the description with a small personal statement, expressing the hope that one day, with the advent of better times, all peoples might see the light and exchange their own laws for those of the Jews, he does not cast his description of the actual festival in allegorical or symbolic terms. The festival is clearly a perfectly real event, a ritualized re-enactment of the collective memory of Alexandrian Jewry.

Josephus, in the first century CE, ascribed huge importance to the Septuagint translation, and therefore to the provision of a suitably impressive account of its origins, and we grant him the credit of supposing that this was not merely because of its service as an antecedent to his own different Greek rendering of the Bible in his *Antiquities*. The historian not only incorporates there a long extract from the Letter (*AJ*, 12.11–118), but he goes so far as to

---

[20] On Aristobulus, see also below, p. 78; p. 98 n. 14. 2 Macc. 1: 10 gives Aristobulus who was 'the teacher of Ptolemy the King' as the addressee of a communication from the Jews of Jerusalem. Perhaps arising from this, Clement of Alexandria and Eusebius associate him with a Ptolemy, generally taken to be Ptolemy VI Philometor (181–145 BCE). For the argument that Aristeas and Aristobulus drew independently on the same tradition, see Walter 1964: 86–102.

[21] Issues set out in Schürer iii: 579–80. See also Holladay 1983–96, iii: 64–5. Full discussion in Walter 1964: 86–102, whose detailed case for the genuineness of the fragments dispelled previous scepticism.

[22] The full *testimonia* in Greek and Latin are in Wendland's Teubner edition (Wendland and Mendelssohn 1900). The patristic material is well-presented in Pelletier 1962: 81–98. And see now Wasserstein and Wasserstein 2006.

invoke the Septuagint enterprise in the work's preface (*AJ*, 1.10–11). He comes back to it in his last work, the polemic *Against Apion* (2.45), as a clear proof of outside interest in the Jewish Law at the highest level.

Josephus apart, the *Aristeas* tradition, as one might expect, underwent repeated reductions and embellishments, which reduced or eliminated a substantial part of the content, while bestowing a miraculous dimension on the translation-event and emphasizing the contribution of divine inspiration. This last was not a feature of Josephus' version, who underplays the sanctity and inalterability of the text; but it had already appeared in that of Philo, who notably here draws upon the Greek language of divine possession.[23] Building on Philo, Christian writing places the translators in separate houses, or cubicles, where, incredibly, they arrive at identical renderings. These are the cubicles knowingly evoked in the lines from Yehuda Amichai at the head of my Introduction, where the poet conflates them with the translation booths of modern conferences. In both cases, terrors lie beneath the superficial harmony. For the ancient translators, the Holy Spirit materializes as assistants, and in some Church writers this intervention elicits from the Hebrew text truths and mysteries which had once been revealed to the old 'Israel' but which were deliberately concealed later by their successors, the later Jews.[24]

It is noteworthy that rabbinic tradition on the Alexandrian enterprise shares with Christian literature some of the miraculous elements, though not the supernatural intervention. It has been suspected indeed that the miracle story originated in Palestinian rabbinic circles from where Christians borrowed it.[25] Tractate megillah in both the Jerusalem and Babylonian Talmud contains a version of the story, and in both cases there is a more or less accepting attitude. The Rabbis knew that adjustments were made for 'King Talmai' (Ptolemy), though how they understood the exercise is obscure, and a variable number—eleven, seventeen, or even

---

[23] For an excellent analysis of this language of divine possession, see Dines 2004: 64–70.
[24] On this influential motif, see further Chap. 9, pp. 282–5.
[25] See the discussion by Wasserstein and Wasserstein 2006: 68–9.

eighteen—of changes allegedly made to the Hebrew Bible is recorded.[26] Some of these alleged changes are not at all apparent to us in the present Greek versions, but one which we can trace is the delightful notion that the Greek term for the Hebrew hare, *arnevet*, had been replaced by the word for 'young (or hairy) of foot' (*dasupous*) at Leviticus 11: 6 and Deuteronomy 14: 7, in order to avoid appearing to mock the King, whose wife, it is explained, had this name. The rabbinic explanation seems to derive from a garbled recollection not of the Queen's name, but of that of the Lagid dynasty, whose founder, Ptolemy I bore the soubriquet Lagos, sounding exactly the same as the Greek word for 'hare'.[27] The Rabbis sometimes thought that the translators had been seventy in number, but sometimes that they were just five (one for each book of the Torah, presumably). Negative attitudes to the translation, including the well-known likening of the day it was made to the day of the making of the golden calf, appear only late in rabbinic literature.[28]

Nor did this negative reaction necessarily affect the popular view. In the Hebrew *Sefer Yosippon*, a mélange of ancient history composed in southern Italy in the tenth century, a version of the sending of the emissaries and of the exchange of gifts appears; and from this much-translated and widely known romance the translation story achieved a place in Jewish consciousness in succeeding generations. The story was also incorporated by some Islamic authors over the centuries.[29]

---

[26] B. *Meg* 9a–b; J. *Meg.* 1.1.4 and elsewhere. For a straightforward summary of the traditions, including a helpful survey of the main rabbinic texts, see Hadas 1951: 73–84. And for the latter at greater length, see Wasserstein and Wasserstein 2006: 31–94. The rabbinic material with its interpretation in modern scholarship is the principal subject of Veltri 1994, a study focusing especially on the two groups of passages which were allegedly altered for 'King Talmai'. For a different interpretation and classification of the passages, see Tov 1999: 1–20, 75–82. See also Baumgarten 2002: 20–8, criticizing Tov, with further bibliography. On rabbinic attitudes to the Septuagint, see further Chap. 9 below.

[27] See further, Chap. 2, p. 89. For a full investigation of this tradition, its value and its aftermath, see Pearce 2007b.

[28] For further details, see p. 304.

[29] The Islamic material is amply covered in the wide-ranging review of the entire tradition by Wasserstein and Wasserstein 2006.

FACT OR FICTION? THE SEARCH FOR HISTORICITY

The scholarly enterprise of catching out Aristeas has an extraordinary and not always savoury history. This reached its climax in works of seventeenth-century scholarship,[30] some of which are still admired today.[31] They purported to expose Aristeas as a fraud, and—far worse—a cheating Jew. The best-known critics of the *Letter*, the outstanding classical scholar Joseph Justus Scaliger, and the churchman and Oxford scholar Humphrey Hody were, each in his own way, virtuoso investigators.[32] Yet their critiques are tainted with astonishing assertions: the *Letter* was not merely fiction passed off as history, but the work of a contemptible imposter, acting true to Jewish type and passing himself off as a well-born Greek. The shameless vanity of the Jews (Aristeas was apparently not alone in his malefaction) had led them to promote their translation without scruple. Thus they had managed to deceive not only their Alexandrian contemporaries but also subsequent generations of unsuspecting Christian readers.[33] Hody, whose

---

[30] This scholarship was preceded by a brief and perceptive observation on the fictitious authorship of the *Letter* (as it appears in Josephus) made by Luis Vives in his 1522 commentary on Augustine's *City of God* 18.42. On Vives, a renowned humanist scholar from Valencia, of Jewish 'conversos' origin, patronized by Henry VIII and employed for a time at Oxford, see Wasserstein and Wasserstein 2006: 241–2.

[31] But it should be noted that Bickerman 1976: 171, after observing that 'the Alexandrian tradition about the origin of the Septuagint came to be challenged after the Reformation and then disproved for historical reasons', went on regardless, and with implicit irony, to mount his own defence of the tradition.

[32] The exposure of pseudonymous works was a major interest of seventeenth-century classical scholars. The most famous example is Bentley's polemic on the Epistle of Phalaris (Bentley 1699).

[33] Hody unhesitatingly exploits his readers' negative assumptions about Jewish character. Thus he writes (Chap. 2, p. 34): 'a qua vanitate minime abhorrent Judaei, qui sine ulla religione, neglecta omni specie veri, mentiri ausi sunt, quasi tota posteritas Midae aures, (quod Tertullianus ait), aptas eorum fabulis assumpsisset'. The Jews had made it their business 'ut Versionis Graecae dignitatem per fas aut nefas extollerent'. (Chap. 3, pp. 40–1). They were 'proni proclivesque... ad figmenta talia', so that 'cum ex aliis exemplis infinitis, tum ex eo liquet' (Chap. 18, p. 265). J. J. Scaliger's employment of similar pejorative language, when he speaks of 'mendacia' and when he writes of the 'fabrications of the Jews' with which no one could be unfamiliar, is noted by Grafton 1998: 32–3. And for the locations of the comments within Scaliger's writings, see Grafton 1993: 416–17, 706–7. The anti-Jewish strand in Hody's polemic surprisingly goes unnoticed by Wasserstein and Wasserstein (2006:

goals were not the same as Scaliger's, is described in the History of the University of Oxford as a man who, after showing early promise with his dissertation on Aristeas, 'applied his learning almost exclusively to religious ends, despite being Regius Professor of Greek'.[34] In fact, Hody's unmasking of 'Aristeas' already possessed something of the air of a theological quest. To discredit the *Letter* was a telling way of undermining the Septuagint's claim to authority as a revealed text. Objections were made by the Dutch scholar Isaac Vossius, at that time resident in England, who had already defended the chronology of the Greek Bible and its claims against the Hebrew Masoretic text, taking an unusual position for a Protestant. Hody responded to the assault made upon him, by reissuing in 1705 his demolition of the *Letter of Aristeas*, on this occasion embedding it within a broader frame of reference.[35]

Scholarship has moved on, even if Hody's endeavours continue to win favourable comment.[36] Passions are nowadays less likely to be aroused by the wars over the biblical text, whether of Christians against Jews or between Christians of different persuasions. But negative implications attached to the 'fiction' label which was for so long pinned to Aristeas as a mark of opprobrium perhaps still linger. We need to go yet one step further, and to remind ourselves that, while Aristeas may have chosen to give his narrative the style and air of a factual account, down even to the inclusion of pretended documents, his contemporaries could hardly fail to have been aware of the conventions within which he was operating. When he solemnly asserts, having recounted the translators' virtuoso performances at the King's symposium, that readers might find this incredible, but that the holiness of the subject guaranteed the truth of everything he had said (*Aristeas* 396), he does it in a tone of artful, almost provocative playfulness which Hody has altogether missed. The ancient

---

254–8), who simply comment on 'the relative absence here of Jewish sources' and express surprise that Hody 'did not seem to know de' Rossi'.

[34] Tyacke 1997: 268. This was not an unusual pattern; a polemicist against the non-juror bishops, Hody was chaplain to two Archbishops of Canterbury. See G. Goodwin in *DNB* (1891) xxvii: 77–8. For an updated entry, see M. Greig, 'Hody, Humphrey (1659–1707)', *DNB* (2004).

[35] On the background to Vossius' first investigation, see Lebram 1975.

[36] For a more critical view, see, however, N. Collins 2000: 115.

readership was sensitive, as we are not, to the literary codes which gave the author this licence.[37]

And yet, one way or another, the question of the story's truth continues to surface and to perplex. This is understandable. At stake is not only the history that we write of the Septuagint itself but also our reconstruction of the culture of Ptolemaic Alexandria, and of both Greek and Jewish mentalities within it. Modern scholarly opinion has been radically divided, with impressive voices on either side. Because the division is roughly on disciplinary lines, the one side has perhaps not taken very much notice of the other side's thinking—a lesson, perhaps, in the consequences of academic compartmentalization. It is perhaps mainly from the ranks of scholars concerned with Ptolemaic history, with Alexandria, or with the foundation of the Ptolemaic Museum and Library that cautious acceptance has come for the tradition of the involvement of Philadephus. Among these were Peter Fraser and, on several occasions, Elias Bickerman.[38] Bickerman constructed a context for the translation by his memorable, if impressionistic, suggestion that the word-for-word translation technique of the Septuagint matched that of the 'dragomans', the official translators of the Ottoman empire.[39] E. A. Parsons' study of the Alexandrian Library, written during the war years and published in 1952, is still worth mentioning in this regard, as well as Luciano Canfora's rather widely noticed contemporary study, *The Vanished Library*.[40] We do, however, find a greater tendency to skepticism on the part of distinguished scholars who have come to the *Letter of Aristeas* as historians of Hellenistic culture, notably Arnaldo Momigliano, Oswyn Murray, and Erich Gruen. Murray writes: 'one may suspect that closer study of the Greek translation itself would

---

[37] Cf. already Hadas 1951: 226: 'Aristeas is not claiming to write history'. And on the problem of fiction as history, see Bowersock's subtle study (1994).

[38] Fraser 1972: 689–90, 700. Bickerman 1976: 121–36, 67–75; Bickerman 1988: 101–4.

[39] On the translation style, and the dragoman parallel, see Chap. 4, pp. 136–9.

[40] Neither Parsons' book (1952) nor Canfora's imaginative study (1989) is wholly reliable, though both are stimulating. Collins 2000 is a monograph dedicated to tracking down the precise date of the Septuagint translation, offering fuller documentation than the earlier works, but also more speculation (cf. also n. 7 to this chapter).

tend rather to disprove than to confirm the story told by Aristeas'. To these three may be added Moses Hadas, in the introduction to his pioneering translation and commentary.[41]

But it is modern biblical research that has most decisively preferred to put Aristeas firmly to one side and to understand the translation enterprise totally in terms of the needs of the Alexandrian Jewish community, to whose leaders the translation was, as the story has it, read out and then presented. These needs were previously defined by scholars in relation to the liturgical practices of the synagogue, but alternative interpretations have now come to the fore.[42] A dismissive line on Aristeas is firmly followed by Sebastian Brock, and recently Benjamin Wright has declared himself eager to jettison altogether the historical baby.[43]

For those of a more accepting bent, Aristeas offers evidence—a commodity in very short supply—about an early phase of the Library and about the atmosphere surrounding it, notwithstanding the text's visible fictional dimension. Even on the lower among the current dating estimates, which would put the book's composition somewhere around 100 BCE, they find in Aristeas a genuine Ptolemaic creation. The formulaic headings to the letters exchanged between the parties appear to show knowledge of official practice, and the decree on the prisoners contains genuine chancery language and some titles of officials are accurate for the period.[44] Such scholars have gratefully taken on board the context evoked in *Aristeas* as evidence for city, court, or library, even without the benefit of a precise date tag, and in doing so they have been content to accept the elements of his narrative, even though context and story are logically not inseparable. On the other hand, even those on the other side, who dismiss the *Letter* and attribute

---

[41] Momigliano 1975: 91; Murray 1975: 123; Gruen 1998: 206–22; Hadas 1951: 52–3.
[42] For discussion of these interpretations, see Chap. 4, pp. 172–4.
[43] Brock 1974; Wright 2006.
[44] Bickerman 1976: 116–28. See Fraser 1972: 974, n. 126 on the chancery phraseology in the royal decree in *Aristeas* concerning the liberation of Jewish war prisoners, and Fraser 1972: 977–8, n. 148 for some examples of Ptolemaic administrative terms in the *Letter*, not all of them entirely transparent in meaning. See also the collection of possibly correct titles for court officials in Kasher 1985: 59, n. 133. The method of dating the work through particular usages remains, however, highly problematic.

the beginnings of the translation exclusively to internal Jewish needs, will still often depend upon him to the extent of allowing themselves to fix the beginning of the translation to some point in the reign of Philadelphus. Briefly expressed but cogent support for the middle ground comes from Josèphe Mélèze Modrzejewski in his history of ancient Egyptian Jewry.[45]

Yet essentially there is no sensible way of choosing between the positions. The story in general lines is not impossible and the most frequently repeated preliminary objection to the account of *Aristeas*, based upon an apparent crude anachronism concerning Demetrius of Phaleron, is less persuasive than appears at first sight. This objection was already raised by Scaliger, and it was developed by Hody, for whose assault this was the springboard. The problem arises because of the information that Demetrius had to leave Alexandria soon after Ptolemy II's accession in 283, banished for having backed the wrong horse as heir-apparent. That would seem to undermine any claim of Demetrius' involvement in a Torah translation commissioned by Ptolemy II. It is not decisive. Historical myth tends to conflate known characters from different periods. The evidence for the banishment is not strong, since our single source for it is Hermippus, by no means the most reliable of biographers. And, finally, it is quite conceivable for the translation enterprise to have been indeed set in motion by Demetrius still under Ptolemy I and then accomplished under Ptolemy II. The Alexandrian Christian writer Clement (*Strom.*, 1.22.148) reported several centuries later that some people ascribed the translation to Ptolemy I and others to Ptolemy II; perhaps the lost voices in the former category had sought a solution to the problem precisely along these lines. Such a sequence would mirror the Library's own development, founded as it was by Ptolemy I and significantly developed by Ptolemy II, who appointed as head of the library his former (second) tutor Zenodotus of Ephesus. It is a further help that we have evidence of Ptolemy II getting credit for the accomplishments of his father: in the Roman period, Pausanias mistakenly ascribed to Philadelphus the acquisition of Alexander the Great's body.

---

[45] Mélèze Modrzejewski 1995: 142–6. But against such a compromise, Dorival, Harl, and Munnich 1988: 77–8.

It is useful to have cleared this objection out of our way. We are dealing with a story which, while clearly oversimplified, is not impossible.[46] Another claim, this time of a positive kind, will detain us just a little longer, in the hope that this too may be laid to rest once and for all.

THE BIBLE IN THE SHRINE OF SERAPIS?

It is intriguing that the Christian author Tertullian endorsed the Aristeas story in the *Apologeticum* (18.8), written around 200 CE, maintaining that 'Ptolemy's libraries, with the actual Hebrew writings', were still to be seen in the Alexandrian shrine known as the Serapeum. His wording is somewhat opaque, but the context shows that Tertullian wishes us to think that the original Greek of the seventy-two was still there within the Serapeum library in his own day. Nevertheless, Tertullian makes no claim of personal observation, and our limited evidence for his life includes no visit to Egypt.[47] He is no more than a hearsay witness. Yet Tertullian's cryptic remark has fed the very widespread notion that the Septuagint was indeed produced for that temple library and moreover that the translation resided from the beginning in a separate collection of texts housed in a distinctive cult centre which, it is surmised, was dedicated in some fashion to 'foreign literature'.

The appropriateness of the location appears to lie in the hybrid nature of the Serapis cult, a veritable symbol of cultural fusion. From the first Ptolemy, the new Macedonian dynasty had made major efforts to come to terms with the overwhelming Egyptian past and especially with the enduring power of the Egyptian gods and with their representatives, the priests. The formation within Alexandria itself, and centred upon the Serapeum, of a brand new cult

---

[46] As we shall see in the following chapter.
[47] For the date of the *Apologeticum* and biographical evidence on Tertullian, see Barnes 1971. It is worth remembering, by contrast, that the unknown author of the *Cohortatio ad Graecos* ascribed by some to Justin Martyr (Chap. 13) claimed to have seen the seventy-two cubicles of the translators when he visited Alexandria: see Veltri 2006: 43–6.

honouring an apparently new god, constructed out of the Memphis worship of Osiris–Apis, reveals the energy and enterprise brought to bear on the task. Serapis continued to have a dual existence: a Greek god on the one hand, an Egyptian deity on the other. The Alexandrian shrine became the city's principal temple.[48] A group of royal statues almost certainly from the Serapeum, belonging to the late third or early second century and representing a successor of Philadelphus and his Queen, are fully Greek in style. So, apparently, was the architectural style of the shrine. And yet foundation plaques for the shrine have been uncovered, of glass, faience, mud-brick, gold, silver, and bronze, which bear the names of Ptolemy III and Arsinoe III in both Greek and hieroglyphic. In conception and perhaps even in their number they belong to Egyptian tradition.[49] This was a place, then, where vastly different worlds were made to meet.

Even if we are inclined to believe that there is something in what Tertullian says, the Jewish texts to which he refers are most likely to have been brought in during the period of the High Roman Empire, when, between 181 and 217 CE, the Serapeum was rebuilt after destruction by fire—perhaps now as a Pantheon, that is to say a temple of all the Gods.[50] And this Severan dating, deduced both from literature and recently and securely from archaeology, makes the restoration contemporaneous with Tertullian's writing. By that time, Judaeo-Christian perspectives were established in the religious 'marketplace' well enough to make sense of the deposition of biblical texts in a temple library of a great cosmopolitan pagan city, over a century before the Roman government turned officially Christian. A remarkable variety of cults and creeds could thrive in Alexandria and live on well into late antiquity.[51]

Apart from Tertullian, allusions to the Ptolemaic deposition are to be found only in the literature of late antiquity; and these are open to the suspicion that Christian speculation about Septuagint origins has

---

[48] On the cult, Fraser 1972: 246–76.
[49] McKenzie, in oral discussion; Grimm 1996: 55, with Fig. 12; Ashton 2004: 22.
[50] McKenzie, Gibson, and Reyes 2004: Sect. 7.
[51] For the religious 'marketplace', see Lieu, North, and Rajak 1992: 1–8. On the vigorous cultural life of late-antique Alexandria from the beginning of the third century CE, see Bowersock 1996. Haas 1997: 13 maintains that 'prior to the fourth century, the pagan community was undisputed in its cultural mastery of the city'.

had a hand in them.[52] The best attestation for the presence of books within the Serapeum complex might seem to be the words of a fourth-century CE rhetor, Aphthonius, a pupil of Libanius, who speaks of 'storehouses... open to those eager to study, an encouragement for the entire city to gain wisdom'.[53] But the contents of the collection here remain entirely vague. It is the fourth-century Christian writer, Epiphanius, who first speaks explicitly of a 'daughter library' and locates it in the Serapeum.[54] To a commentary on Aristophanes by the eleventh-century Byzantine scholar, John Tzetzes, we owe the entire claim that literature pertaining to non-Greek peoples, including that of the Jews, was translated into Greek and placed in what he called simply a 'second library'. Tzetzes conjures up precise figures to show how small this library was by comparison with the main library.[55] Meanwhile, the specific association with the Septuagint, following Tertullian, comes out of an argument made by John Chrysostom, who indignantly points out that the Serapeum can scarcely be regarded as holy, even though the 'translation of the prophetic books' is to be found there 'to this very day'.[56] A modern scholarly surmise has it that the translations of the

---

[52] According to Fraser 1972: 323, surprisingly, 'it seems unlikely that this is an invention'. Casson 2001 does not question the existence of a Ptolemaic library in the Serapeum. Christian speculation continued well beyond antiquity. In a tract published in 1785, the Revd John Blair criticized a theory propounded by Archbishop Ussher and clearly designed to supersede the by-then discredited Aristeas story, whereby the first Greek translation of the Torah was destroyed when Julius Caesar burnt the Great Library, but meanwhile Jews had made a second version, this one including the Prophets, which underwent scholarly vetting at Herod's behest and was deposited in the Serapeum Library on Cleopatra's orders.

[53] In his *Progymnasmata*, the rhetor compares this temple with the Athenian Acropolis. See McKenzie, Gibson, and Reyes 2004: sect. 10, where there is a full translation by A. Reyes.

[54] Epiphanius, *On Weights and Measures*, 11 (*PG* 43, col. 256 B). One modern interpretation takes this to have been a 'lending library'.

[55] For the Tzetzes evidence, see Fraser 1972: 323. Blum 1991: 104–6 (where the complications of the MS tradition of Tzetzes are indicated), and especially the skepticism of Bagnall 2002. Tzetzes' figures are 42,800 scrolls here, as against 490,000 in the Museum. He clearly knew *Aristeas*, but he must also be presumed to have had access to information found in Alexandrian scholiasts.

[56] Tertullian, *Apologeticum*, 18. 8. Cf. above, p. 43. John Chrysostom, *Adv. Iud.*, 1.6. (*PG* 48, col. 851; mistaken reference in Fraser). Chrysostom's sermons against the Jews are dated to the 380s, less than a decade before the destruction of the shrine. See also Fraser 1972: 478, n. 134.

Zoroastrian texts reported by Pliny the Elder were also made for the Serapeum.[57]

To sum up: it is reasonably certain that in late antiquity the Serapeum housed a collection of books. The suggestion was made in Christian patristic circles, in the absence of any real knowledge, that this had originally been an offshoot of the great library. The second book collection was later held to have contained translations of foreign material. It was already asserted by Tertullian that the Bible in Greek and in Hebrew were included within it in his own day, around CE 200. Epiphanius followed suit. It is not excluded that a small library was indeed present in this shrine during the Ptolemaic period.[58] But even if that were the case, the deposition there of any non-Egyptian literature in general, or of the Jewish Scriptures in particular, is not attested and it by no means follows from the syncretistic nature of the original cult. All that belongs to what Roger Bagnall has called 'the library of dreams'.[59] Our literary references are confined to a late period, and it is to this period that the expansion of whatever had previously existed in the Serapeum, as well as the broadening of its religious interests, should be attributed. The Serapeum finally fell prey, in 390/1 CE, to the wrath of the patriarch of Alexandria, acting on the decree of the Emperor Theodosius II, and this date must signify the end of whatever library it had, since the scrolls could hardly have escaped the devastation.[60]

---

[57] See above, p. 27 and n. 6.

[58] The shrine itself is archaeologically dated with certainty to at least as far back as the date of the foundation plaques, during the reign of Ptolemy III Euergetes I (246–222 BCE). It could have existed as early as Ptolemy II, his predecessor. The plan of the temple complex with its surrounding rooms does in fact strongly suggest to archaeologists that a library could have been housed there, at least after the Roman rebuilding of the shrine. There is also no archaeological problem in accommodating an earlier library in the Ptolemaic rooms uncovered within the temple's colonnades, either on the west or on the south side, but no evidence was found for its existence. See McKenzie, Gibson, and Reyes 2004: sect. 7. Briefly in McKenzie 2003: 50–7.

[59] Bagnall 2002.

[60] Casson 2001: 138.

READING *ARISTEAS* AS HISTORICAL MYTH

The author of the *Letter* distances himself from writers who purvey myths, *muthologōn* (322); he dismisses Greeks who invent myths in which men become gods (137–8) and he contrasts the purposiveness of Scripture with things written 'in a myth-like way', *muthōdōs* (168). It is paradoxical, then, that the *Letter of Aristeas* belongs precisely in the realm of what we might readily call 'historical myth', and about this something more must now be said. If such traditions are now understood to be an important element in that 'collective memory' which serves to supply any group of people with its continuing identity, that is in large measure due to the insights developed in the twenties of the last century by the French sociologist Maurice Halbwachs.[61] Historical myths represent an understanding of the past shared within a group and (somehow) among its individual members. Such memories characteristically occupy a space somewhere between fact and fiction. But, for their owners, discrimination between the one and the other is usually immaterial, and indeed it could be counterproductive. Nor does discrimination tend to be a useful exercise for later observers. This kind of remembering supplies a group with an account of the past made relevant to present needs, rendering memory resonant and also flexible enough to be transmitted through generations. Recently, scholars have reflected a great deal on the variety of ways in which 'cultural memory' or 'social memory' (both of these terms doing much the same work as 'collective memory') are preserved, transmitted and put to use in different societies, within spheres such as performance, ritual, festival, ceremonial, and monument. For my purpose, the role played by oral tradition is particularly relevant; but written narratives are also major contributors, not excluding the more 'scientific' kinds of historical scholarship.[62] There is a kind of fraught sibling relationship between

---

[61] Halbwachs 1925; 1950; English versions: Halbwachs 1980; 1992. For a succinct assessment both of the leading critiques of these studies, especially on the psychological front, and also of their durability, see Castelli 2004: 19–21.

[62] The impact of a series of seminal studies of the 1980s is summed up in Connerton 1989. Their prime concern was with modernity, but their application much wider.

history and memory, exceptionally hard to disentangle, and explored with subtlety in Elizabeth Castelli's fruitful re-engagement with Halbwachs from the perspective of ancient religious history (in general) and the study of early Christian martyrdom (in particular). 'Myth' she points out, carries unjustifiably negative connotations in modern parlance.[63]

The classic discussion of memory in the Jewish sphere, Joseph Hayim Yerushalmi's *Zakhor*, is centred on the striking contradiction within Judaism between on the one hand the prominence of national memory and on the other a marked lack of interest in formal history-writing until well into the enlightenment era. But the long-lived debate about that remarkable book has rightly questioned its sharp dichotomy between a people's perception of its past and the writings of its relatively few self-conscious historians.[64] Memory and history are not inevitable opponents.[65]

Some scholars bring to the Hellenistic-Jewish sphere a similarly strict separation between literature and historical record. Erich Gruen finds ingenious construction—and much humour—but virtually no 'history' in the rich store of Hellenistic–Jewish writing, a store which includes not only obviously fictitious expansions of scripture, such as the stories of Joseph and Asenath or Bel and the Dragon, but also the books of the Maccabees—and, indeed, the *Letter of Aristeas*.[66] Yet those works are not all of a kind. Some of them indeed contain precisely the mix of fact and fiction that makes up cultural memory, and surely it is no accident that the Jewish writing of the formative Second Temple period proliferated in creations of the very kind that contributed to the formation and maintenance of a national identity.[67] It could be possible instead to ascribe the characteristic mix of fiction with history in this literature simply to the creative labours of individual authors who had a message to convey

---

[63] Castelli 2004.

[64] Yerushalmi 1982, and for the debate, Carlebach, Efron, and Myers 1998; Myers 1998: 88–9.

[65] The limitations of such a 'stark binarism' are eloquently explored by Castelli 2004: 21–3.

[66] This is a central insight of Gruen 1998.

[67] The topic is a recurrent one in Wills 1995, where such works are not unreasonably classed as novels (of the ancient variety).

and who exploited historical verisimilitude to convey it, as Sarah Johnson proposes in a recent study of 3 Maccabees.[68] But such interpretations fail to account for that crucial oral dimension, the multiple retelling of the stories behind the authors who eventually crystallized them, and which, in some cases at least, are reflected in the plurality of their surviving versions.[69] Creating linkages of past with present, much of this literature is more than the mere exercise of individual prowess.[70] It is no accident that as part of such accounts we tend to be told about re-enactments: the authors emphasize the establishment of festivals of commemoration: in the cases of Purim and Hanukkah those festivals survive throughout Judaism to continue the act of recollection; other festivals, purely local, like the celebration on the island of Pharos of the translation of the Septuagint, are long gone.[71]

Investigating the *Letter of Aristeas* on its own terms, Sylvie Honigman has asked exactly how we should insert our book into the elusive territory of mythologized memory.[72] In order to pin down more specifically the story's function within a particular cultural context, she brings into play the conception of a 'charter myth', a foundation account of the kind which served to assign through narratives of the

---

[68] Johnson 2004, esp. 182–216.

[69] Thus the persecution of 3 Maccabees appears in shortened form in Josephus' *Against Apion*, 2.51–5, there ascribed to Ptolemy VIII instead of Ptolemy IV. Cf. Rajak 2000: 257–72 for an interpretation in terms of an oral-written interplay of the excursus on Moses' Ethiopian expedition in Josephus, *Antiquities*, 2.238–54. This midrashic elaboration is a solution to a puzzling biblical verse about Aaron and Miriam objecting to Moses' Kushite wife (Num. 12: 1), and the story existed in at least one alternative Hellenistic rendering (by Artapanus), which was, however, not Josephus' source. In Josephus' version a piece of Greek ethnographic writing about the Ethiopians has somehow been sucked into what must have been a story of significance to the self-positioning of Egyptian Jews.

[70] Weitzman's study (2005) understands this well. He effectively sidesteps the truth/fiction dichotomy in his sustained interpretation of Jewish historical myth as 'survival strategy'. None the less he still tends to imply that his material is fiction *tout court*.

[71] The Pharos festival is described in Philo's *Life of Moses*, 2.41 rather than in the *Letter of Aristeas*. See above, p. 35.

[72] Honigman 2003: 38–41, 65–91. Honigman would go further, with regard to classical antiquity, taking the radical position that a fact/fiction distinction was not made in Greek historiography. This strong claim requires another, different kind of discussion.

past a place in history to cities and peoples throughout the Greek world and which their owners continued to cherish. She suggests that Aristeas was bestowing a comparable pedigree on the cherished Greek translation of the Jewish Law. We might go even further: if the translated Torah was for Greek-speaking Jews the very core of their identity, then the explanation of how it was translated was the charter myth of their entire imagined Jewish *politeia*, the society that they conceptualized for themselves. There is no doubt that Honigman offers the interpreter of the *Letter* new freedoms and opportunities. We worry less about the difficulty of judging exactly how much of the author's narrative is his own invention and how much is attested.[73] We regard with extra wariness research which builds on claims that one precise element or another of the composite text is its true core.[74] We are better reconciled to a state of uncertainty concerning the document's date of composition, a state from which we are unlikely to be able to escape: perfectly sustainable hypotheses fall anywhere between c.200 and c.100 BCE.[75] Finally, we are encouraged to turn to other questions. The 'facts' are elusive; and in the rest of this chapter I shall focus instead on how the work functions as myth, reflecting the self-positioning of the monarch and the Jews. But since historical myths run the whole gamut, from the entirely legendary to these that incorporate faint echoes of the past and then on to those that weave narratives around well-known historical events and personages, in Chapter 3, by exploring the Alexandrian context, we shall have the opportunity to consider where on the scale Aristeas belongs.[76]

---

[73] We might contrast the approach of Schmidt 1986, a dissertation dedicated to proving that each of the purported documents in the Letter is a 'Falschung'.

[74] Discussions of Septuagint origins surprisingly often extract from Aristeas the assurance of a mid–third century BCE date for the translation of the Torah while rejecting all or much else in the Letter. For a recent textbook example, see Jobes and Silva 2000: 34. See also Wright 2003a: 21.

[75] The arguments for and against the dates commonly considered are nowhere better set out than in Schürer, iii: 679–84. See also now Bar-Kochva 1996: 271–88, arguing for a date towards the end of this period.

[76] The general point is made well by Bowersock 1994: 12, in relation to Rome: 'for any coherent and persuasive interpretation of the Roman Empire it becomes obvious that fiction must be viewed as a part of its history'.

THE 'MEANING' OF THE STORY

As we have seen, the *Letter* has something to say about a number of topics, quite readily identifiable. Its literary agenda is clearly broader than the Torah translation: remarkably, in a narrative of 327 paragraphs, the translators only get down to business in paragraph 300. What has proved more elusive, however, is agreement on where the heart of the book's agenda lies and what might be its central aim. It is perhaps easier to state what the *Letter* is not. *Aristeas* by no means reads as a monolithic, apologetic tract of self-congratulation; it is not constructed in such a way that its every part contributes to the crude political purpose of enhancing the reputation of Ptolemy's Jewish subjects. Nor is the balance and focus of our narrative such as to support the case of a number of scholars, notably Harry Orlinsky, that the 'basic reason' for composing the *Letter* was to 'certify to the divine origin of the Septuagint'.[77] Harping on Ptolemy's central role would scarcely have served to justify the Greek translation in the eyes of Jewish opponents. Still less does the issue appear to be the promotion of any one textual tradition in the Greek Bible over others, at a time when variant versions had begun to proliferate; to argue thus, as some biblical scholars have done, requires extensive reading between the lines, as well as a focus restricted to a very small part of the narrative.

Rather, the *Letter* is an embodiment of Alexandrian Jewish identity, a literary vehicle precisely for its collective memory. That is why a double thread has to be woven into the narrative. On the one hand, the Jews do have a very special relationship with the King: he frees their numerous captives on request, and he even makes their Temple furniture for them. They depend upon him, but he depends upon their God.[78] For this reason, but also because it befits his majesty, he accords those many marks of respect to his visitors, and to the High Priest back in the Temple. The imagined transactions, some more

---

[77] Orlinsky 1975: 94.
[78] Goldstein 1991 sees the author's specific aim to be a demonstration that Jews everywhere were better off under the Ptolemies than under the Seleucids.

plausible than others, echo the aspirations to respect, occasionally realized, of many Jewish communities over the ages in their relations with the ruling power.[79] The evocations of the procedure at court dwell upon matters of etiquette: the formalities of precedence, gaining an audience, the long wait, reduced for the Jewish visitors from thirty days to five (175), the custom of recording everything and storing it in the archives (299). In this setting the Jews, following in the footsteps, we learn, of previous visitors from Judaea, are fed at the royal banquets according to their own religious needs, and it is pointed out that the customary heralds and sacrificers, who might offend their religious sensibilities, are sent away. After that, much is made of the refreshing atmosphere of the island chosen for their labours, which chimes with a widespread interest in the climactic amenities of the sites chosen by rulers for Hellenistic city-foundations.[80]

The felicitous melding of the Jews with their environment is integral to successive episodes. And yet, when it comes to the translators from Jerusalem and also to the Jewish reception of the translation at the end of the narrative, invisible typologies embedded in the overarching structure of the *Letter* come from a different discourse, with echoes of Moses being accompanied by seventy elders to receive the tablets of the Law, and of its acclamation by the entire people of Israel (Exodus 24: 1–7).[81] Following the appearance of the manna, the Divine Spirit rested upon, once again, seventy elders who had been assembled by Moses outside the 'tent of meeting'; they were transformed into ecstatic prophets (Numbers 11: 24–30). In Nehemiah 8, Ezra the scribe reads and interprets (which presumably denotes translation into Aramaic) the book of the Law before the entire community, male and female, of returnees from exile—a community finding its feet in a new environment, just as the Jews in the new city of Alexandria had had to do.[82] The echoes are plain, in spite of differences: as befits the elitist society of Ptolemaic Alexandria, there the

---

[79] Yerushalmi 1995 is a lecture concerned with the patterning of this relationship.
[80] Green 1990: 162, with sources in n. 36 (mainly for Antioch).
[81] The sensitive analysis by Orlinsky 1975 of the working out of the typology of the Sinai revelation within *Aristeas* remains valuable independently of his conclusions on canonization.
[82] Hadas 1951: 39.

audience for the reading from the new translation consists of selected leaders, a representative group from the people and 'the elders of the translators'.[83] Nor, in *Aristeas*, does the session spread over a week (and it does not coincide with the festival of Tabernacles).

It is appropriate for the Exodus archetype, the fundamental model of deliverance in biblical as in post-biblical Jewish thought,[84] to have a special role in a narrative concerned with Jews in Egypt. In fact, the structure of the *Letter of Aristeas* constitutes a kind of reverse Exodus, with hosts of formerly enslaved men, women, and children from Judaea supposedly finding refuge in Egypt, just as they had once fled Egypt. One acute observation recently made is that the narration would have served the valuable purpose of legitimizing return by Jews from the promised land to the 'house of bondage' out of which their God had brought them. That act of redemption from oppression, humiliation, and slavery had come, already in Exodus, and more explicitly by the time to the composition of the book of Deuteronomy, to define their identity.[85] The land that had enslaved their forefathers had become anathema to them, and it was a place to which the law of Deuteronomy (17: 16) had forbidden them to return.[86] The final Deuteronomic curse (28: 68) upon those who do not fulfil the Law and fail to honour the Name is that 'the Lord will bring you sorrowing back to Egypt by that very road of which I said to you "you shall not see that road again"'. The linkage of Egyptian past with Alexandrian present in the mental map of the Jewish community is established beyond doubt by two telling words in Eleazar's prayer for deliverance from a persecution in the city by the later, less-benevolent Ptolemy (the fourth) according to 3 Maccabees

---

[83] The exact meaning of the oddly expressed first sentence of *Aristeas*, 310, describing the three different groups of leaders present, is not clear.

[84] On the Exodus narrative as archetype, see Daube 1963. On Egypt in Jewish memory as symbol of the rejected past, Assmann 1997: 6–8.

[85] See esp. the history summarized in the context of the renewal of the covenant at Deut. 26: 5–9. The required recitation, beginning 'my father was a wandering Aramaean' was subsequently incorporated verbatim as the opening of the liberation story set out in the Haggadah for the Passover seder (which itself is the commemoration laid out in Exod. 12: 14–27).

[86] The connection is explored in Hacham 2005. For the 'non–Exodus paradigm', see also Honigman 2003: 55–6. On the role of the ban of Deut. 17: 16 in the mindset of Egyptian Jews, see now the excellent discussion in Pearce 2007a: 93–7.

(6: 4): 'you destroyed Pharaoh, abounding in chariots, the former ruler of *this Egypt*, raised high in his lawless insolence, with his boastful tongue'. Without the ascription of a show of outstanding philanthropy towards the Jews to Pharaoh Ptolemy Philadelphus, it is hard to see how so total a reversal of orientation could have been achieved.

The incorporation of scriptural detail from Chapter 25 of the book of Exodus into the lengthy *ekphrasis*, which describes the furniture made by the King as a gift to the High Priest, sums up well the double perspective of the *Letter of Aristeas*.[87] And the double thread running through the narrative extends to the depiction of the Jews within it. The Jewish translators of Aristeas are *pepaideumenoi*, men of culture in Greek terms: they are outstanding for their *paideia*, knowledgeable not only in *ioudaïka grammata* but also in the literature of the Greeks (120ff.). Among other things, their abilities fitted them, we are told, to go on embassies. The High Priest is a *kalokagathos*, an excellent man. One of the translators commends watching drama as a suitable leisure occupation. This no doubt reflects, as Erich Gruen has emphasized, 'the circumstances of Hellenistic Alexandria, where Jew of station could attain the highest levels of the education process'.[88] Yet these same translators purify themselves with handwashing and pray before each day's labours; and this handwashing is justified in terms of the *semeiōsis* (symbolism) employed by the legislator (306). Furthermore, we discover very early in the book that Ptolemy's apparently Hellenized Jewish subjects actually include in their number that large component of war captives, whose origins lay in the Judaean homeland and its surrounds. And there, as we discover, life continues to be centred on the Temple, while the twelve biblical tribes are still a live political division.[89] At no point are we allowed to doubt that the Torah

---

[87] This passage includes some of the language of LXX Septuagint 25.23 and 26–8, on which (or a precursor of it) Aristeas is clearly dependent. See the collection of citations from and allusions to the LXX Pentateuch in Meecham 1935: 316–20.

[88] Gruen 2002: 124–5.

[89] Note, however, Bickerman's observation (1988: 34) that these 'patriotic fictions' were not altogether 'without a factual basis'. Thus some post-exilic habitation is attested in areas outside Judaea that had been allotted to Zebulun, Gad, Naphtali, Asher, and Menasseh.

can come only out of Jerusalem—or rather, out of the city which we know to be Jerusalem, but which Aristeas does not name.[90]

OTHER MEMORIES OF THE EARLY PTOLEMIES

One leading motif of the *Letter of Aristeas* recurs in later mythologized reflections of the early Ptolemies, to be found both in Greek and in Latin. Named by Sylvie Honigman the 'Alexandrian paradigm',[91] this motif enshrines a literary pattern about the acquisitive cultural policies of the first three Ptolemies. The parallels are worth exploring, not just because they show *Aristeas* as a precursor of a later Graeco-Roman literary trope, but because of the shared attitudes and memories involved. They help us to understand that the *Letter* has its roots in the traditions of Alexandria, with some basis in recollected reality, and that it cannot be accounted for as the pragmatic invention of an inventive apologist. At the same time, the imaginative development of the traditions suits their different contexts and the differing needs of their recipients.

The theme of importation by royal fiat is the central element in this common motif. Thus, Galen tells a well-known story of how Ptolemy III ordered books to be sent by ship from Athens for copying for the Alexandrian library, and how he then sent back the copies while keeping the originals. And again, there is a curious tale which Tacitus claims to have learned from Egyptian priests, that one of the Ptolemies sent out ambassadors to seek a deity he had seen in a dream, and that these men brought back from Sinope on the Black Sea the cult statue of Serapis, but only after a struggle, for the statue showed repeated signs of reluctance to be moved. To placate the god a special temple, the Serapeum, was built at Alexandria.[92] In both stories, the monarch is made responsible for what was effectively a

---

[90] By contrast, Hadas 1951: 64–5 curiously regards Judaea as insignificant for Aristeas.
[91] See Honigman 2003: 41–53.
[92] Galen 17.1.607–8 (in the *Commentaries on the Epidemics of Hippocrates*); Tac. *Hist.*, 4.83–4. For arguments against the historicity of the 'from the ships' story, see Canfora 1989: 48; Bagnall 2002: 353–4.

theft; and from the first of them, at least, he comes out as a distinctly dubious character.

I suggest that we might explore further the 'Alexandrian paradigm' in Aristeas by bringing into the frame yet another instance, an imaginary letter written by the author Alciphron, once again a work of the Roman imperial period.[93] This piece of prose has some further features in common with Aristeas, for, by contrast with Galen and Tacitus, in neither of these two cases does Ptolemy succeed in getting entirely his own way. The light shed on Aristeas and on the Jewish response to Ptolemy by this interesting feature of the new example will justify a brief exposition of it here.

Menander, the famous dramatist, creator of the Athenian New Comedy, reported on a pressing invitation to court in a letter to the love of his life, Glycera. 'I have received from Ptolemy, King of Egypt, a letter in which he makes the most earnest entreaties, promising in royal fashion, all the goods of the earth.' More precisely, an imaginary letter was put into Menander's mouth by Alciphron, the author of a collection of four books (containing altogether 123 such letters), written in the Greek style of the so-called 'Second Sophistic' trend. We have no biographical information about Alciphron[94] and he is rather rarely read, even now that the literature of that period has come to the forefront of scholarly attention. The Menander–Glycera exchange has been regarded as the height of his surviving accomplishment.[95]

So Ptolemy wants Menander at his court.[96] Menander claims that Philemon, a fellow writer at Athens, has received a similar, but somewhat less stylish, letter. But, for his part, Menander would rather be crowned with the Dionysiac ivy leaves of Athenian dramatic victories, his Glycera looking on, than with all the diadems of Ptolemy. 'Let Philemon go to Egypt.' The declaration expresses not only devotion to Glycera, but supreme self-confidence in the face of a great potential patron.

---

[93] See Rajak 2005a for a fuller study.
[94] See Rosenmeyer 2001, and on Alciphron's literary affiliations, the works cited there, p. 257, n. 4. The most commonly assigned dating is somewhere in the third century CE.
[95] Notably Jackson 1912: 67–96.
[96] Letter 4.18, Menander frag. 569 Kock.

We also have Glycera's reply, a mixture of emotion and calculation evidently intended to typify the female psyche (Letter 19). She has read the King's latest missive, which to her made it clear that the monarch had got to hear about the dramatist's personal life. Ptolemy had surely come to realize that he was striving for the impossible in wanting 'Athens to cross the sea to him...' His mistress is indispensable to the dramatist. For who else could set out the masks, dress the actors, and stand in the wings, fingers crossed, until the audience erupts into applause. She announces, however, that she might consider turning herself into a sailor and accompanying him to Egypt— that is, if he really has to go. And she comes up with yet another suggestion. Menander should delay in giving an answer till the two of them have met with their friends, who happen to be the philosophers Theophrastus and Epicurus, and also until they have consulted both the Delphic oracle and a lady skilled in gastromancy. Meanwhile, let Menander finish up the play in which Glycera figures as a leading character, so that, in this guise at least, he will be taking her with him, if Alexandria is after all to be his destination.

The Menander correspondence is part of a small group of letters in Alciphron's fourth book that evoke not simply moral, psychological, or emotional types or 'characters', not ordinary people or representatives of occupations, like the rest of the collection, but famous historical personages.[97] The extensive production throughout antiquity of the pseudonymous correspondence of famous personages is a related but distinct phenomenon.[98] The historical dimension of that kind of letter has been discussed largely in relation to any possible historical content. It is, of course, impossible to know if there is a factual basis to the incident conjured up here. Glycera was indeed a character in more than one of Menander's plays, and Lefkowitz would argue that the biographical traditions on him, as on other Greek poets, consisted very largely of extrapolations from

---

[97] In this period, the other leading exponents are Aelian and Philostratus, whose fictional letters appear with Alciphron's in the Loeb volume by Benner and Fobes 1949. A Latin representative of the genre is Ovid's *Heroides*, in which the letters of mythological personages are recreated.

[98] Discussed in Rosenmeyer 2001: 193–233. For a comprehensive collection, see still Hercher 1873. A motif from the Hippocratic collection is discussed below.

their writings.[99] Glycera, moreover, appears to be something of a stock name for Athenian courtesans and especially for the mistress of a famous man.[100] If any invitation to Menander was actually issued from Egypt, then it must have come from the first of the Ptolemies, Ptolemy I Soter (305–283 BCE), given that the accepted date for Menander's death is 292 BCE.

Yet, as with Aristeas, there is another dimension to explore, that of mythical memory, for the effect of our diptych of letters depends upon writer and readers drawing upon a received tradition about the Greek past which can be taken for granted. The reiteration of this tradition plays a crucial role in reinforcing a group's sense of its own past, even if its literary treatments range from the most recherché to the seemingly popular.

In these Alciphron letters, we have the imaginative development of a memory, fuzzy perhaps, but a memory for all that. The protagonists are not the voices more commonly heard in this period, those of the great figures of the Athenian fifth century, but voices from the age of Alexander and its sequel. The writer brings nostalgia to his eulogy of Athens, and he plays with a number of clichés, notably the democracy, the exercise of freedom, and the religious cults of Attica (10–11). He vaunts his antiquarian knowledge, alluding to very specific Athenian institutions, to the local geography, and to highlights of Athenian history: 'the roped enclosure ... the feast of pots, the *kerameikos* ...' He crescendos comically: 'the agora, the law courts, the beautiful Acropolis, the Furies, the Mysteries, Salamis nearby, Psyttaleia, Marathon, the whole of Greece in Athens, the whole of Ionia, all the Cyclades.' But in the foreground he puts his critique of the would-be all-powerful Ptolemy, determined physically to pick up elements of Athenian life and put them down in Alexandria. Writing under the Roman Empire, in a period and in a part of the world concerned with defining its own identity in relation to the classical Greek past and possessing its own deep preoccupation with

---

[99] This is the main thrust of Lefkowitz 1981 and see esp. the brief comments on Menander and Glycera on pp. 113–15. Cf. Parsons 1952: 48.

[100] Glycera as a well-known courtesan: Athenaeus 13. 584a; 605d. Mistress of the orator Strepsiades in Aristaenetus, *Epistles*, 2.3; of Alexander's treasurer Harpalus in Diod. 17.108 and Athenaeus 13.586c, 595d–596b: here the same person as Menander's mistress may be intended.

reliving Athens and Atticism,[101] he evokes an earlier moment, the Hellenistic age, in which this imperative existed in a different form, perhaps even more intense and problematic.[102]

We conclude that the seventy-two gentleman-scholars who supposedly put the Torah into Greek for the library of Ptolemy II were not alone in being privileged with supposed invitations from the King of Egypt of a kind which was not easy to refuse. The key to both sets of events is the Egyptian King's automatic assumption that cultural progress is achieved by the physical translocation of individuals; after all, Menander's plays could perfectly well have been performed in Ptolemy's city in his absence. The dramas of Philemon too were surely not beyond reach. But physical translocation is a different matter. There would be an obvious flaunting of power in fetching the author to court, keeping him there as a dependent, and having him write and mount plays to order.[103] More precisely, Ptolemy aspired to a tangible and permanent 'piece' of Athens in Alexandria and this is exactly the point the Alciphron dialogue seeks to press home. The symbolic significance is strong, even if we recognize at the same time the very real benefits of attracting men of talent, of which there were many other famous cases, in the creation of a new city and a new society.

According to Aristeas (176), both a text—the Torah parchments (*diptherai*) written in gold—and its owners/interpreters are brought down from Jerusalem. Thus the Aristeas story incorporates the bringing of books—of the 'from the ships' story—with the translocation to Egypt of learned or creative individuals, as in the Menander/Theophrastus tradition. When it comes to the working out of the narrative, there are again certain similarities between Aristeas and Alciphron: the codes governing the two transactions are comparable. There is the undisguised crudeness of the promise—in the one

---

[101] The classic study is Bowie 1970. See also the major study of Swain 1996. On 'Athenianness' versus 'Greekness', helpful remarks by Whitmarsh 2001: 5–8.

[102] On the relatively scant representations of contemporary Alexandria in the different genres of literature of the Second Sophistic, see Trapp 2004. He plausibly suggests classicizing snobbery as a major reason for this lack of attention.

[103] I am grateful to Markus Asper for pointing out to me the noteworthy lack of evidence for the presence of dramatists in the 'brain drain' to Alexandria. On culture as a tool of Ptolemaic power-politics, see Chap. 2.

case—or the transfer—in the other—of overwhelmingly lavish rewards by the monarch. Correct etiquette is present in the exchanges, as might be expected. But we find, at the same time, a curious directness, with the King himself engaged in the pursuit of his quarry, writing, speaking, and dealing personally with the individuals he desires. This naturally serves to add immediacy to the telling, but it also perhaps reflects the relative informality observable in the courts of the early Hellenistic period.[104]

At first blush, a visible and significant difference might seem to open up between the two narrated incidents. The Ptolemy of Aristeas exudes benevolence, whereas Alciphron's Ptolemy, though his potential generosity is not in doubt, is cast in the shape of an unwelcome intruder into the life of a happy couple. The inconstancy of monarchs and the dangers of their friendship are highlighted (4.14). Indeed one scholar[105] went so far as to suggest that this Ptolemy has some of the unpleasant features of the figure of the stock tyrant. Yet Aristeas too leaves us in no doubt that, for all the extensive goodwill shown by Philadelphus, it was advisable to maintain a certain distance. In the end, this also is a portrait of an autocrat, even if it is one who listens and learns. It is, after all, because Ptolemy is such a ruler that the advice of wise men is necessary to temper his arrogance. We may perhaps think of the witty comment on the limits of Ptolemy II's generosity in the fourteenth of the *Idylls* of the contemporary Greek poet Theocritus: one friend advises another to become a mercenary under Ptolemy, professing the latter to be 'kindly, cultured, passionate, as nice as anyone can be; as a king should be . . . he's generous to many and doesn't refuse when asked—though you must not keep asking' (62 ff.). We are given to understand that an iron fist is concealed in Ptolemy's velvet glove.

As though to depict the dark underside of royal generosity, the reactions to pressure of each of the two groups of celebrated invitees are presented as negative, at least in some degree. This is perhaps the most important point that the two fictions have in common: just as Menander and Glycera prefer to stay in Athens, so the High Priest Eleazar makes a point of insisting that, when their work is completed,

[104] Herman 1997: 199–224.
[105] Bungarten 1967.

the seventy-two wise men must be brought back safely to Jerusalem (46). We learn later that Eleazar's anxiety in parting from them is indeed due to the King's proneness to send for men of talent: the word *metapempesthai* (124) suggests a demand more than an invitation, and the unspoken implication is not just of a temporary sojourn but of guests almost kidnapped. It is indeed with protestations of being driven solely by considerations of the common interest that Eleazar reluctantly allowed the translators to leave Jerusalem in the first place. In the event, they are wined and dined magnificently, but they are not seduced by the delights of the court and they for their part have no inclination to stay. Nor is there any question of their accepting the King's invitation to come again, though this is issued twice before their departure for home, once orally (318) and once in a final letter which puts Eleazar under real pressure not to hinder the delegation if they were by any chance to choose to return. We might think back to the unwillingness of the god Serapis to be carried off from Pontus to Egypt in the Tacitus story.[106]

The 'rejection paradigm' is not a rarity. It appears also in another long-lived Hellenistic story with a continuing existence in the Roman east, that of Hippocrates' refusal to yield to Artaxerxes and leave the island of Cos to go and save the Persian 'barbarians' from the plague. Incorporated in the fictional Hippocratic letters, it there points up even more markedly a contrast between tyranny and freedom. There too an autocrat fails to compel the attendance of a great man. But the specifically Alexandrian theme of cultural appropriation through invitations to distinguished settlers does not figure in that instance, the immediate need being an urgent and practical one.[107]

Ptolemy concludes the *Letter of Aristeas* with the pronouncement that he likes the company of persons of education, and that he prefers to spend his money on this than on vanities (322). A dramatist from Athens was by any account a *pepaideumenos*. But, while it be paradoxical for such praise to be accorded by the Macedonian ruler to the seventy-two somewhat exotic *hakhamim* (sages) from Jerusalem, these men have in fact been rendered by the author of Aristeas

---

[106] See p. 55 above.
[107] For the Hippocratic correspondence, see Smith 1979. Text in Littré 1861. I am grateful to Heinrich von Staden for drawing my attention to this material.

quite as suitable as any Athenians to be contributors to the new Greek metropolis. Their preparedness to present themselves and to be wined and dined, while maintaining their independence, thus reflects their complete fitness; and this very fitness serves to emphasize that their measured cooperation does not extend beyond the limits of their particular pious project.

Our texts are widely separated in time and they reflect widely differing societies and different worlds. *Aristeas* comes out of Alexandria itself, out of the very regime of the Ptolemies. Nor is there any question of a direct connection between the precise content of the two sets of mythologized memories. Yet the juxtaposition has thrown up significant similarities. Each author for his own purposes evokes, with mixed admiration and criticism (though with both ingredients in varying degrees), the legendary but questionable role of the Ptolemies as cultural entrepreneurs. The Jewish text is thus both the earliest instance of a common type of representation and broadly in line with later Greek stereotypes of the behaviour of those monarchs.

So our authors derive comparable benefits from the situations they describe. Each is making a point about royal conduct and in each case the point relates to an issue of cultural identity. If Alciphron is 'about' anything, it is 'about' the glamour of Athens and Athenian effortless superiority: drama, democracy, and a relationship between friends (or lovers) are better than fabulous gifts from a self-interested monarch, with every opportunity that his court can offer thrown in. Just so, the replies of Hippocrates and of the Coans to Artaxerxes oppose wisdom to untold wealth and recall with contempt Darius' and Xerxes' arrogant demands of earth and water from the Athenians (Letter 9).

Aristeas, on the other hand, adds another level of complexity. As we have seen, he represents the Jewish sages as quintessential Greeks, on top of their other attributes, and he thus asserts Jewish participation in the great Alexandrian work of revitalizing and reconfiguring Athenian culture. The Jews are part of that project; decisively they are not Egyptians. But this author also explicitly claims superiority for the Jewish over the Greek tradition: the ostensibly non-Jewish protagonist, Aristeas, his addressee Philocrates, and the King himself, are all at different times shown praising the Jewish God. At the banquets, the sages from Jerusalem are able, like Daniel at the Persian court, not only to outshine all others in wisdom, but most particularly to win the admiration of the philosophers in the company for the adeptness of their off-the-cuff replies (296). The consequence is to open up an unavoidable contradiction, or at least a tension, between the claim of being as good as everyone else, as Greeks, and the claim of being even better, as the followers of a God who trumps all others.[108] Unlike Menander, the Jews cannot afford to indulge in the freedom of simply staying away from the King's table. They come; but they also go again. They present him with the Greek Torah. But they do their work, in every sense, on their own terms. That aptly sums up the way Alexandrian Jews perceived their situation under the Ptolemies.

[108] Cf. Gruen 1998: 216–18.

2

Going Greek: Culture and Power in Ptolemaic Alexandria

The *Letter of Aristeas* combines memory with story in its account of the making of the Septuagint, and above all in its portrayal of King Ptolemy II Philadelphus of Egypt. Understanding, now, something of their interaction, we are better placed to consider the obvious and inescapable question. What should we make of the author's central and remarkable claim that the Torah was translated in the first instance for the satisfaction of a benevolent foreign king? The question may be simple. The answer is not.

The *Letter*, as we have seen, is richly embroidered. Of course there is much in all this that is far better enjoyed than searched with toothcomb for nuggets of truth. A wise reader will not press hard at apparent items of information solemnly presented, such as that series of precise enumerations with which the author equips his narrative. None the less, it is worth noting in passing how regularly the figure of 500,000 books, given by our author as the target holdings of the great Alexandrian library, is produced as one of the (very few) established facts about it, a magic number which has served as the basis of earnest exposition and serious investigation. Many are quite unaware of where this figure has come from. But we have seen that it is no more than the aspiration enunciated by Demetrius of Phaleron in answer to the King's question near the opening of the *Letter*: we are told that 200,000 books is the supposed grand total so far.[1] It perhaps takes an even more rash and

---

[1] Successive edifices, ancient and modern, were built on these non-existent foundations, entertainingly dismantled by Bagnall 2002, who calculates that Greek literature in its entirety will not have filled as many scrolls.

credulous reader to accept the figure of exactly seventy-two for both the tally of the translators and the number of days they took to perform their task. And then there are the names of the translators, which do make up quite a plausible collection but are likely to be invented. Most of them are names of well-known biblical figures. There are also more obscure names from the Bible—Besai (a returnee from Persia with Zerubbabel) and Araunah (owner of a threshing floor in Jerusalem). There is a small admixture of the type of Greek theophoric names favoured by Jews, such as Dositheos and Theodosius. The appearance of reality is perhaps enhanced by the repetition of some names—there are more than one each of Joseph, Judah, Joshua, Samuel, Jonathan, Johanan, and Zechariah. Arsamus, probably the Greek form of a semitic name from the region, also appears twice. The list achieves a fine air of verisimilitude, testimony to the author's skill.[2]

That those seventy-two Jerusalem sages could have accomplished the whole job in the time and circumstances described further stretches our credulity (if indeed we are expected to understand that the translation of the entire Torah was accomplished). Moreover, an assured knowledge of Greek—however oddly the language is used—is displayed in much of the Torah translation, something which would scarcely in the mid-third century BCE have been available to the Judaean outpost: so a significant component of local Alexandrian talent should probably be added to the simple picture of the sages in *Aristeas*.[3] Similarly, the King's single great act of liberation of war prisoners, unsupported by any external source, looks like a simplification of a more complicated reality, validated by the familiar literary device of an elaborately phrased royal decree, and by the apparent precision of his statement of the costs involved—660 talents, a vast sum of money.[4] Finally, the author's

---

[2] The pattern is clear despite a number of corruptions and uncertainties in the manuscript traditions and small differences with the Syriac tradition transmitted in Epiphanius, *de Mens. et Pond.*, 3: these are recorded in Wendland's text. A detailed analysis in terms of the known naming practices of the period was undertaken by Cohen 1984, who argues for their historicity.

[3] This remains true, even on the maximalist view of Hellenization in pre-Maccabaean Palestine presented in Hengel 1974. I owe this point to Jenny Dines. For the Greek formation of the translators, see Chap. 4.

[4] See further below, pp. 79–80.

pride in Judaism has a major impact on his narrative, featuring on almost every page. Eulogy is a characteristic mode and superlatives abound. That a monarch should publicly acknowledge the Jewish God as synonymous with his own chief deity is a popular motif in this kind of literature, figuring notably in the apocryphal tale of Alexander the Great's visit to Jerusalem reported by Josephus.[5] Ptolemy does so more than once, as do his courtiers, Aristeas and Sosibius. The identification has a serious background in Greek philosophy, as we shall see. But the scene as depicted is fantastic.

Yet none of the author's literary or apologetic devices should blur our focus on the bigger picture.[6] That picture, and especially the implications of the role ascribed to the monarch, will be the focus of this chapter. While Ptolemy's involvement may not be demonstrable, I shall show that in this case there is very good reason to take it seriously. The depiction of royal interest fits with the knowledge we derive from many other sources of the cultural politics conducted by the early Ptolemies at Alexandria and of the intellectual concerns of the age. It will emerge that the *Letter* offers rather a convincing explanation for the making of the translation.[7] Meanwhile, on the Jewish side, the production of the Septuagint makes better sense when the realities of life under a dynamic and interventionist monarchy, within the hectic Hellenizing atmosphere of a fast-developing city, are taken into account. All in all, the substantial assertions made in the *Letter of Aristeas* are quite consonant with what we know of the early Ptolemaic environment there—the cultural activities of its kings, the breadth of interest of its Greek thinkers, and the position of its Jews on their mental map. The follow-up to this interpretation, which will appear in Chapter 8, is a reassessment of the impact made by the Greek Torah on Greek literature. The later episodes should not, however, affect our view of the Septuagint's origins.

---

[5] *AJ* ll. 329–39.

[6] As emphasized also by Honigman 2003: 102–5, whose line of reasoning is close to mine at this point.

[7] Cf. Bickerman 1976: 173: 'on reflection, the traditional account is confirmed by the intrinsic probabilities of the case'. My supporting arguments are, however, different.

IMPERIALISM AND CULTURE

The first Ptolemies were rulers of an empire, and the defence of their territorial holdings, won by conquest, was pursued, as is so often the case, by adding to them. Angelos Chaniotis well describes the mechanism at the heart of all of the Hellenistic monarchies: 'the imperialist impulse... which is one of the causes of the never-ending wars, is intrinsically connected with the fact that the acceptance of monarchical rule was founded on war and military power: on the defence of patrimony, the reclamation of lost land, and the conquest of new territories.'[8] The division of Alexander the Great's empire was in a sense never finalized. Alexander himself, under whom some of the founders of the kingdoms had fought, was an ever-present example of ambition. The emblematic type of a boastful man in Theophrastus' *Characters* (23.2) is one who claims to have been on Alexander's expedition. Egypt was the choice of the successor Ptolemy I (323–283 BCE), and it continued to be described as a land 'conquered by the spear'. While not yet technically a king, he made it his business to secure 'three bastions of the Mediterranean east: Palestine, Cyprus, and Cyrenaica'.[9] The holdings of Ptolemy II (285–246 BCE), son of the dynasty's founder, would include all three, but also islands in the Aegean, and parts of Asia Minor. While the chronology of his wars is obscure, most years in the first three-quarters of his reign involved one military campaign or another, and it did not matter that the reality included some severe setbacks. Theocritus, one of the great poets of the age, writes an effusive encomium of Ptolemy II in which he manages to turn into poetry a geographical list of imperial possessions: a share of Phoenicia, a share of Arabia, Syria, Libya, and Ethiopia, together with (all in Asia Minor) Pamphylia, Cilicia, Lycia, and Caria, along with the Cyclades, and the best fleet on the high seas.[10] The court poet

---

[8] Chaniotis 2005: 58. For a high estimation of the importance of Ptolemy's military activities, see also Samuel 1993: 183–4.
[9] Bingen 2007: 24.
[10] Theocritus, *Idyll*, 17.86–94. Gow 1950, in his commentary on these lines, associated the list of conquests with the First Syrian War, which may or may not have been over when they were written. See Bagnall 1976 on the conquests. For a

Posidippus, in the late third century BCE, whose roll of epigrams has recently seen the light of day, similarly conjures up the geography of empire in his use of evocative names: Marathus in Phoenicia, Phocaea in Asia Minor, Paphos in Cyprus, Cyrene in North Africa.[11]

But these early Ptolemies were seeking to impose their empire upon worlds with immensely long histories of grand monarchic rule. Overwhelming displays of power and grandeur were in order for pressing home the impact of victories. Over time, the result of success was the influx of new riches and the growth of fresh opportunity for display, in novel locations, on an increasing scale. The huge wealth of Egypt was one of the Ptolemies' greatest assets, balancing the far larger manpower resources of Asia.

Furthermore, the Ptolemies' self-construction addressed a wide span of audiences. Even their capital, the city of Alexandria itself, which stood as a symbol of Hellenism, was a place of mixed aspect with significant Egyptian features in its built environment and a population which somehow included highly diverse elements. The manipulation by the Hellenistic monarchs of their public image—Seleucids of Asia, Ptolemies of Egypt, and the minor monarchies alike—and the subtle adjustments in their communication with their various subjects, has featured in recent research, with an emphasis on this process as a continual, two-way negotiation between ruler and ruled.[12]

Among the Ptolemies, Ptolemy Philadelphus, son of Ptolemy I Soter (the Saviour), who had founded the Lagid dynasty, probably contributed more than any other to the creation of the new order. The second Ptolemy conceived of every task he undertook on the grandest scale of all.[13] Philo, in a passage of hyperbolic praise of this monarch as the best ever of kings, tells us that 'Philadelphian' was in his day a term applied to any benefaction or construction of

---

concise narrative and assessment, see Hölbl 2001: 35–46; more detailed in Huss 2001. The reign of Ptolemy II is ill-served by our literary sources: the narrative of Diodorus Siculus does not survive and the reign is not covered by Polybius.

[11] See Posidippus 45.1; 46.2; 47.5; 54.3. For the edited texts, Bastianini and Galazzi 2001. Translations and discussions in Gutzwiller 2005. See also the studies in Harris and Ruffini 2004 and in Acosta-Hughes et al. 2003.

[12] See esp. Ma 1999: 179–242 and Ma 2003.

[13] As Turner 1984: 171 reminds us. Vividly evoked in Green 1990: 156–61.

overwhelming magnitude (*Life of Moses*, 2.29). According to the poet Posidippus, the statue of Ptolemy I Soter, presumably erected by his son Ptolemy II, was taller than the Pharos lighthouse. We catch amusing, perhaps even slightly mocking, echoes of this 'gigantism' in the *Letter of Aristeas* (52), where Ptolemy has to be gently dissuaded from presenting the Jerusalem Temple with a showbread table more massive than any predecessor by the reminder that there were prescribed proportions for this holy artefact. By contrast, for another poet, there were no such restraints: when a couch is described, it is a couch which is fabulously superhuman in scale.[14]

We are fortunate to have been left a description of the wildly extravagant procession, the *pompē* of Ptolemy II, held to mark a turning-point in the earlier part of his reign and, if R. A. Hazzard is right, targeted especially at overawing Greek delegations who had been summoned for the occasion.[15] Normally restrained scholars are driven to strong reactions. Peter Fraser writes of an 'astonishing display of ostentation' and Dorothy Thompson of a 'world of hyperbole and extravagance... a colourful catalogue of the wealth of the Ptolemaic empire'.[16] Huge objects wrought from precious metals with baroque elaboration and unparalleled inventiveness were hauled along in the pageant. These included a table of solid silver some eighteen feet in length, four three-legged tables of gold, a gold chest encrusted with jewels, and two tall and ornate silver lampstands. Could Aristeas have been influenced by this list in his own description of the table made for Jerusalem and of the other jewelled artefacts bestowed by Ptolemy on the Jewish envoys? The pageant vividly expressed the aesthetics of luxury. It also conveyed a wealth of meaning, speaking at one and the same time the language of

[14] Posidippus 3.22–3. Bing 2005: 137.
[15] 283/2, 279/8, 275, and 262 BCE are the various dates that have been ascribed to the event, which may have commemorated his father, or perhaps the conclusion of one of his wars. See the appendix on the date of the procession in Thompson 2000. Hazzard 2000: 59–79 argues for 262 BCE as the date by means of numismatic and astronomical evidence, and he interprets the exercise in terms of the diplomatic circumstances of those years. Our source for the description is Athenaeus 5.196b–203b, attributed by him to Callixinus of Rhodes. That author, in Hazzard's estimation, produced his detailed and presumably largely accurate account from a written record about a century after the event.
[16] Fraser 1972: 202; Thompson 2000: 371. Cf. Rice 1983.

Graeco–Egyptian religion—by incorporating divine images in such a way as to assert the dynasty's pretensions to affinity with the gods, and the language of power—by accumulating symbols of the king's claims to global reach. Towns and islands which had been brought under Ptolemaic control figured prominently in the exotic tableaux. A central figure was a god closely associated with the dynasty and also with world travel, the many-faced Dionysus, here represented returning in triumph from India, recumbent on the back of an elephant, surrounded by satyrs and accompanied by the inebriated Silenus, not to mention the trappings of a panther skin dripping with wine, and (another Dionysiac symbol) a phallus nearly two hundred feet long. It is worth recalling how Aristeas makes Ptolemy and Demetrius take the whole of the inhabited known world, the *oikoumenē*, as his field of operation in the planning of the royal library (*Aristeas*, 9).

All conspired to ensure that in Alexandria politics were enmeshed with culture even more tightly than elsewhere. The promotion of learning, of enquiry, and of philosophical and literary activity was a weapon in the Ptolemaic armoury. This is precisely what is echoed in *Aristeas*, and equally in Alciphron's sketch of Menander and Glycera. We have seen that the early Ptolemies, and especially Philadelphus, devised a new and transportable version of the old Greek world and over a period of no more than thirty or forty years, the first monarchs put extraordinary effort into pulling in that remarkable influx of Greek intellectuals, resources, and ideas.[17] But while the intellectual life of Alexandria was self-consciously Greek in its preoccupation with continuing the living tradition of classical Athens and forging disciplines for interpreting that heritage, Alexandria was a city mentally as well as physically open to the outside world.[18] Here, information-gathering reflected a breadth of interest extending beyond any narrow Hellenocentric confines. One group from among Posidippus'

---

[17] For recent evocations of the Alexandrian 'project', see the various essays in the volumes edited by Jacob and de Polignac 2000, and by Maehler 2004. On culture as a tool of Ptolemaic power-politics, the sketch by Erskine 1995: 38–48.

[18] Maehler 2004 ascribes the Hellenocentricity he detects in Greek education in Ptolemaic Egypt to 'cultural defensiveness' in the face of the older Egyptian civilization, of which the newcomers were well aware.

surviving epigrams are the *lithika*, learned nutshell descriptions of fascinating gemstones, ranging from the magnetic rocks of Olympus to Arabian rock-crystal, from Nabataean engravings to Persian lapis and Indian rubies.[19]

This investigative impulse, too, owed much to the legacy of Alexander the Great: scholars and scientists had participated in his spectacular eastward trajectory through uncharted territory, with the purpose of bringing back information not only about places and natural life, but also of foreign peoples. Ptolemy I had created what Jean Bingen called a self-conscious 'symbiosis of his fate and that of Alexander'.[20] It was not by chance that he chose to draw upon his status as a former 'companion' and general to write Alexander's biography. He also arranged for the visible presence of Alexander to serve as a permanent reminder of his example to the city which he founded, by hijacking the funeral cortege on its way from Babylon. The embalmed body seems to have reposed temporarily at Memphis, until it could be ceremonially installed, not, as was expected, in the Siwah oasis at the shrine of Ammon where Alexander had been told of his divinity, but in the heart of Alexandria. Strabo, in his description of the city,[21] says that Ptolemy IV created an alabaster tomb for the remains of Alexander, which lay there in a gold coffin, alongside those of the first of the Ptolemies. Strabo locates the structure inside the royal palace, which, it seems, was not exactly a palace but rather a vast extended complex that incorporated also the Museum and the Library; and it is likely that this was the site of the tomb even before the refurbishments of Ptolemy IV. So the Library for which Aristeas claimed that the Jewish Law was translated sat right beside the city's idealized founder. This was the Alexandrian heart of the Ptolemaic project, both physically and in imagination.

---

[19] For the Posidippus collection as a celebration of the Ptolemies and their possessions, see Stephens 2004; Bing 2005. Poetical aspects of the *lithika* are dealt with in Acosta-Hughes et al. 2004, Chaps. 8–10.
[20] Bingen 2007: 20.
[21] Strabo, *Geography*, 17.1.

DESCRIBING THE JEWS

In various ways, Alexander's inclusive legacy of enquiry extended to Judaism. The impact of his conquests is visible in an association which is at first sight surprising, made both by the scholar Megasthenes, who wrote a book on India, and by the philosophical writer Clearchus of Soli.[22] Megasthenes says that the interpretation of nature found among Jews was shared by Indian gurus or 'brahmans'; while Clearchus actually identifies the Jews of Syria with the philosophers, 'calani', of India. Reaching India had been one of the most dazzling of Alexander's achievements (if the least lasting),[23] and this was why the association of the god Dionysus with India was highlighted in the pageant of Philadelphus, where at the same time Alexander's image brought up the rear, beside the goddess Victory (Nike) and the figure of Athena. So it made sense to explain other notably pious peoples in the light of the discoveries from India. One Indian story concerning Alexander became a paradigm still known to Cicero two-and-a-half centuries later and referred to more than once by him. This was about how the Brahman Callanus burnt himself to death in front of Alexander, evincing no pain and uttering only the statement that he would see Alexander soon. The event was followed by Alexander's own death a few days later.[24] As far as the Jews went, if Alexander did not himself visit Jerusalem, tradition managed to create a story, recorded in Josephus, which diverted his expedition to Jerusalem, took him straight to the Temple and had him doing obeisance before the High Priest—there he was regaled, what is more, with a biblical reading from the book of Daniel.[25] Jews and Indians were thus part of the same exotic, discovered world.

---

[22] Stern i, no. 6 (Megasthenes); no. 7 (Clearchus) from Josephus, CA, 1.179. Megasthenes' Indian history is also attested by Josephus, AJ, 10. 227. The Indian likeness resurfaces in the second speech advocating suicide to his fellow rebels on Masada which Josephus ascribes to Eleazar ben Yair, BJ, 7.351–7.

[23] On Alexander's image in relation to India, see Stewart 1993.

[24] Cicero, Tusc. Disp., 2.52 (and cf. 5.77 for a general allusion); de Div.,1.47. See Bowersock 1994: 71.

[25] For a detailed study, see Gruen 1998: 189–99.

After Alexander, there converged in early Ptolemaic Egypt a number of features conducive to an awareness of the Jewish religion, and more particularly, perhaps, to a Greek response to the Law of the Jews. This targeted interest went beyond the simple eagerness to include the Jewish scriptures in the Library's collection of all the books in the world in the fashion ascribed by Aristeas to Ptolemy (9–10).

We may notice that the translation of the Hebrew Bible is situated within the context of a wider interest in Jews already within Aristeas' own literary procedure. For there is a superficial lack of unity in the *Letter of Aristeas* which we have already noticed. This has elicited scathing remarks,[26] and it has worried even well-disposed readers. As we saw, the business of the translation provides the framework, but occupies little real space, and the bulk of the book is given over to other matters, expressed in a variety of literary genres including splendid examplars of dialogue and of *ekphrasis*. I suggest that this agenda, for all its diversity, might be summed up as opening a number of different windows on Judaism. The varied subject-matter can be seen as serving to explain the point and meaning of the Law that was fetched from Jerusalem. We might perhaps say that the parchment scrolls were a signifier for Judaism itself, and therefore the narrative of finding and fetching them is also an account of how Ptolemy's circle discovered something of what Judaism was about. Mysteries that had previously, as we are told, been scarcely available to Gentiles were now laid open.

Among these mysteries was that of the nature of the Jewish God. Aristeas tells Ptolemy that he has been finding out about the Jews, precisely in connection with the sufferings of the military prisoners, and that 'God the overseer and creator of all things' whom the Jews worship is none other than Zeus and Dis, whose ancient names signified that through him 'all creatures are made alive and come into being' (*Aristeas*, 16). Jan Assmann reminds us that the translatability of the names of deities was a widespread and important principle in ancient polytheism.[27] More specifically, however, there are echoes here of Herodotus recounting the names of the Egyptian

---

[26] For example, Zuntz 1959 and Murray 1975.
[27] Assmann 1997: 44–50.

gods: while unwilling, or unable, to relate any of the stories about them, he explains without hesitation that the Egyptians call Zeus 'Ammon'. There is, furthermore, an even more distinct echo, and that harks back to Plato's dialogue on the subject of names, the *Cratylus*, where Socrates insists that correct names establish the nature of what they name, and states that the combination of Zena plus Dis, while hard to understand, actually both means and correctly denotes 'the cause of life': Zeus is indeed that, and also the 'ruler and king of all'.[28] The Jewish conception of divinity enunciated by Aristeas thus fits particularly well into the framework of Greek theorizing.

THE SCHOOL OF ARISTOTLE AND THE JEWS

The ideas of Herodotus and of Plato on divine names cannot be traced as a direct source for Aristeas, though it is reasonable to suppose that they were under discussion in Alexandria before he wrote his book. In the case of Aristotle, by contrast, we have hints of various kinds of connections with Judaism that go back earlier. In philosophical terms, the school was not at its best at this juncture, and its impact on the higher reaches of Alexandrian thought appears to have been limited. And yet the heritage of Aristotle was in the air. In a non-technical sense, the label 'peripatetic' seems to have been loosely and fairly widely applied to scholars of various types.[29] And there was a tangible and important Aristotelian legacy in the realm of method, for the master had put a very high valuation on collecting, and classifying scientifically, information on a wide front. Among the scholars who came to Alexandria in the early days, a number were Peripatetics, associated in one way or another with the philosophical tradition of Aristotle, and with its special interest in empirical

---

[28] Her., 2.3; 42–5; Plato, *Crat.*, 395e–396a (the parallel is not noted by Hadas). For this important constellation of ideas, see van den Berg 2006: 171–5. At the same time, Aristeas' vocabulary here is notably Septuagintal, when he speaks of God as *pantōn epoptēs* and *ktistēs*, as well as of the captives 'bound in wretchedness' (*sunechomenous en talaipōriais*) (*Aristeas*, 15).

[29] Lynch 1972: 136–7 applies the term 'neo-peripatetics' to those biographers, historians, literary critics, etc.

enquiry and in classification. Aristotle's library was often seen as the precursor of the Alexandrian Library. In the Roman period, Strabo maintained that Aristotle had provided a model for the Ptolemies of how to organize a collection, although he did not believe that the kings had been successful in their attempts to acquire the philosopher's own library for themselves.[30]

For our purposes, it is significant that the Lyceum, Aristotle's school, had a special interest in constitutions, *politeiai*, and therefore in lawgivers. Even those of the 'barbarians' came into the reckoning, along with the systems of different Greek cities: generally the barbarians were not considered up to the mark. In the 120-book catalogue, the *pinakes*, compiled by the librarian–poet Callimachus, there was probably a separate section for *nomoi* (laws or law-codes).[31] That classification could even go some way towards explaining how the Hebrew Torah, which contains much more than the commandments, prescriptions, and regulations, was categorized as *nomos* (with sometimes the use of its plural or of related words) throughout Greek–Jewish thought, a manifestation so ubiquitous that we scarcely stop to think about it.

Josephus tells us that, according to Clearchus, Aristotle in person met a philosophical Jew from Coele-Syria, a man characterized by *karteria* and *sōphrosynē*, who, in a famous phrase, 'not only spoke Greek but had the soul of a Greek'.[32] Few will take that as a historical report, and indeed Josephus himself goes no further than to claim that Clearchus, in a book on the subject of sleep, put this parenthesis about the Jew into his master's mouth. So the book in question is likely to have been a philosophical dialogue, with Aristotle a protagonist of it. Nevertheless, the attribution has emblematic power.

---

[30] On Aristotle's library as model, Strabo 13.608. The tortuous route of Aristotle's library to Rome is recorded in Strabo 12.1.54. But contrast Athenaeus 1.10, who says that this library was owned by the Ptolemies. Lynch's contention (1972: 122–3) that neither the Lyceum nor any other Athenian philosophical school could have provided a model for the Alexandrian Museum, is linked with an insistence upon the essentially religious character of the latter.
[31] For an attempt to reconstruct Callimachus' endeavours as 'bibliographer', see Blum 1991, and esp. p. 135 for the *nomika barbarika*. For a broader perspective, Pfeiffer 1968: 123–34.
[32] Josephus, *CA*, 1.176–83, Stern i, no.7, l.15.

Observations on Judaism are by this means legitimated among the master's successors. The startling statement that the Jew in question, while somehow identifiably a Jew (we are not told how), still possesses a Greek soul, lifts him above any mere barbarians, who are deemed to be in their nature slaves; he is brought, as a Jew, into the charmed circle of Greek discourse.

It is remarkable how much of the enquiry about Judaism of the first period of Greek engagement is associated precisely with Aristotle's Lyceum.[33] Apart from Clearchus, the snippets preserved in Josephus' *Against Apion* include a bemused account of Jewish Sabbath observance by the historian Agatharchides of Cnidus, who was described as a Peripatetic.[34] Although Agatharchides' comments seem to have been somewhat critical, scholars have been inclined to associate a particularly positive Greek attitude to Jews with the early years of the Jewish presence in Alexandria, which waned as time went on.[35] And while we are today more careful about making black-and-white discriminations between 'positive' and 'negative' literary responses to Jews, we cannot fail to notice the extent to which Judaism figured, or at least was thought to have figured, in the Peripatetic mental map in the first stages of the encounter.[36]

Indeed, what is now established as the first real reference to Jews in Greek literature is the discussion of Jewish prayer in the work on piety by Theophrastus, who was Aristotle's leading pupil.[37] We notice too that Demetrius of Phaleron himself, who in the *Letter of Aristeas* is the chief promoter and organizer of the translators' visit, was a well-known Peripatetic,[38] described as an associate of Theophrastus.[39]

---

[33] Suggestive remarks on this by Orth 2001: 108–12.

[34] Josephus, *CA*, 1.209–11; Stern i, no.17.

[35] Note that for Tcherikover 1957 and Fraser 1972: 82–4, the reign of Ptolemy VI Philometor in the middle part of the second century BCE was the high noon of Alexandrian Jewry: see further the discussion in Chap. 5.

[36] As Stern indeed did (i. 131).

[37] As demonstrated by Stern 1973.

[38] On this connection, see Orth 2001: 108–9.

[39] See Fortenbaugh and Schütrumpf 2000: 1–301 for the sources on Demetrius, and esp. 39–41 for the association with Theophrastus. Huss 2001: 230–1 points out that Demetrius was of service to the school at least in the matter to property-ownership, because Theophrastus was a *metoikos* not an Athenian citizen. For a readable sketch of Demetrius' career with some comment on his Aristotelian dimen-

After his banishment from Greece, where he had been regent and reformer under Cassander, Demetrius went by invitation to the court of Ptolemy I, and reputedly it was Theophrastus in person who persuaded the King that the exiled politician could transform himself into a man of letters.

Aristeas (312–14) offers a curious explanation of why the Jewish Law had to date been ignored by Greeks. He mentions two writers, the well-known historian, Theopompus of Chios, and the tragedian and orator, Theodectes of Phaselis, both of whom had sought to quote from the Law. As a punishment for their sacrilege, they had been struck down, in one case by temporary madness and in the other by passing blindness (Aristeas 314–16). The origins of these tales elude us. But the identity of the tragedian is interesting: he was said to have been a pupil of Aristotle's, in the company of the young Alexander, as well as studying at Athens with the orator and educationalist Isocrates.

It is noticeable too that Aristeas' own text contains a good number of Aristotelianisms of a superficial kind, most obviously the striking statement that the High Priest Eleazar was an exponent of the theory of the ethical mean (*metriotēs*, *Aristeas*, 122).[40] Other instances include the following: a statement that men are prone to pleasure which seems to echo the *Nicomachean Ethics* (*Aristeas*,105); a mention of Ptolemy's establishment of local assizes couched in similar terms to Aristotle's account in chapter 16 of the *Athenian Constitution* of how the Athenian tyrant Pisistratus protected agriculture by enabling litigants to remain in the countryside (*Aristeas*, 108–11);[41] the distinction between two kinds of wise men, *sophoi* and *phronimoi* (*Aristeas*, 130); and finally the particular verb used (*energeō*) to describe God's dynamic operation in the world (*Aristeas*, 210).

---

sion, see Mossé 2000. For the supposition that Demetrius supported not only Theophrastus but also Menander, see Green 1990: 72, drawing on Phaedrus, *Fables*, 5.1.

[40] Cf. also *Aristeas*, 211, 223, 256, for less technical endorsements of moderation.
[41] Fraser 1972: 978 follows the identification made by Hadas of an Aristotelian parallelism here, at the same time as accepting the historicity of the statement about Philadelphus.

There may be signs of an Aristotelian derivation also in Aristeas' question about what is most characteristic of kings (notably *Aristeas*, 223). On rather different ground, the assertion that weasels conceive through the ear and give birth through the mouth (*Aristeas*, 165) reminds us of Aristotle's refutation in *On the Generation of Animals* (3.6.5) of exactly this notion. Even the use in an entirely non-technical context of a keyword in Aristotelian philosophy, *prohairesis* (*Aristeas*, 3), in the sense of a considered choice, adds a Peripatetic glow to the writing.[42] An investigation of Aristeas' vocabulary has produced a list of thirty-three terms claimed as distinctively Aristotelian, together with five terms associated with Theophrastus.[43]

Among Hellenistic Jewish writers, the closest to writing philosophy was Aristobulus, presumed to be the addressee of the letter at the opening of 2 Maccabees (1: 11), who is referred to as the 'teacher of Ptolemy'. Five fragments of this author survive, preserved by the Christian authors Clement of Alexandria and Eusebius (in two works).[44] He apparently dedicated his work to the ruling monarch in Egypt, stated by Clement to be Ptolemy VI Philometor (181–145 BCE). Part of Aristobulus' book seems to have consisted of a dialogue with this or another king in which the Jews are shown to have been recipients of royal favours since the Persian period, if not before.[45] The purpose attributed to Aristobulus in the sources is that of showing that Peripatetic philosophy derived from the Law of Moses.[46]

---

[42] The phenomenon, and a number of these examples, were identified by Moses Hadas (1951) throughout his commentary on the *Letter*.

[43] Meecham 1935: 48–9, following in the footsteps of an early suggestion by Thackeray.

[44] For the fragments, see Holladay iii (1995). The sources are Eusebius *Church History*, 7.32.16–18 (citing Anatolius); Eusebius, *Preparation for the Gospel*, 7.14; 8.10; 13.12; Clement of Alexandria, *Stromateis*, 1, 5, 6. For an overall assessment, Collins 2000: 186–90. See also p. 98 n. 14.

[45] On this motif in Aristobulus, see Janowitz 1991: 131.

[46] For an overview of the debate on Aristobulus as philosopher, see Holladay iii (1985): 72–3, 230–2.

THE MONARCH AND JUDAEA

It may be objected that the Ptolemies were autocrats not investigators. The Jews may have been recognized as a fascinating curiosity, but we still have to ask whether the domestication of the sacred text of such a minor population group could conceivably have been thought to contribute to the grand project of cultural acquisition. Could Jews and Judaism have had sufficient positive resonance at Alexandria for the inclusion to pay dividends? A number of factors may be invoked in support of a claim that *ioudaioi*, in both the more specific sense of 'Judaeans' and in the wider sense, 'Jews', merited a place in the Ptolemaic mental map.[47]

First, Syria, and especially the parts of that wider region which included the subdivision of Coele–Syria and the smaller subdivision of Judaea, were crucial to the early Ptolemies. They were border territory, repeatedly contested with their rivals in successive Syrian wars. Ptolemy II's boundaries in this region apparently ran through the Beka'a valley of Lebanon.[48] The fourth Syrian War would conclude with Ptolemy IV Philopator's recovery of 'Hollow Syria' from Seleucid rule by his victory in 217 BCE at Raphia near Gaza (Polybius 5.107.1–3; 3 Macc. 1.). When the Ptolemies were finally to lose control of the region, it would be in a battle fought around 200 BCE at Panium, on the Golan. In *Aristeas*, as we have seen, the release with compensation at Aristeas' instigation of the 100,000 transplanted or imprisoned Jewish soldiers taken by Ptolemy I in 'the country of the Jews', as well as of others captured earlier, is a prelude to the commissioning of the translation. Of these, 30,000 had been selected and settled in garrisons (*Aristeas*, 13). The claim may be overstated but it chimes well with evidence from Ptolemaic papyri of the incorporation of war prisoners of various regions into military units of an ethnically organized army. One surviving papyrus of the relevant period, a deed of 260 BCE, attests to an individual *ioudaios*, Alexander, son of Andronikos, who served in the Ptolemaic army, in

---

[47] Both senses of *ioudaios*, the geographical and the ethno-religious, are applicable at this period; see p. 9.
[48] Ager 2003: 38. Local topography in Grainger 1991.

the post of *dekanikos*. His witnesses, who include other soldiers of the same troop, do not seem to be Jews, and he presumably lived among non-Jews on cleruchic landholdings which will have been allocated to them.[49] It is hard to tell how different a situation this represented from the cohesive structure of the Jewish garrison established earlier by the Persians at Elephantine in Upper Egypt; or from the military colony and temple near Heliopolis established on land granted to the high priestly refugee from Jerusalem, Onias, and his associates, by Ptolemy VI Philometor early in the second century BCE.[50] Most scholars understand the Jewish collective (*politeuma*) of Heracleopolis, whose recorded activities date from the later part of the same century, as another military settlement.[51]

Ptolemaic rule was personal, and a ruler benefited from knowing something of the people and places he ruled. Within Syria and Phoenicia, Hellenistic writers tended to note the Judaean landscape, at least one feature of which stood out as quite extraordinary. The Dead Sea also had economic importance to the ruling power and taken together with its astonishing landscape it is hardly surprising that it becomes at this time a topic of consuming interest. One of the earliest descriptions was that of the important, lost historian, Hieronymus of Cardia, who had apparently been employed by Ptolemy I to supervise the extraction of asphalt there, though it must be admitted that Hieronymus shows no signs of having noticed the Jews anywhere else in his history.[52] This particular topic of discussion evidently exceeds the boundaries of simple ethnographic convention and it seems to arise precisely out of the Ptolemies' attempt to exploit the territory they owned. Though Aristeas does not mention the

---

[49] P. Hibeh, 1.96; *CPJ*, 1.18; the document is extensively emended. For a comprehensive list of 'ioudaioi', named as such, in Egyptian Ptolemaic documentary and literary sources of all periods and involved in various kinds of activities, see La'da 2002: 106–14 and 318. If we allow for possible cases of duplication of individuals, the total will amount to some eighty persons. Some of those, from the second half of the third century BCE onwards, are also described as 'of the *epigonē*' (i.e. 'descent'), and in the opinion of some scholars this term indicates an association with the military.

[50] Josephus, *BJ*, 7.421–36; *AJ*, 13.62–73. On this temple, see p. 98.

[51] For Elephantine, see below, pp. 103, 148–9. On the Heracleopolis dossier, see below, p. 85–6. For elucidation of the military dimension of the *politeuma*, see esp. Cowey and Maresch 2004.

[52] Stern i, no. 5.

Dead Sea, he does bring the disused copper and iron mines of the mountains of Arabia into his overview of the land of the Jews. Since he remarks upon allegations of over-exploitation and, interestingly, damage to the countryside in the Persian period, there is no reason to think that he wishes simply to evoke the Deuteronomic land 'whose stones are iron and out of whose hills thou mayest dig brass'.[53]

Between 260 and 258 BCE (years 26 and 27 of Ptolemy II), Zenon, agent of Apollonius who held under Philadelphus the very high post of *dioikētēs*, financial officer, travelled in Palestine and did business on behalf of his boss and indirectly of the King. The many papyri that have been combined to create his famous archive allow us to trace his journey via Caesarea, through Jerusalem and Jericho, and then across the Jordan and into Idumaea. There is a clutch of documents which concern his transactions with persons in the region, including Jews.[54] Notably, the party visited Birta, the estate of Toubias in Ammanitis across the Jordan. The local significance of this landowner and strongman, who could trace his lineage back to the return from exile and to a dubious character of the days of Nehemiah, was such that Toubias saw fit to send Apollonius letters, written by his scribes in a beautiful large hand. He uses a standard opening with a pagan formula—'if you are well ... thanks be to the gods'—and he explains that he has sent one Aeneas bearing the gift of a eunuch and four named boys, 'of good stock', whose physical features are set out meticulously. It is stated of two of them that they are uncircumcised, while two are circumcised (supposedly less desirable)—and the latter two also have flat noses.[55] Remarkably, there is also the copy of a brief letter addressed to King Ptolemy (Philadelphus) himself, within a letter to Apollonius, and the choice of gifts for the King shows that Toubias had considered the recipient's taste: the King's zoo was famous and Toubias sent Arab horses, dogs, white Arabs, and foals

---

[53] Hadas in his commentary (1951) takes Aristeas 119–20 to be echoing Deut. 8: 9.

[54] For Zenon's itinerary in Palestine, Pestman 1981: 264. For the inventory of documents, ibid., 172–3.

[55] For Tobiah the Ammonite, see Neh. 7: 61–2; Ezra 2: 59–60; Neh. 13: 4–9; Zechariah 6: 10–14.

of wild asses and mules, all tame.[56] As Bagnall and Derow write: 'his gifts are, even if suggested by Apollonios, those of one ruler to another.' That the family did not escape royal attention is amply demonstrated by the fortunes of Joseph, son of Tobias, who, in Josephus' colourful and partly historical family saga, accused all his rivals of collusion and then outbid them for the concession to farm the royal taxes of southern Syria, which had previously been held by a recalcitrant High Priest. Joseph's erotic adventures at court are surely fictitious; less so, probably, the report of the great brutality with which he 'stripped Syria to the bone' (in the words of the court jester) for twenty-two years. Joseph's son Hyrcanus proved even more brazen, in the way he usurped his father's role, and also more reckless in his conduct with the King until forced to withdraw to his own territory; Josephus' tales about the son are even more dramatic and less believable. And Josephus' chronology cannot be made to fit together. But the historian is probably correct when he assigns to the Tobiad family a prominent role in Ptolemaic and Seleucid Jerusalem, where their quarrels with the high priestly Oniad family proved to be a precursor to the Maccabaean revolution. Undoubtedly, these supremely ambitious Jews were deserving of the monarchs' quite close attention.

GRAECO–EGYPTIANS AND THE JEWISH NARRATIVE

The Ptolemies needed in the first instance to maintain their grip on Egypt and its native population. They were not always successful, and for a century or so, beginning with the reign of Ptolemy III, revolts by the native Egyptians were not infrequent. But the Egyptian view of the past was one in which the Jews were implicated.

---

[56] P. Cair. Zen. 59076 and 59075; *CPJ*, 1.4 and 5; Bagnall and Derow 2004: 113–15, no. 65. The letters are dated to year 29 of Ptolemy II. On historical elements in the Tobiad saga, see Gera 1998: 36–58. The partially remains of a small building known as the 'Araq El Emir near Amman are generally identified as the Tobiad residence, mainly on the basis of two nearby graffiti spelling out the family name. On this site, see again Gera 1998: 40–8.

Strikingly, Aristeas himself maintains that he has previously sent Philocrates, the recipient of his present letter, data on this people which he had acquired from the learned Egyptian high priests (*Aristeas*, 6). We have good evidence that Jews engaged with Graeco–Egyptians on this intellectual territory. By far the most important exponent of the endeavour to make Egyptian history accessible to Greeks was the bilingual Egyptian priest of Heliopolis and royal adviser, Manetho of Sebennytus, who won enduring fame for having organized the Egyptian dynastic lists and translated or adapted the priestly books in the early third century BCE. In so doing, Manetho appears to have expatiated, on at least two separate occasions, on his peculiar version of the Jewish exodus (or expulsion, as he believed) from Egypt. Manetho and other writers in a similar vein are cited by Josephus as offensive anti-Semites engaged in one-sided, malicious vilification, and that is no doubt the spirit in which their comments were taken, probably by both sides, when the arguments were revived in the age of Josephus. But the cut and thrust of literary polemic need not have emerged out of implacable hatred. Mud-slinging between the parties might rather suggest the existence of common ground at the time of the first engagement. Contestations of mythological pasts were the stock-in-trade of Hellenistic writing.[57]

From the Greek side, the *Aigyptiaka* (or 'Egyptian Things') of Hecataeus of Abdera, written around 300 BCE, was the first Egyptian ethnography by a Greek, and it facilitated on the intellectual plane Ptolemy I's control of Egypt. The author gave extensive and on the whole laudatory coverage to the departure of the Jews, the colonization of Jerusalem by Moses, and the system of government and way of life that he supposedly established there.[58] It is interesting that the *Letter of Aristeas* (30) specifically invokes the name of Hecataeus of Abdera, rightly or wrongly, as a witness to the sanctity of the Torah.

---

[57] Bickerman 1952 is still a classic study of these exchanges. See further the discussion of Manetho in Chap. 8, pp. 262–3.
[58] Stern i, no.11; Bar-Kochva 1996: 7–43.

A LAW CODE?

Various kinds of documents were translated in the great empires of the ancient Near East. But for obvious reasons law codes, decrees, and regulations were especially given to being expressed in more than one language or to being transferred from one to another, both so that the ruler should be seen to communicate with all of his subjects, and for more directly utilitarian considerations. The Jewish Torah, defined as a subject people's legal system, their *nomos*, would thus recommend itself to the King as a proper object of his attention. It fell within the sphere of meaningful gesture.

Josèphe Mélèze Modrzejewski, who has long reflected upon the legal dimension of the Septuaguint translation, wants to take the official role in the Jewish Torah in Greek well beyond the sphere of gesture, arguing that it may be construed as the commissioning of a practical code to be employed by the regime as a *politikos nomos*, that is to say a subsidiary law for an immigrant group.[59] For the production of such a translated ethnic code, a parallel may possibly be found in a statement in the so-called Egyptian 'demotic chronicle'. This papyrus document, unfortunately defective, records that, at the onset of Persian rule in Egypt, King Darius ordered that a codification of Egyptian law as it had stood at the time of the conquest (526 BCE) be made in demotic, the ordinary language of Egypt, and also that it should be published in Aramaic, the official language of the Persian empire. A different group of Ptolemaic papyrus fragments in demotic from Hermopolis, containing a list of practical legal prescriptions for the use of officials, have been tentatively identified as parts of the old casebook of the Egyptian priests. The last piece in the puzzle is another Greek papyrus from Oxyrhynchus which corresponds in part to the Hermopolis material and which has been interpreted as a loose Greek version of that same code.[60] However, no one has found unequivocal papyrological evidence of the Egyptian law code formally operating as local law-in-action.

---

[59] The fullest discussions of this position is provided by Honigman 2003: 198–213.
[60] Mélèze Modrzejewski 1995: 105–7; Mélèze Modrzejewski 1996: 80–1. Followed by Le Boulluec 2000: 60–1.

In general, we know that the Ptolemies were willing to adopt the existing laws of their subjects. But any hypothesis of a functional role for biblical law as a local jurisdiction within Ptolemaic Jewish communities will be better applied not so much as a primary explanation for the translation, but as a later, secondary stage in the acclimatization of the Septuagint in a world of legal pluralism, and even then, on a very limited scale. Mélèze Modrzejewski's minute and learned analysis of a number of fragmentary papyrological records relating to Jewish litigants of the late third century, falls short of demonstrating the application of any specific biblical law in relation either to personal status or to commercial transaction.[61] A two-stage reading of the legal history fits well with the remarkable new evidence from the recent publication of a dossier of twenty documentary papyri of the second half of the second century BCE, belonging to the Jewish *politeuma* of Heracleopolis in the Nile delta, apparently a cleruchic settlement of soldiers or ex-soldiers with a predominantly Jewish population, and with *archontes* whose executive jurisdiction extended to hearing appeals from neighbouring nomes. The term for a bill of divorce or letter of repudiation (*bublion apostasiou*) found in Septuagint Deuteronomy 24.1–4 makes a remarkable appearance in papyrus 4.[62] A certain Philotas claims that Lysimachus, having sworn to betroth his daughter to him and to hand over a dowry, gave her to another man without the necessary letter of repudiation.[63] Moreover, the legal requirement understood to be necessary for such a letter in the absence of a marriage is in accord with the Jewish law of *qiddushin* but it is not, it would seem, a Greek or an Egyptian requirement. When Jesus speaks against divorce in Mark 10: 4 and Matthew 19: 7 the same Greek term is used. The rest of the language deployed here for the betrothal, marriage, and divorce processes also accords with Greek Deuteronomy, though it is less distinctive. These points of reference sit side by side with the familiar application of ordinary Ptolemaic practice in the dossier here and in papyrus 3. Four

---

[61] Mélèze Modrzejewski 1995: 107–19; Mélèze Modrzejewski 1996: 82–3.
[62] Translating the Hebrew *sefer keritot*.
[63] See Cowey and Maresch 2001: 68–9, with review by Honigman 2002 from the perspective of both Greek and Jewish law and then a response to Honigman in Maresch and Cowey 2003. Further discussion in Cowey and Maresch 2004.

plaintiffs appeal to what they call a *patrios nomos*, the law of their own particular tradition, which could conceivably refer to the Torah, as locally incorporated, but seems rather to designate Greek law as they have customarily used it.[64] Altogether, the principles according to which the officials of the Heracelopolite *politeuma* exercised their jurisdiction remain something of a puzzle. But still the application in the Heracleopolis *politeuma* of at least one Septuagintal norm stands out. In terms both of date and of place, however, we have moved away from the Alexandria of Ptolemy. We shall discover in Chapter 6 that a rich assortment of other new developments belong to this second stage of the Septuagint's life, all of them clustering in the mid-second century BCE. Times had by then changed.

JEWISH NEEDS AND CHOICES

For the Jews, the intellectual environment of Hellenistic Egypt posed a challenge from the start, and an ongoing challenge was presented to successive waves of new immigrants. 'Going Greek' was not only the practice of the best circles in Alexandria, it also filtered down to lower levels and to other towns and villages. This was not just a question of using the Greek language for buying, selling, and litigating. A long word-list from a Fayyum village which appears to be a schoolmaster's book has vocabulary clearly designed to enable his pupils to read Homer and tragedy and thus to assert their membership of the privileged Greek stratum of society.[65]

It was in the interest of a Jewish community seeking to establish itself in a relatively new location to acquire such skills. In a world in flux, there were still openings for those ready to seize them. It was well known that the Macedonian overlords themselves had not so very long ago been newcomers in their homeland to Athenian culture. For Jews, the possibility to go Greek must have been welcome: the alien civilization of their age-old Egyptian enemy could be largely

---

[64] The term appears in papyri 3, 4, 9, and 12. I have been much assisted by Sylvie Honigman's analysis in an unpublished paper delivered in Jerusalem in June 2005.
[65] Fewster 2002: 232.

disregarded: evidence of Jewish use of demotic is lacking. It is a modern fallacy—and still something of a scholarly obsession—to see 'Hellenism' as a threat to them rather than as an opportunity for them to embrace. The Greek translation of the Torah belongs to a group remarkably assured about setting their own limits, as we shall see.

The possession of writings in Greek denoted membership of the Greek 'club'. It was time to open up to the world what before had not only been unintelligible to outsiders but was also viewed, at least by some, as a mystery uncommunicable to the impure. Such a bid for inclusion in the new order swept doubts aside. It is tempting to go a little further. We might suspect that some kind of suggestion on the part of well-connected Jews, perhaps a little prodding, might have initiated the transaction between king and subjects. As an example of the operation of patronage in the Ptolemaic system, we may take two petitions in the Zenon archive, requesting help, directly or indirectly, from Apollonius, the King's highly placed finance minister.[66] It is, we recall, the reception of the scrolls by the Jewish community and especially by its leaders that makes the climax of the *Letter of Aristeas* (310).

A passage from *Aristeas* itself might be cited in support of the notion of a Jewish initiative to the King. This passage seems to say that earlier (and carelessly expressed) Greek versions had preceded the work of the seventy-two. If so, they must have been made within the Jewish community prior to the commissioning of Ptolemy's translation and have been of limited scope: a possible prelude to a large-scale, systematic operation. However, the crucial Greek word, *sesēmantai*, 'marked', is itself somewhat ambiguous, and the vague sentence in which it appears may well be speaking about the previous state of the Hebrew texts and not of any earlier translations.[67]

---

[66] Honigman 2003: 103–5. It is not clear to me why N. Collins 2000: 117 finds any such Jewish involvement incompatible with Ptolemaic orchestration.

[67] The sense in this particular context of the Greek *sesēmantai* (30) is at issue. The verb could at a stretch here mean 'to translate', but it more properly signifies 'to note' or 'write', as asserted by Zuntz 1959: 115–20. Gooding 1963 accepts the last rendering, differing from Zuntz only in taking Aristeas to refer to Hebrew scrolls poorly produced in Alexandria rather than in Jerusalem. For more on the debate, see Jellicoe 1968: 51–2, who comments that he is 'content to leave the exact translation of the

RECIPIENTS OF PATRONAGE

The King's support was a precious mark of that much-desired public acceptance. But there was a more practical consideration as well, to which little if any attention has been paid. The task of translation was a large enterprise in ancient terms, and a difficult one, requiring, under any conditions, substantial labour and therefore significant subvention. The Alexandrian Jewish community could hardly yet have had the means to support its own institutions of learning or its scholarly class. We hear nothing in Aristeas of wealthy Jews supporting the translation enterprise: if any such figures had existed, they would scarcely have failed to achieve recognition in the record. In any event, patronage in a monarchy tends to be monopolized by the monarch, even if delivered by intermediaries; this tendency was even more marked in the overwhelmingly centralized Egyptian state.[68] We have seen, on the other hand, why a Ptolemy and those around him might have wanted to afford such patronage to the Jews. True, this was a numerically insignificant subject group—Aristeas probably needed to inflate well beyond the possible the number of the liberated war captives if this part of his communication was to make any impact. But that was made up for by the geographical significance of the Jewish homeland in Judaea, by their position as a remarkable phenomenon on the scholarly mental map, and by their openness to the Ptolemaic cultural enterprise. Furthermore, a great monarch gained prestige from his control of a foreign law code, irrespective of its immediate practical use or applicability. And a Greek ruler's reputation could be enhanced by claiming that he had made available and useful to Greeks famous and awe-inspiring alien writings. In sum, the intellectual climate made the Jews an attractive topic; geography and strategy made them relevant. Judaism was within the Ptolemaic sphere of interest. Ptolemy's patronage, in the cultural atmosphere encouraged

---

verb an open question in view of the indecisive nature of the evidence'. Note also Bickerman 1976: 191, n. 62, on the use of this word in the second sense in official contexts.

[68] This aspect of the Ptolemaic state is well summed up in Thompson 2003: 108–15.

Cultural Politics of Alexandria

by Philadelphus, allowed grand new ideas to reach fruition, and the Septuagint translation was certainly such an idea.

Whether Ptolemaic patronage is reflected in the translation itself is another matter. Elias Bickerman, with his usual ingenuity, found traces of it. Building on that old scholarly tradition, which stemmed originally from Talmudic explanations accompanying the list of changes wrought in the text by the translator for the benefit of King Ptolemy, he found in the choice of term to denote the biblical hare (*arnevet*) listed among the unclean animals in Leviticus (11: 6) and Deuteronomy (14: 7) a conscious avoidance of echoing the dynasty's name Lagos, whose apparent meaning was 'precisely' hare. This for Bickerman was specifically a case of political caution on the part of those whom he dubbed the 'polite translators' and 'loyal subjects'. Aquila's much later translation, by contrast, had instead not hesitated to use the word *lagōos* (the epic form of *lagōs*). This seductive suggestion has turned out to be not as secure as we would wish when probed. The word preferred in the Septuagint translation is an equally good rendering of the Hebrew, used interchangeably with *dasupous*.[69]

Ptolemaic patronage granted, it would be absurd to seek to explain the translation project exclusively in outward-looking terms. A background of biblical interpretation and creativity was a *sine qua non* for the translators, and that must be sought in Judaism. The scholars from Jerusalem, whether historical personalities or not, neatly symbolize this dimension in the construction of the *Letter*.

Furthermore, whatever the beginnings, we must assume that Jewish ownership of the translated text and its active incorporation into the multifarious activities of a vigorous community were not long delayed, as we shall see. Also from the Jewish side would come the impetus to continue translating the Hebrew Bible, beyond Ptolemy's 'first instalment'.[70]

---

[69] See above, pp. 36–7. The scholarly tradition, examined by Pearce 2007b, goes back to Menasseh ben Israel. Two further political readings by Bickerman, in both cases suggesting that *melekh*, king, has been translated by *archōn* instead of *basileus*, are also placed under Pearce's critical microscope. There are other reasons for choosing the more general term and there is doubt over the Hebrew text or its interpretation in both cases.

[70] For a reconstruction similar to mine, see Orth 2001: 104–5.

Indeed, the scope of that instalment remains opaque. The Greek *nomos*, representing the Hebrew 'Torah',[71] familiarly refers to all five books of Moses, and it has been most often supposed that the whole Pentateuch was indeed included in the original translation project. That remains possible. That the different translated books come from the hands of different translators is a consensus of modern Septuagint study, and it is furthermore highly likely that more than one translator was involved in some individual books, notably Genesis and Exodus.[72] But this lack of uniformity could quite well be the product of the synchronized labour of different hands rather than the mark of translations done over a period of time. For we may safely assume that these hands lacked the perfect harmony claimed for them by the idealizing Aristeas. And we may be sure that they could not aspire to the elaborate system devised for the King James translation of 1611 (no doubt in full consciousness of the Aristeas tradition[73]), whereby the efforts of forty-seven translators (intended originally to be fifty-four) were divided into six separate companies and then brought together in London for three years of scrutiny by a 'general meeting' in which sat two from each company.[74] On the other hand, Aristeas might have had in mind, throughout his discussion of king, scrolls, and translation, no more than some part or parts of the Torah that might be described as 'the Law'—let us say just the religious and purity regulations of Exodus, Leviticus, and Deuteronomy with essential surrounding material; or perhaps the most recent version of the Law as represented by the book of Deuteronomy. It would be nice to see significance in the predominance of Deuteronomy and Exodus passages among the surviving second- and first-centuries BCE fragments—what are probably the two very earliest are from legal sections of Deuteronomy (chaps. 11 and 23).[75]

---

[71] On the equivalence, see pp. 22–3.

[72] Systematic investigation of stylistic variation between books is much to be desired.

[73] As noted by Barnstone 1993: 214. The translators' interest in Ptolemy's commissioning of the Septuagint translation is made plain in their preface, 'The Translators to the Reader'.

[74] On the context to the Authorized Version, see now Nicolson 2003. Daiches 1941 remains interesting, especially for coverage of Jewish input.

[75] See p. 15.

In just the same way as we can only speculate, when we read of the great reform of King Josiah in the Second Book of Kings, as to whether the book of Torah discovered by the king in the foundations of the Temple and read to the assembled people (2 Kings 22) was a whole or just a part of Deuteronomy or indeed something else, with possibilities mooted ranging, again, from the entire Torah to some small excerpt. In the *Letter of Aristeas*, the individual receptacles, whether old Hebrew or the new Greek, are talked of in the plural, whether the term used is *diptherai*, parchments, *teuchē*, rolls, or simply *biblia*, books. This may signify one scroll for each of the five books, or more than that. We do know that, in late antiquity at least, small scrolls as well as large had their place, from the moment when rabbinic regulation forbade the writing even of part of the Torah on anything less than a large scroll, a *sefer*, but, by way of exception, ordained that early chapters of Genesis (the flood) and of Leviticus (the purity regulations) might be put into a *megillah*, or small scroll.[76] Midrashic texts tell us that these were the passages which were used in the early stages of children's education: Leviticus was appropriate 'because the sacrifices are pure and children are pure'.[77] Behind these particular choices lay a very old tradition.

On any account, the Alexandrian initiative under the Ptolemaic aegis was a huge leap forward. As we move on to review the fate of the translation at the subsequent stages of its life, the picture becomes more one-sided, largely dominated by the process of continuation and expansion of the texts, their use among Jews, and their role in reconciling multiple Jewish identities—including, in due course, that of the new group of Christians. 'Pagans' will play a part, but a much diminished one. Yet the role of the ruling power in its very creation would never be forgotten. It would influence Greek-speaking Jews' attitude both to their scriptures and to the world they lived in for many generations to come.

---

[76] J Meg, 74a. See Alexander 1999a: 80.
[77] Lev. Rabbah, 7 and parallels; Avot de Rabbi Natan, version A, 6; Safrai 1976: 951.

3

The Jewish Diaspora in Graeco-Roman Antiquity

Aristeas' account of the origins of the Torah translation encapsulates the essence of enterprise. For translating is not just a negotiation between languages but also a connection between two systems of thought and being. A translation sits between cultural worlds. Where one of the cultures is dominant, making translations is one way for those under its sway to preserve something of their own inheritance. Already true for the Jews in the Alexandria of Ptolemy Philadelphus, this remains the context of the Greek Bible through several more centuries of its Jewish history.[1]

DIASPORA

The situation to which the makers and owners of the Greek Bible were accommodating was, quite simply, diaspora. And the Greek Bible translation was above all a book for the diaspora. The translation served diasporic communities extraordinarily well to connect their constantly renewed tradition, as they understood it, and the world of the ruling power with its dominant Greek culture. Right through the period of its creation, the Jewish diaspora of the west was also in the making. Here emerged the richness of a multiform life, but also the tangled identities, hybridities, ambivalences, and insecurities which we know from later

---

[1] For more on the social function of translations, see Chap. 4, pp. 152–61.

eras. This was, in many ways, the definitive diaspora, in which the broad features of Jewish life and experience over the subsequent 2,000 years were shaped. To a great extent, and for a variety of reasons, it is also a lost diaspora: our evidence is patchy and partial.[2]

The term 'diaspora', widely used nowadays to define the modern situation of diverse groups or peoples, implies not simply the physical fact of existence in many places, but, with that, some kind of adjustment to a division between a homeland (or imagined homeland) and far-flung communities. John Barclay, drawing on recent literature, sums up the features of a diaspora succinctly under three headings: identities are both local and trans-local; cultural self-expression is full of ambiguity; and contestations of power are frequent, be they internal, with other diasporas or (perhaps most telling) with the host community.[3] In terms of a post-colonial consciousness, which valorizes hybrid identities so highly, to be categorized as a diasporic people has become almost a modern accolade—something seemingly to be desired, irrespective of the inherent tensions and of the rarely absent risks of community violence. Barclay's key characteristics are also to be found in the Jewish diaspora of the Graeco-Roman world. There is no doubt that models of nascent diasporic self-consciousness, as well as prototypes of techniques for political and cultural survival and for the forms of quiet resistance available to the unempowered, come to us as the heritage of Greek–speaking Judaism. So indeed does the septuagintal word 'diaspora' itself—a fact which cannot be wholly without significance.[4] Some scholars are troubled by an increasing tendency, especially in the field of cultural studies, to sideline the Jewish diasporic model, whether present or past.[5] For historians, this is scarcely an option.

---

[2] For book-length studies, see Smallwood 1976, Bickerman 1988, Feldman 1993, Barclay 1996, Levinskaya 1996, Rajak 2000, Gruen 2002, and a number of multi-authored works: Overman and MacLennan 1992, Cohen and Frerichs 1993, Isaac and Oppenheimer 1996, Bartlett 2002, Barclay 2004. Among shorter surveys in English, see Stern 1974, Schürer iii, 1–176, Hegerman 1989, Smallwood 1999. The publication of the new epigraphic corpora for Jewish inscriptions, *JIGRE, JIWE* (2 vols.), and *IJO* (3 vols.), is perhaps the most important recent development in the field.
[3] Barclay 2004: 2–3.
[4] See below, pp. 100–2.
[5] Boyarin and Boyarin 2002: 5–32.

This chapter will visit that formative Jewish diaspora, which was indeed the world of the Septuagint. We shall look at the political and social features of the landscape as they emerge from literary and archaeological evidence, and especially at the relationships between Jews and others. Against this landscape, the huge and unwieldy body of translations took shape, determined by the landscape's contours. This survey is necessarily brief and selective; what I offer can be no more than a sketch.

The conventional boundaries will serve our purpose well, and so too the conventional divisions of time. The period of the Second Temple in Jewish history runs from the return of a part of the Judaean population to Jerusalem after Nebuchadnezzar's Babylonian captivity of 587/6 BCE to the Roman sacking of the city in the summer of 70 CE and the destruction of the Temple, consequent on the first Jewish revolt. After two further revolts, one in the Diaspora and one in Palestine in the year 135 CE, Jews were effectively excluded from Jerusalem and the city was rebuilt as a Roman colony dedicated to Jupiter by the Emperor Hadrian. The movement known as rabbinic Judaism (in its first, tannaitic stage) was by then in full swing, though we do not know what proportion of the population was under its sway, and its first, fundamental written texts (Mishnah and Tosefta) were not compiled until around 200 CE. The entire period in Judaism contains huge variety and no orthodoxy. Throughout the period we observe the crystallization of aspects of Jewish society which were to endure with surprising continuity through many centuries.

During those centuries, and over several hundred years, the Greek translation of the entire corpus of scripture was completed by unknown hands, but, after the first Alexandrian episode, always and indubitably for Jews. The land of Israel had a part to play as well as the diaspora in that endeavour, through the continuing influence of its biblical interpretation: fragments of Greek Bible have been found in the Judaean desert and a few Septuagint versions may even have originated there.[6] The relationship between homeland and those outside it was fluid and had been evolving since the first exile.

---

[6] For these fragments see p. 17.

There was always extensive contact. Judaea and Galilee were ringed by Greek cities some of which, like Scythopolis or Joppa (Jaffa), had substantial Jewish populations. The Jews were in fact always a minority in much of Palestine, subject to the same circumstances and the same rulers as Jews further afield; after the loss of Jerusalem, their situation became even more closely comparable to that of diaspora Jews. The Greek language was throughout the period familiar in some degree to many of the Jewish inhabitants of the region, especially those of the upper classes, and even among Jerusalemites.[7] But in the use of the Greek language, what we may still usefully call 'the diaspora' led the way.

There, Jews lived in rural communities, in small towns, and in cities of every size. But most Jews were urban. Beyond local conditions, they experienced the impact of changing suzerains who ruled their kingdoms and provinces with intermittent interference. Sometimes the instability of the rulers, their wars and their changing alliances, brought widespread insecurity and disturbance within which the Jews might be especially vulnerable. In the cities, the polytheistic civic religions were central, alongside the various forms of ruler cult which were much encouraged. Citizenship was all-important for participation in city life, but in an increasingly mobile Mediterranean world groups of outsiders or semi-outsiders like the Jews were a familiar phenomenon, with increasing opportunities for incorporation. Patronage and the system of benefaction ('euergetism') were fundamental to social organization and drove the economic engines. Through the East the Greek language, in its 'common' (koine) form, was the language of Empire, driving underground, and sometimes to destruction, many local languages. Greek rhetoric, philosophy, and literature were the staple of elite education. These were the elements of a relatively unchanging framework. From the Jewish angle, this was a world in principle conducive to accommodation, even integration, without the need for unwelcome compromise, let alone total submersion. In practice, some localities were evidently more hospitable than others, as we might expect: on the basis of the scant evidence, however, that is not a map that we are likely ever to be

---

[7] As comprehensively argued in the magnum opus of Martin Hengel (1974).

able to draw. Even more significant, and central to Jewish memory, was the alternation, sometimes in translocal terms, between good and bad times. The swings depended on a variety of forces, with the stance of the ruling power not least among them. Transformations could be dizzyingly rapid, a phenomenon not unfamiliar from other periods of Jewish history.

It should also be mentioned that the Mediterranean diaspora was not the sole focus of Jewish life outside the homeland. When permitted to return from Babylonia to their land by King Cyrus of Persia in 538 BCE, many Judaeans remained voluntarily in Babylonia. There, communities continued to exist for centuries. They made important contributions to the evolution of diasporic modes of existence, even redefining the very concept of homeland through their halakhic (legal) rulings.[8] But we have little real knowledge of the Rabbis of Babylon until late antiquity, when they were to produce a huge literature in Aramaic, crowned by the Babylonian Talmud, rabbinic learning's most important monument.[9] As we shall see in Chapter 9, some memory of the Greek Bible translation remained in those Babylonian circles.

Around the Mediterranean the spread of Jews in significant numbers came in the wake of Alexander the Great's conquest of the East, and it was accelerated under Greek and then Roman sovereignty. In the century following Alexander's death in 323 BCE, communities of Jewish immigrants settled and rooted themselves in most of the major centres of the eastern Mediterranean. Here too the conventional picture is not far out. The First Book of Maccabees (a piece of Jewish historiography transmitted as part of the Septuagint corpus) chooses to open its narrative with an eloquent—and strongly anti-colonial—account of Alexander the Great's conquests:

He initiated many wars, conquered strongholds and slew kings of the earth. He reached the ends of the earth and took booty from many nations and the world lay quiet before him. And he became proud and his heart was lifted, and he raised a very strong force and with it ruled over countries, peoples and tyrants, and they became his tributaries... (1 Macc. 2–4)

---

[8] For the Babylonian diaspora as construed in the rabbinic literature of late antiquity (mainly among the Amoraim), see Gafni 1997.

[9] For a thorough study of the evidence on Babylonian Jewry, covering also the pre-rabbinic period, see still Neusner 1965–70.

In Alexander's foundation, the city of Alexandria, the Jews claimed to have been there at the start. Before long, their Torah translation was in progress under the auspices of the successor to Alexander's successor on the throne of Egypt.

The second century BCE was perhaps the decisive period for the political and cultural development of the Graeco-Roman diaspora of the Jews—so it is no accident that it was particularly important also for that 'work in progress' that was the creation of the rest of the Greek Bible. Events in Judaea sent waves through the Jewish world, when feuding among the high priestly families and the policies of the Seleucid ruler Antiochus IV resulted in the imposition of a pagan cult on the Temple and the famed military resistance of the Maccabees. The Maccabaean literature also conceptualized for the first time a different kind of response to persecution, the route of martyrdom (not, however, so named), exemplified more dramatically in Chapters Seven and Eight of the Second Book by the figures of the legendary scribe Eleazar and of the mother and her seven sons who perished under torture rather than eat sacrificial meat in response to the King's orders. It is noteworthy that this book, as it has come down to us, is an abridgement of a longer work by an author of diaspora origin, one Jason of Cyrene.[10]

In Jerusalem, the outcome was that the Jewish line of high-priestly rulers established by the rebels (the Hasmoneans) presided over the only period of independent (or semi-independent) rule, and, paradoxically, over the increasing Hellenization of the government for a period of nearly 100 years. In Ptolemaic Egypt, the late third century and the first half of the second century BCE are often seen as the heyday of successful Jewish integration and involvement in public affairs.[11] In most accounts,[12] the far-from-untroubled reigns of

---

[10] On the evolution of the Jewish Greek idea of martyrdom, cf. Chap. 6, p. 000, and see Rajak 2000: 99–133.

[11] In spite of the ascription by the largely fictional Third Book of Maccabees of a major onslaught on the Jews and a disaster narrowly averted to Ptolemy IV Philopator (221–205 BCE). Josephus (CA, 2.53–6) ascribes almost identical events to Ptolemy VIII Euergetes II (Physkon).

[12] For example, Fraser 1972: i. 82–4. Tcherikover et al. 1957: 20–1; Tcherikover 1959: 275–87; Barclay 1996: 37.

Ptolemy VI Philometor (181–145 BCE) and Cleopatra II were the high noon for Alexandrian Jewry. A romance with some basis in fact, incorporated into his *Antiquities* by Josephus, recounts the fortunes at court of several generations of a well-placed family of ingenious Jewish tax-collectors, the Tobiads.[13] And within this period, too, falls the tenure of high military office ascribed by Josephus to two Jewish generals, Ananas (Onias) and Helkias.[14] It has been conjectured that it was Philometor who allocated the special residential quarters of the city to Jews, attested later. Also in Egypt, this century saw the establishment of rural communities, and the building of synagogues, known in the Egyptian context as *proseuchai* ('prayer places'), which are dedicated to the ruling dynasty.[15] The earlier part of the reign had seen the arrival in Egypt of Helkias' father, the dissident high-priestly member of the Oniad family from Jerusalem, through whose enterprise Egypt became home to another Temple. This was a miniature version of the original, located in a sort of mini-Jerusalem constructed at Leontopolis, near Heliopolis in the delta, on the ruins of an old Egyptian temple.[16] Its founder was not just a member of an important branch of the Jerusalem priesthood, but one of the claimants to the traditionally authentic line of Zadok: this was a claim which even the Hasmoneans, who were busy making themselves high priests in Jerusalem, could not match. Probably originally a challenge of the moment, and perhaps achieving little

---

[13] Josephus, *AJ*, 12.160–236. See also p. 82.

[14] See *AJ*, 13. 285. At *CA*, 2. 49–51, the second general is Dositheus, perhaps the courtier and convert Dositheus, son of Drimylos, of 3 Macc. 1: 3. Cf. Kasher 1985: 61. Clement of Alexandria's claim (Strom. 1.22.150.1, also quoted by Eusebius) that the philosopher Aristobulus addressed his work to Ptolemy VI Philometor is widely accepted: see Holladay iii, 94–5. But the Oniad chronology is fraught and the evidence is tenuous.

[15] Some twenty, largely fragmentary dedications are presented by Horbury and Noy 1992: see the index listing p. 276, s.v. *proseuchē*.

[16] Two different dates for the foundation are given by Josephus. The longer of his accounts, at *AJ*, 12.387, is widely accepted; Onias IV, who has failed to become high priest, is there the founder of the temple. But the *Jewish War* (1.33) ascribes the foundation to this man's father, Onias III. For a recent discussion, focusing on the symbolic significance, see Weitzman 2005: 109–11 and 81, n. 33 for the main bibliography. Hayward 1982 is still a useful assessment. See also Bohak 1996; Taylor 1998; Frey 1999; Capponi 2008. On the connections drawn by Seeligmann with LXX Isaiah, see Dines 2007.

more in the end than a local importance—for the Temple gets no explicit mention in the Jewish literature in Greek outside Josephus—this unexpected foundation continued somehow in operation for a remarkable 200 years or more until it was closed by Vespasian in the wake of the Jewish revolt.

In the near East, Rome was becoming a major force to be reckoned with during the second century BCE. So the Jews, both of Judaea and the Diaspora, were coming into Rome's diplomatic orbit and increasingly into areas of her control. The Maccabaean rulers were well aware of this and made early alliances. A sort of triangle was in operation, and the earliest Roman directives to city authorities guaranteeing Jewish freedoms are associated with the Hasmonean John Hyrcanus I who came to power in 134 BCE. The kingdom and city of Pergamum, bequeathed to the Romans in the 130s BCE, seems to have played a central part in the collection and archiving of records of such transactions where they related to Asia Minor. They were subsequently transmitted to us by the historian Josephus.[17] It is not unreasonable to suppose that the large Greek-speaking Jewish communities in this and other great and smaller cities in Asia Minor were also participants in the work of translating the Bible into Greek during this stage of its development. Sadly, however, our sources remain silent, at any rate until we reach the three major revisions of the second century CE, all of them associated in tradition with the work of individuals from this region. The philosophical martyrology known as the Fourth Book of Maccabees, a rhetorical expansion and elaboration of the short martyrology of 2 Maccabees, and perhaps the last surviving Jewish-Greek diaspora work, has now been linked with Asia Minor.[18] By that time, the interaction between Judaism and Christianity is an important extra element on the scene.

In 63 BCE, the Roman general Pompeius Magnus swept through the East and, in the wake of his lieutenants, took Jerusalem and annexed much of Palestine. This was the first of a series of violent engagements with Rome and her agents which naturally sent shock waves through Jewish communities everywhere. The destruction of the Jerusalem Temple in 70 CE, and later the disappearance of Jewish

---

[17] Pucci Ben Zee'ev 1996; Rajak 2000: 301–33, and Rajak 2007.
[18] van Henten 1994.

Jerusalem into the Roman colony of Aelia Capitolina following the defeat in Judaea of Bar Kokhba's rebellion of 132–135 CE, would require yet greater adjustments. A period of uncertainty followed these traumas. One fairly immediate effect, however, must have been to increase the size and critical mass of the diaspora and to facilitate an independent response to the emergent aspirations of the Rabbis to provide religious leadership in the land of Israel.

IDEOLOGY

Reflection upon the condition of exile evolved at the same time as the circumstances of life away from the homeland. The noun 'diaspora' appears first in the Greek Deuteronomy (28: 25; 30: 4–5), and makes some dozen appearances altogether in the Septuagint corpus.[19] The verbal form and its compounds are quite frequently used in this special sense. Deriving from the Greek root meaning 'to scatter', the Greek terminology collects together a number of different Hebrew words, among them a range of terms for exile, disgrace, desolation, and being cast out. Thus a rather more coherent conception is created of the concrete implications of dispersion (over and above the theology) than had existed before. As in the Hebrew Bible, a temporary condition of dislocation is envisaged, to be surely followed by a joyous ingathering and restoration: so, for example, in Psalm 147: 2 (Heb. Ps. 146) on the return to Zion and the rebuilding of Jerusalem; in Isaiah 49: 6 on the suffering servant's future mission to make Israel a 'light among the Gentiles'; or in Nehemiah's passionate prayer of mourning and entreaty in 2 Esdras 11: 9 = Heb. Neh. 1: 9; and, in a free, non-biblical composition, in the prayer ascribed by the author of 2 Maccabees (1: 27) to the priests of long ago, when Nehemiah miraculously restored the altar fire on his return from the first exile. Especially in the prophetic books, this scattering is taken along with the destruction of the cult centre as a state of divine abandonment and interpreted as punishment for the nation's

---

[19] On this vocabulary, see Mélèze Modrzejewski 1993: 65–71. For a complete breakdown of the etymological fields in Hebrew and Greek, see Kiefer 2005. Cf. Chap. 5, pp. 193–5.

wrongdoings—for example, in Jeremiah 41:14–22, after the murder of the Babylonian overseer Gedaliah, or at Daniel 12: 2, foreseeing the deliverance by the angel Michael from the time of unspeakable anguish at the end of days. The writings of the Hasmonean period put a very high valuation on the land of Israel and the authority of Jerusalem.[20] The importance of the sacrificial cult to Second Temple Jews of every hue cannot be overestimated.[21] But something of a more positive representation of the dispersion gains ground in Greek-Jewish writing through the Hellenistic and Roman periods, expressed not only by the Alexandrian Philo but also in the later works of Josephus (*AJ*, 4.115, 14.110). While the latter's first work, the *Jewish War*, had been permeated with the insistence that by the destruction of the Temple and of the city of Jerusalem God was punishing the sins of its inhabitants, in the *Antiquities* Josephus wrote as a resident of Rome and as a writer with broad horizons across the Jewish world and his concern was with other matters.[22] The noun 'diaspora' in its specialized sense is absent from the vocabulary of both of these authors, although the verbal form from the same root makes a few appearances in Josephus.[23] It is to my mind important to stress that neither author yet makes a sharp conceptual divide between Jews in the land of Israel and those everywhere else.[24] On the other hand, both writers make ample reference to an existing or longed-for homeland. Philo, though not Josephus, speaks of an eschatological ingathering; and, while Louis Feldman finds Josephus, for all his unabated devotion to the Jerusalem Temple, singularly uninterested in any post-destruction restoration

---

[20] As emerges from the interpretation of Mendels 1987.
[21] For a high estimation of the sacrificial cult and of the centrality of purification and atonement, see Klawans 2006. D. Schwartz (1996) suggests, by contrast, that the city of Jerusalem had primacy for diaspora Jews, for whom the Temple, even while standing, remained an abstraction.
[22] For Philo, see Pearce 2004a. For Josephus as a diaspora writer, Rajak 2007. For Josephus on exile, Feldman 2006: 695–721. On Josephus' changing perspectives: D. Schwartz 2005. The diverse and continuing rabbinic reflections on relations between the Land of Israel and the diaspora are explored in Gafni 1997 (and see esp. 19–78).
[23] *Diaspora* as a noun meaning 'scattering' in a general sense appears several times in Philo.
[24] Cf. Rajak 2007 and contrast the more theological reading of the Jewish understanding of exile as punishment in van Unnik 1993.

of the city,[25] this elision can be readily explained by that author's special experience and political circumstance.

Membership in the homeland was implicit in the standard appellation for a Jew, *ioudaios/a*, a person from Judaea. It is summed up by Philo's much-quoted statement where, drawing on the Greek vocabulary of colony and mother-city, he asserts that the inherited place of residence was the *patria* of the Jews and Jerusalem their 'metropolis' (*Flacc.*, 46).[26]

DIASPORA LOCATIONS AND POPULATIONS

While Jewish communities were responsive to local circumstances, the interests and concerns of Palestine and the diaspora came together in various spheres of thought and action: the gap in outlook was essentially a matter of emphasis and balance. Moreover, in geographical terms, the boundaries between Judaea and Galilee on the one hand, and the diaspora on the other, were neither clearly defined nor fully definable. The small Jewish territory was ringed by Graeco–Syrian cities in which Jews coexisted with a variety of ethnic groups that followed diverse cults both on the coast and in the Decapolis, beside and across the Jordan. Syria–Phoenicia could be counted a unit with the Land of Israel. Notable among these cities was Caesarea, the capital of the Roman province. Outside the major centres, rural Galilee too, as distinct from Judaea, was a mixed area. An expert on this region can thus quite reasonably ask whether living in Galilee was 'a form of Diaspora existence for a Jew'.[27] The question has, of course, no single or simple answer.

---

[25] See the trio of essays concerned with Josephus' views on the importance of Jerusalem, on exile and on restoration and ingathering, in Feldman 2006: 678–759.

[26] On Jewish use of the Greek vocabulary of colony and mother-city, see Mélèze Modrzejewski 1993: 70. Pearce 2004a argues that, for Philo, Jerusalem had equal status to Alexandria and other centres rather than any transcendent position as the 'true homeland': the mother metaphor is traced as a scriptural image. On the contested meaning of *ioudaios*, see Introduction, p. 8.

[27] So Freyne 2002: 4.

The Alexandrian community remained the most important in the Graeco-Roman diaspora. In spite of harassment and persecution, it maintained a vigorous life until desperately damaged by a large-scale Jewish uprising which occurred in various locations during the reign of Trajan.[28] This community stood out because of its numbers; its strong hinterland of smaller Jewish communities;[29] its visibility in the city (where there were two Jewish quarters out of the five divisions and Jews resided in other areas too); the size and splendour of its synagogue, which was still mentioned with amazement in Talmudic literature;[30] the high status of some members of its Jewish elite (in both Hellenistic and Roman periods); and its creative Jewish–Greek culture, which sprang from, and built upon the Septuagint, but expressed itself in all the major Greek genres—epic, drama, history-writing, philosophy, and rhetoric. We are fortunate in the survival (albeit sometimes in translation into an oriental language) of most of the output of its principal luminary, Philo, the first-century CE exegete, philosopher, and communal spokesman.[31]

Major Jewish settlements were, as we have said, located in the cities of the Roman provinces of Asia (both coastal and inland Asia Minor), in many parts of Greece and the Greek islands, and, not least, in the Egyptian countryside where the pre-Hellenistic Jewish military colonists on the island of Elephantine (at Aswan), established perhaps as early as the seventh century BCE, were joined by new military and civilian settlers in both towns and villages. A window onto the life of some Egyptian Jews (and possible Jews—they are identifiable mainly through their personal names) is provided by a range of documents preserved on papyrus.[32] They relate to business and private affairs of various kinds, but rarely to religious matters. Recently, the Jewish *politeuma* of Heracleopolis in the Fayyum has

---

[28] See below, p. 122.
[29] Detailed account in Kasher 1985.
[30] Tos. Sukkah 4.6; J Sukkah 5.1.55a–b, B Sukkah 51b.
[31] For what is still the best introduction to Philo's copious and complex writings, see Morris 1987.
[32] See Mélèze Modrzejewski 1995. For the documents, Tcherikover, et al. 1957. A revision of this corpus is being prepared by Prof. Y. Fikhman.

revealed in a cache of twenty papyri the workings of its autonomous juridical system.[33]

In the city of Rome, a Jewish community established before the mid-second century BCE was increased to number several thousands, not only by general immigration, but by subsequent waves of enslaved Jewish individuals, many captured during the various Roman incursions into Palestine.[34] Significant numbers were able to acquire full citizenship through manumission in two generations in accordance with Roman law and practice. But prosperity and, still more, social status were surely harder to achieve in the capital than in the provincial cities. Removal to the nearby port of Ostia, where there survives a monumental synagogue building and the names of substantial donors, may perhaps have beckoned, offering, we may surmise, a more ready route to social mobility. The surviving simple and often ill-written epitaphs and the accompanying inscribed drawings from the Roman Jewish catacombs, dating mainly from the third to fourth centuries CE, seem to suggest, even in a religious culture which devalued display and funerary monumentalization, that the deceased and their relatives were for the most part people of quite modest means. Greek, much more than Latin, was the language used by the community, and they probably remained, with some exceptions, speakers of Greek rather than of Latin, in common with a large part of the Roman plebs—and of the first Christians too. A handful of more elaborate sarcophagus burials survive. We find mention among the deceased of officials from eleven or twelve separate 'synagogues' (in the sense of associations) named after locations—Siburesians, patrons—Agrippenses, or trades—Calcarenses (lime-burners). These may not all have existed simultaneously, but it is probable that such groupings were the loci of primary loyalty and that the Jews of Rome lacked any overarching community structure.[35] Its absence would have weakened them considerably.

The extent of the Jewish diaspora in the Roman Empire can be roughly but not precisely mapped, and there undoubtedly existed

---

[33] On these papyri, see pp. 85–6.
[34] On the Jews in Rome, Leon 1995; Rutgers 1995.
[35] Williams 1999b.

communities which have left no trace.[36] But Philo, in words attributed to a letter from Herod's grandson Agrippa I to the Emperor Gaius Caligula, gives a useful conspectus, which we may take to be as complete as the author could make it, since its purpose was to emphasize the great scope of Jewish settlement. Mentioned are

> Egypt, Phoenicia, Coele-Syria, and the rest of Syria too, through to the further inhabited lands—Pamphylia, Cilicia, most of Asia up to Bithynia and the corners of Pontus [the Black Sea area]—and likewise into Europe—Thessaly, Boeotia, Macedonia, Aetolia, Attica, Argos, Corinth, and most of the finest parts of the Peloponnese . . . but also the best-regarded of the islands, Euboea, Cyprus, Crete. I say nothing of the countries beyond the Euphrates. (*Leg.*, 281–4)

Philo here omits Italy, the setting for his text, and also Cyrenaica and Carthage in North Africa.

We know too that the area which was to become the Roman province of Arabia contained Jews too. Communities in Spain, Gaul, and Germany are scarcely attested prior to late antiquity, and the few artefacts of earlier date associated with Judaism have been found here and there are scarcely indicative. Then there were the Judaizers and God-fearers, to be discussed shortly.

For snapshots of life in the Jewish diaspora, we go to individual episodes in Josephus' *Antiquities*, and to the controversial accounts of Paul's troubled dealings with successive synagogues and their leaders in the later chapters of Acts—some threw him out, complained about him to the authorities, and even had him flogged; but at least one synagogue leader was won over. The locations on which momentary light is shed by those two very different sources overlap surprisingly little. Thus, Josephus tells us nothing of the Jews of mainland Greece: had we depended entirely on his writing we would simply not have known of the existence of communities in Beroea or Philippi.[37] On the other hand, an important centre and apparently a collecting-point for the decrees on Jewish privileges cited by Josephus was Pergamum, well known both as a provincial

---

[36] Magisterial survey in Schürer iii, 1–86.
[37] But we do have a handful of Jewish inscriptions from these two cities. See *IJO* 1, Mac 7–10 (Beroea); Mac 11 and 12 (Philippi).

capital and as one of the seven churches of Revelation (cf. Rev. 2: 12–17), yet not a place which fell within Paul's sphere.[38]

When it comes to estimates of Jewish population sizes, the deficiencies in our evidence are even greater, and indeed an ancient historian who has recently tackled the question head-on concludes that the attempt should be abandoned once and for all. He puts it plainly 'I do not believe we have the first notion of how many Jews there were in the ancient world, even roughly speaking; nor do we have the means to discover it'. Philo's figure of one million for the Jews in Egypt may well be no more than a rhetorical flourish, and the startlingly high estimate of eight million Jews for the entire population of the Roman Empire espoused by some rests on extrapolation from a confused medieval statement.[39] The statement ascribed by Josephus to Strabo (in *Antiquities*, 14.114–15) that there was scarcely a place in the empire that did not have its Jews, is equally unverifiable.

JEWISH IDENTITY

Jewish identities in the ancient Mediterranean varied widely, just as might be expected. But it is possible still to speak of common features. The understanding of what was meant by a 'Jew' comprised, as in later ages, both ethnic (or ethno-racial)[40] and religious elements. The Greek designation *ioudaios* had, as we have seen, the primary sense of a person from Judaea; and it is conceivable that it continued sometimes to mean just that. But at an early stage the term served also to indicate descent and cultic membership, and that too continued.[41] In this respect Hall[42] is mistaken in asserting that Jews moved away from 'ethnicity' and into 'culture' when he writes:

---

[38] See Rajak 2007.
[39] McGing 2002. For a maximalist assessment of the population numbers, see Feldman 1993: 293 and 555–6 (n. 20).
[40] The term is that of Buell: 2005: 44–5 (offering a critique of Cohen).
[41] See also p. 8. Cf. Cohen 1999: 69–206, who ascribes the shift from local to religious designation to the forced conversions of the early Hasmoneans.
[42] Hall 2002: 223.

What is interesting is how rarely the 'children of Israel' in this period appeal to a properly 'ethnic' basis of self-identification through genealogy; when they do, it is to pronounce an affiliation with the Spartans rather than proclaim their own distinctiveness... It may be the case that once the Greeks had irredeemably defined Hellenicity in terms of cultural criteria, it was through the medium of culture that the Jews were required to articulate their own specificity.

In reality, the patriarchs and the tribal lineages remained central to the Jewish conception of their own history. It is arguable indeed that emphases on descent and lineage in Israel were early developments, to be traced back to the Persian period when the returnees from exile were identified by family, and the hereditary priesthood became the controlling element in Jewish society.[43]

RELIGIOUS PRACTICE IN THE DIASPORA

In the absence of a central authority, and across a long stretch of time and a wide range of localities subject to diverse regional influences, it might seem rash even to attempt a generalization about diasporic religious practice. If the writ of the Rabbis was limited in Palestine, even in their heyday, this was all the more true of the diaspora. Nevertheless, we can cautiously address the question in terms of a customary minimum requirement for being a Jew. We may derive a modicum of information as to external appearances from the mocking observations of Greek and Roman writers on Jewish practices and conduct. Albeit dependent upon stereotype and hostile caricature, they do serve as some kind of report upon those practices that became the talk of outsiders.[44] It is reasonable to suppose that, as a rule, diaspora Jews saw fit to aspire to the central practices prescribed by the Torah and carried out by the individual within the context of home and family.[45]

---

[43] Stressed particularly by D. Schwartz 1992: 8–9.
[44] Texts collected in Stern 1974–84.
[45] This is not to say there was not a gap between prescription and practice. About the latter, as Seth Schwartz 2001: 67 rightly insists, 'disappointingly little' is implied. On this gap, see also Chap. 6, pp. 227–39.

Male circumcision was the mark of the biblical covenant, and the chief defining mark of Jews for everyone, as well as a source of humour for a wit such as Martial.[46] Sabbath observance was particularly puzzling to pagans, appearing as idleness and folly. None the less, some Jews might seek and receive exemption from the military so as to avoid the need to fight on the Sabbath,[47] and Augustus excused them from court appearances on that day (Philo, *Leg.*, 23; 158; Josephus, *AJ*, 16.27); rearrangement of the grain distributions was another Jewish request. Fasts, both fixed (like the Day of Atonement) or supernumerary, as marks of repentance or mourning, were a visible part of Jewish observance. Roman writers believed that Jews fasted on the sabbath too, and Margaret Williams argues that, while contrary to rabbinic injunction and modern practice, this may reflect a real local practice.[48] The three agricultural pilgrim festivals (Passover, Sukkot–Tabernacles, and Shavuot–the Feast of Weeks) were important and they expressed the connection of diaspora Jews with the land as much as the significance of the Temple in their belief-system. The Levitical dietary laws figure frequently in diaspora narrative, whose authors, no doubt in part with an exhortatory purpose, have the participants avoid prohibited foods or those prepared by Gentiles. Thus, in the *Letter of Aristeas*, the High Priest explains why Moses had seen fit to 'hedge the Jews about with practices of purity in food and drink...' (*Aristeas*, 142). This was not out of respect for mice or weasels or the like, but in order to avoid animals that themselves practise injustice (144–7). In the Pauline literature we are made aware of the challenges posed by abstention from sacrificial meat. Purity through ablution was associated with prayer and, interestingly, in contrast with Palestine, and no doubt for practical reasons, handwashing is better attested than immersion in pools for effecting purification.[49] Intermarriage with unconverted Gentiles was not approved of but no doubt occurred.[50] A passionate convert, like Asenath, daughter of Potiphar, was a different matter

---

[46] Cohen 1999: 39–49; Isaac 2004: 472–4; Abusch 2003. For Martial's epigrams on circumcised slaves, Cohen 1993: 12–16.

[47] On the evidence for Jews in the Roman army, Applebaum 1971; on the meaning of the exemptions: Gruen 2002: 86–7.

[48] Williams 2004.

[49] Sanders 1990: 260–72.

[50] Goodman 1992: 63–6; Barclay 1996: 410–12.

altogether, and perhaps by way of a role model, a popular fiction was dedicated to her romance with Joseph.

Legal rulings made in Jerusalem may conceivably sometimes have been sent abroad, but in general we may readily concur with the protestation of E. P. Sanders that 'diaspora Jews were capable of interpreting the Bible, and that they did not sit patiently waiting for the Houses of Hillel and Shammai to send them their disagreements'.[51] Even in the post-destruction era, the claims to authority of the developing rabbinic movement, with the code for living embodied around 200 CE in the Mishnah of Rabbi Judah Hanasi, are likely to have made few inroads in regions far from their Galileans seats— for all the stories that have come down to us of travelling rabbis. Diaspora inscriptions do not mention rabbis before the fourth century CE at the earliest, and even after that the significance of the label in the epigraphic context is uncertain.[52] It is equally unclear how far the writ of the Palestinian Patriarch, recognized by the government as the representative figure of the Jews there, ran in the diaspora. However, a second- or third-century dedication from Stobi in Macedonia, in which the 'father of the Synagogue' Tiberius Julius Polycharmus 'also called Achurios' gives over the upper rooms of his house to be a synagogue, has a gigantic fine (of 250,000 denarii) to be paid to 'the Patriarch' in the case of non-compliance with the donor's arrangements. The existence of a local 'patriarch' seems highly improbable; but for the Palestinian, given the unreal size of the fine, there is no reason to think that the Patriarch was anything more than a notional authority figure for the Jews of Stobi.[53]

Erwin Goodenough,[54] in a monumental study, sought to construct diaspora Judaism as an independent and highly distinctive religious system, highlighting Philonic allegory, the repertoire of distinctive visual symbols and their possible meanings, and the thoroughgoing syncretism of the many magical papyri which have prominent Jewish

---

[51] Sanders 1990: 256.

[52] Cohen 1981.

[53] See *IJO*, i, Mac1, with the very full commentary of Noy, Panayotov, and Bloedhorn. By contrast, the tomb violation text from Argos in Achaea, *IJO*, i, Ach51, where Aurelius Joses invokes 'the powers' of God and of the Law and 'the honour of the patriarchs' must be taken to refer to the biblical patriarchs.

[54] Goodenough 1953–68.

elements. But the first of these components could hardly form the basis of belief for the ordinary person; the second was much over-interpreted by Goodenough; and the third represents a world of activity shared by Jews, pagans, and Christians alike.[55] Rather, 'common Judaism', in an extension of the felicitous definition of E. P. Sanders, bound Palestine and diaspora together.[56] Until 70 CE, the expected allegiance to the Jerusalem Temple was signalled by the two-drachma (half-shekel) Temple tax, whose collection and shipment was permitted by the Romans, and also through pilgrimage, an act of piety which we happen to know Philo performed once in his life (*Prov.*, fr.2.64).[57] The temple founded by the dissident Oniad high priests at Leontopolis in lower Egypt during the second century BCE appears to have had no importance for Philo, or, at least, he does not mention it in any surviving work. It was no doubt by way of intimidation and to eliminate any possible focus for the remnants of resistance that Vespasian had it closed in 73 CE, after the complete defeat of the revolt in Judaea (Josephus, *BJ*, 7.433–5).

There are weak reflections in the diaspora of the striking religious diversity of second-temple Palestine. Philo talks in *de Vita Contemplativa* of the *therapeutae* of Lake Mareotis who led an ascetic communitarian existence comparable to that of the Dead Sea Essenes.[58] The diaspora Jewish family of Saul of Tarsus might be taken as Pharisaic on the basis of the studies with Gamaliel ascribed to him (Acts 22: 3). And the invective against the Pharisees in Matthew 23: 15 has been interpreted by Martin Goodman[59] as referring to a specifically Pharisaic mission to the diaspora. The dissident Oniad high priests had settled in Egypt in the first half of the second century BCE. The destruction of the Jerusalem Temple probably led to the dispersal of surviving elements of the Sadducaean high priesthood. And, if the rebels of 66–73 can be regarded, following Josephus, as embodying a separate strand or 'philosophy' within Judaism, then we should mention here the information given by the historian concerning the transference of

---

[55] For magic as meeting ground, cf. Chap. 8, pp. 270–6.
[56] The idea is formulated by E. P. Sanders in his classic study of 1992.
[57] On pilgrimage, see Safrai 1974.
[58] On the *therapeutai*, see also p. 229.
[59] Goodman 1992: 61–2.

the activity of *sicarii* to Cyrenaica after the failure of the revolt (*BJ*, 7.437–41). Another divergent tendency is represented by those lax allegorical interpreters of the Law who incurred Philo's strictures (*Migr.*, 89) for proceeding then to disregard it. Yet another was the Jesus movement. It is extremely difficult to assess the impact on Jewish self-definition in the diaspora of the rapid growth and gradual separation of church from synagogue, dependent as we are on Christian voices, but there is no doubt that it was profound.

The destruction of the Temple undoubtedly lent momentum to the development of the synagogue as a source of local self-sufficiency, though it is hard to judge the pace of change. The Greek word *synagōgē* itself means simply 'assembly', or 'association', and the term is found occasionally in connection with pagan groupings. But the synagogue came to be almost exclusively associated with the practice of Judaism, whether referring to the religious community or to its communal building. Apart from Torah reading, study, recitation, and prayer, this became a key physical venue for charitable, social, and political activity.

Archaeologically, the fifteen or so excavated diaspora synagogues have been identifiable less by their design and layout, which lacked uniformity, but rather by the presence of a small repertoire of specific symbols appearing as decorative features—carved, incised, or embedded in mosaic. Alongside the menorah, whether carved or freestanding, the most familiar identifying mark of Judaism were symbols associated with the Temple cult (shofar, incense shovel, ewer) and with the festival of Tabernacles (palm branches, citrons). A Torah shrine, where the scrolls were stored, or occasionally two shrines, can often be located. At Dura Europus, on Rome's eastern frontier, the rich and quite unparalleled sequence of third-century CE biblical illustrations included such striking images as Aaron in front of the Temple, the toppling of the cult statue of Dagon as in the book of Samuel, Ezekiel's valley of dry bones, and Mordecai on his white horse being led by the discredited Haman of the book of Esther.[60] The characters wear a splendid mix of fashions—Persian

---

[60] For the iconographic material, see Hachlili 1998. For the excavations and complete illustrations, see still Kraeling 1956.

trousers, Greek tunics, robes resembling Roman togas. The cycle of biblical illustrations seems to have been organized in a complex system whose message we still cannot fathom. It occupied all the walls of a large hall which was equipped with a Torah alcove surmounted by a shell shape and a decorated ceiling. Inscriptions in both Greek and Aramaic have been found on the site. By contrast, the Stobi inscription sets out in detail the arrangements for turning over part of the private dwelling of Polycharmus to communal use. Assembly in private houses will have been far from unique and had more sources survived we might well have heard of house synagogues.[61]

THE JEWISH COMMUNITY

Commitments from the ruling power were by nature impermanent and subject to local pressures. Swings of the pendulum are literary favourites, following the typology of the new Pharaoh of Exodus, and of the reversals of the plot of the book of Esther, where the courtier Haman secures a decree for the destruction of the Jews, but is then exposed and hanged while the Jew Mordecai is honoured.[62] But in the best circumstances stability and the continuity of rooted communities could surely be achieved in the diaspora, in cities such as Ephesus or Sardis or Syrian Antioch. Very occasionally, a literary vignette reveals the rise and fall of a community, as in the case of Seleucia on the Tigris. It may be, as one scholar insists, that some communities disappeared not through annihilation nor expulsion nor voluntary migration but simply through total assimilation into the rest of the population.[63]

The Alexandrian community achieved a degree of legal autonomy in the age of Augustus, as noted even by an outsider, the Greek writer Strabo: 'an ethnarch stands over them, who administers the

---

[61] The synagogue, as both institution and building, has been much discussed in recent years, including much inconclusive discussion of origins. For the entire field, see first and foremost the monumental study, Levine 2005. For specific aspects, see Fine 1999; Runesson 2001; Olsson and Zetterholm 2003; Rajak 2003.

[62] Gruen 1998 analyses various such tales. For Josephus, Rajak 2005: 92–7.

[63] Bohak 2002.

community and judges lawsuits and takes care of contracts, just as if he were the ruler of an independent polity'.[64] Occasionally, in relation to Alexandria and also to the city of Berenice in Cyrenaica, the term *politeuma*, in the sense of a self-governing unit, makes an appearance.[65] Elsewhere, Jewish groups simply availed themselves of the administrative and social space within the city offered to associations, guilds, and cultic societies of various kinds.[66] *Synagōgē* was but one term for such a collectivity. A marked fluidity in the terminology continued in Jewish circles, however, varying, as far as our evidence allows us to see, from place to place and group to group. Terms such as *synodos*, *syllogos*, *laos* (people), and the Latin *universitas* also occur, and some Jewish groups describe themselves in inscriptions simply as *hoi ioudaioi*, 'the Jews'. *Proseuchē*, 'prayer house' (or literally 'prayer'), apparently coined in Ptolemaic Egypt, appearing in texts from as early as the mid-third century BCE, is still found occasionally in the Roman period.[67]

The honorific titles for the leaders and post-holders of Jewish associations were also variable. Echoing the term by which the wider city described its magistrates, a Jewish community often had its own *archontes*. The synagogue head, *archisynagōgos*, continued through the period as a figure of importance: the honorific and public role of this dignitary emerges from the inscriptions, where liturgical functions and associations are notably absent.[68] The striking presence of some women post-holders in synagogues again has a counterpart in the wider society, in the unusual prominence of independent women in the cities of Roman Asia Minor. It does not follow that they had a liturgical role, much as we might like to think so.[69]

---

[64] Quoted in Josephus, *AJ*, 14.117.
[65] Smallwood 1976 understood the term *politeuma* as a legal definition of status for diaspora Jewish communities. We now have the additional evidence of the papyri from Heracleopolis, attested to Jewish *politeuma*, perhaps of military veterans, dispensing local jurisdiction.
[66] Harland 2003.
[67] For the variety of terminology, see Rajak 2002.
[68] Rajak and Noy 2000.
[69] In the landmark study of Brooten (1982) an active liturgical role is claimed for women office-holders of synagogues.

INTERACTION WITH NON-JEWS

The continuity of communal existence in the diaspora was secured, as we have seen, by pragmatic stances, and, beyond this, by an evident if unexpressed appreciation of the management of plural identities and of the possibilities and the limits of interaction. Accommodation to the environment, and a level of integration into the wider society are generally nowadays seen by scholars as the characteristic pattern.[70]

A fundamental determinant of cultural identity was the primary use of the eastern Mediterranean lingua franca, Greek, as spoken and written language, not only in everyday usage, but also for religious purposes. It is not an exaggeration to say that none of these social manoeuvres would have been possible without the Greek Bible. Translation was from the second century BCE onwards a distinct and important branch of literary activity for the Jewish diaspora, as emerges from the preface to the Greek Ben Sira, where the author's grandson explains how and why, on arrival in Egypt, he laboured to produce a Greek version of his learned grandfather's book of wisdom and instruction. This interest also demonstrates that esteem for Hebrew as holy tongue and national language persisted and it presupposes a functioning bilingualism at least within a scholarly element of the diaspora population.[71]

Such activity at the same time requires a high level of acculturation, but we should remember that this is by no means incompatible with retention of independent traditions. The surviving evidence offers the rarest of glimpses as to how that acculturation expressed itself in terms of Jewish participation in the educational and cultural institutions of the *polis*. But from the literary legacy it emerges that Philo's immersion in Greek philosophy and literature had its counterpart among writers of lesser stature, such as the (anonymous) authors of the Third and Fourth Books of Maccabees and of the Wisdom of Solomon (included within the Apocrypha), or the lost

---

[70] These phenomena are skilfully distinguished in Barclay 1996.
[71] See on the subject of bilingualism, pp. 141–52.

source summarized in 2 Maccabees and named there as Jason of Cyrene, or, again, the pseudepigraphic creator known as Pseudo-Hecataeus. Also revealing are the genres and styles adopted by writers such as Demetrius the Chronographer, Aristobulus the philosopher (known as 'the peripatetic'), Philo the epic poet, and Ezekiel the author of an Aeschylean tragedy on the Exodus. These are preserved in fragmentary form by Clement of Alexandria and Eusebius of Caesarea.[72]

Eschewing a picture of two world views in opposition, expressed by those time-honoured abstractions, 'Hellenism and Judaism', we do better to conceive of the thought of this diaspora as a complex interweaving of traditions, to produce, in the distinctive culture of Greek-speaking Judaism, a fabric in which the threads are no longer separable. Moreover, it is now widely accepted that a process of Hellenization was integral to the development of Judaean society too, even if the extent, depth, and significance of its impact continue to be contested.[73]

In the sphere of material culture, burial practices and the associated epigraphy shed light upon the Jews' adaptation to their varied diaspora environments. Material culture is usually highly open to influence, and indeed the Jews normally adopted the burial patterns and epitaph types used in the wider society, with just small differences.[74] The common artistic styles of tomb decoration were often adopted. Among the more remarkable of the Jewish tombs found in common burial grounds are the twenty-three among the house tombs of the vast necropolis of Hierapolis in Phrygia which are identified as Jewish by their inscriptions or by their Jewish symbols (out of some 360). Architecturally they are no different from the surrounding tombs, and they draw upon the same epigraphic formulae and vocabulary; but fines for violation are to be paid to the Jews, or to the 'settlement (*katoikia*) of the Jews', and deposited in the

---

[72] For this literature, Schürer 1987: 470–704; Holladay, i–iv; Doran 1986; Bar-Kochva 1996. For further discussion of the so-called Hellenistic–Jewish literature, see Chap. 6.

[73] The conclusions of Hengel's impressive study of 1974, which argued for a thoroughly Hellenized Jerusalem, have not gained complete acceptance.

[74] See the useful annotated collection of van der Horst 1991.

Jewish archives.⁷⁵ P. Aelius Glyconianus Zeuxianus Aelianus, in a magnificent synthesis, announces his bequest to two guilds (the purple dyers and the carpet-weavers) so they can commemorate him 'by the grave-crowning ceremony', and by feasts on the festival of the kalends, on the feast of unleavened bread in the seventh month, and on Pentecost.

Within this general conformity in burial practice, Jewish group identity was maintained by a range of subtle cultural markers. In a period where incineration was giving way to inhumation among pagans, Jews practised only inhumation. At Rome, that might be coupled with the distinctive practice of secondary burial of the bones in ossuaries, apparently following the practice prevalent in Jerusalem and its environs. The tunnelled Jewish catacombs of Rome, of which some half-a-dozen are known, foreshadow the extensive Christian underground burial systems and were probably likewise constructed by companies of diggers and developed in similar fashion. One very sizeable Jewish constellation survives, somewhat precariously—the Via Randanini Catacomb on the Via Appia. Here, at least, the strictures against elaborate tombs advertised by Josephus (*CA*, 2.205) appear to have been consciously observed.

Epigraphy supplies our best evidence on participation in city life throughout the period, and certainly after the end of Josephus' coverage. The 2,000 or so surviving Jewish inscriptions include short honorific texts; in these too the Jews, arguably, show a distinctive restraint.⁷⁶ The most elaborate formulations, arguably the most 'pagan', are two noteworthy marble *stēlai* of as early as the first century CE from Berenice in Cyrenaica which attest the Jewish *politeuma* and its archons decreeing honours also to outside benefactors. Marcus Titius, son of Sextus, has run the province with benevolence and skill and manifested a peaceful disposition; he has not oppressed either party; and so the Jews, under a number of named archons, in

---

⁷⁵ The Hierapolis Jewish texts are in *IJO*, ii, nos.187–209 (drawing on readings by E. Miranda). For a discussion of acculturation at Hierapolis, and esp. the Aelius Glykon tomb, see Harland 2006 (using new readings by T. Ritti). See also the full commentary on this text (*IJO*, ii, no. 196) by the editor, W. Ameling.

⁷⁶ Frey's old publication is still necessary. More recently, Horbury and Noy 1992; Noy 1993; Noy et al. 2004. Introduction in Williams 1998a. Studies in van Henten and van der Horst 1994.

assembly on the feast of Tabernacles, decree that he will be crowned by name at every new moon gathering.[77]

By the third century, Jewish town councillors (*bouleutai*) appear in Asia Minor. In assessing their significance, however, we should remember that they appear in a period when civic office was becoming burdensome to the old elites. Our finest source is the famous inscription from Aphrodisias in Caria, perhaps originally part of the doorway of the synagogue, which on one side of the pillar lists the members of an association of 'lovers of learning' and 'all praisers' concerned with 'the relief of grief', and consisting of Jews and proselytes (and two god-fearers), and on the other a group of god-fearers, including a number of town councillors. The dating of this text now seems, however, to be later than was first thought, and nomenclature suggests a date in the fifth century for both faces.[78] The listed occupations of the donors show them to have been of the middling sort: they were tradesmen and shopkeepers, craftsmen, and even entertainers, with goldsmiths probably at the top of the economic scale, greengrocers and butchers presumably lower. We can be sure that the holding of civic office, here as elsewhere, involved at least passive participation in pagan cultic practices, for these were inseparable from city ceremonial and part of every activity. Already in the first century CE, the Jewish ephebes whose names we find in a fragmentary list from Cyrenaica[79] must have been prepared to take their oath by Herakles, patron of the gymnasia.

Some non-Jews expressed interest in and support for the Jewish community by becoming benefactors. Julia Severa, builder of the 'house' where a synagogue was then established at Acmonia in Phrygia, was no less than a priestess of the imperial cult under Nero. The building was subsequently refurbished by three men named on the inscription who bear the Roman *tria nomina*; they may have had considerable local distinction, but they were perhaps just freedmen. Since such philanthropy was a two-way process, we

---

[77] *CJZC*, 71. Cf. *CJZC*, 70.

[78] Publication in Reynolds and Tannenbaum 1987; thorough study with arguments for late dating: Chaniotis 2002. God-fearers discussed in chapters by Kraabel in Kraabel, Overman, and MacLennan 1992.

[79] *CJZC*, 6, col. 2: Iesous and Ioudas, it seems, cannot be other than Jewish names. Jason may also have been a Jew.

may conclude that some Jewish communities were groups to be reckoned with in the civic context. The diaspora synagogue here emerges as an outward-looking institution serving to foster engagement with the world outside.[80]

That there was a more permanent route by which outsiders could mark an affiliation which fell short of full membership of the Jewish group is suggested by the widespread use of the description 'God-fearer', found in variant forms, either as *theosebeis* (as in inscriptions) or as *phoboumenoi* or *sebomenoi ton theon* (in the book of Acts), but surely referring, in both cases, to sympathizers with differing degrees of involvement who had not undergone conversion—some might have gone on to do so, and others not at all. The interest of such persons in Judaism may, again, have been determined as much by social factors as by religious or spiritual inclination. Whether or not this appellation necessarily declares that its holder belongs to a formal and universally recognized category of affiliates to Jewish communities is a puzzle around which inconclusive debate continues. It is at all events clear that judaizing was a highly visible phenomenon, and one in which Josephus takes pride and pleasure. He claims that every city in Syria had both its Jews and its Judaizers (*BJ*, 2.462–3), and also that a large number of the citizens of Antioch in Syria were attracted by Jewish practices and incorporated 'in a way' into the body of the Jews (*BJ*, 7.45). In Damascus, men were concerned by the effect on their wives (*BJ*, 2.560). Certain regional groups of inscriptions, notably Lycian curse texts, show elements of Judaism (or Christianity) so thoroughly mixed up with the local pagan formulae that it is not easy to say whether we should speak of conscious Judaizing by those who wrote them, of traces of Jewish influence, or perhaps simply of a religious mix whose exponents were not even aware of the Judaic elements in their traditions. Worshippers of 'the Most High God', a designation used both for the God of the Hebrews and for Zeus, include the authors of the manumission inscriptions from the Crimean Bosphorus, where the manumitted slaves retain residual obligations 'to the synagogue'.[81]

---

[80] Rajak 2000: 463–78.
[81] See the discussion by Mitchell 1999; see also Gibson 1999, and esp. 96–123.

It would be simplistic to assume that the designations 'God-fearer' and 'Judaizer' always served to identify individuals travelling part of a difficult road towards conversion but stopping short at a particular point. Rather, such descriptions reflected the range and complexity of options and the multiplicity of overlapping identities in the religious 'marketplace' of the Roman city.[82] The word *prosēlutos*, another Septuagint coinage, frequent in the Greek Exodus, Leviticus, and Numbers, is less ambiguous. Becoming a full Jew stood as a real option, and, although converts seem rarely if ever during this period to have been actively sought by Jewish authorities, they were evidently not uncommon and often not unwelcome.[83] There was thus a modicum of competition with the Christian missions. The royal dynasty of Adiabene, converted as the result of the activities of a trader-missionary, went on to associate itself with important donations to the Temple and assistance to Jerusalem, as well as to support the revolutionaries of 66–73 CE. But, for the most part, personal contact or the local visibility of the synagogue brought people to Judaism. Philo praises the courage of the proselyte (his word is *epēlus*, from the same root) who abandoned everything to journey to 'a better home'.[84] Josephus writes that of the many who joined some 'lacked the necessary endurance and fell away again' (*CA*, 2.123). It was not an easy route to take. But, whatever the numbers, this was a mainstream phenomenon. There is perhaps a paradox in the cultivation of such open boundaries by a group whose historic self-understanding fostered self-separation. One might suggest that core beliefs and practices were protected by opening the gate a little way.

THE RULING POWER

The Jews showed a lively awareness of the determining role of the ruling power on their fortunes and an appreciation of the vital importance of governmental support (whatever the kind of government). This is epitomized in the foundation story of the

---

[82] Cohen 1999: 140–97.
[83] As argued in Goodman 1994a.
[84] Philo, *Spec. Leg.*, 1.52; *De Virt.*, 102–8. Cohen 1999: 157.

Septuagint, focusing as it does on the benevolent role of King Ptolemy. A precedent was set by the decree of the Seleucid conqueror Antiochus III to protect the purity and sacred rights of the Jerusalem Temple, with obvious significance for *ioudaioi*, wherever they were. Diplomacy, in which the members of the Herodian dynasty played a leading role, gained for Jewish communities in the Roman provinces the patronage successively of Julius Caesar, of Marcus Antonius, and of Augustus. Synagogues were exempted by Julius Caesar from his ban on *collegia* (associations). In their disputes with their neighbours, communities were assisted by Roman pronouncements which upheld their right to observe their customary practices (*nomoi*) and required regular reiteration. Josephus' *Antiquities* bear witness to the resolute and vigilant manner by which those edicts and decrees of senate, magistrates, or governors of the Roman republican, triumviral, and early imperial period supporting Jews in Greek cities were sought, generated, guarded, and archived.[85] They were a source of pride as well as of practical assistance throughout the period, but needed regular reiteration and renewal. Christian authors were later to perceive Judaism as having legitimate status, making it, in Tertullian's words, a *religio licita* in the Roman Empire, by contrast with the Church (*Apol.*, 21.1), even though the reality was both less formalized and less secure.

CONFLICT

In spite of—or because of—Jewish acculturation, friction between Jews and their neighbours is a persistent feature. At times this was extreme. Anti-Judaism in Hellenistic Alexandria took both literary and popular forms.[86] But it was the Roman annexation of Egypt which sharpened the antagonism between Jews and Greeks, undermining the status of both. Violence erupted in 38 CE, during the very short but provocative reign of Caligula: synagogues were burnt, shops looted, and the Jews herded into what can only be called, with hindsight, a ghetto and

---

[85] Rajak 2000: 301–33; Pucci Ben Ze'ev 1998; Gruen 2002: 84–104.
[86] Schäfer 1997.

Jewish Diaspora

assaulted, with many killed. His successor, the Emperor Claudius, investigated and issued a firm edict which restored the balance between the warring parties, but which still did not shrink from speaking of the Jews in Alexandria as inhabiting 'a city which was not their own', and of the trouble allegedly caused by Jewry generally as a 'general...disease'.[87] In 66 CE, the tensions in Palestine provoked Greek-Jewish violence in a number of Syrian cities. Roman handling of an ethno-religious dispute over the use of space in Caesarea was a trigger for the outbreak of violence in other cities and according to Josephus the whole of Syria became a scene of devastation. Cities sought to 'rid themselves of their Jews', but were uncertain what to do with the numerous Judaizers. Alexandria then erupted, in a repetition of the troubles of the previous generation: the Jews faced not only their frenzied neighbours but also a charge by Roman troops. Before long Jerusalem was in revolt against Rome. In Syria, Josephus selects for honourable mention as a rarity four Syrian cities: Antioch, Sidon, Apamea, and Gerasa, that looked after their Jews in those difficult times. But when Titus called in on his triumphant return to Rome after the sacking of Jerusalem he found a very different state of affairs at Antioch in Syria: a trumped-up arson charge led to the withdrawal of Jewish rights, and mob violence.[88]

In reality, the history of the Jews under Rome was often deeply troubled. Three temporary expulsions of Jews from the city of Rome are recorded: the first as early as 139 BCE and the others under the Emperors Tiberius and Claudius. These measures were consistently ascribed to Jewish proselytizing activity and this, at least as a perception, exacerbated the general religious and social anxiety which induced sporadic Roman actions against eastern cults and against philosophers.[89] Only in the reign of Septimius Severus was conversion to Judaism officially forbidden.

The crushing of the revolt in Judaea of 70 CE led to difficult times.[90] The victory, so important to the Flavian dynasty's fortunes and to their assertions of legitimacy, was celebrated by Rome's issue

---

[87] Tcherikover et al. 1957: no. 153.
[88] For the entire Syrian episode, see Josephus, *BJ*, 2.457–80. For Alexandria, *BJ*, 2.487–98. For Antioch after the war, *BJ*, 7.41–62.
[89] Isaac 2003.
[90] For a fine interpretation of the troubled century following the disaster of 70 CE, see Goodman 2007: 445–511.

of the famous 'Judaea Capta' coins with their memorable image of the captive weeping under a tall palm. It was followed by a formalization, and an effective degradation of the standing of Jews everywhere. Rebuilding of the Temple was not permitted. The consequent diversion of the former temple tax to a new Roman *fiscus iudaicus* drawn upon for the rebuilding of the temple of Jupiter on the Capitol after a major conflagration, its extension to women and children, and its harsh exactions by the Emperor Domitian in the early years (noted even by his biographer Suetonius) could be construed as a collective punishment. Domitian's successor, Nerva, announced in 97 CE via the caption on a special issue of coinage some alleviation of the particular abuses.[91] But we can tell from Egyptian papyri that the exaction continued into late antiquity.

In 115/116 CE, the Jews of the diaspora revolted in waves against both their pagan neighbours and the Roman authorities. The main theatres of disturbance were Cyrenaica, Egypt (Alexandria), and Cyprus (Dio 68.32, Eus. *HE*, 4.2.4; Oros. 7.12.6–7). This is a challenge to the historian. The background was the aftermath of the disastrous revolt in Palestine and Rome's punitive response; conceivably there were Messianic overtones. The wholesale destruction of pagan temples and civic buildings is reported and archaeological traces of such action have been detected.[92] A little earlier than the main revolt (it seems), the Jews of Babylonia had become involved in the successful rebellion of Trajan's newly conquered Mesopotamian province. The Jewish uprisings were suppressed by Roman forces only with considerable effort. The Alexandrian community took many years to recover and some rural communities disappeared altogether.[93] These uprisings were followed, very soon after Trajan's death, by a dramatic uprising in Palestine against his successor, Hadrian, under the leadership of Bar Kochba, 'prince of Israel', apparently supported by some rabbinic leaders. The historical record is poor, but if the Emperor's prohibition on circumcision (whatever its purpose) was

---

[91] For difficulties in interpreting this reform, see Goodman 1989.

[92] The archaeological traces of destruction in the Cyrenean theatre are surveyed, with some overstatement, in Applebaum 1979.

[93] For an exhaustive study of the sources for the Jewish revolt under Trajan, see Pucci Ben Ze'ev 2005.

indeed the trigger for this last major outburst of resistance, as alleged by the *Historia Augusta* (Hadrian 14.2), then diaspora Jews will have been hit just as hard as the Jews of Palestine.[94] The ban was allegedly revoked by Antoninus Pius.[95] The diaspora will surely also have shared experientially the full misery of the aftermath, when the Roman colony of Aelia Capitolina rose on the ruins of Jerusalem and the cult of Jupiter Capitolinus was established on the Temple site itself. If, as rabbinic tradition has it, rabbis were tortured for 'teaching Torah', including the great Akiva, then the shocking news of that too will have travelled far and wide. But in regions close by it could be far more than merely a question of shock waves. The diaspora might be profoundly involved. An enterprising and indefatigable woman named Babatha, whose papers have been found in the Dead Sea cave where she took refuge, probably as a participant in the revolt, and where she certainly perished, was a diaspora resident. She had formerly lived in the village of Maoza at the bottom of the Dead Sea. She owned land in that area, which during the period was taken up into the Roman province of Arabia, and she conducted transactions and litigation according to both local and Roman (though not apparently Jewish) law. One of her two former husbands had come from the oasis of Ein Gedi, in the Judaean wilderness on the western shore of the Dead Sea.[96]

It was only after a century which must be rated as one of its low points politically, that Jewish history perhaps entered, in the second half of the second century CE, a less turbulent era. Most of the excavated remains of diaspora synagogues and their inscriptions belong to the following century and later. At the Roman port of Ostia, it is the late antique phase of the synagogue complex on the edge of the ancient town that has been excavated.[97] Similarly, in the great and ancient city of Sardis in Phrygia, a large-scale synagogue adjoining the city's enormous baths-gymnasium complex was a former civic building, which had been somehow acquired by the Jewish community. The synagogue was elaborately refurbished more than once by donors duly

---

[94] But note the recent rejection of the historicity of this ban by Oppenheimer 2003 and Abusch 2003.

[95] Linder 1987: 99–102.

[96] Publication: Lewis 1989. Goodman 1991 and Isaac 1992 summarize and interpret Babatha's dealings. See also S. Schwartz 2001: 69–71.

[97] On Ostia, see White 1997. New excavations are ongoing.

named on the marble walls and in the floor mosaics whose inscriptions have been laboriously pieced together. Once more, as at Aphrodisias, we have town councillors and god-fearers among the donors. It survived as a synagogue right down to the sixth century. The discovery, in the late fifties of the twentieth century, caused a sensation; and in its final, late-antique architectural form, this synagogue has come, in modern interpretation, to stand as a triumphant symbol of apparent Jewish integration into the life of a major Greek city, and one which remained a prominent centre of late pagan education well into period of the Christian empire.[98] That may be allowed, provided we are aware of the ambiguity of symbols. The physical record may indeed give us a reassuring sense of harmonious coexistence and of the confidence of a community. At the same time the essence of diaspora circumstances lies in powerlessness more than in power, and good relations might easily turn to acrimony. The balance between independence from outside pressures and dependence requires constant adjustment.

This was surely the lesson learnt by Mediterranean Jewry through half a millennium of existence in dispersion. The Septuagint translations, likely, as we shall see in Chapter 9, to be still in use among those in Sardis, bore the stamp of their dual experience. When they adopted the common language it was not only for conversation with others but also, and indeed even more, as a route to keeping their own traditions alive.

---

[98] The full report of the Sardis synagogue has not yet appeared. The Greek inscriptions are published in Kroll 2001. See also *IJO*, ii, 60–145, preceded by an account of the synagogue with bibliography. Hebrew inscriptions are very few and formulaic but they do unexpectedly include one biblical sentence (from Genesis): see Cross 2002. For an early, influential assessment, see the two articles by Kraabel (1992). For an overview of arguments, mainly numismatic, for a late dating of the final synagogue and questions as to the level of acculturation implied, see Rajak 2000: 463–78, Bonz 1990; Magness 2005 (a very late date).

4

Staying Jewish: Language and Identity in the Greek Bible

The linguistic environment in which the Torah translators and their successors operated was that of the Greek *koinē dialektē*, the standard post-classical language of their period. The language they adopted, whether consciously or unconsciously, was the common language with a difference. It is an idiosyncratic, purpose-built version of the language with a most unfamiliar ring to those coming fresh to it.

Translation is always a pragmatic compromise and this particular enterprise was both new and singularly difficult. But still the choice of translation language is unexpected in the light of the perspectives we have gained from the *Letter of Aristeas*. People who had been moved to define their identity in terms of a vigorously Hellenizing environment in a dynamic city might have been expected to translate their sacred text accordingly, and all the more so if they were backed by influential courtiers, endorsed by Alexandrian intellectuals and patronized by the king. We might anticipate that the translation would accord with the current canons of high style, aiming to showcase the best literary Greek writing of its day or at any rate to come as close to that as the translation medium and their abilities permitted. If Jews expected to participate in the Greek enterprise, then what value would there be in a language which appears in its very nature to create a limit and a barrier?

None the less, that remarkable act of royal patronage was, as we saw, acknowledged and remembered with pride but also with a tinge of ambivalence. The Jews had confidence enough to stand back and to let the subtext peep out in their portrayal of the king. The *Letter of*

Aristeas is not an unequivocal expression of conformity.[1] And nor, accordingly, is the translation itself. The double thread, Jewish and Greek, which weaves itself through the narrative weaves itself also through the very fabric of the Septuagint, in its various modes and manners. Aristeas does not doubt that the translators had to come from Jerusalem (even if he seems to avoid naming the city). The Alexandrian Jewish community was of diverse origin, but its members shared the understanding that the source of scriptural understanding was only one. There is symbolic significance in the insistence that interpretation must depend upon men of the High Priest's personal choosing. Such men might indeed be the best arbiters of the meaning of the Hebrew original; but their stamp is also on the Greek replication.

It is in these terms that I shall seek, after exploring other possibilities, to present and to explain the remarkable and distinctive idiom of the translations. An explanation is called for, since this superficially awkward translation language was able to remain more or less a fixture through the centuries—even if we allow for variation among different translators. We can admit that some of these unknown masters could even enjoy occasional linguistic flourishes, such as alliteration or chiasmus; they might exploit metrical effects; they perhaps mitigated repetition with variety in the choice of Greek equivalent for a single Hebrew word; or at the very least they occasionally replaced *kai* with *de*.[2]

Septuagint language, I suggest, encapsulates the paradox of its successive communities, poised between two worlds. It represents a resolution of two powerful drives, the pull of acculturation and the anxiety of cultural annihilation.

---

[1] See Chap. 1, pp. 60–3, on the subtext in the *Letter*.
[2] For the problems and controversies surrounding the interpretation of Septuagint language, with invaluable bibliographical guidance down to 1988, see Harl in Dorival, Harl, and Munnich 1988: 223–66. For more recent discussions reviewed, see Fernández-Marcos 2000: 3–17. For a brief summary by a Greek philologist, see Horrocks 1997: 57–9. For a controversial attempt at a full quantitative analysis, see Walser 2001.

UNDERSTANDING SEPTUAGINT LANGUAGE

Whatever the extent of the Alexandrian first instalment,[3] we can say without a shadow of doubt that it was epoch making. Not least among its innovations was the forging of a lasting method for putting biblical Hebrew into Greek—in effect, the invention of the translation language. The essence of any translation lies in the choice of translation technique. The translators made a cultural choice of what is in broad terms (allowing for individual variations) a word-for-word procedure (in Cicero's often-repeated phrase, a rendering that works 'verbum e verbo') in contrast to the alternative which Cicero calls 'sensus de sensu', 'sense out of sense', in pursuit of a 'dynamic equivalence' which captures the force of what was said rather than the precise structure.[4] In modern technical terms, the Septuagint translation displays an unusually high level of interference from the source language.[5] In simple, if imprecise language, it tends to be 'literal' rather than 'free'.[6]

The translation becomes a matter of course for those habituated to its idiosyncrasies; but it can be trying to read, sometimes obscure, and occasionally unintelligible to those accustomed to literary Greek, be it classical or Hellenistic.[7] Reference to scripture, referring to both Old and New Testaments, as composed in 'barbarian-speak' (*barbaraphōnos*), was something of a commonplace in patristic

---

[3] On this question, see above, Chap. 2, pp. 90–1.

[4] Cicero, *De Optimo Genere Oratorum*, 14. The application of this Roman insight to biblical translation is explored in Brock 1979; Wright 2003a; Troxel 2008.

[5] Interference is defined as 'foreign arrangements of semantic and syntactic structures' by Langslow 2002: 42. For earlier scholarship on the Hebrew–Greek interference, see Horsley 1989: 6–7.

[6] On different types of literalism and the limitations of the term, see Barr 1979. For an attempt to establish a quantifiable set of criteria for measuring the relative literalism of Septuagint units, based on distinctive uses of certain particles, conjunctions, prepositions, and possessive pronouns, see Tov 1999: 219–37.

[7] Swete's Septuagint introduction (2nd edn. 1914) has a short account of Septuagint syntax. The best analysis remains Thackeray 1909. A more modern account is Olofsson 1990b. There are valuable chapters on lexicography and translation technique in Tov 1999, esp. chaps. 6–9. For short case studies with lucid comment, see Janse 2002. See also the works cited in n. 12 below.

writers.[8] For them, of course, the abandonment of the meretricious falsity of rhetoric was a source of pride. Origen had earlier told the pagan critic Celsus how important it was that the apostles 'had no power of speaking or of giving an ordered narrative by the standards of Greek dialectical or rhetorical arts which convinced their hearers'; and he also cited Paul's pronouncement that 'my word and my preaching were not in persuasive words of men's wisdom'.[9] Septuagint Greek was through the centuries treated dismissively, judged simply a debased and horrid form of the language. Wilamowitz's criticism of the 'abscheulichen Septuagintagriechisch' ('appalling Septuagint Greek') appears extraordinary today.[10] The label 'Semitisms', or 'Hebraisms' often carried with it to a degree the implication of solecism, a confusion of languages, a display of ignorance—the touchstone, indeed, of what was once seen as the ineradicable un-Greekness of the Septuagint and of its aspiring community.[11]

Scholarship is now more receptive. Many of the 'Hebraisms' represent a phenomenon perfectly familiar to linguists, that of the 'calque', where a translated word or phrase reproduces in the target language the form and structure of its equivalent in the source language. To take a notable example, the Greek *eirēnē* takes on the senses of Hebrew *shalom*, and thus can 'mean' also 'prosperity', 'health', 'welfare', or even 'news about'. The results can be remarkable, as in the topsy-turvy use of *eirēnē* (peace) at LXX 2 Kingdoms (Hebrew 2 Samuel) 11: 7: *erōtaō eis eirēnēn tou polemou*, 'I ask after the peace of the war', means, quite comically, 'I ask how the war is going'. Here a calque which has become wholly stereotypic operates as a mechanical equivalent in a context where its use could not be less appropriate. Another phenomenon, this time in the sphere of syntax, merits a closer look because it takes us to the heart of the translators' technique. It is well known that paired Greek words are regularly deployed to represent the distinctive biblical Hebrew doubling of the

---

[8] Janse 2002: 341–2 cites Isidorus of Pelusium (*PG*, 78.1080–1), Basil of Caesarea (*PG*, 32.1084), and Theodoret (*PG*, 83.945).
[9] Origen *Contra Celsum*, 1.62. trans. Chadwick; 1 Cor. 2: 4–5.
[10] Quoted in *BGS*: 259.
[11] LEH 2003: p. ix (Introduction) introduces the apparently derogatory term 'translationisms'. The extended discussion in Thackeray 1909: 25–55 is, however, unjudgemental. On the Hebraisms, see also Gehman 1951.

verb in the so-called *qatol qatal* formation: here an infinitive absolute precedes the finite verb, more or less as a matter of course, where the simple finite verb already conveys the essential sense. There are three different ways in which this characteristic formation is replicated in Greek; one way or another, the Greek is moulded to meet the Hebrew. Thackeray's *Grammar* supplies us with some nice statistics. Just twice in the entire Bible we find an exact equivalent to the Hebrew construction, with startlingly non-Greek effect. But, generally, one of several linguistically acceptable types of companion is supplied for the translated verb, which sometimes appears quite redundant or sometimes seems to intensify the sense of the main verb.[12] The additional word, while it cannot grammatically mirror the Hebrew, still serves to ensure that a highly distinctive feature of the original expression is not lost. One technique is the addition of a noun cognate in derivation or at least of related meaning, which might be a dative (Thackeray counted 200 instances) or might (occasionally) be in the accusative case. Alternatively, a cognate present or aorist participle precedes the finite verb (also some 200 instances). Sometimes an adverb is used. There are occasional examples of other devices, but the construction is hardly ever ignored altogether in translation. As we would expect, there is variation in the preferred type of rendering from book to book of the Septuagint, but also inconsistency within books.[13] An example is the rendering of the Hebrew אִם-שָׁמֹעַ תִּשְׁמַע 'if you will hear' or 'if you will obey' in Greek as ἐὰν ἀκοῇ ἀκούσητε, 'if with a hearing you will hear'.[14] Although, as Conybeare and Stock put it, 'here the genius of the Hebrew and of the Greek language coincides', for the usages are 'legitimate' in Greek, the sheer frequency of the occurrence and the high visibility of some of

---

[12] This is sometimes known as the *figura etymologica*. See Thackeray 1908; Thackeray 1909: 47–50; Conybeare and Stock 1988: 56–7, 60–1; Tov 1999: 247–56. Philological analysis in Evans 2001: 128–30 with further bibliography in n. 19. The use of predicative aorist participles in the Greek Pentateuch is also discussed in Walser 2001: 36–8, 151–2.

[13] This emerges clearly from the interesting analysis and tabulations of Tov 1999: 247–56.

[14] Exod. 23: 22, and not infrequently elsewhere. The *NETS* translation arguably adds more than is warranted to the original with 'if by paying attention you listen to my voice'.

the redundancies impress upon the Greek reader that something untoward is afoot.

Both internal and external evidence (including the style of the *Letter of Aristeas* itself) prove beyond any doubt that Greek could be written well enough in the translators' milieu. Indeed, they had enough knowledge of Greek, and specifically the common Greek of the period to have been capable of choosing a more-sophisticated Greek idiom, had they wished to, and to have done things otherwise than they did. Henry St John Thackeray, a master-linguist, appreciated this over a century ago, and new studies continue to provide confirmation of the translators' underlying competence.[15] Suffice it to quote Mark Janse's conclusion to an in-depth analysis of the translators' syntactical peculiarities: 'if they [the translators] were able to deal with such subtleties as Wackernagel's Law, we must assume that they were native speakers of the Egyptian koine.'[16] Trevor Evans investigated in great detail the translators' handling of Greek verbs and he successfully dismissed the simplification that Septuagint syntax is no more than Hebrew syntax transferred to Greek: the tendency is to 'pragmatic functional agreement' much more than to 'mechanical translation equivalents'.[17] Striking examples of erstwhile 'septuagintisms', proven as koine usage from documentary evidence, have emerged from decades of study of the vast corpus of papyri extracted from the sands of Egypt. Modern scholarship rests upon the vigorously expressed insights of Adolf Deissmann, whose research centred on the language of the New Testament but extended back to the Septuagint. He jolted both classical and biblical scholars in the early part of the twentieth century into understanding that the newly-opened-up world of the papyri, together with inscriptions and later Greek literary texts, were a new window open wide into the language of the Greek scriptures and a great resource for understanding them, and that at the same time those scriptures were themselves 'one of the most important

---

[15] Thackeray 1909; Aejmelaeus 1993; Lee 1983; Evans 2001.
[16] Janse 2002: 381. Wackernagel's law, whose correct operation is detected by Janse in Septuagint Deuteronomy and Isaiah, concerns word order in a sentence.
[17] Evans 2001, and see esp. p. 132 for this description.

Language and Identity

documents of Egyptian Greek.[18] Examples on the level of vocabulary, especially technical and semi-technical words, or those drawn from everyday life, especially animal-rearing and work in the fields, were numerous: *aphesis* for an irrigation channel, *genēma* for the produce of the land, are just two common instances.[19] But the formation of words and syntactical constructions were also thus illuminated. In other ways, too, the variety and complexities of koine itself, whose range of surviving material runs the gamut from technical literature to conversation, have come to be better understood.[20] And yet none of this provided a full explanation of what is going on in the Septuagint language.

By way of illustration of how the translation language 'reads', we can do no better than to take what is perhaps the Pentateuch's most signal moment: the revelation of the Divine Name to Moses in a face-to-face encounter at the burning bush. In the footnote below,[21] the text of Exodus 3:15, a verse from God's numinous utterance, is given in the Greek version followed by the Hebrew and then by the English translation from the new *NETS* version. While the Greek translator more or less rises to the occasion, he does so by exploiting rather than abandoning the characteristics of Septuagint diction. Exodus, we may note, is classified among those books in the Septuagint which are translated with relatively more freedom, but that 'relatively' must be underscored, and it can be seen that this freedom, in the linguistic

---

[18] Quotation from Deissmann 1903: 70; see also Deissmann 1927. Contemporaneous, and working on similar principles, see Thumb 1901. Later Moulton and Milligan's *Vocabulary of the Greek Testament* (1914) set about systematic recording of the language of the papyri then known. The most important modern scholar to follow through along these lines has been John Lee. See Lee 1983; also Lee 2003, where the earlier investigation is revisited. For a succinct reassessment by a modern papyrologist, see Montevecchi 1999: 121–33.

[19] Deissmann 1903: 98–100; 109–10.

[20] Horrocks 1997 offers an up to date and authoritative account.

[21] καὶ εἶπεν ὁ θεὸς πάλιν πρὸς Μωυσῆν οὕτως ἐρεῖς τοῖς υἱοῖς Ισραηλ κύριος ὁ θεὸς τῶν πατέρων ὑμῶν θεὸς Αβρααμ καὶ θεὸς Ισαακ καὶ θεὸς Ιακωβ ἀπέσταλκέν με πρὸς ὑμᾶς τοῦτό μού ἐστιν ὄνομα αἰώνιον καὶ μνημόσυνον γενεῶν γενεαῖς.

וַיֹּאמֶר עוֹד אֱלֹהִים אֶל-מֹשֶׁה, כֹּה-תֹאמַר אֶל-בְּנֵי יִשְׂרָאֵל, יְהוָה אֱלֹהֵי אֲבֹתֵיכֶם אֱלֹהֵי אַבְרָהָם אֱלֹהֵי יִצְחָק וֵאלֹהֵי יַעֲקֹב, שְׁלָחַנִי אֲלֵיכֶם; זֶה-שְּׁמִי לְעֹלָם, וְזֶה זִכְרִי לְדֹר דֹּר.

And God said again to Moyses, Thus you shall say to the sons of Israel, The Lord the God of your fathers, God of Abraam, and God of Isak, and God of Iakob, has sent me to you: this is an everlasting name of mine and a memorial of generations to generations.

sphere at least, has very severe limits.[22] A fair selection of noteworthy Septuagintal devices emerges clearly even in this short passage. The rendering of the Divine Name as *kurios*, 'Lord', without the definite article, is the normal practice of the Exodus translator (or translators) as of most others. The names of the patriarchs appear in their Hebrew forms as indeclinable Greek proper nouns. There is a characteristic absence of connecting words between 'God of your fathers' and 'God of Abraam'. Then, the names of the patriarchs are connected by repeated 'and' (*kai . . . kai*).[23] Highly distinctive Greek phraseology conveys something of the rich Hebrew conceptualization of eternity, with the stereotypic adjective *aiōnion* rendering the Hebrew *le-'olam*, 'for ever' (literally, 'for the world'),[24] and this is directly followed by the opaque and un-Greek but resonant combination which the English word-for-word version gives as '[a memorial] of generations to generations'. That represents the pithy Hebrew expression *le-dor dor*, 'to generation and generation', a case where the Greek by no means replicates its Hebrew predecessor word by word but rather evokes it through a slightly different, yet also peculiar, Greek expression. The effect of it all is to highlight this central phrase and its surrounding sentence, and thus to alert the reader to what lies behind it—a Hebrew biblical concept of very particular resonance and significance. The translator hit it off and some of his devices are exploited in abundance through the corpus.

For a second example, thematically related to the Exodus, I take the opening lines of Septuagint Psalm 113, in the Hebrew Bible Psalm 114, 'when Israel went out of Egypt', with the three versions given once more

---

[22] The Greek translation of Exodus is noted for its 'pluses' (words and phrases not found in the Masoretic text) and for the double Tabernacle description at the end of the book, which has suggested to some two translators at work. The possibility of a divergent Hebrew Vorlage is not excluded. For guidance to the issues and the bibliography, the introduction to the translation of this book in the new NETS version is the best resource.

[23] Note, however, that Wevers 1990: 4, in his comment on this phrase, concludes on the basis of a parallel from Samuel that the *kai* which precedes the name of Isaac may in fact have had a Hebrew textual basis.

[24] This adjectival form is recorded in Liddell and Scott but it is infrequent in Greek prose outside the Jewish and Christian spheres. Philo builds on it in his commentary, observing in *de Mutatione Nominum* 12 that in our Exodus passage the *aiōn* is a man-related concept, 'not set beyond memory or apprehension', and that the 'generations' are human, not those of ungenerated beings.

in the note below.[25] Again, we have a passage of evident national and theological significance, and also of great liturgical importance for its role in the Hallel sequence recited by Jews on so many occasions in synagogue and home—a practice of unknown antiquity. The Greek version, interestingly, carries the 'halleluya' superscript, while the Masoretic Hebrew does not in the case of this Psalm in contrast to the three that precede it. Here we find, prominently, as in the earlier Exodus example, those familiar indeclinable proper nouns ('Israel' and 'Jacob') and a range of 'Hebraisms' including *en exodō* (literally 'in the going out', *ti soi estin* ('what is to you?'); and *eis ta opisō* ('to the behind'). We cannot fail to notice, in lines 3 and 4, the superfluous and aurally intrusive repetition of the possessive pronoun *autou . . . autou* ('his').[26] And we observe several examples of new and distinctive septuagintal religious vocabulary: the word *exodos* itself, and the terms *hagiasma* (a sacred precinct or sanctification), and *exousia* (power).[27]

These two sample passages by no means exhaust the roster of types of Hebraism. But we have seen more than enough to get the point. No one could suggest that we are here dealing with ordinary Greek in any of its registers. Septuagint Greek is unique and altogether more

---

[25] ἐν ἐξόδῳ Ισραηλ ἐξ Αἰγύπτου οἴκου Ιακωβ ἐκ λαοῦ βαρβάρου ἐγενήθη Ιουδαία ἁγίασμα αὐτοῦ Ισραηλ ἐξουσία αὐτοῦ ἡ θάλασσα εἶδεν καὶ ἔφυγεν ὁ Ιορδάνης ἐστράφη εἰς τὰ πίσωτα ὄρη ἐσκίρτησαν ὡσεὶ κριοὶ καὶ οἱ βουνοὶ ὡς ἀρνία προβάτων

בְּצֵאת יִשְׂרָאֵל, מִמִּצְרָיִם;   בֵּית יַעֲקֹב, מֵעַם לֹעֵז.
הָיְתָה יְהוּדָה לְקָדְשׁוֹ;   יִשְׂרָאֵל, מַמְשְׁלוֹתָיו.
הַיָּם רָאָה, וַיָּנֹס;   הַיַּרְדֵּן, יִסֹּב לְאָחוֹר.
הֶהָרִים, רָקְדוּ כְאֵילִים;   גְּבָעוֹת, כִּבְנֵי-צֹאן.

At Israel's Exodus from Egypt
    Of Iakob's house from a barbarian people
Judea became his holy precinct
    Israel his seat of authority.
The sea saw it and fled
    Jordan was turned backwards
The mountains skipped like rams
    And the hills like lambs of sheep.

[26] This inescapable feature in Septuagint composition is shared to an extent by ordinary koine practice.
[27] On this phenomenon, see below, pp. 162–72.

peculiar. It is scarcely believable that the word-for-word technique was adopted primarily because of the inhibitions or the limitations of its translators, who, it has been suggested, found it easier to render, basic unit after basic unit, a text which at moments they often could not fully understand. To invent an artificial language in order to cover up the difficulty of solving the odd knotty problem in the Hebrew text would be to crack nuts with a sledge hammer.[28] The complexity of this language seems to emerge more or less fully formed in the translations of the Pentateuchal books, even though there is variation between them and their production may well have been in stages. This is a powerful argument that the language was deliberately created and consciously maintained. A salutary warning of how the crudity of seeming 'translationese' can deceive has been recently delivered by Carlotta Dionisotti for a different language-pairing, in the course of analysing the self-conscious Graecisms that stand out in medieval scholars' translations of non-biblical writings from Greek into Latin.[29] In short, not only may we conceive of something which we can legitimately call a Septuagint 'translation language', but we can identify this as a set of general tendencies which runs across and unifies translators of diverse practice and taste.[30]

Benjamin Wright tackles the meaning of the translation style by way of the famous preface composed by Ben Sira's grandson, who, coming from Jerusalem to Alexandria, made a Greek book (known as Sirach or, by its Latin name, Ecclesiasticus) out of his grandfather's Hebrew work. Remarkably, he begins his work by identifying himself and talking about what he did. This conscientious grandson apologizes that a translation from the Hebrew into another language cannot carry equal power (*isodunamei*) with the original, and especially so when it comes to the translations of 'the law, the prophets and the other books'. Wright takes the point of this statement to be not that the translations fall short of the Hebrew in terms of the meaning conveyed, but rather that they lack the full force and impact carried by the original.[31] Yet the style of the preface itself, Wright goes

---

[28] So Olofsson 1990b: 8.
[29] Dionisotti 2005.
[30] See Harl 1988: 231–3. The point is conceded even by Aejmelaeus (1993 and 2001) who has done much to map that diversity.
[31] Wright 2003a: 11–20 and Wright 2003b; See Ben Sira, prologue, 20.

on to argue, shows the grandson to be a writer who can give his Greek prose precisely those qualities—when he chooses. The conclusion must therefore be that a big difference was perceived to exist between a free composition, like the preface, and the text itself, which was constrained by the need to draw extensively on pentateuchal and prophetic expressions and ideas,[32] and which may itself have sought a biblical authority. For the latter, the Septuagintal translation language, broadly speaking, was appropriate. If Wright is correct, the adoption of the language was indeed a matter of choice. In an extensive body of literature, intended for intensive use and for multiple purposes, such awkwardness would not seem to be advantageous to its users, let alone impressive to the world outside. Excluding sheer incompetence, various explanations on the socio-linguistic level present themselves to explain the reasons for the choice and thus to define the character of Septuagint 'translation Greek'.

One further idea which has finally been consigned to the scrapheap of history deserves mention if only for the allure it once held: that the Jewish Greek Bible translation represents the not-very-elevated everyday communication of Alexandrian Jews, a sort of pidgin language that somehow accorded with an irreducible 'Semititic' essence. H. B. Swete had little doubt about the matter when, in 1900, he explained the background to the Greek Bible in a handbook which was to hold the field for many years: 'the translators were men of Semitic descent with, therefore, innately Semitic habits of thought. They wrote Greek as they doubtless spoke it.' He had worked this out even more precisely:

The Greek which the Jews of Alexandria learned to speak was neither the literary language employed by the scholars of the Museum, nor the artificial imitation of it affected by Hellenistic writers... It was based on the patois of the Alexandrian streets and market—a mixture, as we may suppose, of the ancient spoken tongue of Hellas with elements gathered from Macedonia, Asia Minor, Egypt and Libya.

While no doubt offered in a very different spirit, this fanciful notion has a little in common with that figment of the eighteenth- and nineteenth-century anti-Semitic imagination exposed by Sander

---

[32] See Aitken 1999 on how Ben Sira develops Genesis and Isaiah.

Gilman, namely a degenerate German-Jewish patois, whose exponents, if not fenced off, might debase the true German expression.[33]

As in many other things, Adolf Deissmann was a pioneer in detaching himself from the notion that there existed in Ptolemaic Alexandria a distinct Jewish-Greek dialect outside the Septuagint, insisting that absolutely no conclusion was to be drawn from the 'Hebraisms'.[34] Alexandrian Jews no doubt spoke in all sorts of different ways, depending on who they were and what they were after. But, however they spoke, it was not as the Septuagint is written. Septuagint Greek as we have it is evidently the product of the study, or the translator's cell, or of the 'house of learning' (*oikos paideias*) of the Greek Sirach (51. 23).

TRANSLATION PRECEDENTS AND THE 'DRAGOMAN'

Septuagint Greek does seem to lack sophistication, to breathe a certain naivety. Those who take these qualities at their face value have inclined towards a simple explanation: that precedents for this ambitious new enterprise were limited. Indeed, the translators had few models to follow. In terms of scale, only the translation activity of the ancient oriental civilizations might offer a real parallel, and that would have been a very remote one indeed.[35] In the context of Ptolemaic Egypt, the *Oracle of the Potter*, a semi-literary text of apocalyptic character, apparently composed among rebellious priestly elements and usually assigned to 130 BCE, was translated from Egyptian into Greek.[36] The translator says he did his job *kata ton dunaton*, as well as he was able. This phrase recurs in demotic contracts prepared for Greek tribunals.

---

[33] Swete 1914 [1900]: 9; Gilman 1986, covering both pre- and post-Enlightenment versions of the motif. On notions that Jews were incapable of authentic German expression, see also Seidman 2006: 153–98.

[34] Deissmann 1903: 69. Horsley 1989: 5–40 offers a wide-ranging bibliographical survey of the question of Jewish–Greek in the context of bilingualism. See also the study of Reiser 2005.

[35] On the novelty of the enterprise, see Chap. 1, pp. 24–7. Cf. Brock 1992: 310–11.

[36] Peremans 1985: 252, 6, with bibliography.

Language and Identity

Elias Bickerman liked to think that the Septuagint translators did indeed follow such local practice as was visible to them, and that they laboured under the disadvantage of all trailblazers, a hopelessly inadequate model. He brought into play that figure more often invoked than investigated by scholars, the 'dragoman'. These official translators from and into Turkish played a crucial role in facilitating government in the Ottoman empire down to the modern era.[37] They could acquire considerable authority and were given to diplomatic mistranslations. More loosely, the term may refer to the ubiquitous semi-official interpreter-cum-guide of the Middle East, whether past or recent. Working orally, this type of dragoman can offer, among numerous other services, a sort of ad hoc simultaneous translation, peppered, as required, with commentary or guidance. Proceeding thus, without a written text to follow, does mean dealing with each word or short phrase as it comes. But, equally, such translators resort at times to paraphrases, approximations, and omissions, or to sheer blarney. Bickerman did not stop to sharpen up a picture of the dragoman in operation, then or now;[38] he simply suggested that the 'literal' style of the Jewish translators was in their mould. There he left the matter, perhaps somewhat uneasy about the *deus ex machina* he had conjured up. Bickerman's model is frequently cited. But no support appears to have been forthcoming for his supposition that the dragoman's characteristic *modus operandi* was word-for-word translation. And perhaps this is not surprising.

Trevor Evans looks at extracts from eight Ptolemaic papyri which mention dealings by interpreters, mostly at local level. The term applied to their calling, *hermēneus*, does apparently signify that they are interpreters; but they seem to be involved in a range of activities, most of which do not advance our knowledge of the translation process itself. We find interpreters taking on all sorts of roles as commercial middlemen: one of them, for example, is a guide in the garlic market.[39] This is hardly surprising. But the negative

---

[37] See Lewis 2004: 18–32.
[38] Bickerman 1976: 176. Endorsed by Rabin 1968: 20–6. LSJ gives 'dragoman' as one of the renderings for *hermēneus*. The philological congruence of 'dragoman' with the Aramaic 'turgeman' and its cognate, the classically Jewish 'Targum' has no doubt encouraged the parallel. Cf. for the modern phenomenon, Lewis 2004.
[39] On the semantic value of *hermēneus*, see Evans 2007. Garlic market: *PSI*, 4.332.

evidence to emerge from the enquiry is at least as significant as the positive data. Evans finds nothing that might warrant 'the image of a dragoman standing next to the merchant translating every sentence in turn'.[40] Again, Willy Peremans notes that ancient written translations are remarkably diverse, varying significantly in their degree of literalness: quite understandably so, given their range of functions, for translation was crucial to the inhabitants of Hellenistic Egypt, from the highest to the lowest, and especially in the early years of Ptolemaic rule. Clearly, there was no one simple pattern. Indeed, it may well be precisely because the activity was ubiquitous, small scale, and taken for granted that we encounter explicit statements about it far less often than we might expect.[41]

I would not deny that, as they went about their task, the Septuagint translators were influenced and assisted, perhaps consciously as well as unconsciously, by the everyday practice of professional translators known to them. A translation into Greek, done 'as well as possible', of part of a deed of the sale of some possession by a 'prophet, son of a prophet', in the Fayyum in 11 CE contains a line of untranslated Egyptian job titles. This odd intrusion is better explained by the lack of Greek equivalents in Egyptian than by the translator's inadequacy.[42] It is remarkable that the identical device, to reproduce without translating, is sometimes adopted by the Septuagint translators to deal with special terms such as *manna* or *cherubim*. Conceivably, this is a case of influence from outside practice. Be that as it may, the Septuagint itself mentions an individual interpreter—called *hermēneutēs* rather than *hermēneus*—on just one single occasion, in Genesis 42: 23, when Joseph's brothers come before him in Egypt and they do not recognize him because the interpreter stands between them. Trevor Evans suggests that the Genesis translator here reflects the world of the functionaries and administrators around him.[43] But neither this unknown craftsman nor any other translator reveals the slightest glimmering of a fraternal interest in others of his ilk.

---

[40] Wright 2002: 16.
[41] More surprisingly perhaps, the same was true of Greece in earlier periods: see Janse 2002: 334.
[42] Fewster 2002: 232.
[43] Evans 2007. The Hebrew term in this passage, *ha-melitz*, is not transparent—an intermediary perhaps.

Contemporary day-to-day practice could only have made a passing and subsidiary contribution to helping him meet the huge challenge before him. And the elusive dragoman who flits about the marketplaces and around the pages of scholars does not help us understand how the Septuagint translators fixed on a technique.

A SACRED TEXT

Another route to explaining the character of Septuagint Greek is in terms of the sanctity of the source text. This might be expressed in general terms: sacred writings ought to show that they stand apart; the language in which they were originally expressed is crucial to their exact sense, or to their deepest meaning; religious language should be wooden and incantatory. Similarly, it might be pointed out, it is not uncommon for law to be expressed in archaic formulae. But when it comes to the Bible in Judaism, explanations even more sweeping than these have beckoned, and they are indeed seductive.

No less a figure than Philo of Alexandria encourages this understanding of the relationship between original and translation. As part of his promotion of the Septuagint in the *Life of Moses*, and adjacent to the passage where he describes its origins and the festival in its honour,[44] Philo explains that the Hebrew and the Greek wording stand in a one-to-one correspondence. While the Greek language in particular has many ways of expressing the same idea, when it came to the Jewish law, the Greek terms chosen by the translators matched exactly the Hebrew they stood for, as though in logic or dialectic. This, for Philo, demonstrates them to have been not interpreters (*hermēneis*), but hierophants and prophets, in contact with the entirely pure spirit of Moses. Admittedly, Philo is a witness who belongs, if not exactly to the Septuagint's original milieu, then to a society in the direct line of descent from it, and one still focused very

---

[44] Philo, *Life of Moses*, 2.38–40. See Chap. 1, p. 35.

much on the translations. However, his conclusion merely reveals the transcendental level on which Philo's explanation is here operating. He fortifies, with the argument from language, his own philosophical reading of the inspired character of scripture, whether Hebrew or Greek, and also of the equality of the Greek with the Hebrew. The correspondence theory was simply not intended to function as a realistic description of the Torah translation's texture. An element of the miraculous is included in its very formulation by Philo.

The philosopher's assertion could scarcely be seen as valid on the empirical level. Indeed, the evidence reveals the very opposite to be the case: the same Hebrew term, far from having only one natural equivalent, is to be found rendered in two or more different ways even within the same book. It is not unknown even within the same verse. A notable case is the important biblical word *ger*, roughly speaking a 'resident stranger'. In the Septuagint this is understood as including converts to the Jewish community and it is therefore crucial. In the book of Exodus alone, three different Greek renderings appear: *prosēlutos* (most often), but also twice *paroikos* (a settler, Exod. 2: 22 and 18: 3), and on one occasion an untranslated reproduction of the Hebrew term, *geiōras*.[45]

Harry Orlinsky[46] drew a tight connection between the *Aristeas* narrator's underlying biblical typologies, the phraseology of the description of the community leaders' acceptance of the translation—which he takes to represent immediate canonization by Alexandrian Jewry and, before long, by the entire diaspora—and the 'word-for-word equivalence' method of the outcome, the Greek Torah. From the standpoint of some linguists, too, the Septuagint is readily invoked to serve as a classic example of translation from a 'sacred text', with the special respect for the source, and therefore for the idiom of the source language, that this can imply.[47] Not only was scripture the

---

[45] Exod. 12: 19. Cf. Isa.14: 1, arguably influenced by Exodus. For the variation in these words, see Barr 2003: 527 with Tov 1999: 175. On the general point, *BGS*, 231.

[46] Orlinsky 1975.

[47] So Brock 1992: 311–12, drawing on Jerome's description of his own faithfulness as 'interpres' rather than 'expositor' of sacred text in the preface to the writings of Dionysius, and the implied allusions in that to dicta of Cicero and Horace.

word of God, but exegesis, they point out, could become seriously flawed where a rendering was a little loose. Thus, Janse constructs his analysis of Septuagint language on precisely this interpretative basis, resting, like Orlinsky, on a high concept of sanctity, and especially upon ancient rhetorical utterances about the translation's marvellous precision and perfection, where nothing was either added or subtracted from the original, from which *Aristeas* derives considerable leverage.[48] It is salutary to remind ourselves that Josephus said exactly the same about his biblical *Antiquities*, which is in fact a very freely reworked paraphrase, allowing itself both additions and subtractions.[49] The claim of not adding or subtracting was a commonplace, a formulaic seal of approval. Janse's analysis of the language can stand, but under the rubric of a much-revised explanation which takes a broader view of the meaning and purposes of the translation.

There is much to be gained, as suggested throughout this book, in detaching ourselves from that mindset which puts the Bible in the special category of sacred, or indeed ultra-sacred text; in viewing it as a book, or set of books, not wholly incomparable with others, and Hebrew as a language located in the same sphere as others.[50] Even the term *leshon hakodesh*, which is an earlier name for the language than 'Hebrew', means simply 'the language used in dealing with holy things'. This is not to deny to either of these a share in the attributes of holiness. But it is crucial that in this period of formative Judaism neither the extent nor the implication of a unified holiness ideology has yet crystallized. With regard to texts as physical entities, their primary sanctity lies in their inclusion of the Name of God; and the early papyri show concern over this by their range of strategies for

---

[48] Janse 2002.
[49] See Chap. 7, pp. 252–4. Josephus' version of the Aristeas legend interestingly seems to allow the need for an element of intervention and correction to the translation precisely in order to preserve its quality for ever: *AJ*, 12.108–9. On this ambiguous sentence, see Brock 1992: 309.
[50] See also Chap. 6, pp. 215–16. Cf. the arguments in Wright 2003a: 22–4. Pertinent comments by Dines 2004: 124–8. Sawyer 1999 focuses on the sacred text as a distinct category of writing, yet by no means all the material he brings under this heading is religious in the obvious sense.

dealing with the writing of the Name. Yet, even then, while the earliest fragments of Jewish biblical texts are executed by highly professional scribes, with complete control over their work, and in lettering more elegant, on the whole, than the typical hand of Christian biblical papyri; they are still in a hand labelled more 'documentary' than 'literary', suggesting perhaps that their usage was seen as part of ordinary life rather than belonging to a demarcated zone of the sacred.[51] It is striking that the Karaite Jewish scholars of the tenth- and eleventh-century Arab world, who promoted biblical study and developed sophisticated grammatical tools for this while rejecting the oral law codified in rabbinic literature, were able to challenge 'the [by then] received concept of the sacredness and superiority of Hebrew'. Partly under the influence of Aristotelian theory, they viewed the Hebrew language as one language among many.[52] Here, then, is an example from a different Jewish culture of how dedication to the language of the canonical text can flourish within Judaism without sacralization.

Even in the scripture-soaked world of the Dead Sea Scrolls,[53] an extraordinary freedom in making minor adjustments to the biblical text reproduced in the lemmata of sectarian commentary has been observed by Timothy Lim. Since it does not appear that these all represent alternative text versions, this strongly suggests that even in that rule-bound setting the text was approached not as an enshrined holy object in which every word was sacrosanct but as, within limits, still negotiable.[54] My main point, however, is that biblical texts function in Jewish societies in a variety of ways—perhaps, indeed, the range is even greater precisely because of scripture's pre-eminent position. To explain Septuagint language as simply the natural way of translating a holy book is to close down the discussion far too soon.

---

[51] On material aspects of the early Septuagint papyri, see Kraft 2003 and in more detail at <http://ccat.sas.upenn.edu/rs/rak/earlypap.html> Cf. Introduction, p. 17, esp. n. 21.
[52] Olszowy-Schlanger 1999: 166.
[53] On which see Chap. 7, pp. 245–50.
[54] Lim 1997.

THE INTERLINEAR THEORY: KNOWLEDGE OF HEBREW

Fresh life has been brought to this question by an interpretation that seeks to account for Septuagint Greek in terms of its social function rather than of theology. This is the so-called 'interlinear theory', which is associated above all with the name of Albert Pietersma, and which informs the recently completed *New English Translation of the Septuagint*.[55] The basis of the theory is that the Greek version cannot stand alone because the extent of interference from the 'source language', biblical Hebrew, makes the Greek quite frequently meaningless without close reference to the source. It follows, according to this argument, that the two versions must have been intended to be deployed together. The translation is here understood as originally driven by an educational purpose, that of serving alongside the original Hebrew as a written aid both to studying the language and, simultaneously, to understanding the text. The term 'interlinearity' was at a later stage refined by the theory's proponents, and it tends now to be explained more as metaphor, indicating 'a deeper, less-visual linguistic relationship of dependence and subservience' and 'in no way contingent on the existence of a physical, interlinear entity'.[56] But the central proposition still stands, that the translation provides a word-by-word guide for the student. The theory has strengths, but a number of obvious objections immediately present themselves.[57]

1) Perhaps the most important criticism is that the Greek translations in due course *did* stand alone, in fact sooner rather than later, and they therefore rapidly proved usable and fully intelligible in their ancient context. The comparative case of the Anglo-Saxon Gospel glosses may lie behind the interlinear Septuagint theory, though it is not teased out. But, in that case, gradual but substantial changes were

---

[55] See Pietersma 2002. Briefly set out in *NETS* 2007: pp. xvi–xvii (Preface). Lucid accounts in Boyd-Taylor 1998; Wright 2006. Wright 2003a: 21–5 builds on the theory.
[56] Pietersma and Wright 2007: p. xiv.
[57] As noted by Dines 2004: 52–4. See also the observations of van der Kooij 1999.

made to the original word-for-word renderings before in due course an independent life as vernacular translation apart from the Latin were feasible for them.[58] What emerged as a free-standing book was no longer the same translation. This crucial shift is acknowledged by Pietersma, but without taking account of its power to undermine the basis of the original theory which depended on the supposition that the translation language could only work when accompanied by the source.

2) The degree of interference from the source language tends to be overstated in the context of the interlinear theory. Assuming some familiarity, Septuagint Greek is not hard to comprehend, and it cannot be described as more than very rarely unintelligible. Awkwardness is another matter.

3) Septuagint Greek was not consistently close enough in word order and structure to the source to act as anything like a real interlinear translation (unlike parallels from the medieval world such as the Lindisfarne Anglo-Saxon translation). Word order in particular diverges strikingly. The gap is even greater in one of the relatively freer translations such as Exodus, Job, Proverbs, or Isaiah. But it is always there, and of necessity. A completely interlinear translation is just a dictionary.

4) The addition of literary flourishes, such as alternation, variation, and the echoing of metrical patterns,[59] which even the most austere of translators occasionally produced, would simply get in the way of the translation's functioning as a crib.

5) There is no reason to posit one single purpose for the translation. Indeed a range of intended uses is more probable to justify so major an enterprise.

6) We might expect to find traces of a special consciousness of education and educational processes embedded in the translations if this were the prime purpose of them, but such traces are not particularly apparent. However, as Jennifer Dines suggests, it could be worth looking harder for them.

---

[58] For a good account of the glosses and their development, see Long 2001, Chap. 3.

[59] For sophisticated examples from LXX Amos and Gen. 1: 2, see Dines 2004: 54–7.

None the less, the interlinear theory retains considerable explanatory power and may survive with modification. Whether or not thus intended by its proponents, it readily brings discussion in a concrete and specific way into the sphere of education (be it in a family or a communal context); and, it offers due recognition to the significance of the Hebrew in the background, to the drive for its retention, and to a functional and aspirational bilingualism as the basis for the enterprise. The translation language, in Pietersma's words, 'points the reader away from itself'.[60] Septuagint Greek manifestly 'sits on top of' the Hebrew in a way that would seem to presuppose respect for, and some degree of acquaintance with, the source language as a literary vehicle, at least within its circle of primary users. It could also encourage and facilitate contact in others. The Rabbis' technique for teaching and learning the Hebrew language in an Aramaic milieu has been convincingly argued by Philip Alexander to have been precisely this: acquisition not via grammatical rules but via word-for-word equivalences. Through the Greek, then, both specific knowledge and, equally important, a symbolic attachment to the biblical Hebrew language, with the shared purpose of retaining it as a living force, would be spread more widely through the community.[61] This can be well understood if we bear in mind the 'honorific written and spoken functions' fulfilled by the biblical language throughout later Jewish history. One socio-linguist, Joshua Fishman, talks of the pre-Enlightenment era as one of a 'continuing classical involvement [in literacy in the Holy Tongue], engaged in actively by the ... [male] elite, more passively by every adult male ... and referentially by adult women'. Due to this high valuation and pervasiveness of the classical language, Hebrew, and its role within a very strong, shared ethno-historical tradition, the formation of Jewish languages has followed an untypical pattern.[62]

But what of Hebrew in our period? Throughout the Graeco-Roman era, the Hebrew language, both spoken and written, had a demonstrable ethnic significance for the Jews, in Palestine at least. There losing the language was understood as an irreversible process:

[60] Pietersma 1999: p. xiii.
[61] P. Alexander 1999a.
[62] Fishman 1985: 8–13.

the road to complete assimilation, to ethnic extinction. In many a weak community over the ages the process has indeed been just this. Nehemiah had feared for the little settlement of returnees in Jerusalem, singling out loss of their native language as a consequence of the forbidden marriages he was attacking: 'I saw that some Jews had married Ashdodite, Ammonite and Moabite women. Half the children spoke Ashdodite and they could not speak the language of the Judaeans (*yehudit*) but the languages of the different peoples'.[63] Heller-Roazen's unusual study of the forgetting of languages evokes Jewish anxiety in one other particular time and place, medieval Spain. In the twelfth century, some thinkers apparently felt that using alien Arabic versification systems to write Hebrew poetry would spell the death of the holy language. It is telling, as we shall shortly see, that concern was centred specifically on the transmutation of sound and rhythm and that an essential element of the contemporary Hebrew language was felt to reside in its natural versification. Later, in fourteenth-century Jewish Provence, being deprived of Hebrew was described as tantamount to exile.[64]

In a detailed review of the written and spoken uses of the Hebrew language (in its late classical form) during the Second Temple era, David Goodblatt shows how the role of Hebrew in the construction of Jewish identities enabled it to hold its own against Aramaic. While Seth Schwartz traced a 'talismanic' role for the language back to the Maccabaean period, Goodblatt follows this role further back into the Persian era.[65] The Qumran documents, perhaps from the mid-third century BCE, incorporate archaic linguistic features, notably the

---

[63] Neh. 13: 23–4 (my translation). LXX 2 Esdras 23–4 has the Jews just speaking the 'language of Azotus', not mentioning, as does MT, the languages of the other peoples. LXX may be the older reading: the extra phrase looks like a gloss, tacked on to the end of the Hebrew sentence, an odd positioning unfortunately concealed in standard translations. Which language is here referred to as Ashdodite is not clear, though the survival of a Philistine dialect is conceivable.

[64] Heller-Roazen 2005: 45–51. The concerns are extracted from Judah Ha-Levi's dialogue *Kuzari* and from the sharp criticisms in the responses of Menahem ben Saruq's disciples to the grammarian Dunash ben Labrat. Joseph Caspi spoke of language loss as exile in Provence.

[65] Goodblatt 2006: 49–70; S. Schwartz 1995. Carr 2005 shows effectively how the Hebrew language remained the 'key symbol of indigenous culture', but oversimplifies in understanding the culture to be 'anti–Hellenistic'.

palaeo-Hebrew script employed in a few scrolls, and also some renderings of the tetragrammaton (Divine Name) that avoid the more usual current Assyrian (square) letters.[66] This script is also resurrected in the coins of the Hasmoneans and on those of both revolts in Palestine. The letters of Bar Kokhba, the leader of the second of those revolts, surprised their discoverers by including more Hebrew than would ever have been expected.[67] In the Second Book of Maccabees, which concerns events in Palestine but is itself an abridgement of a work written by a diaspora author, the Jewish martyrs who resist the Hellenizing persecutor Antiochus are several times explicitly said to be speaking in their 'ancestral language', more probably referring to Hebrew than to Aramaic.[68] For Josephus, language is part of Jewish identity, both positively and negatively; the choice of language for particular purposes can matter, even if his undifferentiated use of the term *hebraisti* does not allow us to judge which of the two closely related languages he has in mind at any moment, Hebrew or the Aramaic of Jerusalem and Galilee.[69]

In succeeding generations, Hebrew was a functioning and indeed developing elite language, promoted, as a language of scholarship, to the elevated status of 'holy tongue' among the Rabbis of Palestine.[70] According to a widely cited dictum of Rabbi Me'ir, speaking in the 'holy tongue' ranked with residence in the holy land and recital of the *shema* morning and evening in assuring a person's place in the world to come.[71] The history of the Hebrew language is a continuum, with the intermediate forms of Mishnaic Hebrew developing as a largely written variety out of late biblical Hebrew, in circumstances not entirely clear to us. As for spoken Hebrew, a strong body of opinion now holds that it was in daily use alongside Aramaic during the Second Temple period in Palestine.[72] In any event, even in periods of complete cessation of its use in speech, Hebrew has been fostered as a

---

[66] Campbell 1999.
[67] In brief, P. Alexander 1999a: 73–5. For a longer overview of the role of Hebrew in the period, Sáenz-Badillos 1993: 112–21.
[68] van Henten 1999.
[69] See the discussion in Rajak 2002, Appendix 1: 230–2.
[70] P. Alexander 1999a.
[71] Sifre Deut. 333, Finkelstein p. 383, and parallel texts.
[72] So Sáenz-Badillos 1993; Bar Asher 1998; P. Alexander 1999a.

living *written* language, for personal as well as public communication among the learned, and at times for secular purposes too. Biblical Hebrew, be it noted, is largely intelligible to users of later Hebrew (including the contemporary language) in spite of a great expansion of vocabulary and of syntactical development.

Yet Alexandria was not Judaea. On the common assumption that Hebrew was altogether forgotten in Alexandrian Jewry within a very few generations, the proposition that Septuagint translation style continued for any length of time as a route to retaining a stake in the traditional Hebrew language would be difficult to sustain. But was Hebrew really forgotten? Many languages do indeed give way and die in the face of stronger forces that are able to engulf them. In our world, the tragedy is occurring on a daily basis. A spoken language may be lost to a family group within a generation, certainly within two. Equally languages can resist cultural pressure, and language retention, partial or complete, can be understood as part of a strategy for maintaining, or reasserting group identity, whether used as a daily means of communication or whether carrying some sort of iconic status. As Goodblatt puts it, 'for people who identified as Jews Hebrew was always "their language" in some sense'.[73] And we have nowhere near enough evidence to declare that Hebrew just vanished for the great Alexandrian community in Second Temple times. A few scholars have cautiously stood back from this assumption.[74] And, on investigation, the evidence for the disappearance of the Hebrew language in the face of Greek is not as strong as might be supposed. On the southern border of fifth-century Egypt under Persian rule, the Jewish members of the military garrison on the island of Elephantine used Aramaic as their spoken and written language, for both official and informal purposes. Hebrew had been still alive in the last years of the kingdom of Judah, yet no Hebrew has been found among the Elephantine documents. This seems worrying. But Elephantine is not the appropriate model for us. The uniformity of this military group, and the linguistic affinity of Aramaic to Hebrew both serve to differentiate this case from that of Ptolemaic Alexandria.[75] In addition, the particular character of the three archives

---

[73] Goodblatt 2006: 69.
[74] Treu 1973; Hengel 1974: 62; 101; Kasher 1985: 5.
[75] Porten 1968: 33, n. 27.

found at Elephantine (one family dossier and two sets of communal records) limits the significance of the findings. It is worth emphasizing that the editor of the documents, Bezalel Porten, concludes that the absence of positive evidence for the use of Hebrew is by no means proof that the language was forgotten at Elephantine.

Can we obtain any guidance from a case closer to home, that of the philosopher and expounder of scripture Philo, as well-educated a Jew as one might find in Alexandria, albeit one who flourished nearly three centuries after the dramatic date of *Aristeas*? He deserves our momentary attention because of the interest which has long been shown in the question of his knowledge or ignorance of Hebrew. Samuel Sandmel set out the parameters of the problem in 1978, and they have not changed much. Most of the discussion revolves around the 651 etymologies which Philo employs as an exegetical tool. While working somewhat in the fashion of the Stoic allegorizers, he relies for the most part not on Greek but on Hebrew meanings: Jerusalem means 'vision of peace', Jordan means 'descent', Judah means 'praise to the Lord', Benjamin means 'son of days', Eliezer means 'God is my helper', Laban means 'white'. On the one hand, a considerable knowledge of Hebrew would be required were they to be fresh minted, for most of these meanings cannot be extracted from the Septuagint. On the other hand, critics point to a number of apparent errors and, indeed, a few of Philo's explanations are totally impenetrable.[76] Yet both positions lose their significance if Philo's etymologizing was not his independent work. Whether or not he knew Hebrew, he might reasonably have availed himself of a scholarly aid by way of a pre-prepared name list (*onomastikon*) or of some kind of glossary (*notarikon*) of the kind later absorbed into Jerome's book of interpretations of Hebrew names. Scholars have long been aware of papyri which attest to the existence of such aids, though these need not be contemporary with Philo, and they do not overlap substantially with Philo. However, conclusive proof of Philo's use of them is still lacking.[77] Going beyond the etymologies, D. W. Gooding finds it

---

[76] For a full analytical study, see Grabbe 1988.
[77] See, by contrast, Rokeah 1968, who argues that P. Oxy. 36.2745, a fragment of a list of eighteen Hebrew biblical names beginning with the letter 'i' with their meanings explained etymologically in Greek, itself probably written in the early Christian

telling that Philo's entire exegetical activity is done on the basis of Greek.[78] And Sandmel insists: 'in my work on Philo, I have not found a single instance in which he reflects either the necessity or the reality of having so checked [the original Hebrew].'[79] Against these observations, it is worth pointing out that the very use of etymologies from the Hebrew suggests that the Hebrew source remained a reference point, an object of respect, the perceived authority. Such sentiments of profound respect are perhaps unlikely to have remained purely abstract. Harry Wolfson, whom Sandmel was challenging, founded his own position upon consideration of social realities; and he claimed that the burden is on those who want to argue that Philo lacked all knowledge of Hebrew:[80] 'It is true indeed', he wrote, 'that the Alexandrian Jews found it difficult to preserve the knowledge of Hebrew as the common possession of all the people, but there can be no doubt that provision for instruction in that language was made by them and that the more learned among them had a knowledge of it.' Suzanne Daniel also found it hard to avoid the conclusion that Philo must have known Hebrew, moved as she was by his incorporation of elements of (later) Palestinian *halakhah* and *haggadah* and convinced that this body of material could not have been transmitted at this stage in any other language.[81] On such uncertainties, there is no room for building arguments about the total loss of Hebrew among the intellectual elite of Alexandrian Jewry even in Philo's day, let alone in that of Philadelphus.

A parallel argument concerning the linguistic background to Targum, the interpretive Aramaic renderings of the synagogue readings from

---

era, not only reflects a Hellenistic compilation based on the Septuagint, but represents precisely the material that Philo used. Several blatant misinterpretations stand out even among the few surviving entries, suggesting to Rokeah failures of Hebrew understanding. On the onomastika and the three main papyri, see Grabbe 1988 15–18; 102–8 and (for sample texts) 239–42. The specific connection with Philo is tenuous. The attempted proof by Yehoshua Amir (trans. Grabbe 1988: 233–5) of Philo's dependence on a source through inconsistency in his spelling of the Greek word *perittos/perissos* is intriguing but by no means clinches the matter, at least until the possibility is excluded that the variation is a mere scribal phenomenon.

[78] Gooding and Nikiprowetzky 1983: 89–90.
[79] Sandmel 1978. Cf. Nikiprowetzky 1977: 50–96.
[80] Wolfson 1947: i. 89.
[81] On this argument, see Sandmel 1978: 110.

Torah and prophets, helps us grasp that the need for scripture in Greek does not presuppose its general unintelligibility in Hebrew. During the rabbinic period the Targum was recited by a *meturgeman* (translator) of lower status than the main reader, verse by verse (or three verses by three verses in the case of the prophetic readings) after the original. Their origins appear to go back considerably earlier. While the Targumim are conventionally supposed to have been made for synagogue-goers without Hebrew, Steven Fraade shows how the two voices will have functioned in counterpoint as a bilingual text. The Aramaic never substituted for the Hebrew, and the audience had to be attentive to both. Rabbinic texts further suggest that written Targum may have been involved in private study and in the preparation of the weekly reading, presuming the student's knowledge of both languages and his ability to move freely between the two. This pedagogic practice would in itself have served to strengthen literary bilingualism.[82] The parallel is highly suggestive, even if it is derived from a Semitic language environment and from a Jewish milieu in which the spread of rabbinic influence was on the way to making Hebrew, the language of holiness, the primary vehicle of literary production and scholarly exchange, not to mention the vehicle of their own claim to preeminence.[83] In a subsequent study, Fraade has reformulated these insights in the perspective of the modern descriptive translation theory associated with the name of Gideon Toury, which emphasizes the variety of roles that a translation can play within the linguistic makeup of the 'target culture'. In this second study, the parallel with the Septuagint is explicitly indicated.[84]

For the Greek-speaking diaspora of the fifth century CE, Theodoret, a church writer of Syrian origin, noticed how Hebrew was taught to Jewish boys. Commenting on the particularity of the practice, he says that the Hebrew alphabet is learnt by adolescents in order to enable them to read the scriptures.[85] This is a revealing

---

[82] Fraade 2006b. On the delivery of Targum in the synagogues, see also P. Alexander 1985.
[83] On this development, see Chap. 9, pp. 307–8.
[84] Fraade 2006a, drawing on Toury 2005.
[85] *Quaest. In Gen.*, 10. no.61 = *PG*, 80, col. 165. Millar 2004: 18.

glimpse of an activity about which we would otherwise have had no idea. It is instructive about traditional forms of behaviour, even if no direct inference for our period may be drawn from it.

A small number of scholars have given some thought to the implications of the hypothesis that there existed a degree of bilingualism in Alexandrian Jewry. Notable among them was Chaim Rabin.[86] Bilingualism does not, of course, necessarily imply *equal* control of both languages: one may be far better known than the other: in this case, this would be Greek. Nor does bilingualism imply similar functions for the two languages—many bilingual situations are 'diglossic', where each language has its own function, in a hierarchy.[87] It is reasonable, indeed, to posit the existence of a measure of trilinguality among Greek-speaking Jews, with Aramaic, the middle eastern *lingua franca* over so many centuries, constantly in the background.[88]

LANGUAGE AND CULTURAL RESISTANCE

Could an internal imperative then have dictated this unexpected way of 'going Greek'? We are now ready to put forward a positive proposal: that the very character of this special language in itself served from the beginning as a means of self-identifying, with a primary ethnic indicator, the language of the patria, and self-distancing from Alexandrian society. Absorption into the world of Greek expression was a fact which the 'consumers' of the translation pragmatically took on board but around which they also drew lines.

---

[86] Rabin 1968. Horbury 1994: 17 envisages 'a small scale knowledge of Hebrew in connection with the Bible and prayer', increasing in late antiquity. See also Vergote 1938; Silva 1980; Baumgarten 2002; and remarks in *LEH*, p. x (Introduction).

[87] For definitions, Adams 2003: 3–8.

[88] On the survival of Aramaic in Ptolemaic Alexandria, see Horbury 1994. Fraade 1992 discusses the multilingual world of Jewish Palestine as the background to Targum, and esp. the survival of Hebrew alongside Aramaic. See Le Déaut 1984: 164–5, with further references in nn. 86 and 87, and Joosten 2003 for the possible influence of Aramaic on particular Septuagint renderings, something which Jerome had already noticed.

In other words, Septuagint language in its nature, with its deliberate mirroring of Hebrew balance, syntactic patterns, and semantic structures (even where there is not a one-to-one equivalence) reflects a kind of recalcitrance, a reluctance to accede totally to a Hellenizing 'project', which by the same token could not be ignored. Cultural adaptation went only so far. This contrasts with the 'dissimilation'—emphasizing of differences—which Sacha Stern sees as characteristic of the early Rabbis, who markedly avoided overt cultural appropriation.[89] What is involved in the Hellenistic diaspora is a response to linguistic imperialism which promotes language maintenance not in opposition to, but within, acculturation. Their special Greek, by respecting the source language of the text, serves as an assertion of identity and of the value of tradition for the text's owners. Naomi Seidman speaks of a later Jewish literal translation, that of Aquila, as a 'form of resistance, an overturning of the Greek values he also mirrors...an attempt to trace a Jewish–Greek space, manipulating...Greek to Jewish advantage.'[90] This overtly post-colonial assessment has turned out to be singularly apt for the original Alexandrian translation too. We have noted that Septuagint Greek might have been explicable in other terms—primitive translation technique, respect for the sanctity of the source version, or the educational need for a 'crib'. But we have been obliged to conclude that none of these interpretations offers by itself a satisfactory account.

Since a translation, like any other cultural artefact, is a product of its society or societies, it is reasonable to seek an explanation of the Septuagint translation language in these terms. As a type, the translation falls not within the category which 'domesticates' the source text to the new language but rather within that of so-called 'foreignizing' translations—a term applicable even where the source language is also in some sense the translators' own. Translators who adopt this latter approach express a respectful awareness of the ultimately unbridgeable distance between two cultures. They do this through their unwillingness to compromise more than is absolutely unavoidable the structures and forms of the source language in favour of a

---

[89] Stern 1994: 174–98.
[90] Seidman 2006: 123. For Aquila, see Chap. 9, pp. 290–4.

successful acclimatization to the target language. In advocating 'foreignizing' as against 'transparent' translation in a modern context, Lawrence Venuti's history of translation strikes a blow against what he calls the 'ethnic violence' of the process. The 'foreignizing' solution to the dilemma of translation gained attractiveness at the coming of modern nationalism in the Romantic period, with its emphasis on the vital link between the spirit of the nation and the nation's inherited (or supposedly inherited) language. While Schleiermacher is the thinker primarily associated with these ideas, the complexities of an imaginary satiric dialogue of 1798 by Schlegel will most aptly illustrate the point.[91] When the Frenchman in this dialogue cites favourably the precedent of Hellenic cultural imperialism, the German speaker, who takes the nationalist view still, surprisingly, does not entirely gainsay him. It is inconceivable for the German to remove the Greeks, the very model of perfection, from their pedestal. The chosen model could not be more to our purpose. We see how the issues can be retrojected without difficulty into the realities of the ancient world. In classical antiquity, the Greeks 'domesticated' and absorbed the foreign just as the Frenchman in the dialogue wants to do. The other side is what interests us: for a subject ethnic group which holds its own language as a key marker of identity, and for whom translation is none the less a necessity, 'foreignization' is self-protection against imperialism.[92] The Romantic view of the nation is not a prerequisite for this dynamic to operate.

In principle, of course, a translation must be readable to be functional, and one would therefore suppose that while translators may stretch language to its limits, few can afford in practice to do serious violence to the acceptable usage of the language into which they are translating. In fact, however, attachment to a source (even a completely secular one) has propelled some theoreticians and even translators into extremes not unlike the choice made by the Septuagint translators. Notable among them is A. F. Newman, who produced in

---

[91] Translation of Schlegel 1798, quoted by Venuti (1995: 108) to whose summary of these ideas I am indebted.

[92] This is not to say that 'foreignizing' could not equally be part of an imperialist project. For the German Romantic nationalists, translations that were esp. true to the original could, paradoxically, potentially bring the whole world's goods into the German ambit. See Venuti 1995: 109–17.

1856 a densely archaic English Iliad written in ballad meter. Newman's liberal principles led him overtly to embrace what he saw as the non-Englishness of Homer, to dismiss any notion 'that whatever has a foreign colour is undesirable and is even a grave defect' and, furthermore, to ensure that the qualities of the original should be made available also to the non-learned classes. He therefore sought 'to retain every peculiarity of the original . . . with the greater care, the more foreign it happens to be'. And he declared that 'the English translator should desire the reader always to remember that his work is an imitation'. But the result was far from pleasing to reviewers, who criticized both this and his Horace in terms which might well have been applied to the translators of the Septuagint.[93] For a quarter of a century the pejorative term to 'Newmanize' became a part of the critical vocabulary. In 1861, Matthew Arnold's lectures 'On Translating Homer' insisted, against Newman, that 'the translator must without scruple sacrifice, where it is necessary, verbal fidelity to his original, rather than run any risk of producing, by literalness, an odd and unnatural effect'. This debate, however, was complicated by the particular means of 'foreignizing' which Newman had adopted, an artificial archaism which could be deemed ill-conceived and inappropriate quite apart from its stylistic defects. The creation of 'a natural habitat for the alien presence' through an aged diction was in fact not uncommon, as George Steiner has observed, among English translations of Homer.[94]

The modern history of translation is littered with experiments in fidelity that have sunk under the weight of their own unintelligibility, whatever their theoretical interest.[95] Walter Benjamin, in his short, much-quoted, but extremely complex essay 'the Task of the

---

[93] Venuti 1995: 125.
[94] Steiner 1975: 342. In Steiner's view, Benjamin Jowett's versions of Greek prose authors stand out among translators of Classical texts to adopt this approach.
[95] An astonishing example is a modernist, supposedly homophonic and completely unintelligible Catullus done by the Zukovskys and commented on by Venuti 1995: 214–24. More important, but also because of its extensive commentary, was Nabokov's 'literal' Eugene Onegin, of which the author wrote: 'to my ideal of literalism I have sacrificed everything: elegance, euphony, clarity, good taste and even grammar.' See Steiner 1975: 315 and Barnstone 1990: 48–9, who points out that, this exercise apart, Nabokov was a prolific and effective translator.

Translator' conjured up the theoretical construct of an ideal translation which adhered totally to the parent syntax. For him the perfect prototype was to be found precisely, and exclusively, in an interlinear version of the scriptures.[96] But the ideal was, he declared, also an impossibility.

The Septuagint translators occupy a distinguished place in the line of seekers-for-the-impossible. Their product was far beyond a mechanical school text. But neither was it a doctrinaire exercise. The translation language they forged worked and survived because it did a job. Inscribed within the language itself is an assertion of communal independence which made it possible for the translations to serve as a vehicle for quiet cultural resistance. And in the following chapter we shall see how this resistance is expressed through content as well as form.

I have framed in this manner our encounter with Septuagint language because it serves to emphasize the point I wish to make, that we see the sense in this creation when we view it as part of a constellation of choices. This choice is the perhaps more gradual but none the less deliberate sequel to the initial decision, as I have reconstructed it, of cooperating with the regime in the making of a translation. Both decisions can be related to the situation in which the Jews found themselves in Alexandria. They dealt effectively with the challenge. Recourse to a technique that was knowingly, and constructively, Hebraized paid homage to Hebrew in the very process of 'going Greek', each of them crucial elements in the constructed identity of an Alexandrian Jew. It is indeed paradoxical that, while the acquisition of an important translation might seem prima facie to be destructive to the survival of the original text and of the source language, the process may in fact work positively. If the translation is perceived as, as happened here, to merit constant extension, improvement, and correction, there has to be a scholarly class to bring this about and that class at least will foster contact with the original sources.

---

[96] Benjamin, in translation by H. Zohn 1968: 82; published Venuti: 2000: 23. The often-cited original, 'Die Aufgabe des Übersetzers' was published by Benjamin in Heidelberg in 1923 as an introduction to the German translation of Baudelaire's *Tableaux parisiens*. The translation by Zohn, ironically enough, sometimes distorts the meaning of the original. For an exposition which takes account of the many twists in Benjamin's thinking, see Barnstone 1990: 240–59.

Language and Identity 157

But why *this* language? It is one thing tentatively to suggest that the 'feel' of the Hebrew is evoked by it, another to indicate how this happens through the chosen translation technique.

I suggest that one way in which this purposeful choice makes an impact on the modern reader is on the auditory level, and this will have been very much more marked in the ancient context. The profound dependence of biblical verse and prose on the aesthetics of sound, the 'oral register', in the Hebrew Bible has been explored by Susan Niditch,[97] and linked to the position of the biblical authors at the intersection of oral and scribal cultures. Arie van der Kooij identifies reading aloud, *anagnōsis*, as an essential element in the method of interpretation practised in Jewish scribal circles.[98] None of this is to deny that scripture's main mode of transmission among Jews, at any rate since the Persian period, was via texts written by scribes.[99] Martin Jaffee ascribes to the Rabbis a process of 're-oralization' of a culture that had come to make heavy use of the written text.[100] Interestingly, the rabbinic appellation for the Bible in its entirety, *mikra*, comes from a root meaning 'to cry out, call, summon'; the noun appears frequently in the Bible to describe a convocation of the people for the primary purpose of hearing a reading. This contrasts with terms such as 'Bible' (from *ta biblia*—books) or the English 'scripture' which of course means 'writing'. For most people most of the time through most of antiquity the Bible was a heard text. Large tracts of the Bible could only have been known to many through memorization: Jewish rates of literacy may well not have been much different from those in the wider population, and it is even argued by Catherine Hezser that they were on the low side of the norm for Graeco-Roman societies.[101] The literacy of

---

[97] Niditch 1996.
[98] See the remarks on p. 49 on the role of orality even in the transmission of what was a written text par excellence. Cf. van der Kooij and van der Toorn 1998: 219–22.
[99] On the scribes of the Persian period, see Schaper 1999. On the consistent importance of writing in the Jewish conception of scripture from at least the fifth century BCE, Sawyer 1999: 50–8.
[100] Jaffee 2001: 17. And see also P. Alexander 2003.
[101] Hezser 2001 is a comprehensive investigation of Jewish literacy in this period.

many was in any case limited or partial.[102] For everyone, including the highly literate, there were major difficulties in unrolling and keeping open with both hands a scroll of sufficient size to contain even a single biblical book (as would have been the norm). The general absence of verse-dividers and even word division made reading very slow: there are some signs of their appearance towards the end of the Second Temple period BCE.[103] As if all that were not enough, the production of scrolls whether from woven and glued papyrus or from animal skins, and even the manufacture of ink, involved lengthy and costly processes.[104] Thus, outside the liturgical context, citation from memory was essential for scholars before the era of the great medieval Jewish codices. In this respect, Jewish readers and writers were in the same position as all other Graeco-Roman intellectuals. Feats of memory which to us seem extraordinary were probably not uncommon. The epitomator who turned Jason of Cyrene's five-volume book into 2 Maccabees says that he is offering convenience, *eukopia*, to those who wish to commit the whole of the history to memory.[105] It is suspected that Paul knew very large portions of the Greek Bible by heart.[106] All this implies a relationship through sound.

A modern poet, John Hollander, writing from the perspective of the King James Version's English, captures so well a modern English reader's impression of the Hebrew Bible's 'song' as to deserve a substantial quotation:

> The verse of the Hebrew Bible is
> strange; the meter in Psalms
> and Proverbs perplexes.
> It is not a matter of numbers, no
> counting of beats or syllables.
> Its song is a music of matching, its
> rhythm a kind of paralleling.
> One half-line makes an assertion;

---

[102] This is a central argument in Harris's study (1989); see esp. pp. 5–21. For the resulting debate, see Hezser 2001: 18–26.
[103] There are some traces of them in the Minor Prophets Scroll: see Kraft 2003.
[104] See Roberts 1983, and, for the Jewish milieu, Haran 1983 and Haran 1985.
[105] 2 Macc. 2: 25.
[106] So Wagner 2002: 20–8.

> the other part paraphrases it;
> sometimes a third part
> will vary it.
> An abstract statement meets with
> its example, yes, the way a wind
> runs through the tree's moving
> leaves.
> One river's water is heard on
> another's shore; so did this
> Hebrew verse form carry across
> into English.[107]

Probably the first thing one notices about Septuagint Greek is the unremitting chime of an accumulation of phrases or clauses tied together by the connective 'and': *kai* (representing biblical Hebrew's basic paratactic structure, with *kai* representing *ve-*). We saw a small example from this in the sample passage from Exodus 3. In Greek, the replacement of at least some of these strings by combinations of subordinate and main clause would be expected. As Anneli Aejmelaeus points out,[108] the reader divines by intuition that something is going on. In fact, that process is more complicated than is immediately apparent, for she is able to show that in reality 'it is not the degree of parataxis that matters', since non-Septuagint Greek can also be highly paratactic. What is special about the Septuagint is its concomitant extremely sparing use of the Greek particle *de* and scarcity of participial constructions, which take the translation a good deal further away from the flow of any normal Greek.

Together with this feature come other audible effects evocative of biblical Hebrew, some of which were present in my two examples and in my earlier description.[109] Repetition serves to attract attention, as do linguistic irregularities. So the reader will be affected when these features are combined in the translators' reproduction of the Hebrew infinitive-absolute-plus-verb construction which I described earlier.[110] More than one method is used to address this aspect of the

---

[107] Hollander 2001: 26, quoted in Bloom 2007: 22.
[108] Aejmelaeus 1982 is a book-length study of Septuagint parataxis.
[109] See above, pp. 131–3.
[110] For this feature, see above, p. 129.

biblical language.[111] On a few occasions, the translation (Greek verb plus adverb) is just a normal Greek construction which renders the meaning adequately. But, mostly, special devices are called into play. In two instances (out of the entire Hebrew Bible) an exact Greek equivalent actually appears, with a notable triple instance at Jeremiah 44: 25 (LXX 51: 25): 'And do we shall do... and remain you will remain... and do you will do'.[112] The most common solutions found by the translators are less 'literal' than the Jeremiah type, but they still stretch Greek usage. We would describe them as idiosyncratic outside the Septuagint context: 'with theft I stole'; 'with witness he witnessed'; 'with stones he will be stoned'; 'with blessings you will bless'; 'returning I will come'; 'blessing I will bless you'.[113] Finally, a surprisingly persistent aural impact is made by what is linguistically a relatively trivial feature: both prose and verse are characterized by the ubiquity of those redundant possessive pronouns.[114]

It has been from time to time observed that homophony, similar sound, is an occasional reason for the choice of a particular Greek equivalent.[115] So, for example, in two places *(kata)skēnoun* is adopted for speaking of God choosing to 'settle' the people in the Land, rendering the Hebrew *shakhan*.[116] The process is especially interesting where the matching of meanings is defective, as when *tokh*, 'oppression', is rendered as *tokos*, usury.[117] The effect is usually through the matching of consonants, and it is unquestionably aural. But the clear and indisputable instances are not numerous enough to allow us to make a great deal of a phenomenon which, in any case, could only have affected those who anyway knew the Hebrew scriptures rather well.

But we have seen enough to be sure that, while the actual sound of the Greek sentences may not exactly replicate the Hebrew,

---

[111] The following analysis and examples are derived mainly from Tov 1999: 247–56.

[112] In this verse, too, the impression is enhanced by the intertwined exact rendering of verbs linked to their cognate nouns.

[113] Gen. 40: 15; 43: 3; Num. 23: 11; Gen. 18: 10; 22: 17. Thus the two types of solution are either, verb plus (usually cognate) noun; or, even more oddly, Greek participle followed by finite verb of the same Greek noun.

[114] They represent the Hebrew possessive suffix.

[115] Examples, analysis, and a critique of earlier studies in Tov 1999: 165–82. Cf. Barr 1985.

[116] Num. 14: 30; Ps. 37 (36): 3.

[117] Ps. 55 (54): 12 and Ps. 72 (71): 14.

reminiscent rhythms ring out through it. It is a question often of prominent and audible patterns which function as stand-ins for their Hebrew counterparts. The translators manage to fulfil Walter Benjamin's requirement that 'a translation, instead of resembling the meaning of the original, must lovingly and in detail incorporate the original's mode of significance, thus making the original and the translation recognizable fragments of a greater language, just as fragments are part of a vessel'.[118]

Furthermore, substantial variation within the general pattern among groups of books or within books, which would seem to reflect different translators, demonstrates the translation language to be also a flexible tool. Minute investigation of Septuagint translation technique has begun to yield the rudimentary profiles of these nameless workers, who can be individuated by a range of criteria, such as the extent of intertextuality to which they are disposed, and their level of concern with solving knotty problems in the Hebrew, rather than according to the more familiar but very slippery measure of 'literalness'. Anneli Aejmelaeus concludes from her statistical analysis of clause connection in selected samples of Septuagint Greek that 'free renderings' are 'like fingerprints that the translators have left behind them. By these fingerprints it is possible to get to know them and to describe their working habits, their actual relationship with the original and their talent as translators'.[119] These anonymous figures faced the usual decisions that translators have to make about sentence structure, linkages, and individual words. A few manifest strong aesthetic impulses—the Job translation has even been reckoned elegant and the Isaiah translation sophisticated; others, it is fair to say, show limited interest in the artistry of their writing. The Psalms translator, on whom many others draw for vocabulary and for quotation, is surprisingly faithful to his original, and because of this he is apt, frustratingly, to flatten the poetry and weaken the power of the Hebrew expression. That emerged all too clearly from the second sample we looked at earlier, the arresting opening of Hebrew Psalm 114.[120]

---

[118] Benjamin trans. by Zohn 1968: 78.
[119] Aejmelaus 1987: 362.
[120] See p. 133.

VOCABULARY AND HISTORY

It is a paradox that the translators' conservatism allowed at the same time a highly creative usage of Greek. Adherence to a relatively close translation went together with word-formation and semantic innovation on an unusually large scale. This is a distinctive cultural practice of the first importance. To an extent, the translators were able to fulfil Walter Benjamin's stipulation that faithful translators expand and deepen the language into which they are translating (which he supposes will be their own language) by means of the language of the source.[121] The fruits of this achievement are rather familiar, for this inventiveness has given us terms which are still alive in the word stock of many languages today. They have travelled various routes, often via that Jewish–Greek channel of the New Testament, and sometimes via borrowings into the Latin of the Vulgate.[122] 'Diaspora', 'proselyte', 'idol', 'ecclesiastical', 'devil', 'hagiography', and 'holocaust' are but a few of the English derivatives of Septuagint language. In some of these cases, especially the last, there has been a decisive shift from the Septuagintal meaning, while in others, the movement has been small.

New terminology and new meanings emerged through the courage and ingenuity shown by successive Septuagint translators in designing new tools for their trade. This repertoire was an expanding and developing resource, a central part of their translation technique. My purpose in discussing it here is not in the expectation of capturing, and still less explaining that elusive technique with all its interrelationships and permutations—that is a specialized and complex task.[123] Still less is it my purpose here to follow where such as Anneli Aejmelaeus tread, in seeking to beat a path to the workrooms of those translators. It is not possible for us to look at more than a handful of examples, and even those in brief. But an insight into the process gives us a grasp of exactly how the translators constructed a bridge

---

[121] Benjamin trans. by Zohn 1968: 80; repub. in Venuti 2000: 22.
[122] Cf. Sawyer 1999: 91–5.
[123] For current work on the subject, see Olofsson 1990b. Recent developments are summarized in Dines 2004: 52–4.

between their two worlds and in doing so created a new cultural artifact. Their language and its history are at the heart of their work, and also one of their chief successes.

It has sometimes been felt that the translation enterprise must have had smaller-scale precedents.[124] Mainly, this appears to be due to the difficulty that some have in believing that a religious Jewish community could function for even a moment in a predominantly Greek-speaking environment without putting at the very least its cultic and spiritual keywords into Greek. The coinage of terminology must therefore have come as a first and very early stage. The hypothesis seems to be unnecessary, in the light of the linguistic developments that we have already traced.[125] A pattern of trilingualism continuing over several centuries is a likely scenario. Furthermore, an elaborate conceptual vocabulary is a rarefied need, hardly called upon for most of life's requirements. And ritual observance is receptive to foreign diction. It is rather when complex material begins to be translated that the urgency of evolving systematic functional equivalents in the new language is going to arise. The translators deserve their due.

Enquiry into the changing word-stock and patterns of lexical choice permits the Greek Bible to yield up some of its secrets, but there is a warning tag attached. James Barr's classic polemic, *The Semantics of Biblical Language*,[126] had a major effect in waking scholars up to the absurdities and the hazards of the kind of approach to the study of meaning which reads group mentality into the histories of individual words. Barr engagingly exposed the presumption which underlies work of this kind, the belief that words carry an inner as well as an outer significance, thus enabling the structure of the Hebrew or of the Greek (or of any other mind) to be discerned, as it were through their respective vocabularies. Apart from the 'Humboldtian metaphysics', as Barr called them, behind such operations, they are patently vehicles of more or less explicit theological endeavour, and at worst of political ideology. Simple semantics are

---

[124] So, for example, Siegert 2001: 38, drawing upon the argument that consolidation of the Genesis vocabulary would scarcely have been possible otherwise. Dorival, Harl, and Munnich 1988: 228 gives a cautious endorsement: 'il est vraisemblable que le lexique des traducteurs n'est pas né de la seule invention des traducteurs'.

[125] See pp. 145–52.

[126] Barr 1961.

ensnared into strange forms of service. The biggest repository of such scholarship remains the prized *Theological Dictionary of the New Testament*, which remains a standard reference work, both in the original German and in English translation.[127] The purpose is made explicit in the title. Special attention goes to the key words of Christian theology, such as *pais theou* (son of God), *eucharisteō*, *hairesis*, or *apostolos*. For all their immense learning and usefulness, the extended entries tend to read as progress towards a goal. One example of many is the entry for the word *laos*, the word which, from Homeric antecedents, is taken up in the Greek Bible as the term for the people of Israel, and then subsequently in the New Testament. The *TWNT* entry, written by the anti-Semitic Hermann Strathmann, opines that the Jewish concept was diminished by the addition of the idea of chosenness and that it was left to Christianity to 'protest' and to correct the 'regression'.[128] It might be thought that a certain emphasis on the Christian material could be justified by the dictionary's academic objective, which was, after all, understanding the language of the New Testament for the 'new Israel'. Yet the original title already made it apparent that not just plain lexicography but 'sacred lexicography' (in the apt phrase employed by Wayne Meeks) was at stake, with salvation history as its goal; and today it is perfectly clear that the implications also run well beyond the sphere of theology. Meeks relentlessly exposes the links between belief, scholarship, and politics in the biography of its creator, the Protestant scholar Gerhard Kittel. The *Theological Dictionary* researched Jewish scripture in the perspective of the 'Jewish question', and in the service of the Third Reich.[129]

In this kind of ideological lexicography, the Septuagint has played a special part. It could be understood as bringing new Hebraic content to Greek words, by way of preparation for the Christian impress which they were to receive and thus to prepare the way for the new dispensation by facilitating the fusion of Judaism with

---

[127] Kittel and Friedrich 1932–79 (*TWNT*). Ten-volume English edition (*TDNT*), Kittel 1964.
[128] Highlighted by Meeks 2003: 540.
[129] Ibid., esp. 534–44.

Hellenism.[130] The objective is more innocuous but perhaps just as clear, in the asides of C. H. Dodd, whose series of studies in *The Bible and the Greeks* was, along with Kittel, a butt of Barr's assault. Dodd devoted considerable attention to the term *nomos* and his spadework is not to be dismissed. But, by way of a parting shot, after concluding it to be clear that *nomos* is 'the normal and regulative meaning' for Torah in Hellenistic Judaism and covered 'the whole of the O[ld] T[estament] use of the word', he wrote as follows:

> Thus the prophetic type of religion was obscured, and the Biblical revelation was conceived in a hard, legalistic way. In thus rendering the term, the translators are no doubt reflecting the sense in which their community read the Hebrew Bible, but their rendering helped to fix and stereotype that sense. Where thinkers bred in Hellenistic Judaism sought to escape into a religion of greater spiritual freedom and spontaneity, it was not by way of return to the prophetic idea of Torah, but by taking up a fresh attitude to religion conceived as Law.[131]

Barr's assault on such higher flights of fancy, of doctrine, or of prejudice, is deservedly a classic. His criticisms, however, may today usefully be nuanced, and his commentary on the Greek Bible's word pool, in abeyance for a generation, need not be outlawed. Thus Barr scorns interpretations of the preferred Septuagint adjective for 'holy', *hagios* (as against the regular Greek terms for 'sacred', *hieros* or *hosios*)[132] that understands its evolution as governed by a deliberate distancing from pagan cult and its language. Yet the persistence of *hagios* and its compounds, together with the striking production of

---

[130] On the use and abuse of the Judaism–Hellenism dichotomy, and on the problems of dechristianizing our narrative, see the remarks on pp. 6–9, 280–8. And for LXX as *praeparatio evangelica*, see Chap. 9, p. 287. By contrast, Meeks 2003 shows how Gerhard Kittel resisted the agenda of the history of religions school who wanted to interpret the rise of Christianity not theologically but historically, and in the context of the surrounding religious world. Kittel by contrast saw the essential task to be stripping primitive Judaism of Greek, assimilatory elements so as to return to a pure, biblical form; in *TWNT*, this task had its lexicographical counterpart.

[131] Dodd 1935: 34. For remarks on Dodd's approach to 'theologically-motivated exegesis', cf. Tov 1999: 257–69. On the term *nomos*, see Introduction, p. 22.

[132] Barr 1961: 282–5. For a highly public use of *hosios*, see Sotades' apparently widely known obscene epigram on Ptolemy II: 'You are pushing the point into an unholy (*hosiēn*) hole', quoted by Plutarch, *de Liberis Educandis*, 11a and Athenaeus, *Deipn.*, 14.621a.

neologisms such as *hagiasmos* (which appeared in our Psalms example) and *hagiasma*, do suggest that there was much more at stake than a simple requirement for the suitable equivalent for the Hebrew *qadosh*. A new web of meaning was being forged. In fact, *hagios* with its long-lived cognates, *-i/asma/ -ia/zw/-asmos/*, not only represents that Hebrew root *qadosh* and its derivatives, but also assists in the translation of at least a dozen other roots.[133] It is not a simple stereotype. Those cognates are not forms known in ordinary Greek, although the *-izw* termination is occasionally found in the classical language.[134] The root tends to connote, following its most frequent Hebrew counterpart, an object set apart either positively or negatively. The use of the neuter, in both singular and plural, to refer to the Temple, and the literal transference of the Hebrew superlative to produce the Greek formation *hagios hagiotatōn*, as a name for the Holy of Holies, are good instances of the creation of a semi-technical vocabulary. Their application to the Jerusalem Temple perhaps ensures the popularity of the *hagios* terms, which become indispensable to Philo and Josephus. The author of 4 Maccabees is particularly attached to their cognates, even coining his own. As for the standard Greek *hieron*, that is more rarely used in relation to Judaism; but it is noteworthy that 1 Esdras returns to make it a term of preference for the Jewish cult. We are almost able to trap language in the making as it moves to a new cultural context.

With suitable caution, we may now proceed to a few further, well-known examples. For the altar of the Israelites, Septuagint prefers the strange-sounding *thusiastērion* (as against *bōmos*, the obvious Greek word). Suzanne Daniel has demonstrated the consistency of this preference.[135] It is thus unsurprising that both *thusiastērion* and *hagios* emerge as value-laden terms in the New Testament. *Thusiastērion* refers to the Jewish cult but also has figurative uses in the New Testament, where we find it in Hebrews (and then in later literature).[136] Similarly,

---

[133] *hagios* and its derivatives are explored in Gehman 1954.

[134] On the problem of these causative coinages as possible equivalents to Hebrew *hi'fil* and *pi'el*, see Tov 1999: 195–202. Janse 2002: 370–5.

[135] Daniel 1966. And see further van der Kooij 2003.

[136] See Meecham's commentary on *Aristeas* in Meecham 1935: 193. Cf. Bar-Kochva's attribution of special significance to Pseudo-Hecataeus' choice of *bōmos*, not the expected *thusiastērion* in Bar-Kochva 1996.

holokautōma, the word used for what is sacrificed or for the sacrifice itself, representing *zevach, mincha,* or *'olah,* is a new noun which appears for the first time in the Greek Bible, and which was in due course to be adopted into Jewish–Greek writing and freely used by Josephus: only the verbal form, *holokauteō*, appears in classical Greek. We must of course bear in mind that only a small proportion of what was written in classical and Hellenistic Greek now survives, and we have therefore to admit the possibility that the noun too appeared in Greek literature now lost to us. Conclusions in this area can never be more than tentative.

To take a different type of case, in the realm of God–man relations, we find a previously known but unexpected Greek word, *diathēkē*, annexed by the translators to be the standard equivalent for *berit*, the supremely important 'covenant' between God and Israel that was made with Noah and with Abraham, that in the latter case promised possession of the Land of Israel, that was invoked and reiterated many times, and that every generation entered into through each and every circumcision. This lexical adoption is made in preference to the related word *sunthēkē*, which would be a more natural choice; it had the advantage of standing apart from everyday usage. *Sunthēkē* would probably have been the ordinary Greek word at this time to describe a compact between parties, while *diathēkē* normally means 'will' or 'testament'. The translators did not invent an entirely new sense, but they rather drew on something already there in a minor way: 'agreement' is a possible sense for *diathēkē* already in classical and apparently in Hellenistic coinage.[137] The result of their choice, then, is the creation of what is virtually a technical term, an old word given a new, specialized meaning. The term frequently appears in the composite *kibōtos tēs diathēkēs*, 'ark of the covenant'. Even more interestingly, from as early as Genesis, the old Greek is occasionally willing to describe agreements other than the covenant with Israel, and even agreements among Israel's enemies, by the term *diathēkē*.[138]

[137] At Aristophanes, *Birds*, 440, the sense seems to be an 'agreement'. See Lee 1983 for koine evidence.

[138] For example, Gen. 21: 27 and Ps. 82 (83): 6: observation and examples from Tov 1999: 92–3. But it does not seem right to describe this as a 'second dimension', i.e., secondary usage, given the existence of occasional Classical and Hellenistic precedents.

By contrast, the later translators, Aquila and Symmachus, are equally comfortable with the less-specialized *suntheke*—in Aquila's case, it would appear, even more so.[139] It is unsurprising that for Josephus *diatheke* has only the familiar sense of 'will' or 'legacy': one of the chief purposes of the rewriting of the Bible in his *Antiquities* was to produce a version of scripture that read quite differently from the Septuagint, composed in high (or reasonably high) literary Greek. The ark itself is for him simply *kibōtos*, a box. Josephus, moreover, avoids calling the covenant with God *suntheke*: he either uses circumlocutions or else, mostly, chooses not to talk about it at all.[140]

This open-ended category of septuagintal coinages and distinctive terms are varied even in their origins: as we have just seen, some are neologisms, new inventions; others are words with some slight classical Greek antecedents; some, again, are quite ordinary Greek words used in new ways, described as 'semantic neologisms'. In the Septuagint itself, we have to reckon with the very marked variation in practice between different translators, and sometimes the patterns are quite intricate. A notable example is that *qahal*, the people of Israel as an assembled body, is translated exclusively by the word *sunagōgē* in the first four books of Moses and largely so in the prophets, but exclusively by *ekklēsia* in all the historical writings and virtually exclusively so in Psalms. This seems puzzling, but we must allow that different translators simply have their own preferences and that there are not always explanations to be found. We may not conclude, simply on this basis, that the translators of the prophets, or of any of the prophetic books, shared a background with the translators of the tetrateuch. It may simply be that the former modelled their style on that of the latter; at what level and by virtue of what kind of motivation such a choice will have been made, it is often beyond our capacity even to speculate.

In similar fashion, the translation of 'slave' or 'servant', represented by the one Hebrew word *'eved*, wavers between *pais* and *doulos*. The

---

[139] For Aquila's methods, see Chap. 9, pp. 290–4. For analysis of this and other political and legal terms, the 'Demetrios' database of the AHRC Greek Bible Project is a specialized tool: see <http://www.rdg.ac.uk/lxx/>.

[140] Feldman 1998: 154. Josephus plays down to some extent the covenantal dimension of the Land: see Attridge 1976: 78–92 and for the debate on this topic Amaru 1994; Spilsbury 1998: 70–1.

translations of the books of Job and Proverbs have sometimes been ascribed to the same person, but a close analysis has revealed a dramatic dichotomy in lexical preferences.[141] 'Fear' [of God] is *phobos* nineteen times in Proverbs, only twice in Job, where we find that *theosebeia* ('piety') is used, along with cognates of the verb *deidein*, 'to be afraid'. In the spectrum of words meaning 'wisdom', 'understanding', 'knowledge', naturally indispensable and very frequent in books of so-called Wisdom Literature, the Hebrew *da'at* is rendered by *aisthēsis* ('discernment') on twenty-two occasions in Proverbs, but entirely by other words in Job; while *binah* or *tevunah* are *phronēsis* ('judgement') fifteen times in Proverbs, yet only twice in Job. To cap it all, that old favourite, *paideia*, standard Greek for 'education', which is so essential a part of Ben Sira's wisdom vocabulary (and about which so much nonsense has been written), makes twenty-eight appearances in Proverbs, twenty-two of them as a rendering of *musar* (traditional ethical teaching); on the other hand *paideia* simply does not figure in Job, where it is also to be expected. Such divergences of preference are a very marked feature of Septuagint as a corpus, and a peculiarly difficult feature to explain with any confidence. The dates, locations, and preferences of translators and their communities must all have something to do with them. The line between conscious and unconscious choice, between what was intended and what could not be avoided is not one to press. And within the realm of intention, how are we to decide between exegesis, theology, literary taste, outside influence, and even sheer perversity, as motivating factors?

As to the subsequent history of the reshaped vocabulary, that too is varied. Some words simply do not seem to make the grade within surviving Greek–Jewish literature: they figure scarcely or not at all. And there were winners and losers among words. There are a few which vanish from sight. The literary register of a text was evidently a material factor in the vocabulary which its author accepted or rejected. It would seem that some features of the characteristic Septuagint translation language simply did not sit well in the newfangled later Greek–Jewish literature, where stylistic aims tended to matter

[141] Gammie 1987.

and literary aspirations were higher. Sometimes, variants of original Septuagint words seem to have come on stage later on, and to have fared better than the original term. Indeed, there appear, as far as we can tell, to have been several waves, or generations, of vocabulary formation. The Greek Daniel (in both versions), Esther, and 1 Esdras reflect the evolution of what might be described as a second stratum of special vocabulary.[142] Greek terms virtually absent from the Pentateuch, and scarcely represented in the other books, may well be found as common currency in this group; they may well recur in some of the translated apocryphal books, especially 1 Maccabees (but also to a lesser extent in the Second and Fourth Books of the Maccabees), Judith, and Tobit. New coinages also still arise. A nice example is the clutch of interrelated, almost onomatopoeic negative terms to connote impiety and impious action, *dussebein, dussebeia, dussebēma, dussebeis*, obviously invented as extra-strong antitheses to the central Jewish–Greek term *eusebeia* (for various Hebrew terms), which appear in 1 Esdras, and in 2 and 3 Maccabees. *Asebeia*, by contrast, had been favoured by the Septuagint prophets.[143] It is also significant that independent coinage outside the Septuagint as we have it was taking place from an early date. Thus the term *exagōgē* for Exodus was adopted by the Alexandrian Jewish writer Ezekiel 'the tragedian', though the translator of Exodus uses only the verbal form *exagō*.[144]

One contributor to all these developments was no doubt changing fashion in the use of the Greek common language, the *koinē dialektē*, in the wider world—itself a topic on which there is much for linguists still to discover. That distinctive predilection for coining new words may be common to this period, and not, as it may seem to us, unique to the Septuagint. Dorothy Thompson makes the connection and gives a number of parallels:

---

[142] Talshir's (1999) study of 1 Esdras is a valuable resource for the analysis of this vocabulary. She believes, however, that the translator did not know existing translations of Ezra-Nehemiah and Chronicles, and thus was not consciously diverging from them.
[143] Cf. Talshir 1999: 265.
[144] *Bible d'Alexandrie*, p. 26: Exod. (Introduction).

The complex vocabulary and syntax of both official communications and legal writings suggest the development of both a legal and a bureaucratic jargon. Existing Greek vocabulary was extended in meaning (*skepē* for example coming to mean not 'cover' but 'patronage' or 'protection') and the use of unusual vocabulary, of abstract nouns for instance (*sykophantia*, 'sycophancy', *philautia*, 'selfishness', or *antilēpsis*, 'defence or succour') or colourful and unusual verbs (*skullesthai*, *diaseiein*, or *perispān* are all terms used for 'to harm'), in legal and bureaucratic writing suggests a professional system in which training and practice served to complicate and even to mystify. If some of the bureaucratic words are found also in contemporary literary usage, in the Septuagint or in Polybius, suggesting their adoption into the koine of the Hellenistic world, the same fortunately cannot be said of the complicated sentence structure which combines with linguistic usage to typify the documents of the Ptolemaic administration.[145]

But if the translators availed themselves of the linguistic customs and fashions of their day, they also showed resourcefulness and even audacity in developing and extending them. Perhaps the influence was not entirely one-way. Might we imagine that the Septuagint translators' creative talent in deploying language could somewhere at some time have served as an example to those outside the Jewish community who needed to find new ways of saying things in a new society?

To understand the lexical choices made by the Septuagint translators as dictated purely by the linguistic need to find an intelligible equivalent for everything in the Hebrew would scarcely be tenable. Whatever the initial drive behind them, the characteristic Septuagintal neologisms, in both the abstract and concrete spheres, allowed the expression of more layers of sense and suggestion than standard, 'correct' Greek usage could have done. It would be a great loss altogether to exclude explorations of Septuagint vocabulary as a tool for understanding their world. The ascription of new semantic range and associations to the existing Greek lexicon is a highly distinctive feature of their work. Its innovative flair deserves recognition. The further extension of this vocabulary into Hellenistic-Jewish writing is a fertile field for further exploration.[146] On both sides now,

---

[145] Thompson 1994: 77.
[146] In relation to Philo, Cohen 2002 makes an interesting start.

there is general acceptance that, ultimately, profiles of the distinctive Septuagintal terminology will extend further than its immediate context, and well outside Jewish Greek. And, beyond that, there is the larger framework to consider: the self-referential functioning of the 'great code' of the Hebrew Bible, in which books, verses, and expressions are interrelated in multiple relationships, marked by both extensive repetition and self-conscious divergence.

FUNCTION AND EVOLUTION

A community of observant Jews is exposed to that code in more than one way; and we should expect that to be so however different were the circumstances for Greek-speaking Jews. What is more, the central activities of Judaism are intertwined and scarcely separable: Josephus in *Against Apion* speaks of the practice of regular Torah reading as a learning process. Targum, the Aramaic translation with its midrashic expansion and explanation, is an educational tool. In later Judaism, worship is also study, and study is worship. This provides a useful perspective in which to imagine *how* the Greek translation language would have made its impact. There is no question of alternatives here. Both liturgical and educational settings must have played their parts. In gatherings of Jews, be it within synagogues or elsewhere, Torah readings for the festivals and probably on the Sabbath will have been taking place from the beginning of our period. Jutta Leonhardt emphasizes that for Philo teaching was the most important activity, rather than reading *per se*.[147] The institutionalization of readings from the prophets (in the Jewish, wider sense) came later, attested only in the period of the writing of Acts (presumably the end of the first century CE). The attempt by Thackeray to track the evolution of the later books of the Greek Bible translation by matching up internal evidence with the later cycles of *haftarot* (weekly prophetic synagogue readings) was therefore not successful, though it was an

---

[147] See Perrot 1988, McKay 1994, and Leonhardt 2001.

interesting failure.[148] The material evidence[149] could in principle give us clues, for the overall dimensions of a scroll can sometimes be deduced from the column width in a fragment, and that in turn might give some indication of its function: a large scroll is less likely to belong to a private individual and more likely to have had some public role. Sadly, the pieces are neither sufficiently substantial nor plentiful enough for sensible conclusions to be drawn from them.

A possibility to consider is that Torah readings were done in Hebrew and Greek together. Since the origins of the Aramaic interpretative translation known as Targum, so important in late antiquity, are also lost in mists of history, we cannot be confident that incipient Targumic practice could have provided some sort of exemplar. Nevertheless, the public translation mentioned in connection with Ezra's reading to the people from the scroll of God's teaching (Nehemiah 8: 8) is sometimes taken to be the first appearance of Targum, which therefore would have been in operation as early as the fifth century BCE. Such a role for the Greek translation would have been feasible even if the Septuagint acquired an independent status within a relatively short time, thus differentiating itself from Targum (which had always to be read in conjunction with the Hebrew).[150] In education, we must think of group study by adults, as in the Hellenistic disciple group,[151] or of the Qumran community model, or that of the scribal school or the *bet midrash*, as much as of children's schooling. In all these contexts, reading aloud, memorizing, and close attention to small units of a text were the order of the day.[152] And we are now looking outwards, for, after the first generation, translations were surely generated in

---

[148] Thackeray 1923. Now a remarkably close coincidence has been demonstrated (Cohen 2007) between Philo's citations from the prophets and the series of synagogal readings from Isaiah (*haftarot* of consolation) of the weeks which precede Yom Kippur. This does suggest that the beginnings of the cycle were in place in Philo's day, even if not the complete system as Cohen claims.

[149] See Kraft 2003, and cf. p. 158 above.

[150] For an extended exploration of points of comparison and contact, see Le Déaut 1984.

[151] Cf. L. Alexander 2002 on the 'spaces' within cities which Christian teachers and philosophers alike found for their operations.

[152] For scribal reading aloud and interpretation as the background to the translators' methodology from the earliest phase, see van der Kooij and van der Toorn 1998.

other Jewish centres, including Jerusalem, and received throughout the diaspora.

Translation activity continued apace, alongside independent composition, over a period of perhaps three centuries (if we are to assign an early date to the first beginnings), and we shall return to consider the significance of this activity later.[153] Suggested chronologies remain profoundly insecure. This insecurity extends not only to the assignation of approximate dates or periods on the basis of supposed hidden allusions to historical events or of use by outside authors (themselves of uncertain date), but even to proposing relative chronologies. The apparent dependence of one book on another, used by scholars as a peg on which to hang a chronological sequence, may sometimes equally well be turned on its head, or else it may reflect a more complicated cross-fertilization.[154] This is particularly applicable to the Psalms, which themselves quote much from other books. The process of composition will surely also have been assisted by rudimentary word lists and glossaries, adding in some cases the possibility of mutual dependence on the same resource.[155]

It appears that translation work continued actively through the second century BCE. The *personae* of the translations of political prophecies in Isaiah has been hypothetically related to the international situation of the Seleucid era and in particular to the situation during the Maccabaean crisis of the 160s BCE or more recently to the impact upon Egypt of the invasion of Antiochus IV.[156] The prologue written by Ben Sira's grandson, who was his Greek translator, gives us a date for his arrival in Egypt of the thirty-eighth year of the reign of King Ptolemy Euergetes (i.e., Ptolemy VII Euergetes Physkon); this was probably the year 132 BCE and certainly had to be a year before 116 BCE when Ptolemy Physkon died. The other absolute dating we

---

On teaching and learning in Alexandria, see Cribiore 1996. More broadly in the Hellenistic and early Roman worlds, see Morgan 1998.

[153] pp. 224–6 and pp. 309–12.

[154] The current consensus is tabulated in *BGS* 111–12. These issues have been investigated by the work of the AHRC Greek Bible in the Graeco-Roman World Project. For the debate on interdependence, see Barr 2003, criticizing Tov 1999: 183–94.

[155] Such as the fragment discussed above, p. 149, and see also p. 254.

[156] Notably by Seeligmann 1948, esp. 4; 82. Further discussion in Troxel 2008.

have, from the colophon added to the book of Esther in some manuscripts, puts the bringing of this text to Egypt in the fourth year of Ptolemy and Cleopatra, which must be either 114 BCE, 78–77 BCE or, just possibly, 48 BCE, since these are the only times a Ptolemy and a Cleopatra sat together in the fourth year of joint rule on the throne of Egypt.[157] A few distinctive items of Roman administrative vocabulary appear in the Greek Daniel, the most notable of these being *hupatos*, the unmistakeable Greek term for a Roman consul.[158]

Such an extended period of production may mean not so much that it took a surprisingly long time for the translations of the prophets to emerge—a 'prophetic gap' as it has been nicely called[159]—but rather that activity was concentrated at a lower level, by contrast with the public and highly visible beginnings of the enterprise. We might envisage much piecemeal production of local or private translations by groups and individuals, and perhaps formalized, complete texts of individual books being produced in response to special situations or needs. Sometimes two versions of one book were produced, as with the two versions of the biblical Ezra-Nehemiah, nowadays known as 1 and 2 Esdras. The use of adapted Septuagint language was also extended beyond the core texts to additions to existing books, and also to some further translations, such as the history of the wars of Judas Maccabaeus and his successors told in 1 Maccabees, which was translated, as can be proved, from a Hebrew original in an essentially septuagintal style. This demonstrates as well as anything the functionality and durability of the translation language as a framework, and its significance for the continuity of Jewish identity in changing circumstances. A number of these books will figure in the following chapter, and in Chapters 6 and 7. I shall return to consider further the role of the texts in the life and culture of Greek-speaking Jews.

---

[157] For both these dates, see Schürer iii, 506–7.
[158] *hupatos* figures in both Septuagint and Theodotionic versions.
[159] Coinage by Dines 2004: 50.

5

Representing and Subverting Power

The Greek Bible has much to say about the world's rulers—appropriately enough, given that one of them took the credit for its inauguration.[1] Subsequently, a convergence of elements fuelled this concern, encouraging responses ranging from adulation to rebellion, and we find these reflected in all manner of Jewish writing in Greek, inside and outside the Septuagint corpus. Religious, literary, and political factors combine here. Writing meshes with social circumstances. Successful texts were used and reused, interpreted and reinterpreted, worked and reworked, adapted to different contexts. To take a striking example, the late biblical book of Daniel is made up of two parts, generally described in commentaries as 'court tales' and 'apocalypse'. Much of the court tales section (chaps. 2–7) has come down to us not in Hebrew but in Aramaic. This section itself appears to be a composite. The apocalyptic last chapters, by common agreement, were composed in the midst of the Maccabaean crisis in Jerusalem of the 160s BCE, its author unaware of the Temple's final liberation and rededication.[2] But it, too, actually consists of successive different episodes. Greek translations of parts of the book may have anticipated the issuing of a complete Greek version. But before long there were two such versions in existence, and also other Daniel stories in circulation, among them the popular tales of Susannah and the Elders and Bel and the Dragon.[3] We cannot expect in such a text

---

[1] For a variety of recent approaches to this rich topic, see the papers in Rajak et al. forthcoming and also Gruen 1998: 189–245.
[2] For an excellent brief account of these developments, see Collins 1998: 85–115. On the historical dimension, see Millar 1997.
[3] On which, see below, pp. 188–9.

to find more than momentary one-to-one correspondences between event and history. What we can do is to examine ideas and sentiments encapsulated in the compilations and translations as they have come to us, as well as the language in which these are expressed, where possible exploring their meaning in relation to other texts and to the broad experiences which many of their ancient Jewish readers will have shared.

TALKING ABOUT KINGS

A wide Jewish-Greek vocabulary was evolved for power, both as an abstraction and in its various concrete embodiments. Techniques were devised in the literature for talking about divine omnipotence in relation to and by comparison with the mighty of this world, and also for talking about how this power expressed itself, in the defence of God's people and against other deities and their images. These were major themes already in the Hebrew Bible, which was equipped with a collection of stereotypes and a wide range of terminology, and Greek equivalents had to be found for these. But there appears in the Greek translation, over and above that, a tendency to expand yet further upon the problems of power, as well as an increased preoccupation with the exercise of authority and with standing of the temporal kind. These are often displayed in what appear to be small adjustments to the arrangement of the original Hebrew units, to wording or even just to word order. While we need to be aware that such disparities might be the product of a different Hebrew original rather than of any translator's choice, we are on reasonably safe ground if we assess each disparity on its merits, keeping a watchful eye on textual variants and on the history of the book in question.[4]

In the books of the Septuagint corpus, rulers are remembered, listed, portrayed, compared, analysed, addressed, praised, and criticized. They appear in many guises, from the epigrammatic style of

[4] Modern Septuagint scholarship has been transformed by the evidence of the great diversity of Hebrew text forms current at Qumran. The question of the relationship between Septuagint and Hebrew text forms is well explained in Fernández Marcos 2000: 67–2000.

Greek Proverbs, through the deliberately cryptic allusions of Greek Daniel, to the pious exhortations of Ecclesiasticus (much but not all following the cue of the Hebrew Ben Sira) and on to the dramatic presentation of a fearsome persecution in 3 Maccabees and 4 Maccabees. The Hebrew Wisdom tradition, from Proverbs on, already had a special affection for sharp comments on the conduct of the powerful as well as prudential with (not always consistent) advice as to how to deal with them. The tradition was a long one in the ancient near east, and commonplaces accumulated; but, for those exposed to the vagaries of rulers, such wisdom could have had immediate practical value whenever it was reiterated.

Then, in the Hellenistic and Roman periods, exploration of the nature of monarchy appears in a much wider range of genres in Jewish writing,[5] becoming a favourite subject of speculation and imagination. It is hardly surprising that so much of the *Letter of Aristeas* is taken up with the extended banquet scene, where the sages from Jerusalem teach one of the greatest Egyptian monarchs how to rule—essentially by imitating and subordinating himself to the God of Israel. Even God's servant Moses is, as we saw, a king in Philo.

The preoccupation with rulers surfaces in small details as well as in large themes. In the Septuagint Job, the three international friends, the provoking comforters of this 'great man (*eugenēs*) of the East' are assigned the titles of royalty. They are identified, both in the translation of the narrative and in the concluding genealogy, which exists only in the Greek, as Eliphaz the king of the people of Teiman, Baldad the tyrant (*turannos*) of the Sauchians and Zophar, the king of the Meinaeans (Job 2: 10 and 42: 17e). The effect is to locate the story firmly among the highest echelons of middle-eastern society, but also to convey the point that, for all their high status, none of these notables can solve the problems of cosmic injustice nor bring any relief to the sufferer. Later rabbinic midrashim provide only a partial parallel for the royal designation of Eliphaz.[6]

Septuagint Proverbs 24: 22a is a sharp and vivid attack on the cruel and arbitrary responses to which kings are prone. 'The king's tongue is

---

[5] See already the reflections embedded in the *Letter of Aristeas*, and discussed in Chap. 3.
[6] Midrash Tanhuma (Vilna 1899: i. 166); Targum Yerushalmi to Gen. 26: 12.

a sword, and not one of the flesh . . . if his wrath shall be provoked he devours men's bones and burns them up as a flame, so that they are not fit to be eaten by the young eagles.' The message is that a king is unfathomable, don't thrust yourself forward; with patience he can be broken down. Even the bad ruler can be trumped in the end. This is additional to the Masoretic Hebrew, but since it reads as though translated it may reflect a different original rather than a Greek 'plus'.[7]

One explanation for this interest is theological, the perennial need to position earthly kings in relation to the divine ruler. A supreme divinity is often and usefully invoked to endorse kingly majesty; and yet, to be deposited in a hierarchy, even as second only to the Almighty, does lay down limits for the king's stature. 'It is through me that the mighty are mighty; through me that tyrants rule the land' says personified Wisdom in Septuagint Proverbs (8: 16), and through Wisdom speaks God. The reverse problem also arises: short of recourse to mysticism, it is difficult to find ways of defining and describing that supreme divinity except through the language of human monarchy, which might seem to diminish the divine and to overvalue the human. Moshe Halbertal, exploring links between monarchy and 'idolatry', suggests that the Hebrew Bible's intensive application of human kingship language to God resulted in an ongoing dilemma which coloured the Jewish approach to mortal kings and which had a big part to play in fostering ambivalent attitudes to them.[8] But what other language was there? These considerations would seem to apply in equal measure to the Greek Bible.

But the question is not just God-talk. In post-exilic literature a real interest manifests itself in how kings should govern and what it is like to live under them—the questions, in fact, which are the root of political theory, and also of so much of the existence of any vulnerable subject. Both Jewish kings and foreign rulers could mean trouble for a Jewish community. The Jews had accumulated, recorded, and recycled layer upon layer of experience of both sorts. After the return from the first exile in Babylon the fate of Jewish communities, both in the diaspora and in Jerusalem, became in many new ways dependent on the vagaries and the capriciousness of their overlords. The Jews

---

[7] Studied by Aitken in Aitken 2007.
[8] Halbertal and Margalit 1992.

perceived themselves as a subject people both in their own country, and also, increasingly, because of their spread 'among the nations'. Stories of courts and kings do somehow engage with real problems.[9] Their content may be a source of fun and entertainment.[10] Acts of the imagination nevertheless do important pragmatic work for their creators and readers, and they are, as Steven Weitzmann has compellingly reminded us, part of the time-honoured Jewish art of survival.[11] Fictions and fantasies are a route to adaptation. And they are also a form of embedded debate and investigation.

Essentially Jews contributed to kingship literature because it mattered to them acutely. A summary of their situation might run as follows: they understood that self-preservation meant retaining the favour of the ruling power of the day; but they had few illusions about where they stood. Things would not always be easy; bad times were inevitable. It was necessary therefore to understand their controllers, to avoid complacency, and to develop the repertory of their own responses.[12] And it was necessary, in doing this, to retain a sense of their own worth, to reassert their own values, to preserve a free and independent spirit.

It is worth reflecting on why the translators and the Greek Jewish authors who followed in their wake evince far less interest in the life of the *polis* than in monarchy. They evidently knew enough about its institutions to borrow as a designation for the people of Israel the old democratic word for the people's assembly, *ekklesia*, an inspired choice whose huge future they could never have predicted. A concrete answer presents itself. Jews tended to have to appeal over the heads of the often-hostile local city authorities to the more distant suzerain, who exercised the decisive influence over their fates.[13] In

---

[9] Rajak et al. 2007.

[10] Gruen 1998: 189–245 has alerted us to many instances of humour in such narratives missed by previous commentators.

[11] Weitzmann 2005: 9–10, 14–5.

[12] Gruen 1998: 189–245 focuses effectively on the first of these needs and his picture of the interaction between 'Kings and Jews' is thus a more cheerful one than mine.

[13] On the Alexandrian delegations to Rome after the violence under Gaius Caligula, and on the Roman decrees maintaining Jewish rights in the cities, see pp. 119–20.

both the Hellenistic and Roman periods the power of those city authorities had severe limits. There is perhaps mileage, too, in a literary explanation: kings symbolize regimes of every kind, they display the workings of power in its pure, untrammeled form, they are government laid bare.

The translators and authors did think hard, then, about the issues surrounding kings. For them, furthermore, the terms of reference were particular, because the Greek language of divine power has its own connotations, different in resonance and reference from the Hebrew. The societies in which the various translators lived were far removed from the worlds represented in most of the Hebrew Bible. They did not seek wholly to elide the difference, though they did engage in sporadic updating of the original in terms of contemporary political language. In those books of the larger Septuagint corpus that were composed in the Second Temple period rather than inherited from earlier times, the Greek translators, or in some cases original authors, had the greatest scope to express themselves on such topics, and therefore those books inevitably play an important part in this chapter.

WISDOM AT COURT

'Listen therefore, O kings, and understand; learn, O judges of the ends of the earth', begins chapter 6 of the Greek composition known as the Wisdom of Solomon. The words in the first part of this book are put into Solomon's mouth. It may not seem surprising, therefore, that firm advice is there given by the king to his fellow monarchs, the proud rulers of the world, whose arrogance is evoked by a strong onomatopoeic word, *gegauromenoi* (exulting), rare in biblical Greek, as they lord it over the masses (*ochloi*). They had better remember that not only does their rule, *kratesis*, come from God and their *dunasteia* from the most high, *hupsistos* (the alternative term *pantokrator* appears only once in Wisdom), but that their use of it will be scrutinized (*exetasei*) by Him according to the criterion of justice. They are also called *dikastai*, delegated judges, as it were, of the ends of the earth (an expression favoured by the Greek Psalms). They are best advised to guard the law, *nomos*. The key is Wisdom, which starts with the knowledge of God, and leads to holiness; that achieved, their thrones and sceptres can, it is promised, last for ever—*eis ton aiona* (6:1–21). In both time and space therefore, a cosmic scale is operative. There is no separate concern at this point with the fate of Israel.

In such a manner, the Wisdom of Solomon begins to tackle the theme of royal power. One of the most read of the apocryphal books, this is an elaborate and carefully composed essay in the established biblical wisdom tradition, but with its teachings no longer presented as brief apothegms, as in the book of Proverbs, but in rhetorical expatiations. It represents a marked development in the genre of wisdom literature. The book speaks to Greek philosophical interests, but it is perhaps most distinguished for its fine elaborations of biblical themes and imagery in a manner which some have called midrashic.[14]

Two notable examples from other genres deserve mention at this point. Our theme emerges vividly in the debate among the sleeping king's bodyguards in the book of 1 Esdras. This is a Greek translation of the book of Ezra, somewhat different and apparently more up to date in its lexicon than the main version which appears in the Septuagint. In the English Protestant Bible, 1 Esdras forms part of the Apocrypha. The Hebrew/Aramaic Ezra is closely followed in this translation, but it is topped and tailed, beginning with the account from Chronicles of Josiah's Passover, and ending with a small extract from the book of Nehemiah.[15] In the highly diverting conversation about what is the best thing in the world, visibly evoking in format the comparison of constitutions in Herodotus's third book (80–2), the contest is between the respective powers of the king, women, and wine. To assert the claim of the first, a graphic picture of absolute rule is painted. The king is supreme over all those men who have power in the world (*huperischuousi*), dominating land and sea (*katakratountes*—note the intensifying prefix). An accumulation of three verbs is reserved to describe the king's control: *huperischuei kai*

---

[14] Gilbert 1973 and now Grabbe 1997.
[15] For 1 Esdras, see the commentary of Myers (1974) and the two studies of Talshir (1999 and 2002).

kurieuei... kai despozei. People make war at his bidding; they build mounds, walls, and towers. The rest of humankind farm, bring him their produce, and pay tribute (*phoroi*). If he orders people to kill, they kill; or likewise to make desolate or to build. So both his people and his armies (*dunameis*—a word which in Greek has also the basic sense simply of 'powers')[16] obey him (*enakouousin*). He eats, drinks, and sleeps while people are obliged to stand around. And yet the king is entirely subjected to his women, on whose every word he hangs. His courtesan Apame takes the crown off his head and slaps him in the face. This whole show serves, of course, only to enable every other form of power to be trumped by the non-contestant from outside— truth, or, to be more precise, the truth of God. All three other claimants, when it comes to it, are *adikoi*, without justice; and, of the three, it is monarchy which is the serious contender, with wine and women as amusing foils. Truth, we are taught, and the lesson is couched in biblical terminology, is at the end of the day—one might perhaps say a little late in the day—to be identified with the *ischus kai hē exousia kai hē megalaiotēs tōn pantōn aionōn*, 'the strength and power and greatness of the eternal'. The Vulgate's Latin version of the concluding sentence has remained with us: *magna est veritas et praevalebit*. This story was incorporated into his history by Josephus, who was writing his *Antiquities* at the end of the first century CE, into his account of the period, and he followed 1 Esdras quite closely, allowing space also for the debate.[17]

Two Greek versions of the book of Esther have come down to us, and the freer of the two, the Septuagint version (known as the B text), contains six major additions to the Masoretic Hebrew Esther, which substantially alter the balance of the book and add to its length by some two-thirds, bringing both narrative elaboration and religious elucidation. This state of affairs suggests a high degree of fluidity in this late biblical book.[18] Again, Josephus exploited most of them towards the end of the biblical narrative of the *Jewish Antiquities*.[19] In these

---

[16] Cf. p. 188.
[17] On Josephus' use of the Greek Bible, see pp. 252–4.
[18] For the Greek Esther, see Clines 1984; de Troyer 2000; and de Troyer 2003: Chap. 1.
[19] Josephus, *AJ*, ll. 184–296.

additions, we are rarely far from royalty. In the first, Artaxerxes sends a letter, in which he, and at the same time the book's composer, offer the king of kings the opportunity of expatiating on his own self-image. This ruler sees himself as *epieikēs* (mild or perhaps fair-minded), and is proud to be the ruler of an empire one could travel safely across, one which embodies an ideal of universal peace that spreads throughout the *oikoumenē*. It is often maintained that two regnal decrees were the only ones of the six additions to Esther to be written originally in Greek, rather than translated from Hebrew. In the case of these pseudo-documents, purporting to emanate from the royal court, the style and technical vocabulary are thoroughly convincing to scholars. In fact, we do not need to assume that the rather different style of the other additions suggests a non-Greek origin; it has perhaps not been quite appreciated that Semitisms, apparent or real, are no kind of guide, given the way in which the curious Septuagint translation-language, with its echoes of Hebrew syntax, became itself a language for free composition.[20]

Another of these six additions to Esther opens with a prayer offered by Mardochaeus/Mordechai (addition C, 13 ff.). As is well known, there is no mention of the name of God in the Hebrew Esther, but here things are different, and God appears (as he often does in the Greek Bible) as helper, *boēthos*, and protection, *skepē*.[21] Artaxerxes has just sealed the fate of the Jews. They are all to die on one day on 14 Adar, because their hostility to the regime, manifest in their perverse laws, threatens the stability of the empire. God's power is naturally foremost in Mardochaeus' mind and on his lips, and the language is the customary political vocabulary, but in reverse application. In this value system, *philodoxia*, ambition, a commendable characteristic for Greeks, is utterly disclaimed by Mardochaeus. God knows that this is not his motive for resistance. His sole reason is to avoid idolatry, which would be entailed by bowing down to the evil minister Haman (famously described in the Greek Esther as a Macedonian), a human being who has arrogated power to himself. 'I did this so that I might not hold a man in greater honour than God.'

[20] Davila 2005.
[21] On this, see de Troyer 2003: 25–8.

Esther's prayer follows. She has taken off the garb of her *doxa*, here an unnecessary form of external splendour (14: 2). She is about to go in to the king unbidden to plead for her people, and face the lion (24). She invokes God as *kurios*, as Israel's *basileus* (14), as He who has power over all (30), but also as helper, *boēthos*, in extremis, when the heathen seek to destroy God's people and his altar, and his house, while opening the mouths of those who praise empty things (*mataiōn*), who would elevate for ever a king of flesh and blood (*sarkinos*). Israel's separation from all *ethnē* in the days of her own forefathers is recalled. For herself, Esther thinks it important to declare that she has not eaten at Haman's table, or participated in the king's symposium, or drunk the wine of libations (*oinos spondōn*), presumably with reference to her intermarriage. Her meeting with the king enthroned comes in addition D: in all his glory, and he is awesome and terrifying, but God makes him gentle.

The court atmosphere depicted is unspecifically orientalizing: Bickerman points out that most of the customs described could attach to any court. But we do have, from its colophon, an indication of date for the Greek Esther translation: we are told that in the fourth year of Ptolemy and Cleopatra the translation was brought to Alexandria by Lysimachus of Jerusalem; but, of course, it need not yet have been in its final form.[22]

THE VOCABULARY OF DIVINE RULERSHIP

Defining God in the terms appropriate to an earthly ruler does not, then, inevitably diminish the deity. On the contrary, the formulation may be so turned as to measure divine power against all other. This supremacy is then proved by the divine management of the fate of rulers: 'he slew great kings (*krataious*), Sihon, king of the Amorites and Og, king of Bashan and all the kings of Canaan' writes Psalm

---

[22] On the playing up of oriental features in the Jewish depiction of monarchs and their courts, see Alexander and Alexander 2007. On the specific setting and on the dating, Bickerman 1944 and Bickerman 1950a. The possible dates are either 114 BCE or 78/7 BCE or 49/8 BCE, with the middle of the three most likely.

134.²³ The mechanism is generally straightforward: kings elevate themselves (the key verb *hupsoō* is used); then God brings them down, they find themselves in fetters, and He tells them what their offence was. A clear statement of this sequence can be found in the speech of the comforter Elihu at Job 36: 7–9; Olofsson has noticed that the Greek version underlines rather than softens God's destructive activities and that *tapeinoō*, to bring low or abase, is a word well liked in the Septuagint translations which serves as a rendering for several Hebrew equivalents.²⁴ The proper stance of kings is to hear and to recognize that they are slaves. David is God's thrall. Job in his misery is insistent that this is how things are (Job 36: 11). In the vocabulary for this process the term is avoided. The appropriate Greek terms for the pride that comes before a fall, *hubris*, together with words derived from it, are very useful to the creator of the Septuagint Job, as also to the Proverbs translator. The terms are used, at least occasionally, by the translators of most of the prophetic books. They appear, too, in the Wisdom of Solomon and in the Maccabaean literature. But it is interesting that they are totally avoided by the Torah translators and in the historical books.

This is not the place to enter into the theological territory of the Septuagintal names for God, let alone the philological complexities of their Hebrew exemplars.²⁵ The point worth making here is that the translators evolved a set of compounds and combinations which lifted their language beyond the prosaic reference points of the ordinary power-language of the day. This Greek terminology appears to render concrete and immediate the more shadowy and dispersed power suggested to the later reader by the Hebrew original, though we are hardly in a position to know whether ancient readers were affected by the Greek in similar ways to us, let alone to sense how the Hebrew reverberated in ancient Israel. C. H. Dodd²⁶ contrasts *kurios ho serapis* and other such examples from pagan cult with the distinctive, absolute use of the term which rings through the Septuagint and confidently concludes that in this very word alone is lodged

---

[23] = Heb. 135; and cf. Ps. 135 LXX.
[24] Olofsson 1990a: 20–1.
[25] For a recent study, see Rösel 2007.
[26] Dodd 1935.

'a manifesto for monotheism'. In the manuscripts as they have come down to us, the written word *kurios* (lord) is the most frequent translation choice; often it is folded into the arresting phrase *ho kurios ho theos* (the Lord the God). But since these are Christian manuscripts, the matter is not quite as straightforward as it may seem. Scholars have noted that surviving fragments of apparently Jewish texts put the Hebrew tetragrammaton (the four letters spelling the Divine Name) in one form or another into the Greek wherever the word *kurios* appears in the Septuagint.[27] The most striking of these are the somewhat mysterious four Greek letters ΠΙΠΙ; another is to put four letters of the palaeographic Hebrew alphabet inside the Greek. It is still probable, however, that Jewish readers of the period enunciated the Name, thus written, as *adonai* or else as *kurios* (depending on which language they were using).[28]

Pantokratōr, 'ruler of all', offers a more graphic definition of the scope of the divinity's power, and it has become a technical term in a way in which its Hebrew semantic counterpart, "*adon hakol*, does not during the biblical period.[29] The active exercise of authority is graphically evoked. But there is a theological trap to be avoided in interpreting the change. The claim that a conception of 'universalism' here creeps into Jewish thought via a new Greek-influenced understanding of the Jewish God is, once again, to read Jewish history 'as a preparation for the Gospel'.

The Divine Name *Ho theos ho hupsistos*, the God most High, appears very rarely in the canonical books with the exception of Psalms, but frequently in the apocryphal books, where it has gained ground in a dramatic way. This term corresponds closely to the Hebrew *'el 'elion* and is the natural rendering of it, although there is no one-to-one correspondence between the chosen translations. Here we find the translators happy to bend to their own needs a conception resonant also in pagan religious life, as a name for Zeus or a description of the supreme deity of certain groups of

---

[27] With a small number of exceptions where what seem to be fragments of Jewish papyri follow Christian usage. On this phenomenon, and esp. the ΠΙΠΙ form found several times in P. Fouad Inv. 266, see Introduction, p. 17 n. 21. and the literature cited there.

[28] So, with certainty, R. Hanhart's introduction to Hengel 2002: 7–8.

[29] See the wide-ranging study of the term by Montevecchi (1956).

worshippers. The term effectively evokes both a physical location and a non-physical elevation.[30] Indeed, the verb *hupsoō* is used in a metaphorical sense translating various Hebrew verbs from Genesis onwards, though in the vast majority of cases there is a connection with the Hebrew root *rom*. The word makes a rare appearance in a similar sense in the historian Polybius (5.56.12). In Josephus we find it employed in the *Jewish War* in such a sense five times, which is interesting, even if the application is to puffed-up mortals rather than divinities. The metaphorical use of the very unusual noun form *hupsōseis* figures at Psalm 149: 6, rendering *romemot*—the elevation of God through the singing of his praises. In New Testament texts there is an important theological twist and the eschatological element comes to the fore: John especially exploits a double allusion to the crucifixion and the final ascent.[31] Interesting speculations are prompted by the use of the ordinary noun *hupsos*, 'sublimity', as a keyword in literary criticism by a philosopher of the early Roman imperial period, Longinus (or Pseudo-Longinus), who famously stands out among pagan writers for quoting from the opening of Genesis.[32]

Yet the more graphic means used in the Hebrew Bible to communicate the terror of the exercise of divine might may also be exploited in the Greek versions. The simple word *dunamis*, 'power', and its cognates are extremely frequent throughout LXX, extending even to the coinage *dunamoō* in a few instances in Psalms, Ecclesiastes, and Daniel, with apparently wider use in Aquila's version. There is nothing unusual about this vocabulary (for all the theology that can be built upon it), and it sits comfortably within Greek religious language. What is remarkable is its prominence in the Jewish texts.

The changing rendering of 'Lord of hosts/armies' illustrates the complexity of the patterning of choices. The non-Pentateuchal Hebrew *adonai tzevaot* ('Lord of Hosts') has three Septuagintal renderings, appearing in three different groups of books: the transliteration *sabaot* (Isaiah and occasionally elsewhere), *pantokratōr*, in the Pentateuch, the other prophets and 2 and 3 Kingdoms; and, finally, in various books,

---

[30] See the full study in Mitchell 1999.
[31] See Chap. 7, pp. 246–8, for the use of the Septuagint in the Gospels.
[32] See Chap. 8, p. 269.

but especially Psalms, *theos* or *kurios tōn dunameōn*. The noun *dunamis* has on occasion a concrete application in Greek, functioning in a quite straightforward way in Greek historians to refer to the forces (hosts) or supplies available for a particular war, be it of men or of weapons; however, it is very unusual to have the word standing entirely on its own to mean simply 'army', as Meecham seems to suggest. Why then does no translator offer the more natural *tōn stratiōtōn* for 'of the armies'? Dodd[33] maintained that *dunameōn* was meant to evoke angels, or lesser divine beings under divine subjection, a sense in which the word undoubtedly appears in Jewish and Christian literature, but support for this interpretation of the stock phrase is scant. Again, explanation may elude us, but the technique of the translators is becoming familiar: their hallmark is to mould a special vocabulary out of familiar units which together trump the ordinary language of political power. The results, at first glance naive and clumsy, were remarkably successful.

Despite new-fangled solutions, depictions of God's power do not always shrink from the apparently archaic biblical anthropomorphic imagery of the mighty hand and the outstretched arm. If anything, the Septuagintal tendency is to multiply the effects over and above the Hebrew (if we are to judge by the Masoretic text at any rate). Thus Deuteronomy 3: 24 in Greek offers a doublet for one Hebrew word for 'greatness'—*godlekha*—and two words for arm instead of one. Those famous anthropomorphisms and anthropopathisms have been separately studied for several of the Greek books[34] and the findings are not at all predictable. It has been argued persuasively that Psalms maintain the anthropomorphisms even where not strictly 'necessary', that is to say where they could easily be handled as mere aspects of language and ironed out.[35] The shaking of the earth by God is vividly evoked in many Psalms, and in Greek the verb *saleuein/saleuesthai* (to cause to shake/totter) retains the anthropomorphic image here.

Yet new types of power terminology keep coming in. The noun *exousia* is not found in the Pentateuch and only rarely in the biblical

---

[33] Dodd 1935.
[34] Orlinsky 1975; Soffer 1957 (Psalms); Wittstruck 1976 (Deuteronomy).
[35] So Soffer 1957.

books. Its precise sense in classical Greek is 'capacity', 'formal authority', 'right', but also, from the fourth century CE on, 'office' or 'magistracy'. It functions as the translation of *memshala* or of cognates of the late biblical Hebrew root *shilton*, representing, one might say, the less awesome and more formalized depiction of divine control. It looks as though here fashions in Greek language have led the way and that the word's shift of meaning and increased currency in later Greek writing is what has led to its adoption by the Septuagint translators at a certain stage: they used it also for the temporal power of rulers or their delegates.

When God's might is proved against the idols, the preferred Septuagint Greek term for the latter, *eidōla*, is well chosen. In classical Greek the word means a phantom, a shadow, something false, by contrast with *eikōn* and *homoiōma*, which denote the actual likeness, or *agalma* and *gluptos*, a carved statue. These other terms taken from pagan ritual are not absent from the Septuagint: they do figure sometimes in the Septuagint. Thus, *eikōn* is used where Daniel requires variation in his terminology for the various images involved in the story; *homoiōma* appears, along with *eikōn* at Deuteronomy 4 in Moses' exhortation on the subject of graven images, gluptoi/. But both Philo and Josephus take up the Septuagint use of *eidōlon*. Daniel (both Greek versions) occasionally has the form *eidoleion*, in which he is followed by 1 Maccabees.[36]

On God's power in relation to the Jewish monarchy, Psalm 88 (Heb. 89) is a key text, a discursive poem, which expatiates upon the elevation of David, God's slave (*doulos*),[37] and of his throne, over that of all the kings of the earth. Though chosen and anointed, David is rejected by his subjects, that throne hurled to the ground. The Psalm begins with an extensive declaration of divine power, and as we have come to expect, in the Greek version, its use of the vocabulary of politics tends to render the more numinous Hebrew language of strength.[38] However, the Greek version is in general very close to

---

[36] *TWNT* describes the function of the special word *eidōlon* as polemical, part of an intensifying campaign against idolatry.

[37] *hupsoō* is used again in l. 25, for *tarum karno* which is thus not translated literally here.

[38] Note esp. at l.14 *ho brachion meta dunasteias*, for *zero'a 'im gevurah*.

the original. In the vocabulary applied to God's commandments, we may note especially the interesting word *krima*, apparently the standard Hellenistic Greek term for a decision or judgement.

THE KING'S ANGER

The words used to describe the anger of an all-powerful overlord work in similar ways, but there is a philosophical dimension which adds extra and interesting twists. The God of Israel, effortlessly victorious in any clash or in any comparison with mortal rulers, was a conspicuously angry God. This could not be brushed aside, for all the contorted protestations of Aristeas. Philo followed certain Greek philosophers in ascribing to his deity the same lack of passions they did to their gods. But then he could only explain the God of Genesis 6: 7, whose wrath was such that he was ready to blot out his entire creation, by resort to the strained suggestion that this description was a mere ploy designed to frighten the foolish and the incorrigible.[39] God's wrath, like everything else about him, was not subject to strictures; only, at most, to anguished theological reflection. The language of anger from above thus possessed a thick extra layer of meaning for Jews. And the imperative of establishing proper distinctions produced a place on their agenda for the critique of ordinary mortals, however powerful, who presumed to trespass on this territory. Greek-speaking Jews therefore received a challenging mixed heritage, and we can observe them shaping it in different creative ways, as an expression of their Janus-like self-identity and of their ambivalence towards the ruling power.

It is perhaps not surprising that the Hebrew Bible has an extraordinarily rich vocabulary for anger. Among the available terms, one particular verb, *ḥarah* (burn), together with the related noun *ḥaron* have special roles in denoting the heat of God's wrath. These words

---

[39] For Aristeas, see above. For Philo, see esp. his tract *Quod Deus Immutabilis Sit* 51–2; 68.

are also intensified in the combination *ḥaron aph* or *ḥaron apo*, the 'heat of [his] anger'.[40]

The overwhelming majority of the appearances of these combinations are with reference to divine anger, with a small number of exceptions. Of fifteen uses of the term in its special sense, two alone are in the Pentateuch, two are in Judges, and there are interesting small clusters in Samuel and Job. The terrifying punishments inflicted as a result of intense divine displeasure, and their educative and redemptive force for Israel, are a familiar and recurrent motif scarcely requiring illustration. An anger which is to some extent anthropomorphized fuels the enduring conception of a sin–punishment cycle, whose beginnings are perhaps to be associated with the Deuteronomic stratum in the Hebrew Bible, but which makes its presence felt across the entire literature.

This powerful motif does not disappear in Jewish–Greek biblical, or parabiblical literature. The Septuagint translation did not seek to replicate the graphic force of the preferred Hebrew terms for divine anger. However, they did what they could inventing a fine combination, the 'anger of his fiery spirit'. Though unfamiliar in Greek literature, this became more or less the standard Septuagintal rendering.

Thus divine anger is made to stand apart from the anger of the human ruler. On the worldly plane, by contrast, Greek motifs of description and categorization serve our literature well. The standard philosophical drive to distinguish the good king from the tyrant lies behind a line of powerful representations of tyrannical anger, found in especial abundance in the non-translated books. The Second and Fourth Books of Maccabees deal dramatically with an explosive confrontation with a monarch. Antiochus IV interrogates, tortures, and executes seven brothers, their mother, and an elderly priest for refusal to abjure Jewish practices during the religious persecution in Judaea in the mid-160s BCE.[41] It is in 2 Maccabees, itself an

---

[40] And both can also stand on their own. It is sometimes suggested that this puzzling term refers to fire emanating from the nostrils, but that is difficult to sustain given that in a few cases it does apply to a human agent.

[41] On the literary form and content of both 2 and 4 Macc., van Henten 1997: 17–82. Translation and commentary in Hadas 1953.

abbreviated version of the lost history in Greek by Jason of Cyrene, that the literary tradition about these events has its starting-point, within the brief compass of two narrative chapters (6 and 7). Faced with the promised and just anger of God, Antiochus' self control is blown to the winds. He becomes enraged (2 Macc. 7: 39), and this facilitates his perversion and enables him, we are told, to treat the last brother to be killed with even more brutality than the others. His offer of wealth and personal royal patronage (2 Macc. 7: 24), that is to say, all those advantages which mark out and guarantee his own standing in his world, are scornfully rejected by the victims, who thus reveal that they set his royal position at nought. The youngest brother's confidence that God has the power to provide for them anew, even though the king has taken away from them every last thing under his control, makes the final mockery of the king's authority. The spilling over of Antiochus' facile and furious reaction is brought into opposition with God's delicately balanced wrath. The much-discussed assertion made in 2 Maccabees (7: 33) that the anger of the living God will last only a short time, just enough to shock and educate his people and then it will cease, is in keeping with the Hebrew prophets' conception of a finite process of chastisement set in motion by terrifying but temporally limited divine displeasure. The tyrant's anger is explicitly contrasted with that kind of anger which operates in association with justice (*dikē*).

TOPPLING IDOLS

During the second half of the first millennium BCE, the fate of Jewish communities became in many new ways dependent on the vagaries and the capriciousness of their overlords. The Jews understood themselves to be a subject people, scattered 'among the nations'. The diaspora condition became a permanent reality after the non-return from Babylon of many Jews, when Cyrus allowed them to return. Others settled in Egypt. 'Diaspora', as we have seen, is a concept originating in the Greek Bible, and it is a very different word from any of its Hebrew equivalents. Mélèze Modrzejewski has neatly underlined the historical significance of the difference in perspective.[42] Diaspora can be positive or neutral. However, when diaspora is explicitly presented as a punishment, in a text like the Greek book of Baruch which was written under the impact of the shock waves emanating from the fall of Jerusalem, then the distinction can dissolve between the Hebrew and the Greek conceptions, and the misery of losing the homeland and your freedom becomes apparent.

What the post-exilic condition brought out, the circumstances of the Greek and then the Roman worlds greatly emphasized. While diaspora communities were minorities dependent most immediately on the goodwill of their neighbours, behind that lay the ruling power with whom lay the ability to safeguard their position—or not. Imperial rule was epitomized in the traditional literature by heathen kings, whose godlessness was expressed in their arbitrary and arrogant behaviour; and notably also, in that world, by the demand for veneration of their gods or of their own images. So another well-liked biblical topic now gets more firmly connected with representations of monarchy, a preoccupation with the pathetic feebleness of idols. In post-exilic literature, the kings were regularly, and graphically, epitomized by their idols.

This is a response to any kind of foreign rule, but it is perhaps especially closely related to the conditions of diaspora existence, and the connection had already been made in the (presumably post-exilic) book of Deuteronomy (4: 27–8). It is perhaps a telling point that the Deuteronomist assumes the consequence of the threatened dispersal of Israel to be that they will worship other Gods in other countries. The exile therefore brought about a renewed need to fight the attraction of foreign cults (Deut. 4: 27 ff.): *kai latreusete ekei theois heterois, ergois xeirōn anthrōpōn* . . .

The Lord will disperse you among the peoples and you will be left few in number among the nations to which the Lord will lead you. There you will worship gods made by human hands out of wood and stone, gods that can neither see nor hear, neither eat nor smell. But if from there you will seek the Lord your God you will find him.

---

[42] Méleze Modrzejewski 1993: 68–9; cf. Chap. 3, pp. 100–2.

A Gentile environment which seemed readily to absorb those cults became a fact of life. Maintaining their identity required that Jews construct themselves as standing apart from them. The motivation was social as much as religious. They needed to feel empowered to hold out against the seductions of conformity which this environment might throw up as well as the pressures from all around and from above. There might even be compulsion on the part of the rulers or of their ministers to engage in polytheistic worship. So paradigms for endurance, patience, and detachment, and also, if it came to it, for resistance were called for.

Psalm 151 is a psalm not included in the Hebrew canon, but handed down in a range of forms and languages, including parts of a Hebrew version from Qumran which is longer and more elaborate than the Greek version.[43] This is clear evidence that we are dealing with what was originally a Hebrew composition. Evidently, the summary version became popular in Greek. This Greek psalm differs in metre and approach from the canonical psalms in Greek: the Septuagintal syntax is thus not entirely explicable in terms of the Hebrew language original. That this is a late biblical composition, in both languages, is clear from the intervention of an angelic figure and also probably from the device of an autobiographical thread. The poem has been thought by some a Maccabaean song of triumph. It should, in any case, probably be read allegorically, as conveying with great vividness Israel's need for God's protection, without which she cannot compare with her 'brothers', taller and more handsome, *kaloi kai megaloi*. *Mikros ēmēn en tois adelphois mou* are the first words of the psalm. But God, it continues, took pleasure in David and anointed him. Then David went out to meet Goliath who cursed him in the name of his idols—*en tois eidōlois autou*. But David decapitated him, removing Israel's disgrace. The poem takes advantage of the Septuagintal equation whereby the Philistines are usually called *allophuloi*, simply, other nations, foreigners. Evidently, before ever this Psalm was written, a circumlocution has made this troubled

---

[43] Ps. 151 A and B are col. XXVIII of the collection 11QPsa = 11Q5. On the Hebrew Ps. 151, see Talmon 1989: 244–72. On the Greek version, see van der Kooij 2001; discussion also in Aejmelaeus 2001.

relationship the archetype of Israel's dealings with Gentiles.[44] Here, through his God, the little David, a king-to-be, is empowered both to outshine his brothers and to confront not a giant (Goliath is neither named nor thus described) but the spiritual power of the Philistine cult statues.

The *allophuloi* were here inseparable from their idols. And, indeed, the parabiblical Jewish literature in Greek evinces extraordinary passion over the subject of graven images. This too develops out of a series of strongly expressed passages in the Hebrew Bible and, again, goes on to surpass them. We find a veritable repository of texts in different registers and different genres, building on biblical patterns and usually on biblical language, but expanding and exploring the familiar theme of the hollowness and powerlessness of graven images, and their predicted doom. The contrast between these lifeless statues and the living God is a biblical commonplace, omnipotence set against total futility. The point is often made through the depiction of the cult image as a man-made object, with a focus on the craftsman's act of creation, especially in the major invectives of Isaiah and Jeremiah. 'Their idols', wrote the Hebrew Jeremiah, 'are like a scarecrow in a cucumber patch. They cannot speak. They have to be carried, for they cannot walk'.[45]

A new dimension of power is introduced in the Greek period. When invective against idol-worship is coupled with the critique of earthly kings an important new connection is made. Since kings are themselves powerless in the face of God, dependent wholly upon Him, as hard as they try to prop up themselves and their regimes with cults and cult statues they discover that they have also to prop up, quite literally, those very statues. Thus, the agenda of idolatry is brought into the arena of political life, and, since the Jewish–Greek imagination saw that arena as occupied by autocratic monarchs, also into the heart of the Jewish enquiry into the nature of kingship.

---

[44] The equivalence is disentangled in Lieu 2002. The section about the Philistines is cut off in the Hebrew version so comparison is not possible.

[45] Jer. 10: 5. The unexpected comparison to a scarecrow (or perhaps just an upright post) is absent from our Greek versions which, in the case of Jeremiah, differ substantially from the Hebrew. But it has found its way into the Epistle of Jeremiah (69). See already Deut. 4: 27–8; and see also Ps. 115: 3–8; 135: 6–7; Isa. 40: 18–19; 44: 9–21; 46: 5–7.

However, it was not only that Jews were now living dangerously, scattered through a world populated by false gods. We cannot overlook the fact that the Maccabaean period saw the homeland too fall subject to a governmental whim, when Antiochus IV had a pagan cult, the 'abomination of desolation' (as Daniel put it), installed in the Jerusalem Temple, as part of an introduced Hellenization. Consequently, waging war on idolatry was at the forefront of the first Maccabaean campaigns in Judaea and of the propaganda of the Hasmonean successors of Judas and his brothers, as we find it echoed in the First Book of Maccabees. The author (or perhaps the Greek translator) of 1 Maccabees, writing towards the end of the second century BC or near the beginning of the first, has it not only that Mattathias (father of Judas and his brothers) together with his followers destroyed the pagan altars up and down the country, where many Jews had 'worshipped idols' (2: 46) as the first act of insurrection against Seleucid rule, but also that the altars of other peoples were demolished. Thus, at Azotus, Judas pulled down the altars and burned the carved images (*ta glupta*) of the Philistine gods (5: 68). In addition, we are offered the curious information that idols are removed from the garments of the dead. At Gezer (south-west of Jerusalem) Simon purified the houses where the idols stood (13: 47), suggesting that uncleanness attached in a special way to the images themselves. All this was a precedent to the eventual cleansing of the Temple when it was restored to the Jews. Even in their homeland, the Jews had been set to become a subculture, and the long arm of the imperial ruler had closed in.

It is in the book of Daniel that the most impressive of all the literary idols appear, both in dream and reality. The final form of the book dates to the Maccabaean crisis, even if it contains earlier material, especially in Chapters 1–7. A huge, golden, partly anthropomorphic image created by Nebuchadnezzar to assert and embody his glory and supreme power and to cow his people who must all bow down to it at the sound of music (Dan. 3) is trumped by Daniel and his associates through their simplicity and their faithfulness to their own traditions. They are simply not afraid of the king or of the persecution he unleashes in the name of the idol which embodies his own pretensions. The resolution of this episode is comfortable for Jewish readers—the king's conversion to the worship of the all-powerful Jewish God. The tales and visions in the first section of Daniel are not much imbued with the millenarianism of the prophetic later part.

Daniel was evidently one of the most popular of all biblical personalities in Hellenistic Judaism and in early Christianity. Josephus regarded him as the best of all prophets because he attached times and dates to his prophecies.[46]

There are two different Greek versions in existence—to the delight of textual scholars—and Josephus himself used the version linked with the name of Theodotion. Curiously, it was this version too, or at least something very close to it, that was the version which was to find its way into the Septuagint manuscripts in place of the expected 'old Greek', in a situation unique to the text of this particular biblical book. The explanation is not clear, but at any rate Josephus seems to reflect what was normal practice by his day. Finally, in the earliest Christian art, Daniel in the lions' den and the three youths in the burning fiery furnace are widely used as symbols of the believer's readiness for death and divine redemption.

Additions to the canonical book, which is already itself a conflation of different tales, proliferated and spread. Some were composed in Aramaic, like part of Daniel itself, and some probably in Greek; all of them put the hero Daniel centre-stage. Perhaps the best known is the story of Susannah and the Elders. We shall look only at one of the two parts of Bel and the Dragon, an addition in all the Greek texts.[47] In this tale of Daniel, set within the Persian empire and located in Babylon, the foolishness of a king is exhibited for all the world to see as a simple schoolboy experiment provides embarrassing proof of the uselessness of his god. The mockery of the cult statue is perhaps in the line of descent from the representation in 1 Samuel of the statue of Dagon in the Philistine temple at Ashdod, which, when the

---

[46] Josephus, *AJ*, 10: 267. Actually, the prophecies are not quite as precise as Josephus suggests, and millenarian speculation through the ages has interpreted them in a hundred different ways. For Josephus on Daniel, and for the history of interpretation generally, see J. J. Collins 1993: 72–123 (by A.Y. Collins).

[47] On Bel and the Dragon, see Collins 1992; Bergmann 2006. Bergmann effectively puts the story into the context of both biblical and post-biblical idol-discourse, suggesting that the post-biblical literature is less connected to professions of faith and more to rational discussion of the question of idols' lifelessness.

captured ark of the covenant is placed beside it, collapses and falls apart (1 Sam. 5:5; 1 Kingdoms 5:4-5). A graphic illustration of this scene is part of the decorative scheme of the Dura Europus synagogue. But the Babylonian gods had a special need for feeding. Bel was in the habit of receiving the completely absurd quantity of twelve bushels of fine flour, forty sheep, and fifty gallons of wheat every day. The King could not understand why Daniel did not perform *proskunēsis* before him, and was firmly told that this young man did not honour *eidōla cheiropoiēta*, but only the living God who created heaven and earth and had the *kuria* of all flesh. The King asserted Bel's claim to be a living God by pointing to his daily consumption. But Daniel just laughed and said that Bel was merely clay inside and bronze outside, and had never eaten anything. By spreading ashes over the floor of the temple, Daniel was able to prove to the King that the seventy priests of Bel, together with their wives and children, had been entering the temple, not through the sealed door but from below. They consumed the entirety of Bel's daily ration. Not only were the priests executed by the enraged King (at least in one of the two text versions, the so-called Theodotionic), but the statue of Bel met its destruction and the King converted to Judaism. In the second part of the story, a cult statue of Bel in the shape of a great snake is crammed with food to bursting; but this time Daniel has to be rescued from the lion's den by Habakkuk the prophet. Claudia Bergmann directs our attention to a particular emphasis on food and consumption in Second Temple Judaism, vividly exemplified here.

Within and around the Bible, the Jeremiah literature had considerable prominence in the Greek and Roman periods. The book of Jeremiah itself was structurally modified in Greek translation, producing a different order of chapters. Literature around the theme was added. In general terms, there can be no doubt that we witness here a response to the catastrophes of Jerusalem. Two texts, the book of Baruch and the so-called Letter of Jeremiah, have remained associated with the wider biblical corpus. The generic character of their authors' expression is such that we are not permitted to make more specific identifications of date or location, though there is a good case for locating Baruch after 70 CE. For our purposes the pseudepigraphic Letter of Jeremiah, of which a fragment has been found at Qumran, is pertinent, for it is yet another tirade against graven images, supposedly associated with Babylon, but with a clear message for later readers.[48] No doubt Jeremiah's authorship in chapter 10 of the biblical book of one of the more extended prophetic assaults on idol-worship is what lies behind this invention. The Letter of Jeremiah is written in a simple, clear Greek, with some biblical resonances in its phraseology. What is interesting is that this subject is deemed appropriate as advice to the Jews exiled in Babylonia, that is to say, as a guide to dealing with diaspora circumstances. The manufacturing processes of idols arouse particular interest. A new and symbolic theme is the processes of decay to which they are prey:

> their hearts are eaten out... for creatures crawl out of the ground and devour them and their clothing. When their faces are blackened by the smoke of the temple they are quite unaware of it. Bats and swallows and birds of all kinds perch on their heads and their bodies and cats do the same. From all this you may be sure that they are not gods, so have no fear of them. (6: 21)

The corruption of priests, prone to steal the silver and gold in which idols are bedecked and even to hand it on to the temple prostitutes, is, it seems, another novel theme (12; 28; 33). Impurity is tangible; idols are touched by menstruating women and those fresh from childbirth. But what is particularly interesting in this work is the mechanism by which God's power is set against the powerlessness of the idols. Repeatedly, we are told that idols cannot make and unmake kings, setting up, as it were, a tripartite power relationship (34; 52; 66). Within the tripartite comparison it is better to be a king, who can at least prove his courage, than a sham god (58–9). Graven images cannot fight against kings (56). Nations and their kings can look at them and see that they are but the work of men's hands (52). In the end, all these splendid statues will rot away, and they will have incurred nothing but contempt.

The Wisdom of Solomon, with which I opened, is also in principle undateable, except that its apparent exploitation in the Pauline literature offers a possible *terminus ante quem*. It has been associated by a recent editor, David Winston, with the period of the Emperor

---

[48] For the Epistle of Jeremiah, see the introduction, translation, and commentary by Moore 1977.

Caligula's imposition of his own image on synagogues and his proposal to do the same in the Jerusalem Temple with a cult statue of himself. More broadly, the vocabulary of the book has pointed to a first century date. David Winston in his commentary on Wisdom[49] identified thirty-five words which did not occur earlier. The use of the single word *thrēskeia* to mean 'cult' has also suggested a date in the period of the early Roman Empire when that usage became commonplace. Both lines of argument are insecure: it is especially difficult to build upon a word found already in Herodotus in the required sense, as is the case with the word *thrēskeia*. Nevertheless, the author's preoccupation with the cult of images in the world around him is striking, and there may well be echoes in his denunciations of the Roman cult of the emperors, as we shall shortly see. The excursus springs from a discussion of the punishment of the Egyptians at the time of the Exodus, which is ascribed in large measure to their grotesque practice of animal worship. This makes it likely that Wisdom was composed in Egypt. The attack widens, and the rejection of the true God is put forward as the root offence committed by the world's wicked and foolish men (12: 27).

There follows what is probably the most extended exploration of the worship of images and its meaning in Greek–Jewish literature, ranging from theoretical reflection to unrestrained invective, from citation to exegesis. Some legal-style (halakhic) discriminations are made: a wooden vessel may be a source of justice, and it is then a blessing, but in the case of an object of worship, both it, for daring to be called a god, and its maker are accursed (14: 7–9). The structuring here, as in much of the book, is in terms of biblical parallelisms, and it is noticeable that the Greek, while not Septuagintal, creaks somewhat at the joints. Idol-worshippers perjure themselves and offend against what is pure (*hosiotētos*). There is a fascinating description of the carving of an image from a useless piece of wood, closely modelled on Isaiah 44: 9–20. In the Greek, the development of the theme may be described as a detailed expansion on the word *cheiropoiētos*, made by human hands, a word regularly applied where graven images are criticized, notably by the Isaiah translator (and also by

---

[49] Winston 1979.

Paul). Then we are offered a summary of the kinds of uses to which such a wall-mounted statue made by a craftsman might be put (13: 11ff.), the forms of human distress which drive people to supplication, and the different favours asked of gods. This distinctly human, indeed psychological, approach diverges from the biblical models.

Several themes stand out. All are remarkable for the blistering hostility with which a fundamental feature of Graeco-Roman life is regarded; and this in a work, as we said, quite strongly influenced by Greek philosophy. Idols are the source of all immorality, of *skandala*, snares (a distinctive Jewish–Greek use of the word, which underwent further development in Christian literature), and of the destruction of life. Bloodshed, the murder of children, every kind of warfare and of obscenity, and immorality come with their cults. We expect divine retribution to be brought against them as well as their makers (14: 11). And, most pertinent, human susceptibility is exploited by *turannoi*, who turn their cult, *thrēskeia*, into law, transporting images of themselves to their distant subjects; the similarity and the verisimilitude and attractiveness of the sculptor's work are explained as being in a direct relation to the success of the cult in evoking loyalty. Here the specifically anthropomorphic character of Graeco-Roman cult images is brought to the fore, as well as their specific role within the practices of the ruler cult. The Roman emperors are known to have shipped their images around the provinces.

Among the literary products of the period that had no Hebrew originals some did but others did not become attached to the Septuagint corpus. The preoccupation with idolatry is shared between both groups. The rewritten Bible which survives in Latin under the name *Liber Antiquitatum Biblicarum* labours, according to Howard Jacobson, 'to highlight idolatry where it is present and to add it where it is not present'.[50] There are none the less a few occasions where the author has omitted idol-worship that does appear in the Bible,[51] and that divergence from the text leads Jacobson to suggest that this author intends his readers to understand the concept of idolatry in a special and wide sense, as a descriptor for any kind of

---

[50] Cf. also Jacobson 1996: 246. Cf. Murphy 1988.
[51] See, for example, *LAB* 18: 13–14 compared with Num. 25: 1, on the worship of Baal Peor, with the commentary by Jacobson (1996) on this passage.

faithlessness to God and his Law. Again, in the romance of Joseph and Asenath, the daughter of Pentephres, priest of Heliopolis, is presented as a woman who worships 'dead and dumb idols' and defiles her mouth with their sacrifices. She must become converted to be accepted by Joseph in marriage—indeed even to be kissed by him—and this elaborate conversion is preceded by a lively scene in which she throws her idols out of the window.[52] In the Third Book of Maccabees, in an account of an onslaught on the Jews by a crazed and drunk Ptolemy, the resolution of the crisis is followed by the execution of 300 'defiled' compatriots (3 Macc. 7: 15): presumably they had lapsed and worshipped Dionysus as required by the King.

It is fair to say, however, that the ordinary non-Jewish worshippers are, by contrast, relatively exempt from personalized criticism, except perhaps on the score of weakness. It is not they but the practices around their cults which are to be shunned. The threatened destruction is visited in graphic fashion on their gods and appears to be limited to those gods. The Jewish reader is to be persuaded by every device of rhetoric and argument, through the emphasis on images, that all other gods are not only powerless but actually non-existent. And yet they are to be feared and loathed. Tyrannical rulers characteristically impose their cult and must be resisted. All this serves to establish the standing of the Jews, in the strongest possible fashion, in terms of the power of the Jewish God, and to prepare them for the possible need for refusal; yet not to turn them against those outside.

This voice is not entirely new. The Hebrew Bible, and especially the prophets, already contain memorable critiques of idol worship, while the prudential advice offered by the authors of Wisdom writings had deep roots, not just in the Hebrew Bible, but in the traditions of the Near East. Nor am I suggesting that the open attacks on monarchs are confined to the Septuagint. Precedents are to be found already in the Exodus story, in the narratives of the judges of Israel and, again, in the Hebrew prophets.[53] Habakkuk (1: 11) said that kings everywhere worship their own might. Isaiah mocked the vanity and arrogance of the Assyrian king (10: 13–14). But it was in the Greek

---

[52] On idolatry in Joseph and Asenath, in comparison with Philo, see Pearce 2007a: 38.
[53] On this theme, see the interesting discussion of Maddox 1998.

literature of the late Hellenistic and the Roman period that the two themes were firmly brought together: the ultimate powerlessness of rulers and the grotesque absurdity of their cult images.

LITERATURE AND SUBVERSION

We may perhaps be surprised at the evolution of this discourse of open critique of other cults. The texts we have surveyed, with their crumbling or toppling images, their undermining of institutionalized systems of worship, their denunciation of priests, and their lambasting of kings, vaunted the power of one race alone by vaunting the power of its God. Admittedly unspecific in reference, many of them were all too graphic in their depiction and perfectly transparent in meaning. John Barclay[54] has presented the Wisdom of Solomon as 'an educated and deeply Hellenized exercise in cultural aggression'. He does, however, also remind us that this same book has at times been read as a document whose main thrust is not aggressive at all, but rather to persuade Jews to adapt to Greek culture.

What consequences did the composers of these texts intend or envisage? A wide circulation of readers must have been both intended and achieved, given the proliferation of material and the multiplication of versions. That the committed readership was indeed largely located within the Jewish communities seems on all counts likely.[55] A number of the texts I have discussed could conceivably be read as some kind of call to arms. By expressing hatred and contempt for alien cults, by dwelling on the evils of rulers, by means of constant reminders of God's saving grace, it would theoretically be possible to provoke readers to militancy, to incite revolution—surely a provocation to the local authorities at the very least. An interpretation is conceivable which traces a straight line from the reading of Daniel to the diaspora Jewish revolt under Trajan.

There are, however, strong objections to such a reading. Most obviously, we are obliged consequently to ignore the prominent

---

[54] Barclay 1996: 186.
[55] For pagan knowledge of the Greek Bible, see Chap. 8.

vein of cautious realism that runs right through the varied sample of utterances in different genres presented in this chapter, and of similar passages which might have been selected. Caution, watchfulness, and reconciliation with the current order are the first line of defence recommended explicitly or implicitly by their authors, even when they criticize prevailing evils and conjure up oppressors. Regrouping and resolution are regular outcomes of imagined conflict. Angry monarchs repent, convert, or are superseded. Detestation of idols does not turn into an invitation to attack their worshippers. Power is a fact of life, its misuse finite.

In addressing texts which inscribe traumatic circumstances or acute tensions, conjectural association with real events is a temptation hard to resist, and such passages are often seen as the product of some particular national crisis. Thus, for example, in seeking to show that the court stories in Esther and in Daniel reflect real exilic circumstances, W. Lee Humphries suggests that each of these books has a basic, earlier stratum written when good relations between Jews and the Persian government prevailed with trouble coming only from feuds at court.[56] To these has been added a later stratum written when things had turned much nastier, in the late Seleucid period. Writers—and translators—do indeed respond to circumstances. But the relation between the events inscribed in their narratives and events on the ground cannot be one of direct, one-to-one correspondence. Depictions of crises do not necessarily arise from situations of crisis: there are reasons for them to be thought useful and to be found appealing in good times as much as in bad. In our case, even if the need for reaction to extreme pressure might for some never arise there was still great value for Jewish communities in recognizing the possibility that it might do so and in representing their world accordingly.

On the practical level, remembering past oppression was conducive to being forearmed. Such a motivation is often invoked today among Jews and others as a reason for remembering catastrophes. Taking a longer view, there is advantage for the long-term survival

---

[56] Humphreys 1973: 220–3. For a detailed attempt to relate Daniel to the changing fortunes of the Jewish community in Judaea, see Gammie 1976. For a full introduction to the components of the book of Daniel, J. J. Collins 1993: 1–71.

and the solidarity of the group in conjuring up past enemies and evoking challenges successfully surmounted. Philip Davies expressed this insight well in connection precisely with the court stories in Daniel: 'we can presume that the preservation of distinct values and identity by a sub-culture in an imperial cultural milieu, whether hostile or not, requires conflict in order to sustain itself; lack of conflict aids assimilation.'[57] The most useful narratives, then, are precisely those which act as a deterrent to complacency by depicting both the worst of possibilities and the most vivid of reversals. Moreover, dramas with satisfactory endings provided excellent lessons in the benefits of piety. In the best circumstances, such scenarios could be confined to the realm of memory or imagination while peace and harmony prevailed outside.

These texts then, for all their vigorous criticism and unrestrained mockery of the fictional powers-that-be, are not crafted as incitements to rebellion, nor as active encouragement to Jews to set themselves at odds with their rulers; they are able to serve, paradoxically, just as well as an encouragement to adjustment to the status quo. Far from implying that 'the rulers of the earth' should be overthrown, the fundamental reserve in our texts towards those rulers' pretensions, and especially towards their claims of divinity, is coupled with an endorsement of their assured position in a hierarchy which has the true God standing at its summit. The exploitation of Greek philosophical models of bad kingship and of traditional stereotypes of what distinguishes the tyrant from the good ruler serves precisely to validate the need for the latter. Looking ultimately inwards as much as outwards, these texts serve to develop Jewish strategies for cultural and religious self-definition and group preservation. They subvert values and critique institutions in a coded discourse.

This may seem to be a high-risk policy. It can be objected that in a context of autocracy any publicly visible attacks on any deified rulers would be deemed treasonable. For even if, in reality, Hellenistic kings or Roman emperors did not come into face-to-face confrontations with Jewish heroes—they were figures remote in the extreme for

---

[57] Davies 1991: 163.

insignificant inhabitants of distant provinces—still the limits of the possible were revealed by direct intervention in the affairs of the Jews of a Seleucid king in the shape of Antiochus IV or of a Roman emperor in the shape of Claudius (who in a supposedly pacificatory letter describes the Jews of Alexandria as a disease, *nosos*, in the world).[58] And again, there might have been protection in the passivity and inaction of governors and of local officials, whose general approach to the exercise of responsibility was to step in as little as possible and act only when they had to.[59] Yet the transactions surrounding the decrees on Jewish rights issued to provincial cities by senators and governors and recorded by Josephus reveal that the pressure of local disputes and the Jewish requests for protection often enough put the Jews into the spotlight. What assurance was there then for Jewish groups or individuals that the invectives they were reciting and texts circulating would escape the suspicious eyes of enemies and of the authorities? Why did the translators, authors, transmitters, and readers take such risks?

One explanation offers itself. We may point to the esoteric nature of the Greek biblical corpus, brought about by its changing yet enduring language or linguistic idiolect, that peculiar version of koine Greek which is in effect a new translation language and which we studied closely in Chapter 4. Even where that idiolect was not called upon in its full form, as for example in the Wisdom of Solomon, a highly allusive and idiosyncratic vocabulary could still be deployed, creating an enclosed environment for these utterances. Moreover, beyond the fundamental phenomenon of language, but still grounded in it, this literature denies easy access by virtue of its intertextuality. Any one text is only completely understood in terms of multiple allusions and resonances. What could outsiders make of the confidence with which those anonymous creators conjured up

---

[58] The Emperor Claudius' policy, as expressed in the surviving papyrus fragment of his Letter to the Alexandrians (and in a somewhat different form in two edicts cited by Josephus) was apparently successful in bringing the violent ethnic disturbances inflamed by his predecessor to an end. See *CPJ*, ii. 153; Josephus, *AJ*, 19. 280–91.

[59] As, for example, when Pliny as special imperial legate in Bithynia wrote to Trajan that he was obliged to take action because of the increasing problems created by the growing number of Christians in his province, but that he had never done so before: Pliny, *Letters*, 10. 96.

kings whose rule could last for ever, or of their perverse re-evaluation of *doxa*, or their strange expressions for holy things? The full sense of the words could not be conveyed to readers not nurtured on the language and the biblical precedents. While vocabulary and thought developed, as we have seen,[60] in the course of the post-biblical period, still the new and the old formed a complete continuum.

In the event, we quite rarely find the ascription of disloyalty, still less of treason, among the many critiques of Jews in Greek and Roman writers.[61] The common charge laid at the door of Judaism (and later of Christianity) in Greek and Latin writers (and presumably in daily life) of misanthropy and xenophobia could easily have taken that turn, but apparently did not do so. This is, by contrast, precisely the turn taken by the anti-Semitism of the modern nation state, whose staples have been accusations of double loyalty, conspiracy, subversion, and revolution.[62]

Thus the Greek Bible could serve as an effective manual for life under foreign rule, above all for those living in a country 'not their own'. Not only that: this element of the texts could play a part in assuring their enduring centrality and vitality. Within the spread of genres could be found an impressive and ever-growing array of representations of the forces behind governments and the fate of subjects, of power and powerlessness from which principles—and warnings too—might be derived. These passages combined the discourse of accommodation with the spirit of independence. Both discourses were essential for survival of the individual and of the group. Independence complemented accommodation, helping especially to build up a compensatory self-esteem. This review of representations of power in diaspora biblical literature has brought out a spirit of criticism and a potential for subversion stronger than the strand of acquiescence. That may usefully counterbalance the emphasis of recent accounts of the Jewish diaspora as a model of

---

[60] See Chap. 4, pp. 162–72.
[61] Feldman and Reinhold 1996: 357–8, in their collection of Greek and Roman citations critical of the Jews, under the perhaps somewhat modernizing heading 'lack of patriotism', cite only Apion's charge, from Josephus at *CA*, 2.68, that the Jews caused conflict and sedition.
[62] For a brief and helpful summary of the phenomenon, see Shain 1998: 60–83.

contented integration and self-confidence.⁶³ On the other hand, I have stopped short of defining those outbursts through which the author of the Wisdom of Solomon likes to shake his readers as reflections of open antagonism and experienced conflict.⁶⁴ A more integrated reading leads us to allocate to such documents a place along the spectrum of writings of non-active resistance. The users of this literature, to be found in many different places over several centuries and under a succession of regimes, were well-served.

⁶³ Notably Gruen 2002. Cf. also the interpretation of J. J. Collins 2000, where he proposes associating the raging polemic of Sibylline Oracle 5 with the diaspora revolt against Trajan.
⁶⁴ As in Barclay's description: see above, p. 204.

6

The Uses of Scripture in Hellenistic Judaism

The Jews are frequently called 'people of the book', a description which is apt enough, even when the book is quintessentially a scroll or scrolls and when a conception of oral (rather than written) transmission has since late antiquity underpinned Judaism's endless enterprise of commentary on 'the book'.[1] As a matter of history, the particular application appears surprisingly late, and its origins, paradoxically enough, lie in the Quran, where Jews (or occasionally Christians) are addressed as *ahl al kitab*.[2] It is a label which, in any case, has done yeoman service. '[In] historical Judaism, the central task of exegetical tradition is to demonstrate the capacity of Scripture to regulate *all* areas of life and thought', writes Michael Fishbane in introducing his classic study *Biblical Interpretation in Ancient Israel*.[3] James Kugel has made us aware of how each generation saw its own interpretation of Scripture as, simply, scripture.[4] Yet another very influential scholar, Moshe Halbertal, has fruitfully applied the concept of a 'text-centred society' developed in other theatres of intellectual history, to the Jewish sphere and especially to rabbinic Judaism in all its phases. There, Torah (the five books of Moses) was without doubt the underlying source, while, in time, Mishnah, Talmud, and probably some of the midrashim—all outgrowths of the

---

[1] On the emergence during the rabbinic period of the concept of the 'twofold Torah', i.e., oral and written, see Fraade 1999.

[2] For the Islamic application of the term 'people of the book' to the Jews, see Stroumsa 2003: 153–5.

[3] Fishbane 1985: 3.

[4] The approach is exemplified throughout the work of Kugel, and see esp. Kugel 1998, with a summary in the work's preface. Kugel engages in close readings of interpretations and their interconnections.

Torah which rest firmly (in one way or another) upon it—acquired their own massive authority and, indeed, Halbertal maintains, a distinctive kind of canonicity.[5]

From this base, we can now move on to find out what role the Greek translated Bible could have played in the lives of the 'people of the book'. Mindful of the outstanding importance of the Bible, and of biblical interpretation in Jewish tradition generally, it is tempting to transfer these assumptions without more ado, and to stake out this feature as the determining principle also of Hellenistic-Jewish culture. A sharp and significant contrast with mainstream Graeco-Roman culture then takes shape. This step has been taken often enough. As an example of a quite familiar kind of assertion, I can do no better than to quote the most authoritative reference work in the field, the new English edition of Emil Schürer's classic *History of the Jewish People in the Time of Jesus Christ*. Here we read that 'the basis of all Jewish–Hellenistic culture is the old, anonymous Greek Bible translation known as the Septuagint... without it the religion of the Greek-speaking Jews was as unthinkable as the Church of England without the Authorized Version'. The fourth German edition of Schürer's original work had instead spoken, as might be expected, of Luther's translation.[6] This pair of supposedly interchangeable parallels serves well enough to convey how a particular form of scripture can be fundamental to the evolution of a creed. But their interchangeability already exposes their vagueness. Moreover, Schürer's supposition that what differentiated Greek-speaking Jews from Jewish users of Hebrew or Aramaic was a distinctive brand of 'religion' is an odd one. Might the sub-text be that the former group was on the road to being illuminated by the Christian 'religion'? In a rather different spirit, Victor Tcherikover called the Greek translation of the scriptures the 'cornerstone on which the entire edifice of Jewish Alexandria rested'.[7] With the second statement it is harder to disagree; yet it is no more than the very beginnings of understanding.

We have no licence simply to assume that a particular pattern of relationships with the scriptures was the common property of Jews

---

[5] The application is worked out in Halbertal 1997, and see esp. pp. 1–10.
[6] Schürer iii: 474; Schürer 1901–9, iii: 424.
[7] Tcherikover 1959: 348.

across the language divide; in Judaea, in the rest of Palestine, and in the Babylonian and the Graeco-Roman diasporas alike; and through more than half a millennium of turbulent events.[8] Many societies and groups have nurtured indispensable texts, and these texts can be embedded and do service for them in diverse ways.[9] The task of this chapter is to ask what specific forms were taken by that text-dependence in the world of Greek-speaking Jews. How important were the scriptures to them? What difference did scripture make? First, we need to delimit the world we are talking about and to satisfy ourselves that we may reasonably consider it, for all its diversity, a cultural unit. Then we shall observe how its literary heritage is concerned with recycling biblical ideas and narratives. From the various kinds of surviving evidence, we shall go on to build as best we can a picture of the role of the Bible in society and in individual lives, taking due account of the inadequacy of our evidence, of underlying problems, and of questions that remain unanswered. In the second of the two chapters devoted to this topic, we shall look at new ways of throwing our evidence into relief.

PRELIMINARIES: CANON AND CANONICITY

But first, a matter of description. Why is the important, seemingly apposite, and much-discussed question of the 'canon' and the 'canonical' scarcely visible in my discussion? Do these terms not sum up what I mean? Why not speak of 'canonicity' rather than 'centrality', 'authority', 'uses', or 'engagement'? Would we be speaking of essentially the same thing but in more appropriate and meaningful, more 'biblical' terms? We have already seen that there existed no specific 'Alexandrian' canon of the Greek Bible, different in content from the evolving Hebrew corpus.[10] Nevertheless, the overlapping completion

---

[8] But for a more carefully nuanced sketch of the picture in the Graeco-Roman diaspora, see Barclay 1996: 424–6.

[9] Stock's study of 'textual communities' in medieval Europe (1993) has been influential in stimulating study of the social role of canonical texts.

[10] See Introduction, pp. 21–2.

of the Hebrew scriptures and the process of their crystallization into a single entity is not irrelevant to their Greek counterparts. We would expect to find some reflection of that situation in the Greek milieu. And, indeed, in a soft sense, the answer to my question is positive: the vivid presence of the Bible in the culture does make it reasonable to speak loosely of 'canonical status'. But, if we attempt to apply the concept in its full-blown sense to this context, we are in trouble.

'Canonization' comprises a range of elements—fixing the content of the group, fixing the text, ascribing a superior kind of authority to a master text or list of texts (with their interpretations). The extent and pace at which the first two of these crystallized during our period for the Hebrew Bible, let alone for the Greek Bible, remains an open and debated question: the last section of the tripartite Torah was evidently still open and variable; the prophetic section too may not have been closed; some even argue that the Torah, for the Qumran sect at least, contained books outside our Pentateuch.[11] As Jennifer Dines writes: 'it is easy for later perceptions of the sacrosanctity of Scripture to be retrojected, but this should be resisted'.[12]

The last of the three elements in canonization means something very like 'centrality'. And in this third sense the topic of this chapter could almost have been described as the varieties and functions of canonicity. Yet I am positioned both before and beyond canonicity: that is to say, before that late date when full biblical canonicity can with confidence be said to have been firmly established among Jews, and beyond the wall of sanctity raised by the word 'canonicity'. It is worth remembering that the concept of a 'canon' as applied to scripture is not native to Jewish articulation. As James Barr[13] quite baldly puts it, 'the word "canon" is a Christian term; moreover, when used in this sense it is a rather late Christian term, not found until about the fourth century CE. There is no ancient Hebrew expression meaning "canon".' Still, the term has been more or less acclimatized in modern discussion of the Jewish canon of the Hebrew Bible, which

---

[11] For a recent and radical approach to the problem, see Campbell 2000.
[12] Dines 2004: 125.
[13] Barr 1983. Another scholar to make this point is Barton (1986: 44), for whom 'the word "canon" itself is a most inappropriate term to describe the scriptures of Jews and Christians in the first few centuries of our era'.

has been lively and constructive, and it is unnecessary to object to it on that score.

The discussion still, however, leaves basic questions unresolved. The library of scrolls found at Qumran has opened up the interesting possibility that different groups within Judaism had different lists of books they held sacred. The corpus of books regarded with special esteem by the Dead Sea sect included the book Jubilees, a rewrite of part of Genesis which incorporated the sectarian solar calendar; a remarkably large number of fragments of Jubilees have been found at Qumran.[14] On the other hand, the conservative position, of a closure well-nigh complete by 70 CE, has not been entirely rejected.[15] And now Menahem Haran once again proposes a very early 'canonization' in Judaism, though one that worked differently from Christianity, functioning not by weeding out but rather by the prompt adoption of new holy texts which were essentially anthologies of old documents. He contends that the related religions—all three monotheistic religions in fact—used very different routes to achieve the same result, a canon to all intents and purposes.[16]

At the heart of the debate has been the question of the fixing of the 'Prophets' section[17] which, in the Hebrew Bible, includes also the post-pentateuchal historical books. It is quite likely that in the Second Temple period the category was even more inclusive, with perhaps Psalms within it at the time of the Maccabees. Most scholars would admit that the third section of the Jewish division of the 'canon', the 'writings', must have fluctuated until two or more centuries later. And even at that late stage, when something did change, David Stern suggests,[18] closure was not an official determination but simply a de facto development, through what was read and what was not, in liturgical as in educational contexts. As for the conceptualization of sanctity, that was understood essentially as a matter of levels

---

[14] For one vigorous statement of this position, see Campbell 2000.

[15] For the conservative approach, Leiman 1976, updated by Kamesar 1993, but already criticized in detail by Barton 1986: 21–95.

[16] Haran 1996: 7.

[17] Examined at great length by Barton 1986: 21–55. Lim 1997: 3–4, with nn. 2–5, conveniently summarizes the opposing positions. Barr 1983: 54 ff. remains illuminating.

[18] Stern 2003.

of holiness. At some point before the middle ages, everything about the physical text, and every word written in it, indeed the lettering itself (square Assyrian) became a holy thing and an object of reverence.[19] But our period sees no attestation of this. Nor is there any precursor of the distinctive—and still puzzling—rabbinic concept of books that through their holiness 'defile the hands'.[20]

Using terms such as 'canonicity' suggests that we are dealing with a text that was placed on a lofty pedestal. 'Canonicity' easily shades into orthodoxy of approach, and even rigidity. Characteristic to Judaism's intimacy with the Bible is, rather, a very wide range of attitudes and of kinds of engagement, from the most profound to the light-hearted or even frivolous, which were not seen as inappropriate for a holy text. Yehuda Amichai, the great Israeli poet whose lines open this book, captures the essence of his own relationship with the scrolls of the Law and that of the Jews through the ages in a stanza that appears to be flippant but has a serious meaning:

> The Jewish people read Torah aloud to God
> All year long, a portion a week,
> Like Scheherezade who told stories to save her life.
> By the time Simchat Torah [the Rejoicing of the Law] rolls around,
> God forgets and they can begin again.[21]

There were degrees of holiness, too: Torah, the word of God through Moses, requiring greater reverence than the prophets—who in turn required considerably more than some of the 'writings'. The issue is often therefore better defined in less loaded cultural terms.[22] It is the different ways in which people live with the books they treasure.

Robert Alter has shown beautifully the depth and significance of the Bible as a literary model in Jewish literature through the ages, feeding the imagination at every level in a manner which was 'more dynamic and multi-faceted than its doctrinal function would

---

[19] See Green in Neusner and Green 1989: 7–22.
[20] On which see Beckwith 1985, and Goodman 1990.
[21] Yehuda Amichai, 'God changes, prayers are here to stay', stanza 9, from Amichai 2000: 42 (trans. Bloch and Kronfeld). Simchat Torah, the festival of the Rejoicing of the Law, marks the annual recommencement of the cycle of weekly readings.
[22] Cf. Stroumsa 1998: 10.

require'. This Jewish kind of canonicity is, for example, vividly ascribed by Alter to the leading nineteenth-century Hebrew poet (Hayyim Nachman Bialik), a writer from a traditional background who worked in a secular literary medium with modern literary and cultural goals and often wrote on modern subjects. In the case of Yehuda Amichai—for all his surface irreverence—interactions, often troubled interactions, with a biblical past and overt biblical themes are even more frequent. Because this kind of canonicity is built into the history of the Hebrew language itself, whose word stock, phrases, and images are inescapably biblical, it presents ever-renewable opportunities, as well as never-ending demands.

Alter speaks tellingly of 'a power of canonicity that is not limited to doctrine or strictly contingent on belief in the inspired character of the texts invoked'.[23] Here he extends the meaning of the term beyond the sense generally given it in biblical studies. He writes against a background in which this broader concept of 'canonicity' has acquired a vigorous secondary existence, a development to which he himself has been a contributor. The modern or post-modern role of the erstwhile literary canon of 'great' works, indispensable to our culture, continues to be the subject of much examination, introspection, questioning, and argument. All this would bring yet further content which would divert us from our purpose here. The neutral term 'centrality'[24] expresses in simple fashion what is needed here and will serve my discussion well.

THE HELLENISTIC–JEWISH TRADITION

It is proposed in this discussion to take Greek-speaking Jews as a single entity. Is this justified? The term 'Hellenistic Judaism' is conventionally applied not just to the Jews of the Hellenistic era proper, but—for want of a better term—to the entire diaspora which is the subject of this book, the whole gamut of Greek-speaking Jewry from Alexandria to the Crimea, from 300 BCE to 600 CE

---

[23] Alter 2000: 60.
[24] 'Centrality' is also the term chosen by S. Schwartz 2001: 240–3.

(Sardis).²⁵ Arnaldo Momigliano maintained that 'there was a distinctive brand of Hellenism which was Jewish Hellenism. There were entire communities which, even though they considered themselves Jews and practised the Jewish religion, spoke Greek, thought in Greek and knew hardly any Hebrew or Aramaic. For at least seven or eight centuries, Greek remained the alternative cultural language of the Jews'.²⁶ Language for Momigliano is a decisive criterion, and this, he pointed out, justifies a special focus on Jews for whom Greek was the primary language. Most of these people were to be found around the diaspora proper, but the description could also apply to Jewish inhabitants of Greek cities within and around Palestine. Indeed, on the view maintained by Martin Hengel in his epoch-making and controversial *Judaism and Hellenism*, Greek culture had penetrated even Judaea to such an extent by the turn of the third century BCE that Momigliano's dictum might almost have been true of certain residents of Jerusalem itself.²⁷ In broad terms, however, we are talking about the culture of the Jewish diaspora, within which, for this purpose, must be included the Christian communities that grew out of it and that produced the books of the New Testament.

As we saw in Chapter 3, we are talking about a long line of Jewish life lived through Greek, embodied in a long line of written self-expression in Greek.²⁸ The line forms a tradition, because contributors demonstrably build on the work of predecessors. This does not mean that all of them could possibly be aware of all those that had gone before; but it does mean that even from our damaged record we can discern a cultural community, of writers and therefore of readers, continuing through time and of course through differing circumstances. Thus Gregory Sterling, investigating the reception of Philo's

---

[25] This diaspora is described in Chap. 3.
[26] Momigliano 1990: 25.
[27] Hengel 1974 (in English trans.).
[28] Schürer, as reflected still in the revised version (vol. iii), separated 'works originally composed in Greek' from those written in Hebrew and Aramaic. Though criticized, this has proved to be far-sighted. While assignations can be a good deal more arbitrary or hypothetical than they appear, we are provided with an immediate overview of the Jewish–Greek tradition and the division allows significant patterns to emerge.

treatises among Greek-speaking Jews (as well as pagan philosophers), concludes (if tentatively), on the basis of passages showing striking literary similarities, that they were known in Egypt, Syria, and Rome.[29]

What has come down to us looks like a broken line with a number of spurs. Entire texts have disappeared over time, a notable instance being the Maccabaean history of Jason of Cyrene in its original form, of which the book we know as the Second Book of Maccabees is an abridgement. There is no reason why there should not be lost works whose existence we do not even know about.[30] Many important and apparently early contributions to this tradition exist for us in tantalizing fragments, representing vestiges of lost historians, philosophers, poets, and dramatists.[31] These were transmitted highly selectively via earlier excerptors of the Roman period, notably Alexander Polyhistor, a scholar of wide-ranging curiosity in late republican Rome.[32] Subsequently, in the first Christian centuries, indirect citations were included in their own writings, and for their own purposes, by patristic writers. The most important of these was Eusebius, in the *Preparation for the Gospel*; but already before this the Jewish citations had played a part in Clement of Alexandria's anthology, the *Stromateis*.

Josephus, when he debates the relative antiquity of Jews and Greeks as part of the defence of Judaism in his *Against Apion*, draws on a number of such writers, sometimes labelling them, surprisingly, Greek rather than Jewish, as he should have done and as they surely were.[33] Thus he includes among the 'Greek' writers who, he claims, had known about and made mention of the Jews, the name of Eupolemus. And excerpts surviving in the Christian sources

---

[29] Sterling 1999, with the main evidence coming from Sibylline Oracle, 4, the Testaments of the Twelve Patriarchs, 2 Enoch, 4 Macc. and Josephus.

[30] The point is made well in Vermes and Goodman 1984.

[31] Full primary sources and exposition of all these writers in Schürer iii: 470–704, or Collins 2000. Discussion of the major figures under the rubric of 'apologetics' in Sterling 1992: 137–225.

[32] Freudenthal's study of 1879 is still the point of reference for Alexander Polyhistor, not yet replaced.

[33] Josephus, *CA*, 1. 218. The historian at this point may have chosen to use a purely linguistic definition of the description 'Greek' to the advantage of his own argument.

from a work by a writer of this name describe its subject as 'the kings of Judaea' and highlight the achievements of David and Solomon. Another small excerpt, concerning Abraham and somewhat different in spirit, has in modern times been assigned, rightly or wrongly, to a 'Pseudo-Eupolemus', possibly a Samaritan.[34] Along with Eupolemus, Josephus also names 'the elder Philo', probably to be identified with a poet said by Eusebius to have authored a poem on Jerusalem; of the poem we know nothing more than the title. A second poet, Theodotus, who told the story of the abduction of Dinah, sister of Joseph, and his brothers, and its gruesome consequence, the massacre of her abductors' people the Shechemites by Simeon and Levi, also figures in Josephus' roster of outside writers in Greek aware of the Jews.[35] Elsewhere, Josephus ascribes to a certain Cleodemus Malchas[36] an interesting genealogical line of the descendants of Abraham which runs not only to Jews but also to the Carthaginians; and Josephus' quotation from Cleodemus is in turn quoted, once more, by Eusebius, for essentially the same purpose as Josephus has quoted it. The fragmentary writers and Josephus are, then, links in a chain of Jewish writers in Greek, even where they are mis-described. They appear to be bound by the common purpose of making sense in Greek historiographical terms of a Bible-based version of the Jewish past.

Another lost writer was apparently a source for Josephus but did not make it into the Christian record, and he remains nameless. This is the writer inelegantly dubbed Pseudo-Hecataeus in modern scholarship. The real Hecataeus of Abdera was a scholar who worked for Ptolemy I and interpreted Egypt for him. Josephus ascribes to that important literary figure a cluster of quotations which includes a not entirely unrealistic description of the Temple and which concludes with the tale of a Jewish archer's scornful and witty demonstration of the absurdity of reading omens—he simply stepped forward and killed the bird that was meant to be a portent.[37] A minority of scholars have accepted that the entirety of the material was written

---

[34] For alert assessments of both of these writers, see J. J. Collins 2000: 37–50.
[35] Josephus, *CA*, 1.216; Eus., *Praep. Ev.*, 9.22. J. J. Collins 2000: 57–60 insists, in the face of older opinion, that Theodotus was probably not a Samaritan, if only because of his lack of enthusiasm for Shechem, the Samaritans' main city.
[36] Josephus, *AJ*, 1. 239–41.
[37] Josephus, *CA*, 1. 183–205.

by the genuine Hecataeus, but many others[38] detect behind part of the whole narrative the work of an apologetic Jewish author—hence the label 'Pseudo-Hecataeus'. That same author may also have produced the book on Abraham which Josephus ascribes to Hecataeus in the *Antiquities* (1.159). In Pseudo-Hecataeus, then, we have another link in the chain.

At the same time we cannot help noticing that Josephus has nothing to say about some of the most striking figures among the earlier Jewish, or at least apparently Jewish, writers in Greek. It would appear that he simply did not know about them. In other words, the tradition does not run in a broad and open stream. Ezekiel, author of the *Exagoge*, a tragedy on the Exodus in Aeschylean mould, complete with a vision of Moses sitting on the throne of God as well as the appearance of a magnificent and wonderful phoenix, must have been a most remarkable talent.[39] Yet there is not a hint of him in Josephus' copious writings. Nor do we hear a word about several prose writers whose striking Hellenizations of Jewish tradition he might have been expected to embrace. Demetrius, sometimes dubbed by moderns 'the chronographer', liked setting and solving puzzles, much like the later midrashists. He asked, for example, how it could happen that the Israelites were unarmed in Egypt but armed in the desert (the answer being that they acquired the weapons of the drowned Egyptians). A certain Aristeas (not the author of the *Letter*) went in for the kind of knowledgeable exegesis which identified obscure biblical individuals with more familiar personalities of whom rather more was known, another technique of rabbinic Midrash. Thus he made the suffering Job into the son of Esau and then identified him with the obscure figure of Jobab in Genesis 36: 31–3. That compelling biblical figure was indeed often assigned by Jewish commentators to the patriarchal period, perhaps a mark of his appeal in the Greek tradition. Another member of this group of authors, Aristobulus, was labelled a Peripatetic philosopher; he apparently defined the divine voice as an abstraction and God as a metaphor, anticipating philonic allegory.[40] Above all, Josephus appears

---

[38] See, most recently, Bar-Kochva 1996, an intensive, book-length study of the question.
[39] Eus., *Praep. Ev.*, 9.28–9.
[40] On Aristobulus as a Peripatetic, see p. 78.

not even to have had any inkling of the work of Jason of Cyrene, nor any knowledge of the surviving, abbreviated version of his history of the Maccabaean revolt which makes up 2 Maccabees and which, as it happens, mentions Aristobulus in his opening chapter; alternatively, if Josephus was aware of it, he must have had a very strong reason indeed for not incorporating anything from it into his narrative of the wars of the Maccabees and of the Hasmonean rulers, either in the *Jewish War* or in the *Jewish Antiquities*.[41]

The patchy pattern which confronts us should not be a surprise. The transmission of literature under ancient conditions was erratic at the best of times, and it is in the nature of diaspora that communities are widely dispersed. It complicates the picture further that some Greek–Jewish texts were evidently routed through Jerusalem. Again, the fragmentary historian Eupolemus is often, and reasonably, identified with the ambassador whom Judas Maccabaeus sent to Rome. The translator of the First Book of Maccabees from Hebrew into Greek (but in a distinctly biblical idiom) is likely to have been Jerusalem-based. The Second Book of Maccabees, in its existing abridged form, is politically focused on the Temple to an extent which suggests at least a close association with Jerusalem. We must suppose either that Jason, the original author of the full history, was a Cyrenian who came to Judaea, or else that his work had a reception there, leading to a refocusing of the abridgment.[42] All this again makes it necessary to conceive of the tradition as an intricate series of relationships rather than a simple linear development.

The tradition I am marking out finds its twin culmination in Philo and Josephus. These are magisterial and voluminous writers, and most of what they wrote has been preserved for us (again through the agency of Christian scholars). Each of them has the uniqueness of a great creator, which makes it particularly difficult to treat him as

---

[41] On the absence of any trace of 2 Macc. from Josephus' writings, see D. Schwartz 2004: 58–9 suggesting that small points shared between the two narratives but not with 1 Macc. are too unimportant and too few to be significant. Goldstein 1983: 26–7, n. 80 maintains that Josephus demonstrably knew the abridgement of Jason of Cyrene's work but chose not to use it because of its anti-Hasmonean slant.

[42] So Doran 1981. D. Schwartz 2000 finds the city to override the Temple even in 2 Macc. On differences in historiographical slant between diaspora and Judaean writing, see D. Schwartz 1999.

typical of their times. Inevitably, though, we shall depend upon them in the rest of this chapter.

It will already have become clear that if there is one unifying factor which allows us to talk of a tradition, this lies not in its singleness, but primarily in its consistent engagement with an authoritative literary corpus, the Greek versions of the Hebrew Bible. What is in question is of course not simply scripture, but scripture in Greek. The biblical books in their original Hebrew form may have been the ultimate symbolic point of reference even for Jews who themselves were entirely ignorant of the language.[43] But it is the distinctive Greek version which can claim to be the common diaspora heritage. We meet it, as we have already begun to see, at every turn.

THE GREEK BIBLE AND JEWISH LITERARY PRODUCTION

As we have seen, Hellenistic–Jewish literature comprises different types of text, and these are hooked into the scriptures in different ways. And yet we find scarcely a single writer who is *not* somehow hooked into them. This will be visible in the following sketch which outlines the main kinds of relationship with scripture to be found in Greek–Jewish writing.

To begin at the beginning, the *Letter of Aristeas* is perhaps the quintessential surviving piece of Hellenistic–Jewish writing and also one of the earliest. This embodied, as we saw, the collective memory of Alexandrian Jewry and it served as the 'charter myth' (to use Sylvie Honigman's term)[44] of the Septuagint translation. It is noteworthy that the legend contained in the *Letter* is adopted both by Philo and by Josephus, who use it to illustrate arguments of their own. Josephus retells the narrative part of the *Letter*, sticking very closely to the text, while Philo summarizes and embellishes, elaborating the miraculous dimension of the story. Earlier, that other philosophical writer,

---

[43] As argued in Chap. 4.
[44] The concept of 'charter myth' is developed in Honigman 2003 and discussed here, at Chap. 1, pp. 49–50.

Aristobulus, had somehow included the same translation story in his exposition.[45] If the 'charter myth' was so crucial and ubiquitous a tradition, the translation must itself have had a very high importance.

'Rewritten Bible' appears to describe nicely a good part of the output of the Hellenistic–Jewish tradition. This term, brought originally into play by Geza Vermes, is now very widely adopted to cover adaptations of biblical material in a variety of styles, showing varying degrees of respect for the form and content of the original.[46] The description is not without its problems, especially when we have to decide how to define its limits, but so far as we can tell it characterizes well enough, in its wider usage, the vestiges of Hellenistic–Jewish material that have reached us via Josephus, Clement of Alexandria, and Eusebius. There we see displayed a range of techniques for developing or embellishing the source. The scope is considerably wider than the Torah alone, as we have already seen, covering not only patriarchs but also kings and other figures of obvious interest such as Job and his daughters, or the prophet of the destruction of the first Temple, Jeremiah; or, again, famous edifices (notably, again, the Jerusalem Temple and—an earlier marvel—the Tower of Babel). Detailed chronological computations and synchronizations are sometimes offered, covering the *longue durée*. Also quite characteristic are elaborate genealogies linking the Hebrews to one another and to the rest of mankind. The treatment ranges from close verbal analysis to simple allegorical readings in which a symbolic meaning is extracted from stories which might otherwise perhaps have seemed simplistic or disturbing. One caution is necessary: as Robert Doran has acutely observed, 'since Eusebius was concerned with the earlier period of Jewish history and with the knowledge that non-Jews displayed of the biblical tradition, the preserved fragments necessarily deal with the Bible',[47] which may give us a somewhat misleading impression as to the real range of interests of the diverse group of

---

[45] On Aristobulus' version of the Aristeas story, see Chap. 2, p. 78.
[46] Vermes 1959; and see the important discussions of P. Alexander 1988, and Bernstein 1998. On 'rewritten Bible' in Greek, there are apt remarks in Bernstein 2003.
[47] Doran 1986: 248.

writers on which he drew. But even allowing for this bias the roster is overwhelming.

The description 'rewritten Bible' also suits further Hellenistic–Jewish material, such as the novelistic love story of Joseph and the Egyptian Asenath. There a strong romantic element accompanies an unusual conversion story, in which a mysterious honeycomb has to be consumed, from which an angelic figure summons a swarm of bees, before Joseph will agree to a marriage which Pharaoh goes on to bless. All this develops out of the spare statement in Genesis (41: 45) that Pharaoh gave Joseph for a wife the daughter of Petephres, priest of Heliopolis (in the Bible Potipher(a) the priest of On), at the same time putting him in charge of the whole of Egypt.[48] Considerable freedom was often taken with the biblical subject-matter by the Jewish–Greek authors, as Carl Holladay has stressed.[49] The kinds of elaboration they engaged in were sometimes in keeping with the other-worldly speculations which we find in Jewish texts of the period written in Hebrew and Aramaic. Among Eupolemus' cast of characters, for example, was the angel Dianathan, who told David that he was not to build the Temple. This author also adds an exchange of letters between Solomon and Vaphres king of Egypt to the correspondence mentioned in the books of Kings and Chronicles; and he modifies biblical chronology by turning Eli into a high priest of the days of Solomon.[50] Such a sometimes mystical, sometimes fanciful, but by no means frivolous approach is utterly at home in the genre of 'rewritten Bible' surviving in other ancient languages, just as it is characteristic of the haggadic midrashim (scriptural commentaries) in later centuries.[51]

The production of works in the 'rewritten Bible' mould was closely intertwined with the translation process itself. That 'work in progress' (as it has been well described) embodies a notable phenomenon, whereby later Greek translations demonstrably share vocabulary and phraseology with the those of the Pentateuchal

---

[48] For an introduction to this interesting and undateable novella, see J. J. Collins 2000: 103–12 and 230–8. Kraemer 1998 offers a full-length study. Bohak 1996 reads the story as a veiled promotion of the Jewish temple of Leontopolis. Cf. Inowlowski 2002.
[49] In Holladay 2002; van der Horst 1988.
[50] See Wacholder 1974.
[51] For these techniques in a Second Temple milieu, see esp. Fraade 2006b.

books or with other translations which would seem to have been made in an early phase, especially, and understandably, Psalms.[52] Emanuel Tov has made a beginning of gathering and analysing these intertextual associations, suggesting how some Greek books served as a kind of master document and provided a repertoire of terms and concepts for other, presumably later, translations. The data are revealing, even if the direction of particular dependencies may be uncertain.[53] A high degree of intimacy with the substantial parts of a previously completed corpus of translations is implied.

Copying, correcting, and improving the quality of the relationship between source and target texts are other activities included under the general rubric of translation. Much scholarly attention has been paid to the evidence of endeavours to make corrections in the light of an available Hebrew text. This, it now seems, was going on as early as the first century BCE, if the recent earlier dating of the Minor Prophets scroll fragments found at Nahal Hever beside the Dead Sea is correct.[54]

Furthermore, a language for self-expression was forged by the Greek Bible. The translators devised a vocabulary and with it a range of concepts that could not, in the nature of things, represent exactly their Hebrew prototypes. Greek words were deployed in specialized meanings and neologisms were regularly created. The list is a sizeble one and we have already had occasion to consider it.[55] Here we need only recall that different Greek Jewish authors used the vocabulary in different ways. Some terms had greater exposure than others, some a longer life than others. Here too, the routes of transmission were, once again, not uniform. It is often when we explore that basic level of individual lexical units that we are struck by the pervasive influence of the Greek Bible on its communities of Jewish users.

---

[52] Tov 1999: 183–94.
[53] As James Barr pointed out. See Barr's critique of Tov in Barr 2003.
[54] As revealed by Barthélemy 1963, whose central conclusion on the scribal activity involved is still widely accepted, although with an earlier date for the documents than he proposed. For the authoritative publication, see Parsons in Tov, Kraft, and Parsons 1990. The succinct account in Dines 2005: 3–4 and 81–4 is helpful.
[55] In Chap. 4, pp. 162–72.

Last but far from least, citations, whether verbatim or approximate, are an important vehicle for the diffusion of this special vocabulary and more broadly for asserting connection with the source text. Exact citation and close allusion to biblical material is found in nearly all the literary texts in my survey. Some texts are more dependent on them than are others, but it is worth pointing out that biblical echoes or exempla can have a special value as markers in works which do not follow traditional templates but rather appear as more-or-less Greek, in form and character. It is highly significant that we find a repertoire of biblical allusions and citations even in works as 'unseptuagintal', and as late as the Third and Fourth books of Maccabees, which were probably composed during the Roman period. These allusions and citations are scattered through the books. They are particularly appropriate to prayers and, unsurprisingly, in 3 Maccabees they cluster above all in the prayer of the priest Eleazar, uttered as the Jews are being herded into the amphitheatre by the tyrannical King Ptolemy (IV) where they are to be trampled upon by inebriated elephants.[56] But perhaps most memorable is the listing of biblical exemplary figures which appears in the conclusion of 4 Maccabees, an intensely rhetorical short book which recounts the confrontation of an aged priest, a mother, and her seven sons with the persecuting tyrant-ruler Antiochus and their tortures and successive deaths. The writing is a combination of philosophical dialogue, oration, and moralizing characteristic of the Second Sophistic movement in the Greek cities of the high Roman Empire. But the martyred mother closes her passionate exhortation with a veritable sermon, a *derash torah*, in which, as she makes a point of telling us, she repeats the teachings of her late husband from 'the Law and the Prophets', offering paradigms of courage, and quoting a chain of familiar words of inspiration for those who suffer. From Isaiah (43: 2) she declares: 'even though you go through the fire, the flames shall not consume you'. From Psalms (34: 19) she reads: 'many are the afflictions of the righteous'; From Proverbs (3: 18) she adapts the very familiar description of Torah as 'a tree of life'. With Ezekiel, she asks 'shall these bones live?', and she concludes by combining Deuteronomy 30: 20 with Deuteronomy

---

[56] 3 Macc. 6: 2–15.

Scripture in Hellenistic Judaism

32: 39: 'I kill and I make alive. This is your life and the length of your days.'[57]

TEXT AND USERS: SCRIPTURE IN ACTION

We have surveyed a Jewish literary output which does indeed reveal a distinctive and very highly privileged role for the Greek Bible among Jewish–Greek writers and readers. Adherence to an extensive sacred text of a particular kind, accessed in the form of a translation, must have major implications. If text-centredness has its types and gradations, the many different roles that a key text might play within a society are in reality conditioned at least as much by the character of the society as by the nature of the text. It does not matter that devotees are prone to see things differently, often all too eager to attribute control to the unchanging dictates of the scriptures which bind them. To investigate scripture as a social artefact is not to deny its status as perfect truth for many, nor to overlook the absoluteness of their conception of the text as the word of God and the most profound reality, or the highest philosophy. There are still questions to be asked about the mechanisms of use and about the functions performed by the texts for those who cherish them.[58]

Unfortunately, not only is the legacy of the Jews of the Graeco-Roman diaspora severely battered, as we have discovered, but what remains is of a kind that relays little direct information about what communities did, still less how people conducted their lives as individuals. Nevertheless, we can expand our reconstruction in some measure out of our same surviving texts together with a handful of inscriptions and even more sparse images. I shall go on

---

[57] 4 Macc. 18: 10–19. The last of the quoted sentences is cited also in 1Q22fl 2.4–5. It should be noted that some scholars have regarded the final chapter of 4 Macc. as a later addition. For commentaries on 4 Macc., see Hadas 1953; Scarpat 2006; de Silva 2006.

[58] S. Schwartz 2001: 66–8 insists on the gap between ideology and reality in relation to the influence of Torah on life. For the lists of biblical men and women used as examples (both negative and positive) in Philo's *de Virtutibus*, 198–210 and in the *Allegorical Commentary*, 3. 65–106, see Borgen 1997: 40–7.

in Chapter 7 to suggest that a comparative analysis in terms of broad typologies is a resource which offers a route to filling out the story and to putting our evidence in perspective. But the first task is to outline what the sources tell us about scripture in action.[59]

1. The written Torah was itself an iconic object. The supreme importance of the physical text was manifest on several dramatic occasions at the time of the first Jewish revolt. One of these took place at Caesarea in May 66 CE, where, when Roman troops could not (or would not?) control the disturbances that ensued after the desecration of a synagogue, the local Jews removed the Torah from the synagogue and fled with it to a village eight miles away. Caesarea was formally a Greek city and control had recently been awarded by the Romans to the minority of Greek inhabitants. This text (which is described by Josephus in his usual fashion as a book, *biblion*, rather than as a scroll) may even itself have been written in Greek.[60] The episode was an important one, which Josephus regards as marking the start of the revolt against Rome. In a different context, the crude figurative representations of what are evidently collections of scrolls lying on their sides in an *'aron* (scroll-cupboard) which decorate a number of the inscriptions of the Jewish catacombs of Rome, and also fragments of gold glass artefacts found there, are witness to the importance of the physical Torah a century or two later.[61]

2. Moses the lawgiver, as the author or transmitter of the Torah (sometimes the one, sometimes the other) served as the ideal figure, the culture hero par excellence of the Hellenistic–Jewish imagination. He was the prophet who had seen God face to face, who had heard his voice, and who had been told his name. Philo called Moses an interpreter (*hermēneus*), but also, in the *Life of Moses*, a king.[62]

---

[59] Borgen 2001 interprets Philo's *Embassy to Gaius* with such a purpose in view, finding there evidence for the incorporation into life of various aspects of 'outer tradition', broken down into 'verbal', 'behavioural', 'institutional', and 'material' tradition.

[60] Josephus, *BJ*, 2.284–92. Josephus has no term for 'scroll', and elsewhere too he speaks either of books, *biblia*, like the ones Titus gave him on the fall of Jerusalem (*Life*, 418), or else simply of *nomos*, the Law, as when it is carried in the Flavian triumph (*BJ*, 7.150).

[61] Depictions in Leon 1995: Plate 20, Fig. 34; Fine 1997: 155.

[62] Pearce 2004b: 37–40; Calabi 1998: 2–9.

Here, Philo presents the roles of lawgiver, prophet, and high priest as the accompaniments of kingship.[63] At times, Moses' uniqueness is expressed in strong spiritual terms: he is the 'dearly beloved of God' and the hierophantic enunciator of his sacred truths. In the biblical narrative of Josephus' *Antiquities*, Moses has the more down-to-earth persona of ruler, statesman, and general.[64]

When Greek–Jewish writers of a more universalizing bent, such as Artapanus (if indeed he should be regarded as a Jewish writer),[65] preferred to stress Moses' role as a culture hero, inventor, and benefactor of humanity, this only increased his stature. In the *Exagoge*, the tragedy on the Exodus ascribed to Ezekiel, there is a memorable and mysterious moment where God, a protagonist in the drama, vacates his throne temporarily in favour of Moses.[66] For the Alexandrian Jewish 'extreme allegorizers' alluded to by Philo, Moses seems to have been quite simply the teacher who had revealed all wisdom.[67] For the *therapeutai*, those Egyptian ascetics in their community beside Lake Mareotis, Moses was a choirmaster.[68] As the leader of the defining event of the Exodus from Egypt, Moses was as much the founder (*archētes*) of the nation as Abraham. So, for Philo, Abraham's journey from the land of his fathers (interpreted spiritually by Philo) and his adventures in Egypt had merely prefigured the Exodus, and it was Moses who put his seal on everything that Abraham had achieved.[69]

3. The Greek Bible was the source of the Greek–Jewish sense of history, a building-block of identity.[70] This shines out of Josephus' writing, through his professions in the first book of *Against Apion*

---

[63] Philo, *VM*, 1.334.
[64] See Philo, *Spec. Leg.*, 1.41. On the figure of Moses in the Graeco-Roman world generally, see Gager 1972; on Josephus' representation of Moses see 'Josephus' Moses' in Rajak 1975, online at <http://pace.mcmaster.ca/York/york/dissert.htm?id=13>; also Feldman 1993: 374–442.
[65] For recent doubts on the identity of Artapanus, see Jacobson 2006, and, further, Chap. 8, p. 266.
[66] For a full commentary on Ezekiel, see Jacobson 1983. A more recent discussion is offered by van der Horst 1988.
[67] Taylor 2003.
[68] Philo, *Vita Cont.*, 87.
[69] Philo, *Migr.*, 1; *de Abr.*, 60–106; 275–6. For Moses v. Abraham, see Pearce 2007a: 94 and n. 69. On the defining role of the Exodus, cf. Chap. 1, pp. 000.
[70] See the discussion of 'the Jewish sense of history' in Rajak 2000: 11–37.

and equally through the structuring of the past in his *Jewish Antiquities*, where almost half of the twenty books are a rewriting of the biblical narrative.[71] The evidence suggests that Josephus used both Greek and Hebrew Bibles to assist him in this endeavour.[72]

4. The mental furniture of literate Jews was biblical when they expressed themselves in Greek at moments of crisis and drama. One might think of the ready use of moral examples and helpful quotations even in unlikely places—for example, in the desperate and learned appeal, which Josephus ascribes to himself, delivered from the walls of Jerusalem to the besieged inhabitants and recalling in detail occasions on which God had wrought miracles to rescue his people from Egyptians, Philistines, Assyrians, and Persians, in contrast to occasions when their sins had brought about the capture of Jerusalem by Babylonians, Seleucids, and Romans (*BJ*, 5.375–419). He is writing, of course, in Greek, and it is to be supposed that Greek-speaking Jews would be among the readers of his *Jewish War*.[73] The picture must have had resonance for them. The Bible in their minds will have been the Septuagint.

5. Public expression as recorded in inscriptions, whether commemorating the dead, protecting their tombs, recognizing donors and benefactors, or settling scores, drew on the rich resources of the Greek Bible formulae, for phrases and occasionally for longer quotations. In three or four epitaphs from Rome we find, in slightly differing Greek translations (which itself is a matter of interest) a phrase from Proverbs 10: 7. 'may the memory of the righteous ones be for a blessing'. Widely used in later times, we may suppose that this was more familiar already in the commemorative expression of late antiquity than our limited evidence allows us to see.[74] Curse formulae characteristic of a judaizing (though not necessarily entirely Jewish) milieu in Phrygia (in central Asia Minor) deter tomb violators by referring darkly and cryptically to the 'curses of

---

[71] On Josephus' Jewish 'archaeology', see Rajak 2000: 241–55.

[72] See below, pp. 253–4.

[73] Although recent scholarly emphasis has fallen on Josephus' Roman orientation, there is evidence of intense interest in the Greek-speaking diaspora in the events of the revolt and of Josephus' connections in elite Jewish circles there. See Rajak 2005b.

[74] *CIJ*, i. 201, 370, and 86 = *JIWE*, ii. 307, 112, 276. For this commemorative formula and the significance of the translational variation, cf. Chap. 9, pp. 305–6.

Deuteronomy'; they may not have expected comprehension on the part of those in whom they wished to instil fear. On two occasions offenders are threatened by the 'sickle of the curse', in obvious reference to the 'flying sickle' which will wreck the houses of malefactors according to the Greek version of Zechariah (5: 1–4).[75]

Most remarkable are a pair of almost identical inscribed two-sided tablets from Rheneia, a small island that served as a burial ground for the bigger island of Delos. Each of these showed a pair of uplifted hands on each side with palms facing forwards, an image found also in Delian pagan epigraphy. The unusually early date of the inscriptions, ascribed palaeographically to the second or early first century BCE, gives them particular importance. They call upon the Most High God who sees everything, and his spirits or angels (*pneumata*), to avenge the innocent blood of an unfortunate girl—Heraclea in one case and Mart(h)ina in the other—treacherously murdered, apparently poisoned. The appeal is made on the day when every soul humiliates itself, a phrase which echoes the description of the Day of Atonement (Yom Kippur) in Septuagint Leviticus (23: 29). This is indeed a day on which it is appropriate to settle accounts, even if not quite in the way hoped for here, and many commentators have understood the statement literally as referring to that most solemn of all days. Apart from this remarkable phrase, an impressive cluster of septuagintal verbal echoes, first identified systematically by Adolf Deissmann, suggests that the users' contact with scripture was quite direct.[76] Still, we should not forget that these formulae could have been prepared by a purveyor of curses for a client who grasped rather less of them than their originator.

6. Supremely important as the Jerusalem Temple was for the majority of diaspora Jews, scripture was prior to Temple, since

---

[75] Deut.: *CIJ*, ii. 760 and, by implication, *CIJ*, ii. 770: 'the curses written below ...' = *IJO*, ii. 172 and 173; also now *IJO*, ii. 174. The reference is to the famous lists of curses Deut. 27 and 29 pronounced by Moses on those who do not obey the law. Zechariah: *CIJ*, ii. 768 and 769 = *IJO*, ii. 175b and 176: the Masoretic text has a 'flying scroll'. Discussion in Strubbe 1994.

[76] *CIJ*, i. 725a and b; *IJO*, i, Achaea nos. 70 and 71, pp. 235–42; Deissmann 1927: 416–23; Gager no. 87, p. 185; van der Horst 1991: 148–9. The echoed phrases are from Exodus and Numbers, and distinctive language is shared with Job, Esther, Sirach, and 3 Maccabees.

there were laid down the prescriptions for its construction, for its maintenance (including the Temple tax paid by all adult Jews), and for the Temple cult in all its aspects.

7. The Greek Torah was the chief (and perhaps sometimes sole) determinant for Greek-speaking Jews of Jewish practice and observance, which were probably governed by a pragmatic interpretation of the requirements laid down in the five books. Circumcision was not in doubt. Nor was some version of the dietary laws of Leviticus and Deuteronomy. In the *Letter of Aristeas*, when an explanation is offered, in response to alleged widespread curiosity, of 'the legislation concerning foods and drinks and wild animals regarded as unclean', the climax of the explanation is the symbolic intent in the Lawgiver's teaching (144–52). The permitted animals are wild and carnivorous, and 'procure their food with injustice.' The forbidden animals are gentle and, because they 'part the hoof', they inculcate discrimination between right and wrong. But even when the interpretation is allegorical, the foundation is in the admonitions of scripture, explicitly referred to (155) and of course in its very precise requirements. Philo writes that on the Sabbath none of the ordinary business of life was to be conducted and no one was to give or receive anything (*Leg.*,158). More specifically, one was not to light fires, till the ground, carry loads, act as a juror, demand the restoration of deposits, or recover loans (*Migr.*, 91).

8. The Greek Bible was the source of Jewish practical ethics in the diaspora. We might invoke those verses in archaic Greek which purport to be the work of the Greek gnomic poet Phocylides (and are therefore ascribed to a 'Pseudo-Phocylides').[77] No mention is made there of Jews, Judaism, the Law, or scripture. The expected critique of idolatry is absent. But the influence is clear of Jewish traditions on issues such as assisting the poor, humility, treatment of the enemy, burial of the dead, and abhorrence of homosexuality (the last given a rather prominent position). And when we come down to the detail there are propositions derived from the Septuagint in a straightforward way, such as the injunction to keep away from false

---

[77] See van der Horst 1978; also in Charlesworth 1983: 565–82; Schürer iii. 688–92; Barclay 1996: 336–46; Collins 1997: 168–74.

witness,[78] or to give just measure (*metra nemein ta dikaia*).[79] Some precepts are drawn from the wisdom literature and the prophets.[80] Since Jakob Bernays brought his skills of detection to this work in 1856, the author of Pseudo-Phocylides has been generally regarded as a Jew. If we are looking at a pagan Greek Judaizer, who had become absorbed in the Jewish texts and fascinated by aspects of Jewish morality, then this individual has taken so much of Judaism on board that it comes to much the same. Another moral principle in Pseudo-Phocylides (184–5) is the widely enunciated abhorrence of infanticide. Philo drew this unconditional ethical imperative from Exodus (21: 22–5) and his is the only extended surviving Jewish perspective on the ubiquitous ancient practice of infanticide, which he utterly deplored and which he attacked on three separate occasions, always in the most emotive of terms. Probably addressing a Jewish readership, and speaking ostensibly to the male population, his vehemence is such as to suggest this was no abstract matter. Adele Reinhartz may well be right in suggesting that in reality Jewish practice was not uncontaminated by the surrounding *mores*.[81] None the less, this was a clear ethno-religious marker both in Greek–Jewish discourse and in the perception of outsiders, and for the topic to have so forcibly caught the attention of the likes of Tacitus (*Hist.*, 5.5), Jewish behaviour cannot have diverged entirely from Jewish precept.

9. The Greek Torah, most often described in Greek as *nomos*, may well at times have served as a source of law, referred to in the jurisdiction of Jewish courts.[82] The editors of the dossier of twenty papyri from the organized Jewish community (*politeuma*) of Heracleopolis (P. Colon. 29) have noted the most surprising use there of the Septuagint term for a deed of divorce, *bublion apostasiou*, as well

---

[78] Pseudo-Phocylides, v.12. cf. Exod. 20: 16, Deut.19: 13–19, Prov. 21: 28, etc.
[79] Pseudo-Phocylides, v.13, cf. Deut. 25: 14, Lev. 19: 35.
[80] See van der Horst 1978: 122, who writes: 'the LXX origin of these verses is very clear'.
[81] Reinhartz 1992. See Philo, *Spec. Leg.*, 3.110–19, and also *de Virt.*, 131–3 and *VM*, 1.10–11.
[82] On *nomos*, see pp. 22–3.

as an apparent smattering of other Septuagintal terms in the second half of the second century BCE.[83]

10. It is often emphasized that in a text-centred society the authority of the text conferred status on its interpreters—be they scribes, or teachers, or even translators. Without the labours of such as these, the scriptural collection could not have remained relevant to changing circumstances.[84] Hermeneutics overcame 'the cognitive dissonance, the distance and tension between conceptions reflected in the old scriptures and present perceptions'.[85] The translators who followed the original seventy-two remained invisible, as is the way of translators, though they must have been considerable scholars. But perhaps the attention lavished on those semi-legendary characters is already telling. We do not really know who were the authoritative interpreters of Torah for Greek-speaking Jews. But a programmatic statement of Josephus, from the personal statement which concludes his *Antiquities* (20. 264), seems to be intended to apply universally, beyond the confines of Palestine. He says that only those able to interpret the Law are reckoned as wise among the Jews. In inscriptions, a sprinkling of personal titles that evidently denote scholars appear, but not before late antiquity, when the influence of the Rabbis of Palestine was spreading outwards. The term *nomomathēs* (student of the Law or of *halakhah*, perhaps) figures twice among the epitaphs of Jews buried in the Jewish catacombs of Rome. There too we find a 'father of the synagogues' who is a *mathētēs sophōn* (student of the sages, probably representing the Hebrew *talmid hakham*). The vow of Samoe (Samuel?), priest and *sophodidaskalos* (teacher of wisdom), was found recorded in mosaic in the very centre of the great Sardis synagogue.[86] That we do not encounter more such figures may be put down to the limitations of the epigraphic record.

11. Torah reading was the focal point of the synagogue, contributing greatly to its communal prominence, and powering its

---

[83] On the Heracleopolis dossier, see Chap. 2, pp. 85–6.
[84] Fishbane 1985 is a study of how the mechanism of reinterpretation operates.
[85] Stroumsa 1998: 10.
[86] Rome: *CIJ* (2nd edn.), i. 333, 113, and 508 = *JIWE*, ii. 68, 374, and 544. Sardis: *IJO*, 2. 63 (dated to c.500 CE). These texts are helpfully brought together in Williams 1998b: 33 and 50–1.

development.⁸⁷ Josephus spells this out in relation to his own period, praising the regularity of the practice. Torah study, among the other activities of a pre-70 CE, Greek-speaking Jerusalem synagogue, is attested in the famous Theodotus inscription.⁸⁸ The book of Acts (13: 14) depicts Paul hearing the Sabbath reading of the Law and the prophets at the synagogue of Antioch in Pisidia and the depiction is surely accurate, at least for the time of the writing of the book. Archaeology amply reveals the presence of an immovable, stone Torah shrine in most of the later synagogues. Earlier synagogues will have had a wooden construction.⁸⁹

12. Obligatory prayers were limited in the pre-rabbinic world, but the role of prayer, both public and private, was greatly expanded during the Graeco-Roman period, and we may presume that this touched the diaspora too. It is significant that Second Temple Jewish literature, in Greek as well as Hebrew, is replete with finely written prayers in which formal elements are combined with creative spirituality. To take just one case, it is not purely for literary reasons that the Greek version of the book of Esther⁹⁰ includes among its additions the eloquent prayers of Mordecai and Esther uttered at the most desperate moment of the crisis. Judith Newman has brought home to us the extent of 'scripturalization' in Greek–Jewish literary prayers, and especially, once again, in their use of exempla. In the book of Judith (9: 2–14), which survives in Greek, the heroine, before going in to kill the Assyrian general Holofernes, prays to the God of her ancestor Simeon, invoking his bloody revenge and Israel's triumph over the polluting foreigners who had raped 'a virgin'. The reference is to the abduction of his sister Dinah by the people of Shechem in Genesis 34—a prayer implicitly appropriate to the utterer's gender—but Simeon's is the only name mentioned, and readers can be expected to supply the story. In 3 Maccabees (2: 2–20) the prayer of the

---

⁸⁷ Levine 2005: 146–55. See also van der Horst 1999 for early evidence of Torah reading.
⁸⁸ For a re-examination of the Theodotus inscription, vindicating the accepted pre-70 dating, see Kloppenborg 2000.
⁸⁹ On synagogue shrines as a unifying (if not universal) feature in synagogues: Rutgers 1998; Levine 2005: 351–6.
⁹⁰ On the Greek Esther, see above, Chap. 5, pp. 183–5. These prayers make up Addition C.

High Priest Simon that the king of Heaven save the sanctuary from desecration by the arrogant Ptolemy, originally written in Greek, recalls three models of unsuccessful brute force—the giants of Genesis, the Sodomites, and the Pharaoh of Exodus. It is fair to say that these authors do not so much seek to elucidate the biblical sources as to put their serviceable exempla to use. The understanding is that, as Newman puts it, 'a recurrence of the biblical past was possible in the present'.[91] The procedure echoes the art of allusion deployed to such powerful effect in the Hebrew prayer text fragments from Qumran (not all of which need have been originally written within the Dead Sea community), but here, as befits the historical genre, the prayers both contain and are embedded in narrative, they are imbued with rhetoric, and the allusions are by no means as subtle or as profuse.[92] While we can hardly suppose that those literary representation accurately reflect the way Greek-speaking Jews actually prayed, the significance of continuities in technique and even in content with later liturgy is rightly emphasized by Newman.[93]

13. Devotion to the Torah is spelled out as the driving force of Judaism. Dedication to the Law of God, that is to say the Word of God, is the best expression there can be of love for the Divine Name. In Hellenistic Judaism this claim is articulated in the form of an idea of immense future significance, the exemplified concept of martyrdom—though it was left to Christian discourse to supply the label. Jewish–Greek narratives represent repeated heroic examples of resistance to tyrannical oppression. By preferring to die than to infringe the Law, and also, in the case of the mother of the Maccabees, to urge their children to die, they establish that the Torah rates above life and they set an example which was meant constantly to inspire, if only rarely to be followed. In the first century CE, this doctrine is spelled out. It is striking how often Josephus insists that Jews will endure every kind of derision and will suffer torture even unto death rather than transgress the *nomos*: he sometimes embeds the explanation in his narrative, but at other times he makes general statements of great

---

[91] Newman 1999: 11–17 and 117–200.
[92] For Qumran prayer, Chazon 2000a; Chazon 2000b; Chazon 2003a; Chazon 2003b.
[93] Newman 1999: 210–14.

Scripture in Hellenistic Judaism 237

resonance, notably in the *Against Apion*, where he aspires to sum up the essence of Judaism.[94]

This is an impressive dossier, even allowing for what we do not know. An important question arises about missing persons. Looking beyond the elite, we are bound to ask whether knowledge of the Bible in Greek was the attribute to an equal extent of male Greek-speaking Jews of all classes all the way down, let us say, to a Jewish slave who had been one all his life. Our authors take us just part of the way. Philo was proud that on the Sabbath places of instruction in virtue stood open in 'every city' (*Special Laws*, 2.62). Josephus sings a similar tune through the global language about the importance of the Law to the entire body of the Jews which he deploys throughout the second book of *Against Apion*. He has no qualms in castigating Greeks for the elitism and exclusivity of their philosophies.[95] The existence of such non-elitist ideologies already marks out a distinctive quality of Judaism. But they do not tell us how people behaved. We might also reflect upon the oral dimension of biblical transmission and translation practice, since this meant that the scriptures, albeit copied by scribes and studied in written form by scholars, were heard by many more people than could read them. We might also suggest that not all the surviving Jewish-Greek literature belonged to high culture: the conversion story of Joseph and Asenath is a kind of Jewish novel; and the ancient novel tends to be categorized as in some sense a 'middlebrow' product. Again, private inscriptions, especially simple epitaphs, open up a somewhat wider sphere than the restricted world of high literature. For all that, we have to admit that our grasp does not extend much beyond the upper echelons of society; but this limitation dogs so much of ancient history.

Uncertainties should not be overlooked in the final reckoning. Yet they do not undermine the powerful impact of the 'scripturality' that emerges from the remains of the heritage of the Hellenistic Jews. We have no reason to doubt the endlessly renewed value of the

---

[94] Josephus, *CA*, 1.42, 2.218, 232, 272, 292. Cf. *BJ*, 2.152–3; *AJ*, 15.288. On Jewish–Greek death for the Law, see esp. Van Henten 1997 and Rajak 2001: 99–133.

[95] Josephus, *CA*, 2.169: those who held similar views of God to the Jewish legislator did not see fit to divulge their views.

Septuagint to them. We cannot question the devotion of its people to the translated book. At the same time, we shall find as we continue that this particular world of Judaism had its own distinctive mode of text-centeredness, set within certain parameters, in keeping with its circumstances.

7

Parallels and Models

What, in the end, are we to make of the text-centredness, the 'scripturality' that emerged strongly from the previous chapter's review of Hellenistic Jewish culture and practice? For all the vividness of the impression, the evidence available to us constituted a very small corner of a picture now irreparably lost. Parallels and models are resources for interpreting what we do see, and that will be the route pursued in this chapter.

The role of scripture in Jewish society has been compared, sometimes perhaps unthinkingly, to that of the Homeric poems in the world of the Greeks; although we shall find significant differences, the contrast is illuminating. However, a different kind of comparison, drawn from within Jewish societies of the period, will provide the perspective needed to add depth to our picture, setting mainstream Hellenistic Jews beside two even more dedicated groups of users of scripture in antiquity. It may be worth adding, in view of modern preoccupations, that 'fundamentalism' in a real sense is rather rarely in question, since revered texts achieve and hold dominance most effectively by being endlessly reinterpreted. In this way they can serve, as they have in Judaism, as an adaptable, multi-purpose resource for life.

THE PARALLEL WITH HOMER

The Greeks too had their foundational literature in the shape of the Homeric poems, essentially the *Iliad* and *Odyssey*. In late antiquity the story of the Septuagint translation was in fact conflated with

Hellenistic traditions about the collection of the scattered Homeric epics and about their editing under the auspices of the tyrant Pisistratus in sixth-century BCE Athens.[1] Homer is often spoken of as the Bible of the Greeks, in the sense that the Homeric poems too were the basis of education, of much imaginative creation, even occasionally of decisions between states. Josephus, in his demonstration of the superiority of Jewish culture to Greek, never actually likens the two bodies of literature, but he does invite the comparison almost immediately after the opening of his *Against Apion* (12) when he declares Homer's poems to be indisputably the Greeks' oldest creation. It should be added, however, that the parallels immediately diverge, with Josephus pointing out that in reality Homer's works come from as recently as after the Trojan War and that they were allegedly even then transmitted only in oral form, leading to inconsistencies within them that (in the historian's view) the Bible entirely lacks.

But perhaps, despite Josephus, Homer's unrivalled position in Greek literature and society can help us understand what the Greek Bible meant for Greek-speaking Jews.[2] Might there even be a genetic connection between the social roles of these two core texts in societies that evolved over the same period, at no very great distance from each other? The Bible translation proves that Greek-speaking Jews were involved in the Greek educational process from almost the earliest days in Alexandria, so there existed ample sites of contact. And it has been reasonably suggested that the translators framed their task in terms of the techniques which the Alexandrian grammarians had developed for editing Homer.[3]

Margalit Finkelberg has little hesitation. She sums up the status of Homer thus: 'these poems became the universally accepted frame of reference, in fact, the only frame of reference in which the cultural language common to all those who belonged to ancient Greek civilization was formed, and therefore an inseparable part of the identity

---

[1] The merging of the two traditions is discussed at length in Veltri 2006: 81–90.
[2] See Finkelberg and Stroumsa's Introduction and Finkelberg's contribution in Finkelberg and Stroumsa 2003.
[3] Van der Kooij 1998; Honigman 2003: 47.

of those who saw this civilization as their own.'[4] Homer could, like the Bible, be understood simply as history.[5] Homer too could be claimed as the source of all knowledge and wisdom. To all that, it may be added that the Mishnah itself appears to allow some sort of comparability between Homer and the biblical books in the report that the Sadducees accused the Pharisees of saying that biblical books 'defiled the hands', but not so Homer.[6] Moreover, some semblances of a parallel development may be discerned. Thus, while in the Second Temple period, biblical works or works in biblical style were still being produced by Jews in profusion such as would have made the imitators of Homer deeply envious, in rabbinic Judaism, by contrast, the books of the Bible, established as foundational, were no longer an object of imitation. It has been asserted that just the same pattern set in with regard to the position of the Homeric epics in late Hellenism.[7] And, finally, some experts have identified a tradition of allegorical interpretation as distinctive of Jewish culture in Greek, and comparisons have been drawn with the sophisticated allegorical readings evolved by Greek (and subsequently Christian) readers of Homer, who were particularly troubled by the crude activities of his Olympians.[8] Allegory is an interpretative strategy which preserves the authority of a text whose literal meaning may be problematic for new generations of readers. Already a simple form of the allegorical approach appears in *The Letter of Aristeas* itself, when the High Priest expounds the dietary regulations.[9] We see another early stage in the development of this method in the exegesis of Aristobulus.[10] But the culmination of this technique lies in the great series of allegorical

---

[4] Finkelberg and Stroumsa 2003: 5.

[5] Cancik 2003: 119.

[6] M.Yaddaim 4.6. Homer here would by implication be the outsiders' equivalent of the Bible. But note that there are variant readings, and even if one of the two forms 'Hamiros' or 'Hamarim' were to be shown to be correct the reference would not necessarily be to the poems of Homer.

[7] Stern 2003: 237–9. On the role of Homer in later Greek literature and art, see the detailed study of Zeitlin 2001.

[8] On the Homeric allegorizers, see Dawson 1992: 23–72; Lamberton 1986.

[9] Cf. Chap. 6, p. 232.

[10] On the character of Aristobulus' exegesis, see Janowitz 1991: 130–3; J. J. Collins 2000: 186–90.

expositions of Philo of Alexandria. For him, this is a fundamental tool for looking, with open eyes, beneath the surface of the words and beyond the outward nature of the world. And Philo attests also to the practice among Alexandrian intellectuals of a more extreme form of allegorical interpretation of the Law than he himself found acceptable, one which rejected the literal interpretation altogether, as he rarely did (*Migr.* 88–94).[11] James Carleton Paget suggests that Alexandrian Jewish allegory is 'an attempt to de-particularize the Hebrew Scriptures through the lens of Middle Platonism': to do the scriptures justice it is necessary to address the soul rather than the body. The Exodus from Egypt itself was for Philo, as Sarah Pearce demonstrates, at a very deep level understood as an escape from the 'land of the body' with its senses, passions, and corruptions.[12] But the technique also follows, it is often claimed, in the footsteps of Homeric exegetes, especially in fact those of Pergamum (rather than Alexandria).[13]

Philo's Greek education was profound, as was his commitment to philosophy. And Philo could not have stood alone, devoid both of teachers who could influence him and of readers who could understand him. Yet there are major contrasts—more fundamental, I would argue, than the similarities—between the way Homer worked for the Greeks and the way the Bible worked for the Jews— contrasts, indeed, which Philo would have been glad to admit. Homer's high status simply cannot match the supremacy and ubiquity of scripture in life. Philip Alexander's cautionary words deserve attention.[14] Suggesting that 'the Homeric epics are ... perhaps not the most ... fruitful comparator to the Torah of Moses in the Greek world' he offers three major contrasts which help explain the greater centrality of the Hebrew scriptures for their users. While Alexander is

---

[11] On the 'extreme allegorizers', see now Taylor 2003. Cf. Goulet 1987 for the suggestion that there existed 'pre-philonic Philonic commentaries'. On Philonic allegory alongside literal interpretation: Pearce 2007a: 29–33.

[12] Carleton Paget 2004: 151. Pearce 2007a is a study of the 'land of the body' in Philo.

[13] Carleton Paget 2004: 152–3. In the end, however, Carleton Paget has to admit that it is almost impossible to connect our Jewish material with any specific products of Alexandrian culture, since rather more of the former has survived than of the Greek philosophy and the literary exegesis from that environment.

[14] P. Alexander 1998b: 130–1.

concerned with the later rabbinic period, they are largely relevant to our period too. First, there is a large difference in genre, since the biblical books, whether in Hebrew or in Greek, patently manifested virtually every genre and type of writing—not just poetry and narrative. Second, and very visibly, there is Torah's embrace of (in rabbinic parlance) *halakhah*, that is to say law and precept and their interpretation, constituting a detailed and prescriptive guide to life. And third, a fundamental difference lies in the pre-eminent standing of Moses, a figure above criticism, within the entire scheme. There could never have been such a figure in Homer, where gods and mortals alike are full of flaws and weaknesses. I would add to Alexander's points the observation that in pre-rabbinic Judaism the biblical corpus is all-encompassing, while Greek drama, for example, exploited many myths and traditions of all kinds which had little or nothing to do with the Homeric cycle. We must conclude that, if the Homeric parallel advances our understanding of the role of the Greek Bible in Hellenistic Jewish society, this is more by way of offering perspective and contrast than because of any deep congruence. The question deserves deeper study, but the differences that have emerged already serve well to highlight the social power of the Jewish holy books even in their Greek form. It is again Josephus who provides us with the telling image of opposition: Plato admired and 'crowned' Homer, but he banned him from the ideal state of the *Republic* because his badly behaved gods stood in the way of *orthē doxa* (*Against Apion*, 2.256). Even in the remotest of fantasies there was nothing dispensable about the Bible.

A COMPARATIVE APPROACH TO JEWISH BIBLICAL CULTURES

The uses of the Bible in contemporary Jewish communities of other kinds offer a different kind of perspective on Hellenistic Judaism and different techniques are needed to generate a useful comparison. It will be illuminating to cast our net widely, and from among the Jewish societies that fostered the Greek Bible we should not exclude the early Christian groupings, still closely linked to Judaism and broadly informed by this same biblical culture.

It would seem that the spectrum of scripturality as it plays itself out in Judaism has at its extremes two radically different types. On the one hand, the kind of text-centred culture we have so far been exploring refers and defers to scripture as its master text, speaking to central cultural values and governing certain core activities. Scripture is intimately and at least fairly widely known, so as to be readily drawn upon in writing. On the other hand, some social groups go much further than this and are involved in a dynamic, intense, and pervasive relationship with a set of writings which they believe to have been revealed to them and with which they experience a highly privileged relationship. Theirs is an existence of constant and engaged study and response; they are steeped in the writings—'text-soaked', we might say. These are the men and women who truly live by the eloquent words of Psalm 119, the great exposition of devotion to Torah: 'O how I love your teaching. It is my study all day long'.[15] The differences in degree between the two types are so great as to become differences in kind. My categories are perhaps congruent with those 'two types of exegetical tradition' identified by Michael Fishbane, one 'dignified by its verbal origins in Scripture, the other dignified by the religious community which lives by Scripture and whose customs can therefore be regarded as a form of non-verbal exegesis'.[16] It would seem that the second type of exegetical world produces a depth and complexity of relationship with the texts which the first alone could never achieve.

I shall explore this dichotomy by means of a three-part contrast between different kinds of Jewish society, looking temporarily across the language divide. An extreme case is provided for us by the Qumran sect, a Hebrew and Aramaic-based, secluded, interpretive community located in the land of Israel, with strong apocalyptic and even mystical strands in its world view. The second case is the Jesus movement, or rather circles within it; there is nothing controversial

---

[15] Ps.119: 97. The Jewish Publication Society translation cited here is truest to the spirit of the Hebrew. LXX Ps. 118: 97 has *ton nomon sou* for the Hebrew 'your Torah' and *meletē* for the Hebrew 'study' or 'conversation'.

[16] Fishbane 1985: 3 (Introduction).

Parallels and Models 245

about placing the earliest Christian writings within the cultural spectrum of Hellenistic Judaism, whatever the ethnic origin or the degree of separation from Jewish practice of their originators. Finally, we shall return to what, in my terms, is the mainstream Hellenistic–Jewish tradition.

The producers of the literature written at Qumran, who may also be deemed the users of its much broader non-sectarian library, offer a vivid example of a text-soaked community, a grouping which saw itself as a 'house of Torah' (CD, 20.10). Not only was the biblical corpus for them a 'cherished inheritance' but their overriding preoccupation, as Fishbane well expresses it,[17] was 'with a vast labour of learning and elaboration... a living commitment to the truth and significance of Miqra [scripture]'. The intended purpose of the copying and recopying of a multitude of texts over several centuries was the unceasing use of the entire community in study and interpretation, and unceasing absorption in the twofold revelation given directly to the community alone defined its holy identity in its desert exile. The Community Rule ordained that 'in the place where there are ten men let there not be lacking a man who studies the Torah day and night continually, concerning the right conduct of a man with his companion. And the many shall watch together for a third of every night of the year, to read the book, to study law, and to pray as a community'.[18] Menahem Kister speaks of a post-classical world, in which the entire Bible was there to be alluded to, interpreted, reworked and actualized.[19] He also points out that allusions to scarcely any works outside the Bible can be found at Qumran. And the sectarians were the inspired interpreters.[20] The guarantee of the inspired quality of sectarian interpretation lies in the direct exposition by God to the Teacher of Righteousness of the meaning of prophetic mysteries.[21] And this 'post-classicism', if that is what it is,

---

[17] Fishbane 1988: 340.
[18] IQS 6.6–8. The translation was made by Fraade 1993: 56, as part of his study of the sect's self-understanding as recipients of true Torah.
[19] Kister 1998.
[20] For an overview of the sect's self-understanding, Talmon 1989 is still enlightening.
[21] 1QPHab 7.4–5.

still involves a sense of participating in the fulfilment of those mysteries.

It is thus not surprising that Qumran texts of diverse genres and types, whether specifically sectarian or apparently non-sectarian, engage actively in the creative process of biblical interpretation. Our repertoire of genres has grown now that all the fragments can be studied: reworking or retelling of narrative, wisdom, prophecy, and poetry combines with exegesis in seemingly limitless profusion.[22]

In assessing the specific impact of the Bible in Greek on the New Testament writings, the study of the very numerous citations has naturally enough been in the forefront. In many cases, allusions, imprecise verbal echoes, combinations of phrases, and adaptations have been considered alongside precise quotations, and distinguishing between these different categories is in itself a never-ending challenge, necessary for students of textual history or trackers of theological nuances. To follow the immense literature on this subject is fascinating and there have been major achievements in the field, which I shall not list now. But it is also frustrating, because so much of the work has been directed to very specific objectives. As Krister Stendahl wrote: 'the study of quotations of the OT standing in the NT can have many functions and the way in which it is handled is in part coloured by the purposes the various students had behind their studies.'[23]

What is interesting for my quest is that each book or group of books in the New Testament displays its particular preferences among Old Testament texts, and each throws up its own distinctive and complex way of relating to those texts. Thus, in the Synoptic Gospels, eighteen of the forty-six distinct quotations are peculiar to Matthew (including the eleven special quotations preceded by a quoting formula); but only three each to Mark and to Luke. Nine out of twelve quotations in John are unique to him. The twenty-three quotations in Acts fall almost entirely in the speeches. The Pauline Letters contain seventy-eight direct quotations, but of these

---

[22] As displayed in Bernstein 2003. For the complete corpus translated with commentary, Vermes 2004.

[23] Stendahl 1968: 40.

seventy-one are in Romans, 1–2 Corinthians, and Galatians. The Pastoral Epistles scarcely quote at all. Revelation does not quote directly, but has more Septuagint phraseology than any other book.[24] There are, of course, multiple explanations for these observed patterns.

Thus, Luke is steeped in Septuagint language and terminology in a very special way, as demonstrated by Albert Wifstrand,[25] and he explains the remarkable phenomenon of Luke's 'Septuagintisms' in vocabulary and syntax—which used once to be thought of as Semitisms—as manifestations of an aspiration to the 'dignity' of a 'sacred text'. Alternatively, we might look to the Bible-soaked mind of someone formed by an actively engaged, text-centred community. That is not to say that all Luke's contemporary readers would have been of this kind.

The fact remains that, of the New Testament books, the great majority are suffused with Septuagint material. According to Swete's still invaluable Septuagint introduction,[26] we can find direct citations (under his definition) of every biblical book in the New Testament, except Ezra, Nehemiah, Esther, Ecclesiastes, Song of Songs, and a few Minor Prophets. At the same time, over half of these citations are of Isaiah and Psalms. The Epistle to the Hebrews is a fabric woven of quotations and allusions, almost sixty in all, again, and especially, from the Psalms. These are handled with traditional tools of Jewish exegesis—interpreting one passage in the light of another, argument from silence, comparison, antithesis, argument *a fortiori*, and deductions from the common etymology of names such as Melchizedek or Salem.[27] Overall, the absorption is such that we are impelled to describe the authors and their core readers, for all their diversity, as members of bible-based and text-soaked communities. Here 'the Bible was the touchstone not only of the New Testament writers' religious teachings but also of their total life and culture'.[28] Perhaps

---

[24] Swete 1900: 391–2.
[25] Wifstrand 1940 (in Swedish); trans. in Wifstrand 2005. See also the discussion by Loveday Alexander (2005), to whom I owe my awareness of Wifstrand's work.
[26] Swete 1900: 26.
[27] Karrer 2006, with further bibliography; and see also commentary by Attridge 1989, and especially pp. 23–5.
[28] Ellis 1988: 692. Cf. now, with an assessment whose significance goes beyond Luke–Acts, L. Alexander 2004.

they did not always address groups or individuals all of whom were equally capable of participating in and responding to that textuality: in the case of the recipients of most of Paul's Epistles, many probably lacked 'hearer competence'.[29] But still their authors were clearly formed in such a milieu: even the unique genius of Paul requires a context. Within the New Testament, then, we have reflections of Greek-speaking communities of a special kind. Like the Qumran sectaries, they read the Bible through the filter of relevance to their own ideals and fortunes. Authoritative interpretations were offered by their teachers.

In this respect, therefore, the New Testament corpus is significantly similar to the Qumran corpus. It is even the case that a comparable selectivity in preferred sources for citation or echo occurs among individual works within the Qumran corpus. George Brooke has exposed a striking pattern of preference.[30] Genesis, Deuteronomy, Isaiah, and Psalms are the texts found in the largest number among the scrolls (followed by Exodus and then Jubilees).[31] And the last three of these are indeed also often quoted. But, to take a couple of examples, in the Hodayot (hymns of thanksgiving) and similarly in the Damascus Document, the Minor Prophets are also notably influential. The latter also makes significant use of Numbers and Ezekiel, as well as of Hosea and Micah in the Admonition section. The former, on the other hand, have little from Numbers, but draw on Jeremiah and Job. Diversity in the subject-matter of the compositions may not provide the whole explanation. A pattern of pathways and preferences in the choice of reading and memorization within an extensive corpus familiar to all may well be characteristic of compositions emanating from groups that interact constantly and meaningfully with their texts. Where the central text for a community is not in fact one holy book but a large and unsystematic corpus, devotion to a selection of preferred texts within it could be more meaningful than a thinly spread attachment to the whole. We must imagine that the affections of individuals and of groups shifted over time.

[29] As pointed out to me by Ed Sanders. Cf. Wegner 2002: 33–9, on the 'hearer competence' of Paul's Roman recipients.
[30] Brooke 1997.
[31] A distribution list of the fragments among the biblical books is provided in VanderKam and Flint 2002.

SITUATING HELLENISTIC JUDAISM

That most Hellenistic–Jewish writers manifested constant respect for biblical literature through their choice of subject-matter, and the frequent display of intimate knowledge is plain enough. Furthermore, this is the gesture by which the authors publicly defined themselves as Jewish writers. We can without hesitation call them 'text-centred'. There may have been some gap between the writers and readers. But the writers, at any rate, apparently know some, if not all, of the Greek Bible well, and they use it inventively and creatively.

And yet their culture is not 'text-soaked'. Admittedly, Hellenistic–Jewish writers have been caught using the same kind of interpretative techniques as the Qumran *pesher*-type commentaries when they cite Bible in Hebrew or weave allusions together in 'exegetical systems'. This is well illustrated by Dimant[32] in relation to the theologically laden application of phrases from the Song of Moses in Deuteronomy to the martyred brothers' prayer in 4 Maccabees 7: 6. Dimant's claim is that biblical allusions are used by authors writing in Greek in very much the same way as the Hebrew and Aramaic authors. The claim has to some extent to be qualified, however, in the light of her own demonstration of a rather widespread tendency among the writers in Greek to avoid direct biblical citation and to prefer allusion, except in directly cited prayer (distinctly reminiscent of the practice of Acts).

That there existed common techniques of interpretation is undeniable. But the similarities are formal and do not run to the essence of what constitutes *pesher*, a consistent and assertive application of the biblical 'message' to the writer's own day. We are left with a clear sense that the creative energies behind the work produced in Greek lie somewhere else. As a group, the Greek–Jewish books are distinct in their overarching formal attributes, including their wide range of genres, many of which are, quite simply, accepted genres in Greek literature. They are also distinctive in what they lack: extended accounts of visions and apocalypses are thin on the ground. Again,

---

[32] Dimant 1987: 3–6.

there are appropriate preferences among them for particular forms of interpretation. Thus, even the most Hellenized of these writers are fond of typology: one thinks of the Exodus motif threading its way through the *Letter of Aristeas*,[33] of the Deuteronomic sin-and-punishment models in the narratives of the First Book of Maccabees combined with those from Kings, or of the Esther paradigm underlying the persecution story in the Third Book of Maccabees. As mentioned, Greek–Jewish writers use direct biblical citation surprisingly little, favouring indirect allusions, and, even more, forms of rewritten Bible and the imaginative exploitation of biblical themes. There is, thus, a marked difference in what we might call the dynamics of interaction with the original, at least if we are to use what survives as a sample.

In writing of scripture as a model for language at Qumran, Fishbane aptly speaks of the creation of a 'thick archaic texture'[34] through the interweaving of Hebrew passages, and by means of the special resonance created by the richness of the intertextual associations. The associative richness of Qumran writing in various modes, from poetry to *halakhah*, is an absorbing topic of current study.[35] Such density and interpretative complexity cannot be found even in the most 'biblical' of surviving Jewish compositions in Greek.

The fundamental contrast between the two broad types of text-centred community may be summarized, and in some measure explained, by saying that the main thrust in Hellenistic–Jewish literature is typically not inward, towards community building and resistance to the environment, but outward, towards making connections. The main challenge for its authors was from the beginning to generate new forms of fusion of their two received literary heritages, themselves subject to continual reinterpretation. They needed to be at home in both.[36] Carl Holladay[37] has highlighted some pointers to the level of competence in and grasp of Greek literature

---

[33] Recently explored in a new and fruitful way by Hacham 2005.
[34] Fishbane 1988: 356.
[35] For a review, see Bernstein 1998 and Bernstein 2003: 226–38. A recent study which engages theoretically with the complexities involved in evaluating allusions in the liturgical sphere at Qumran is Chazon 2003b, citing earlier literature.
[36] A point effectively brought out by Barclay 1996.
[37] Holladay 2002.

evident from the fragments of the Hellenistic–Jewish writers, notably Theodotus' freedom with Homeric language and conceptualization, and Ezekiel's awareness of dramatic technique.[38] This, of course, reflects their education.

PHILO AND JOSEPHUS

It is perhaps the life's work of Philo of Alexandria which sums up this duality best. There is very little in Philo's oeuvre, as it stands, that does not arise out of interpretation of the Pentateuch,[39] whether by means of the allegorical system of which he was the great master, or, as in some of his commentaries, more directly.[40] Whether or not he knew much of the Hebrew language, his working tool was Greek and the Greek Torah was for Philo an inspired text, seemingly reckoned as a valid equivalent to the Hebrew original.[41] He did not write commentaries on the rest of scripture, though he did from time to time cite or allude to different Psalms. Among other rare non-pentateuchal references are three to the 'song' of Hannah, for him an inspired prophetess.[42] We could not wish for a more eloquent exponent of Judaism, as he understood it to have been enunciated in the five books of Moses, than Philo in his various types of commentary, at the heart of which lies the creation of man in the image of God and also the fate of the Jewish nation. His vision unequivocally includes the ritual observances and the Temple cult. And yet it hardly needs saying that Philo's philosophical method and even his ethical

---

[38] Cf. van der Horst 1988; Doran 1986.
[39] Exegesis was even spotted (see Borgen 2001) within Philo's late political work, *Legatio ad Gaium*, apparently part of what was once a greater whole. The Philonic authorship of the fragmentary *de Providentia*, which strikingly draws its proofs and exempla from Greek history, is contested. See the commentary of Hadas-Lebel 1973.
[40] On Philo as biblical interpreter, see the masterly summary of Amir 1988, and for full-length studies, Nikiprowetzky 1977; Borgen 1997.
[41] And so, presumably, for Philo's circle of readers, as observed by Mendelson 1982: 18.
[42] See Runia 2001: 117 on Psalms in Philo and also on Hannah.

formulations placed him firmly within the Platonic tradition; they were indeed themselves a major contribution to that school's articulation of its central ideas—absolute good, the dichotomy between the darkness of the world of the body and the light in that of the spirit, the definition of the virtues and the virtuous life, the role of contemplation. The allegorical technique itself, which represents his characteristic though not his sole method of interpretation, can be associated with similar tendencies in the Stoicism of his period. His enthusiasm for harmonization, however, did not prevent Philo, at least towards the end of his life, from attacking 'Greeks', and also what they stood for, a set of ideas and beliefs which he was ready to describe as 'Greek'. This is a marked feature of his treatise *On the Contemplative Life*.[43]

Flavius Josephus, who exemplifies a different kind of bi-cultural attachment to the Greek Bible, represents a different paradigm. The biblical narrative of the first half of his *Antiquities* came out some half-a-century after Philo's last works, somewhere in the 90s CE. Varied as Josephus' concerns and writings were, we have already had occasion to note how from his earliest writing scripture was a central resource, and how a seemingly unforced recourse to quotation emerges as an underlying habit. In the case of a Jerusalem priest and self-professed Pharisee, this surely meant the Hebrew before the Greek Bible; from the latter he was inevitably therefore more distanced than Philo. Nevertheless, Josephus could hardly have conceived of his later work, the *Antiquities*, in which the entire first half is a rewritten Bible, let alone written these books, had the Greek translations not existed. And he wrote this work as a diaspora Jew who had moved far from his Judaean roots.

Josephus' paraphrase, though much studied as exegesis and literature in its own right, is not often brought into discussions of Septuagint matters. The authoritative 1988 handbook by Harl, Dorival, and Munnich, for example, has very little to say about his *Antiquities*. There is an obvious reason for this: that Josephus' particular genre of paraphrase is

---

[43] On the latter, see Taylor 2003: 42–3. On Philo's stance vis-à-vis Greeks and Jews, Birnbaum 2001. On his Jewish perspectives, see still Wolfson 1947; and also Mendelson 1988; Cohen 1995; Niehoff 2001.

helpful only very intermittently when pressed into service as a witness to the underlying text-type. His rewriting, particularly extensive for the Pentateuch, makes it for long stretches impossible to chase up individual words or phrases, or to make any inferences about the structure of his source or about the ordering of material there.[44] Josephus claims to offer an accurate translation of the Bible into Greek: *metaballo* ('convert') is the commonest Greek verb used by him to describe this activity, and *methermēneuō* ('interpret') is another.[45] We know that he takes this claim seriously, because it figures in the preface to the entire work (1.5) and it is subsequently repeated more than once. But he does add, subtract, embellish, and modify, time and again: probably he regards this as a legitimate part of his role as translator-interpreter.[46] His stylistic adaptation, his modernization, his rationalistic explanations are influenced both by the rhetorical practices of Greek historians and by midrashic traditions which he incorporates in a manner sometimes reminiscent of the Aramaic Targum.

Josephus probably knew much of Hebrew scripture by heart and we may imagine that he also had scrolls in front of him as he worked—perhaps even those very ones which Vespasian allowed him to remove from fallen Jerusalem. His working methods and precise sources are not made explicit. None the less, the first ten books of the *Antiquities* reveal sufficient septuagintal expressions of a kind which could hardly be arrived at independently, and we also find the occasional replication of telling errors. We conclude that Josephus indeed drew on the Greek Bible as well as the Hebrew. It is implausible that his use of the Greek will have been other than direct,[47] though it is conceivable that he benefited from some sort

---

[44] On the principles of this rewriting, the authoritative studies are the two separate collections published by Feldman in 1998, and especially see the systematic overview in Feldman 1998a: 3–220. Rajak 1975 and Attridge 1976 were pioneering works on the topic. On Josephus' use of a text of Samuel clearly related to that known at Qumran, see Ulrich 1978 and 1999a.

[45] Feldman 1998: 45–6 analyses the implications of these different verbs.

[46] The gap between profession and execution may be variously explained. For an exhaustive list of the possibilities, see Feldman 1998: 37–46. For a new suggestion, in terms of Greek conventions, see Inowlocki 2005.

[47] The hypothesis of an intermediary source, which German scholarship used to favour, has happily now fallen into oblivion. See especially Hölscher 1916.

of Septuagint-based onomasticon or glossary for certain technical terms and for the Hellenization of some Hebrew names. Papyrus fragments attest to the existence and use in late antiquity of lists of this kind.[48] But Josephus often added declinable terminations to names, replacing the Septuagint's preference for leaving proper names in a Hebraizing, indeclinable form. These already reveal the historian's preoccupation with style.

Furthermore, Josephus actually incorporates into his own biblical narrative some sections of the Greek Bible corpus which were either originally composed in Greek or else had been translated from Hebrew or Aramaic into relatively non-'septuagintal' Greek. Thus, his version of the Esther story comes with several of the septuagintal Greek additions, adding not only to the piety but also to the dramatic qualities of the masoretic Hebrew. Again, this suggests that the move away from Septuagint style was a major consideration for this author. And that is surely why it was possible for Josephus to present the rewritten Bible of the *Antiquities* as a new and unprecedented venture, which he does eloquently and assertively. While the changes were in an obvious way designed to be palatable to the audience of 'Greeks' whom the author likes to address, the meaning of this transformation for a Jewish–Greek constituency is plain. They now had a Bible that could take its place in the roster of Greek literature, catering to the more sophisticated taste of the age, which no doubt some of them shared, and also catering to their own pride. The contrast between this style and the more familiar registers of Bible-based Jewish Greek writing has been well described by Loveday Alexander.[49] If, as she suggests, biblical Greek represented for Jews writing in Greek their own kind of classicism, then the defection of Josephus from Jewish to Greek classicism, through his choice of the Atticizing high style, was all the more significant.

---

[48] See the discussion in Rokeah 1968 of a papyrus fragment which appears to be a late antique example of such an onomasticon. The author argues that this list was the source of Philo's etymologies. Cf. Chap. 4, pp. 149–50.

[49] L. Alexander 2005.

THE BIBLICAL CULTURE OF HELLENISTIC JUDAISM

Philo, Josephus, and their predecessors were in effect making bridges for themselves between the different worlds which combined in their minds and lives and those of fellow Greek-speaking Jews, and which combined to make up their identities. The engagement with interpretation through translation also nicely epitomizes the culture of these communities, diverse as they were. The labours of their literary and scholarly elites constitute an enterprise no less important nor less impressive than that which comes from the heart of one or other of the traditions they lived with. Bridges suggest traffic in both directions—not only from Hebrew to Greek, but also from Greek to Hebrew. In Jewish memory, those bridge-builders have been greatly underestimated. I would contest the implicit disparagement by Chaim Rabin of the 'essentially alien character of Hellenistic Judaism, receiving isolated principles, but without the attendant intellectual atmosphere'.[50] In relation to the Jewish textual heartland, it might seem that the Jewish output in Greek was secondary, its writers as the led rather than the leaders. But it is scarcely possible to assert this without falling into a circular argument about what is centre and what is periphery. Rather, we can see Greek-speaking Jews as participating honourably in what E. P. Sanders has described as 'common Judaism', and as linked to those other Jewish worlds of Palestine and of the diaspora through a shared dedication to the Bible, but one which they expressed in their own way.

The constraints of living as a minority demand vigilance in the defence of traditions; self-imposed boundaries are sought and constantly redefined. For Greek-speaking Jews, the scriptures were an effective tool for this purpose, from which other tools could be derived. Yet there is no reason to think that the people of the diaspora huddled around their Torah—or, rather, their *nomos*. Far from it. While the Greek Bible catered to the Jewish identity of Hellenized Jews, it also, and paradoxically, provided the intellectual route by

---

[50] Rabin 1968: 21.

which Mediterranean Jews became more 'Hellenized', because it ensured that the entirety of their lives, including their religious lives, could be lived in Greek.[51] The Greek language gave access to a vast section of the known world. Moreover, while it is clear that, for participation in Hellenistic–Jewish culture to be feasible, study and interpretation of the Bible, or at least of Torah, would need to have had a large place in the life of an elite Jew, we also have to allow that the very same Jewish urban elite was able to interact with its Greek counterpart and to share in their cultural life. In the case of Philo, Alan Mendelson draws not only on the content of the writings themselves, but also on the philosopher's explicit statements about *paideia*, to conclude that the upper crust of Alexandrian Jewry in his day participated in a full Greek education, centred on grammar, rhetoric, and philosophy, and at least in the pre-Roman period, based in the gymnasium.[52] If their Jewish identity was not the sole or even sometimes the core identity of most Hellenistic Jews, scripture could not be the exclusive basis of that group's education and religio-cultural activity and the role (and rule) of Torah could not take undisputed primacy in their hybrid thought-world. They were engaged in a balancing act.

Thus, it might be said that Greek-speaking Jews lived *with* Torah, rather than fully *by* or *through* Torah, by contrast with the greater involvement and intensity of the text-soaked Qumran sectaries, or with large parts of the Jesus movement that evolved amongst those very Jews. Nevertheless, the debt of Greek-speaking Jews to their constant companion, the Greek scriptures, was immeasurable, as was the contribution of that companion to the balancing act that they had to perform to ensure their continuity and survival as an ethnic and religious minority. The companion had, among her many other merits, the ability to stay in her place.

Paradoxically, again, it was the spread of the Jesus movement that opened up new stimuli in the Jewish diaspora for a more totalising brand of text-centred existence, such as had up to then characterized Judaea. While this took place among Greek-speaking Jews, new waves

---

[51] One of the few to spot this paradox was Treu, in a study (1973) well ahead of its time.
[52] Mendelson 1982.

from Judaea were influential. The changed relationship with scripture came now, however, with a radical redefinition of what such an existence entailed. Subsequently, for the Christian movement, including some Jewish Christians, the corpus of authoritative and essential texts would itself be dramatically enlarged by the production of new books with a claim to authority and then by the canonization, at the end of the second century CE, of the books of the New Testament. For the rest of the Greek-speaking Jewish world, the old literary favourites continued to serve, as we shall see in Chapter 9.

8

The Bible among Greeks and Romans

We have explored the Greek Bible's many-sided role in the lives of Jews, and to some extent early Christians. But did scripture in Greek continue to function as a bridge between cultures? What legacy did that Greek-sponsored first translation, the momentous enterprise sparked by Ptolemy's patronage, deposit among the Greeks? Here there should be fewer complications. Many have answered with a resounding negative. 'No Hellenistic poet or philosopher quoted it', writes Arnaldo Momigliano: he had absolutely no doubt that 'Gentiles at large' just did not interest themselves in hearing the Jewish narrative in the words in which the Jews themselves expressed it. Had they cared to do so, history would have taken a very different course.[1] In recent times, only a very few scholars have had the temerity to challenge the consensus, notable among them John Barclay.[2]

It is usually supposed that Greek and Jew just went their separate ways. While, according to Noah's blessing, the 'words of Torah may have been heard in the language of Japhet [i.e., Greek] inside the tents of Shem [i.e., among the Jews]', in the tents of Japhet things were very different: there those words, even in the language of Japhet, remained inaudible.[3] So, despite the emergence of Torah in Greek,

---

[1] Momigliano 1975: 90–2, criticizing the delusions of certain scholars. For interrogation of the silence, at least to the extent of considering whether 'les thèmes bibliques pouvaient être de bonne heure connus des Grecs, contrairement à ce qu'admet la doctrine dominante', see Mélèze-Modrzejewski 1988: 573.

[2] Barclay 2002: 140–3.

[3] The reference is to Noah's blessing, for not looking at his nakedness, on his son Japhet (Gen. 9: 27), whose name is etymologically linked to 'enlargement' and also to 'beauty'. Shem was the father of Javan (Gen.10: 2) and Javan was traditionally the progenitor of the Greeks (his name perhaps evoking 'Ionian', becoming the Hebrew

the two parties are pictured as heading relentlessly into that division which has allowed 'Hellenism' still to stand as the antithesis of what is essentially 'Judaism' down to this day. The antithesis has done extensive cultural work and it is has been endlessly invoked in European discourse, among Christians and among Jews equally, in many milieux and registers.[4]

A fresh look at the evidence is all the more desirable now that the roots of that constructed dichotomy are increasingly under scrutiny. It is timely to probe that alleged silence, to try and figure out how complete it really is. Our route is mainly through literature. I shall consider authors who seem to incorporate some knowledge of biblical material, and, in particular, biblical material in Greek, not simply of the Jews as a nation or Judaism as a cult or Jerusalem as their mother city. We shall find that, while the trawl is quite slight, some echoes at least are there to be picked up by the sharp of hearing, and they will call for explanation.

The first port of call is Alexandria and the aftermath of the first translation. We then move forward in time, and in due course beyond the confines of Egypt, tackling the problem on a wider front.

PTOLEMY'S LEGACY

There are indeed detectable signs of disappointment in Jewish circles at the lack of immediate positive response to the translation among outsiders. The non-recognition of the Hebrew Bible in the high Greek literature prior to the translation is a worry expressed by the author of the *Letter of Aristeas* himself. He felt called upon to explain away this little problem—if the book was so great, why hadn't anyone

---

name of Greece). Rabbinic interpretation took this passage to permit the (enlargement of) the Torah into the (beautiful) language of Greek; this was more particularly linked to Aquila's translation. Cf. p. 290 below.

[4] On the polarity, see the essays in Engberg-Pedersen 2001; and Rajak 2001: 535–7.

known it before? Writing perhaps somewhere in the middle of the second century BCE, he might well be thought to be speaking, by a familiar kind of transference, of the situation in his own day as much as of the past. He explained matters by recalling obscure traditions about two Greek writers of the fourth century BCE, Theopompus the historian and Theodectes the tragedian, who paid a high price for their illegitimate enquiries. One became mad for thirty days, and the vision of the other was severely damaged for some time—signs of divine displeasure (*Letter of Aristeas*, 314–16).

Subsequent generations of Hellenistic–Jewish apologists, carrying on down to Josephus, put themselves to great trouble to dredge up evidence of early acquaintance and respect. In the first book of his polemic *Against Apion* Josephus counters or anticipates at great length the hostile claim that if the 'best' Greek historians had not read the Hebrew scriptures then those scriptures could hardly be truly antique and significant. 'I shall endeavour', he writes, in introducing his work, 'to set out the various reasons which explain why our nation is mentioned by a few only of the Greek historians; at the same time, I shall bring those authors who have not neglected our history to the notice of any who either are, or feign to be, ignorant of them' (*Against Apion* 1.5). In due course he musters for the reader's scrutiny a ragbag of quotations from Greek witnesses, starting with the barely historical Pythagoras and going on to Herodotus' report on how the Syrians and Phoenicians learnt the practice of circumcision from the Egyptians, or perhaps the Ethiopians (*Against Apion* 1.161–218).[5] Some of these quotations have more in them than others, but in general they should be seen as attempts to write the history of thought in a fashion meaningful to Jews.[6] In spotting references to Jews and stressing Jewish priority, they contain an indubitable touch of wishful thinking. But it is unfortunate that in reaction to these sometimes crude apologetics, the modern fashion has swung too far the other way.

But still, should we not have expected more? Reflecting on the major losses in our inheritance of Hellenistic-Greek writing, we

---

[5] This passage is illuminated in Barclay's introduction and commentary: Barclay 2007: 91–5.

[6] See Borgeaud 2004.

clutch at straws and suggest that our picture is distorted: the crucial texts, we may claim, have just disappeared. This is not easy to sustain. Was it, then, simply impossible to break through the fear and terror once experienced by Theopompus and Theodectes? Yet other replies, perhaps more rational, suggest themselves. The most commonly offered reason is the barrier created by style, the peculiarities of the translation language, designed, as we have seen, to fulfil internal needs. Momigliano's simple formulation is not untypical: 'it was bad Greek'.[7] On the Greek side, we might point to the importance of divisions and canons of genre in classical Greek writing, which produce a kind of segregation of subject areas: each to its own genre. On this interpretation, literate Greeks who were perfectly well aware of the Bible simply had no context in which to give voice to this dimension of their knowledge. For, whatever the initial Alexandrian plan had been, the spheres of Greek and non-Greek culture never really merged in Egypt. The translated Jewish scriptures, while themselves Greek documents, belonged to the oriental legacy, and they were therefore not suitable material for absorption into the high Greek literature.[8] We might also think in terms of rapid cultural change. Following an age of enquiry and openness at the dawn of Alexandrian culture, there was a narrowing: perhaps, by the time the Torah had got its library catalogue number, taste had moved on. After all, there is not even a claim that the Greek translations of the rest of the biblical books were deposited at all, prior to the (dubious) statements of Church Fathers, notably the late third-century CE Tertullian, about finding the Torah in the temple library of the Serapeum.[9]

These solutions, in varying degree hypothetical, may at least serve to put to rest immediate anxieties about the credibility of the *Aristeas* narrative's central claim.

---

[7] Momigliano 1975: 91.
[8] As expressed, for example, in the *separate* temples built by the Ptolemies outside Alexandria for the old Egyptian gods, Thompson 1988: 106–54.
[9] On Tertullian and the Serapeum, see Chap. 1, pp. 43–6.

THE EXODUS CONTROVERSIES

Careful reading can take us further, bringing to light fragments of dialogue which suggest that, while the response may have been limited, the oblivion was not total. Remaining in Alexandria, we turn first to passages ascribed to a Graeco-Egyptian writer, Manetho, who can claim the credit of being the founder of Egyptian historiography. He played the role of interpreter of native traditions to the first Ptolemies. Some have judged that Manetho derived from the Greek Torah a grasp of the Jews' foundation stories inasmuch as they concerned Egypt, on which he proceeded to put his own perverse interpretations. Writing in Greek in the early third century BCE, this Egyptian priest described the Exodus from Egypt as the enforced departure of a collection of lepers and other polluted people, under the leadership of a certain Osarseph (i.e., Joseph). It is fair to say that counter-arguments to the claim of dependence here have also been offered. First, it is maintained that Manetho scarcely reflects actual knowledge of the Bible, given that his story is, to put it mildly, rather different, and that nothing more than a vague awareness of the Passover ritual need have reached Egyptians. And, second, we are reminded that the book of Exodus may not even have been translated into Greek when Manetho wrote.[10] Against this it should be pointed out that neither Manetho's dates nor those of the beginning of the translation are actually known to us. Furthermore, what we cannot doubt is that we pick up here the vestiges of an active exchange between two opposing sides; a framework stood ready into which the details embodied in the Septuagint version will sooner or later have been dragged—probably sooner. Amos Funkenstein puts Manetho's version of Exodus into the category of 'counter-history', that is the process of 'reading an adversary's most trusted sources against the grain'. So, the Jewish settlement in Goshen becomes a leper colony and the 'mixed multitude' a bunch of outcasts, while Moses simply turned Egypt's good customs upside down.[11] To turn a text upside

---

[10] Schäfer 1997a: 146, arguing against Kasher.
[11] Funkenstein 1993: 36–7. 'Reading...against the grain' is a phrase taken from Walter Benjamin.

down, you have to know something of it; indeed, it could be argued that you do better if you read it quite attentively.

We can find traces too of the continuation of this exchange. For the attitudes of Manetho and his like apparently left their mark on the Septuagint version in the form in which our manuscripts have transmitted it. This we see in a very striking omission of any mention of the disease of leprosy at Septuagint Exodus 4: 6–7, where it ought to come. In the Hebrew, Moses receives a divine sign when he inserts his hand into his garment, as bidden, and it turns white and leprous; but the hand is instantly healed when he puts it inside his garment again. The Greek version merely says that Moses' hand became like snow, without saying why. Ezekiel 'the tragedian', an Alexandrian Jew who wrote plays about Moses that looked like Aeschylus, and other Jewish–Greek writers too, follow suit in the succeeding centuries. That is unsurprising, as even from their pathetic surviving fragments it is clear that they knew and used the Greek Bible. The important point for us is that the modification presupposes an expectation that the Greek Exodus would be noticed by potentially hostile critics, an expectation real enough to call forth a decisive response. The response may seem to be minor, but to change even a word of scripture was not a small thing.

Moving on in time, it is likely that Josephus' literary butt, Apion, head of the Alexandrian Museum in the mid-first century CE (and well known to powerful Romans), was another Graeco-Egyptian who knew something of the Greek Exodus. John Gager suggested long ago that *Against Apion*, 2.25, cited by Josephus for the purpose of refutation, is a destructive version of Exodus 24: 16.[12] There, Moses spends forty days on the mountain, covered by a cloud, before coming down with the Law and rejoining the seventy elders. Apion has it that Moses ran away and hid like a coward on mountain Sinaios, which lay between Egypt and Arabia. Josephus is unlikely to have been the first Jewish debater to offer a firm response to this challenge. The attentions evoked by the Exodus controversies may not have been exactly welcome to their Jewish participants. None the less, the degree of hostility presupposed need not have been as great as it

---

[12] Gager 1972: 124.

seemed to Josephus long afterwards. Derogatory versions of the Exodus narrative did not cease proliferating—several are to be found in the opening chapters of Tacitus' *Histories*. But by then the reasons given for the Jews' departure from Egypt, and the events ascribed to their journey, were quite divorced from anything in the biblical version.

FURTHER ECHOES: ALEXANDRIA AND EGYPT

It is not often noticed that Peter Fraser, the greatest modern authority on Ptolemaic Alexandria, retained a perfectly open mind on the possibilities of biblical influence. In the obscurity of a footnote, Fraser suggests that two separate sentences from the Hellenistic historian Agatharchides of Cnidus, found in the historian of the Roman period, Diodorus, are genuine echoes, even if not exact quotations, of the Greek Bible. In one case the echo is of the account of the parting of the Red Sea in Exodus, and, in the other, of the resonant words from Ecclesiastes (12: 7) about the end of life and the 'return of the spirit to God, who gave it'.[13] The difference in precise wording in the latter case does not undermine a thought-provoking similarity.[14]

Perhaps not quite as persuasive is a suggestion about a line in an epigram of Callimachus which was revived by Fraser and which has now been given some prominence in a restatement by Luciano Canfora. The great Alexandrian poet jokes about a woman who has given him an oil lamp vowed on her daughter's behalf to the Canopian god, and in grandiose fashion he says of her 'O evening star, how have you fallen (*epeses*)?' perhaps reflecting and adjusting Isaiah's

---

[13] Fraser 1972: 517. It is fair to observe though that Agatharchides writes not of God but of the spirit, *pneuma*. Fraser remarks that Agatharchides appears not to have been particularly well disposed to Judaism even if he was not as hostile as Josephus (*CA*, 1.205–12) makes out.

[14] Menahem Stern (Stern i, no. 17) is doubtful, and excludes both citations altogether, while Munich in *BGS*, 17 supports his own scepticism with the observation that LXX Ecclesiastes is generally thought to have been translated long after Agatharchides, a judgement about which there is no certainty and which can in any event only apply to our existing Greek version.

famous, though rather more solemn exclamation about Lucifer (14:12): 'how he has fallen (*exepesen*) from heaven, the day-star, son of dawn'.[15] It is not clear how it should affect our judgement on this verbal echo that the evening and morning stars made conspicuous appearances within Ptolemy Philadelphus' great procession, that vast and hugely expensive extravaganza, designed to celebrate the regime, its conquests, and its gods, whose memory was to redound through the centuries.[16]

We are well aware that the Greek Bible provided subject-matter for a number of writers in Greek of the Hellenistic age, most of them apparently associated with Ptolemaic Alexandria, none of them known to us by more than a small selection of excerpts preserved by indirect transmission. These are the fragments of the so-called 'Hellenistic–Jewish authors'.[17] They have been much studied, but there are two fresh observations to be made. First, we should remember that even the very names of most of these writers would have been lost, and nothing of their writings would have survived, had it not been for an indefatigable scholar of wide sympathies in late republican Rome, known to us as Alexander Polyhistor, who, as his name suggests, presented data on a large number of ethnic groups and nations including the Jews. I do not know of anyone who has tried to argue that this collector was a Jew; and yet he seems to have had a good deal of interest in the history of the Jews.[18] On the other hand, it is presumed that any author who is cited by Polyhistor, and thence subsumed into Christian tradition, and who manifests a close

---

[15] Callimachus, *Epigrams*, 16.4. The Canopus divinity associated with the lamp is probably Adonis or Serapis: see Fraser 1972: 1000–2, n. 255; Canfora 1989: 43 and 103. Cf. Dorival in *BGS*, 14. However, Fraser rejects other formerly mooted parallels: Callimachus, *Hymn to Apollo*, 6–7 with LXX Ps. 23: 7; and Theocritus, *Epithalamium of Helen*, with phrases in Song of Songs.

[16] Cf. Chap. 2, pp. 69–70. The report comes to us from Athenaeus 197d. The point is noted already by Seeligmann 1948: 100 and by Fraser 1972: 1001; see Thompson 2000: 375.

[17] We have no conclusive evidence that even these writers, generally referred to by the collective label 'Hellenistic–Jewish', were in fact all Jewish. It is rarely observed that this is no more than an assumption derived from their subject-matter. Neither of the Christian sources from which our fragments of them derive, Clement of Alexandria nor Eusebius, makes any statement about their identity. For more on these writers, see the discussion in Chap. 6.

[18] The same point has been made by Barclay 2002: 242.

engagement with biblical traditions, must have been Jewish, or else—which comes to much the same thing in this period—Samaritan. However, the affiliation of Polyhistor's sources is nowhere stated. Indeed, Josephus, when he has occasion to mention three such writers,[19] actually speaks of them as Greeks, *Hellenes*, while praising them for having a better sense of truth and falsehood than most non-Jews. Part of the basis for modern scholarship's presumption of the Jewishness of all the authors cited by Polyhistor is precisely the conviction that only Jews could or would have deployed detailed knowledge of biblical narratives, themes, or interpretations. We are dealing, in fact, with a circular argument here. Among this cast of characters is the extraordinary Artapanus who, if a Jew, was one who had a remarkable involvement with Egyptian polytheism.[20] At the very least, then, we should note the shakiness of one of the supposed cornerstones of our understanding of Hellenistic Judaism. Once we discard the blanket certainty that the Greek Bible had absolutely no impact outside Judaism in the Hellenistic world, our evidence configures itself afresh.

Papyri can help just a little. An interesting reflection has been offered about one of the oldest biblical fragments on papyrus, dated to somewhere in the second century BCE.[21] The scrap known to biblical scholars as Deuteronomy 957, containing some twenty verses of the book of Deuteronomy, was found as part of a mummy's cartonnage, or wrapping, along with Greek literary texts, including a fragment of the *Iliad*. Dines asks how a carefully written biblical scroll could end up in this situation? Religious sanctions prohibited its being sold to a paper dealer or deposited in a rubbish heap. One explanation of the physical evidence is that it reflects possession (and reading?) of the Jewish scriptures by non-Jews, who naturally would

---

[19] The writers are Demetrius (wrongly named as Phalereus by Josephus), Philo the Elder, and Eupolemus: see Josephus, *CA*, 1.216–17.

[20] Coincidentally argued very recently by two scholars almost simultaneously: Jacobson 2006 and Zellentin 2008. Feldman 2002: 316–17 also hinted at the possibility of a non-Jewish Artapanus, but did not return to the suggestion. Contrast two very coherent Alexandrian Jewish scenarios constructed for Artapanus in Collins 2000: 37–46 and Gruen 2002: 201–12.

[21] Dines 2004: 5.

not hesitate to recycle the material in due time. Jews would never willingly do so—even a defective scroll had to be appropriately disposed of.

From the later books of the Bible, we find reflections of the well-known story of the judgement of Solomon in the dispute between two recent mothers each claiming to be the mother of the one surviving newborn: his solution, of course, is to identify the real mother through her reaction to his staged suggestion that the baby be cut in half. A similar story appears in an Oxyrhynchus papyrus dated apparently to about the same period as Apion. But the story is there attributed to Philiscus of Miletus, a well-known rhetorician of the fourth century BCE. No explicit association with Hebrew tradition is made in the papyrus. Another version, this time in Latin, carries a similar boy-cutting story where the child has been moved from one bed to another: this appears in no less a work than Petronius' *Satyricon* (79–80), also without attribution. It is by no means impossible that influence from the Greek translation of the book of Kings fed into the story some time after Philiscus.[22]

THE ROMAN MILIEU

Even the cautious Menahem Stern, in his monumental collection of texts by Greek and Latin authors on the Jews and Judaism, saw real significance in the adoption by Ocellus Lucanus, a Roman Pythagorean of the second or first centuries BCE, in a discussion of the value of sexual intercourse, of the Greek terminology in Genesis 1: 28 for the peopling of the earth.[23] *Poluandreisthai* and *plērousthai* are the key Greek words. We might wish to suggest that in the sphere of philosophical or scientific thought allusions to Jewish texts could be more at home.

---

[22] P. Oxy vol. 41, 1972, 2144. Josèphe Mélèze Modrzejewski concludes that Philiscus himself somehow knew the Bible, calling his 1988 study 'Philiscos de Milet et le jugement de Salomon: la première reférence grecque à la bible'.

[23] Stern i, no. 24, who invokes Richard Walzer (1949). The key word *plērousthai* appears in one MS version; see Dorival, in Dorival, Harl, and Munnich 1988: 17–19.

Later, perhaps in the first century CE, this impression is substantiated when we come to the author of the book *On the Sublime* (probably not the third-century CE Platonist Longinus to whom the book has traditionally been attributed) and the famous lines in which he combines and adapts three verses about the command for the creation of light and (a non-biblical addition) of dry land from the first chapter of Genesis. Thirteen words in the text come directly from the Greek Genesis. The apparent quotation is introduced in a manner different from that of other quotations of non-Greek origin in this part of the text.[24] Longinus holds up the words of the 'lawgiver (*thesmothetēs*) of the Jews' as a model of noble writing about divinity, comparable with Homer on Poseidon. It has been judged clear by the best commentator on this passage 'from the way he expresses himself, that his acquaintance with Moses was by no means confined to this quotation'. Here then, for the first time, a pagan author reveals that he is aware, if not of the exact identity of his biblical reference, than at least of the Mosaic associations of his citation.[25] To assume the author was himself a Jew has been a desperate attempt on the part of those who cannot accept the alternative. It is indeed conceivable that Longinus should borrow the crucial words from a predecessor who does figure elsewhere in his work, a Sicilian rhetorician called Caecilius. But, still, the identification of this Caecilius with a Jewish ex-slave, mentioned by Plutarch as having been owned by the Caecilius who had been quaestor in Sicily to the corrupt governor Verres, is a wild conjecture.[26] Surely the motivation behind the stitching together of that fabric of invention must be precisely the perceived need to explain how a serious Greek author is found quoting Jewish scripture. A Jew conveniently surfaces at whose door knowledge of the Greek Torah can be laid, because it is assumed that no highbrow Greek could be responsible.

---

[24] I owe these observations to Jenny Dines.
[25] Stern i. no. 54. This is accepted as a genuine citation by Dorival.
[26] *Tēn de doxan ioudaios.* See Suda s.v. Caecilius. Plutarch's depiction as a Jewish freedman in his *Life of Cicero* (7.6) of the quaestor Caecilius, involved some two generations before Augustus in the business surrounding Cicero's prosecution of Verres, seems to arise from the confusion of two individuals on Plutarch's part: Stern i. 566, Schürer iii, 86: 701–4; Momigliano 1975: 91.

Indirect lines of transmission between the Greek Bible and Longinus might of course be posited; and Jewish involvement could be conjured up here too. The observation made in a recent study that the quasi-citation need not come from direct knowledge of the biblical passage is accompanied by the not unreasonable comment that it looks as though it belongs in one of the succinct biblical 'rewritings' much practised by Hellenistic–Jewish authors. If that is so, it remains the case that Longinus will have read, if not the Greek Bible, at least a form of rewritten Bible, which, for my argument, is worth almost as much. It is also worth noting that there are interesting parallels between the choice of expression of 'Longinus' and a late Hellenistic–Jewish treatment of the creation which does survive: I refer to the emphatic statement made by no less a figure than Josephus near the start of his *Antiquities* (1.15) about the fineness of the conception of God entertained by the Jewish lawgiver, the *nomothetēs*, as he calls him.[27] The point is that on any interpretation we see in 'Longinus' evidence of the penetration of verbal echoes of scripture to the world of elite Greek literature. John Barclay aptly points out that the fact that Longinus merely alludes to the relevant sentences in Genesis suggests an expectation that readers might be familiar with them.

The last in our line manifests the most extensive acquaintance with the Greek Bible of all pagan thinkers. This is the Pythagorean Numenius of Apamea, who was active near the end of the second century CE. Clement, Origen, and Eusebius are in agreement both on his interest and on his intense admiration for Moses as philosopher and as prophet.[28] It was especially in teasing out the implications of the Deity as perpetual being (*ho ōn*), in accordance with the Septuagint's rendering of Moses' revelation at the burning bush, that he revealed his profound engagement as well as familiarity with the text.[29] In his famous description of Plato as 'Moses speaking Attic Greek' (*attikizōn*), often cited by the ancient authorities, Numenius

---

[27] For the Hellenistic–Jewish flavour of the Longinus citations, I am once again indebted to the analysis of Jenny Dines. For the Josephan parallel, see Stern i. 364.

[28] See Stern ii. 206–16.

[29] So Burnyeat 2005, in a detailed philosophical interpretation of the fragments concerning Moses and the nature of being.

was, I suggest, perhaps alluding with gentle criticism to the distinctly non-Attic idiom of the Moses of the Septuagint.

The age of Numenius was one of intense engagement between philosophies and religions. Something new was in the air. Nevertheless, much was dependent upon Hellenistic models and especially the philosophical heritage. The Hellenistic era had provided at least as many opportunities for cultural contact. And cultural contact there already was. It would be absurd to claim the books of the Bible, in whatever language, were literature in which pagans without a special interest would be able to immerse themselves. Yet they were familiar with it at various levels. There were literate pagans, above all philosophers, who, quite simply, did have an interest sufficient to take them some distance into the Jewish writings, whether for praise or for criticism or out of curiosity. They were able to do so because the books of the Bible were part of their world and were not an unknown entity. And, perhaps too, the spirit of Ptolemy reawakened from time to time.

THE WORLD OF MAGIC

So much for literature, high or not quite so high. That might seem to be the end of the story; but there is one further direction in which to look. Widening our horizons, we turn to a world that is slippery and dangerous not only to its users but even to those who study it. I refer to the sphere of magic, of incantations and spells, as these survive for us in written form. Magic is the great meeting ground, where social classes, ethnicities, and religious systems intermingle. The surviving ancient magical texts provide us with a tantalizing zone of contact where we may glimpse formulae, wordings, and even citations apparently shared by Greeks, Egyptians, Jews, and subsequently, of course, Christians too. But Jews seem often regarded as the super-experts. The most extensive Greek incantations which survive are on papyri, found very largely in Egypt, and often of a date considerably later than what is thought to be their original formulation. It is remarkably common for these incantations, and also for amulets, lead tablets, and similar vehicles, to incorporate biblical material in

Greek, to the extent where they even produce a few exact quotations of significant length.[30]

Within spells and alphabetical concatenations, which at first blush may strike us as pure nonsense but in which have been found systems of symbols and persistent traditions,[31] we see a juicy array of divine names, derived from the Greek versions of the Hebrew appellations of the Jewish God—Iao, Sabaoth, Adonai, Eloi, Eye, the Pantokrator—as well as many angelic names, familiar and unfamiliar, and telling pronouncements of the type 'I exorcize you in the Hebrew language'.[32] A charm in one magical papyrus reads: 'I am Moses, your prophet, to whom you committed your mysteries which are celebrated in Israel; you showed forth moisture and aridity and every kind of nourishment. Listen to me! I am the messenger of Phapro Osoronophris. This is your authentic name which was committed to the prophets of Israel.'[33]

Given the widespread acceptance that Hellenistic material is embedded in the later compilations, there should be no question of excluding the Greek magical texts from any enquiry about reactions to the Bible among non-Jewish Greeks. It will be more difficult to decide what to make of them. The common Mediterranean lingua franca of magic is thought to stretch far back and to have been always characterized by a good deal of interpenetration. There is every reason to think that in the Hellenistic period elements adopted from the Bible already played a prominent part.[34] The reasons for this influence are not far to seek: the distinctive, backward-running Hebrew alphabet (to whose twenty-two letters the Jews themselves were in due course to attribute profound meaning), the profusion of

---

[30] P. Alexander 1999b: 1071.
[31] For a sympathetic account of the power of gibberish in so-called *voces mysticae* (i.e. seemingly unintelligible words) and of *characteres* (collections of letters), see Gager 1992: 8–11.
[32] The best short survey of the entire field of early Jewish incantations and magic books is still the chapter by P. Alexander (1986), with a useful list of Greek papyri containing Jewish influence. Cf. P. Alexander 1999b. Betz 1997 finds it almost impossible to distinguish Jewish material in four Greek magical papyri concerned with healing. On the attractions of Jewish magic in a Christian environment, see Wilken 1983: 83–8.
[33] *PGM* V. 108–18. Cf. Gager 1974: 142.
[34] Observed by Schäfer 1997: 19–43.

angels and names of angels in Jewish parabiblical literature, the mystery surrounding the names and descriptions of the God of the Hebrews (as in the charm just quoted), and the power that accrued around the figure of Moses, prophet and guardian of God's revealed mysteries, to whom was entrusted knowledge of the Divine Name.[35] The vivid images of Solomon, regularly classified as a magician,[36] of Abraham, the other patriarchs, and Joseph, of David, all played their part. Since they lived in and through the biblical stories, in essence, this adds up to the benefits of ownership of some of the most powerful, and certainly the most extensive, texts in the business. Within the sphere of Jewish magic, abundant use of biblical quotation and allusion was in all periods a defining characteristic, as we see clearly in the magical material in Aramaic, Hebrew, or other languages from late antiquity, above all the famous magic bowls from Mesopotamia.[37]

There has been a revolution in recent years in our understanding of Jewish magic, especially through the recovery within rabbinic literature of the *hekhalot* tradition which gave birth to Jewish mysticism, through the accumulation of powerful arguments for its early origin and exploration of its boundaries with magic. Again, extensive research into the incantations on the late antique magic bowls, with their long multilingual texts and their repertoire of extraordinary images of devils, chickens, and the like has opened a new window on the phenomenon.[38] Such advances are of course not confined to the study of Judaism. These near-universal practices have been pulled inwards from the margins of history, to be allowed, now, a role at the very centre of many, if not all, past societies—a 'counterculture' perhaps.[39] Perceived by the powerful to have a potential for subversion, magical practices existed, generally, in an enduring equilibrium

---

[35] Instances of formulae in the papyri on the theme of the revelation of the Divine Name are given by Gager 1972: 142–6.

[36] On Solomon as an expert in magic, see Torijano 2002.

[37] Naveh and Shaked 1993: 22.

[38] The essays in Schäfer and Kippenberg 1997, esp. the papers by Schäfer and Gordon, offer insight into the methodological debates and the nature of the evidence. For a different approach to understanding the boundary, in relation to the sphere of ritual, see Graf 1991.

[39] See Gager 1994 on 'counterculture'.

with approved forms of cultural expression. It is clear to us today that spells, love charms, amulets, recipes, potions, cures, incantations, curses, exorcisms, and adjurations of demons were popular in the 'best' social and religious circles. While officially discouraged, kept separate, and often condemned by religious authorities, magic was, quite simply, everywhere; and in practice it was not always eschewed even by insiders of those same religious hierarchies. That is as true of Jewish conduct as of any other, in spite of strenuous and unqualified biblical prohibitions.[40] Conceptually, the boundaries between magic and religion were fluid, and they shifted as required in any particular context. Peter Schäfer finds it to be a distinctive feature of the Jewish conceptualization of magic that it is not outside 'religion', but an element within it. Even where the undesirable and feared 'other' was thought to be intruding, control and containment were the preferred tactics, not exclusion. Thus, the early Jewish mysticism of the *hekhalot* literature is deeply grounded in scripture, and this mysticism works its way into rabbinic texts; but at the same time the literature incorporates techniques and forms of expression freely drawn from the practitioners of magic.[41] That spectrum of practices is intangible and esoteric in its very nature. Over time, the many elements of the scene become invisible.

All this increases the claims on our attention of the biblical echoes in magical texts, however peculiar the forms in which this material appears there. But how did the spells work? Lost stories of interaction between people exist behind the written words of the magic texts; yet they are stories too deeply concealed in the surviving multi-layered compilations for us to do more than guess at them.

The possible transactions involved are well illustrated from one of the better known magic texts, a bilingual (Latin and Greek) love charm of the third century CE, inscribed on a lead tablet discovered at Hadrumentum (or Hadrumetum) in North Africa.[42] Jewish origins

---

[40] The key text is Deut. 18: 9–14. Schäfer 1997: 28–33 examines the significance of this and other key biblical statements.

[41] The basic study of the connection between the two in the early period is Schäfer and Pomerance 1992. Also Schäfer 1997: 19–43. How early an origin should be assigned to the *hekhalot* literature remains controversial.

[42] Audollent 1904: 373–7 (text); Deissmann 1903. Translation, bibliography, and discussion in Gager 1992: 112–13.

have been inferred for this charm from an intimacy with Bible and *haggadah* (stories, essentially) which seems to emanate, as Philip Alexander puts it, from 'a well-stocked memory'. On the other hand, that the client was non-Jewish is suspected from her name, Domitiana, and that of her man, Urbanus. And finally the garbling and misspellings in the manuscript are taken as evidence of a non-Jewish copyist.[43] This is not unreasonable guesswork. John Gager, by contrast, is uneasy about even such tentative proposals. He writes that, while the language of the charm is reminiscent of the Septuagint and other Greek–Jewish texts, and the God of Israel is the only deity invoked, 'there is no need to assume that either the client or the professional was Jewish, though both may have been'. The language, he believes, may by this time have entered the common culture. The clients were perhaps non-Jewish freedmen.

With a small number of documents that carry biblical resonance we can go further. One such explicitly asserts that it is designed for Jewish use. This is the relatively straightforward 'Prayer of Jacob', which includes various magic formulae alongside a magnification of divine power, but also has the request to 'the Lord God of the Hebrews' that he should 'maintain the one who possesses this prayer, who is from the stock of Israel and from those who have been favoured by you'. There is no obvious pagan (or Christian) intrusion into this particular text.[44]

It is generally supposed that another, significant part of the 'trade' consisted of Jewish practitioners producing spells replete with Hebraic formulae for the use of non-Jews. This is likely to have been a common scenario, and for understanding the transmission of Septuagint terminology it is important. But this still only takes us so far, for the thinking of the participants constantly gives us the slip. How can we know whether those non-Jewish recipients had any notion of—let alone respect for—the origins of the biblical words, phrases, names, or allusions in their spells? What did they believe them to be?

An alternative model is a chain of transmission in which non-Jewish practitioners, rather than clients, 'borrowed' recipes or spells

---

[43] P. Alexander 1999b: 1074–5.
[44] *PGM*, XXIIb. Translation by D. E. Aune, in Betz 1986: 261.

from Jewish magicians. That would require no more than an indirect relationship between Jewish purveyors of magic, always highly respected figures, or indeed any Jews, as 'middlemen', and the non-Jewish population at large. Where concatenations of biblical phrases contain markedly 'un-Jewish' elements there has indeed been a strong tendency among scholars to assign them to a 'pagan' compiler. Thus the famous *hebraïkos logos*, a modern name derived from the ancient wording given to a section of the great Paris magical papyrus which describes itself as the charm of a certain Pibechis,[45] shows precise knowledge of the Hebrew Bible and of *haggadah*, in its formidable adjuration against a demon in the name of 'the God of the Hebrews', of 'the Great God Sabaoth' (using biblical language), who is praised by the heavenly power of angels and of archangels'.[46] The continuing assemblage of designations is awe-inspiring: the God 'who appears in fire', 'He that is in holy Jerusalem before whom the unquenchable fire burns for all time with his holy name', 'He to whom the wings of the cherubim sing praises', and (in this case alluding, it has been suggested, to an otherwise unknown aggadic tradition) of 'the seal which Solomon laid upon the tongue of Jeremiah and he spoke'. The spell also talks graphically of God as the redeemer from Pharaoh, of the ten plagues, of the pillar of cloud, 'through whom the Jordan drew back and the Red Sea which Israel crossed became impassable'. The latter is a clear evocation of Psalm 114: 3.[47] In a doubling of the Jewish tradition of seventy languages, or perhaps a reference to the midrashic 140 nations of the world, God also 'revealed the 140 languages and distributed them by his own command'. The recipient is even enjoined not to eat pork so as to stay pure because the spell is preserved 'among pure men'. But still there are enough improprieties for Philip Alexander to declare: 'no Jew (or for that matter Christian) would have referred to "Jesus, the God of the Hebrews", or misspelt "Israel" as "Osrael". Nor, it might be thought, is a Jew himself likely to have referred to the incantation as a

---

[45] *PGM*, IV, 3009–85. Translated in Betz 1986: 96–7.
[46] On the biblical references, see 'The Great Magical Papyrus of Paris and the Bible' in van der Horst 2006: 269–79.
[47] Cf. van der Horst 2006: 277.

"Hebrew spell".[48] E. R. Goodenough, who believed that his exhaustive explorations had unearthed a lost 'Hellenistic' Judaism with its own radically divergent, syncretistic, and mystical orientation, would have regarded none of this as beyond the pale for Alexandrian Jewry.[49] Few have followed him down that road. More prosaically, it is not inconceivable that Jewish purveyors of magic operating with a sharp eye for the preferences of the non-Jewish market lie behind the resonant phrases of the *hebraïkos logos*. When it comes to magic, however, few assertions can be more than tentative. The web is utterly tangled.[50]

For all that, the Greek magical texts from Egypt and elsewhere do leave a powerful impression, not to be disregarded, that religious and ethnic boundaries have scant significance inside their world. This impression may well in some ways reflect the realities of daily life better than more structured and formal types of written evidence. Magical practices, however opaque, represent a zone where the Jewish–Greek Bible was in some sense a known entity, not wholly invisible to outsiders. The operation of this zone, as I have tried to reconstruct it, implies a degree of awareness in non-Jewish circles at least of the Bible-based nature of Jewish religious conceptions, and perhaps of considerably more.

CONCLUSION

The sum total of Greek and Roman biblical echoes that we have recovered may seem a scant haul, even if bigger than expected. It is still a lot more than nothing. To have found such signs at all, some

---

[48] P. Alexander 1999b: 1074.

[49] Goodenough is generally deemed to have failed in his larger objective, but his multi-volume study (1953–68) remains a treasure house of source material for this kind of study, textual as well as visual, and a useful reminder that we should remain open minded. Note especially the extensive study of charms and amulets in vol. ii. Goodenough 1998 is a useful abridgement by Jacob Neusner, with introduction.

[50] See Alexander's own words of caution (1986: 345–6) on the possibility of unpacking the conglomerate of motifs in magic texts: in the end 'it is simply magic'. An analysis in terms of a spectrum of degrees of Jewish content might be productive.

lingering ripples, perhaps, of those which once moved outwards from the first translation, confirms for us, should confirmation be needed, that the Septuagint did not emerge from or into the confines of an enclosed ghetto. A basis of curiosity and awe may be inferred in Greek circles sufficient, in the first place, to generate the dynamic of the sponsored translation and the public reception of the Jewish Bible in the early stages of Hellenism. The intense and experimental encounter between the Greek establishment and the Jewish Bible which came at the dawn of Hellenistic culture dimmed during succeeding generations. In the later stages of the encounter in Alexandria, it was as often as not antagonism that fuelled responses to the Jewish narrative. The Romans, for their part, may rightly be accused of cultural myopia and obtuse monolingualism.[51] None the less, it was within the framework of the spread of Roman domination that the Jewish scriptures again attracted an apparently increasing amount of thoughtful notice. In this same framework, the emergence of Christianity was to effect a dramatic change.

[51] This is a central argument in Momigliano's classic study (1975) with which my discussion opened.

9

The Septuagint between Jews and Christians

The first half of the second century CE was a period of contrasts and contradictions, and sometimes disasters, for the Jews of the Mediterranean basin. Some Jewish communities in the Roman east recovered from the trauma of the Temple's loss and Jerusalem's destruction and they were apparently able to flourish. In other places, there was renewed violent resistance to Roman rule accompanied by urban conflict with non-Jews.[1] First came the suppression in four theatres of war of the desperate revolt of 115–117 CE against the Romans under Trajan which led to the collapse of four centuries of rich Jewish life in Alexandria. Then, some twenty years later, came the repercussions of the crushing in Judaea of the Bar Kokhba revolt of 132–135 CE by the legions of Trajan's successor, Hadrian. The re-founding of Jerusalem as a Roman colony and the exclusion of Jews from living there will have had deep significance also for the diaspora. Among other things, it meant that hopes of a rebuilding of the Temple in the foreseeable future fell away dramatically.

According to the accepted timetable, it could have been as late as this that the enterprise of translating the Hebrew Bible into Greek was concluded, perhaps in the land of Israel and perhaps in the diaspora, with the production of Greek versions of Ruth, Ecclesiastes, and Lamentations, and also, as we shall see, with the making of fresh Greek versions. But by now the Christian church was transforming the landscape. While it has been possible for us to consider the New

---

[1] For further details of the conflicts, see Chap. 3, pp. 122–3.

Testament's uses of the Greek Bible within the framework of Hellenistic Judaism, by the second century a separate evolution was well in hand. But most Christian groupings leant as heavily as ever on what was now the Septuagint, and they made this collection very much their own. We have early evidence of tension with Jews precisely over Greek texts. In Justin Martyr's *Dialogue with Trypho*, whose dramatic dating is the time of the Bar Kokhba revolt, we read how Christian interpreters claimed to have the authentic version, uncorrupted by Jewish distortions, thus, in this as in other ways, laying claim to the heritage of Israel.[2] In his *First Apology*, Justin implies, in a highly confused pronouncement, that the Jews failed to understand the real meaning of the Septuagint, a translation arranged by Ptolemy from texts sent him by King Herod; they had forfeited their right to possession of it through Bar Kokhba's mistreatment of Christians and through their blasphemous denial of Christ.[3]

In this chapter, I shall begin by exploring the ideological and historical reasons for the extraordinary durability of this view. They are an interesting and important story in themselves. Then I shall systematically examine the lynchpins of the abandonment theory: the twists and turns in the Christian versions of the Septuagint translation-legend of the *Letter of Aristeas*; the role of the proselyte translator Aquila; the allegations in Justin Martyr's *Dialogue with Trypho*; further evidence from patristic writers and from Christian legislation; and the use made of rabbinic evidence. I shall then offer a new reading of how and why Jewish attitudes to the Greek translations developed in new and very creative directions, in the first part of the second century CE, without needing to abandon the old Greek texts.

It was a distinguished New Testament scholar, C. F. D. Moule who, with admirable objectivity, called the process by which the early Church adopted the Jewish scriptures in Greek 'one of the most remarkable take-over bids in history'.[4] Moule's readiness to call a spade a spade deserves much credit. Appropriation was indeed what transpired. But the simplicity of the statement may also be

---

[2] On the dispute embodied in the *Trypho*, see below, pp. 298–301.
[3] Justin, *First Apology*, 31, and see Adler 1990: 3–4.
[4] See Jellicoe 1974: pp. iv–v (Prolegomenon). Equally frank was Martin Hengel (2002: p. xii): 'the Christians snatched it away from the Jews'.

misleading, suggesting as it does a single act, a conclusive change of ownership accomplished at an early stage in that enormously complicated process of the 'parting of the ways'. With different spins on it, this same account has gained extraordinarily wide currency.

A model so immovable requires inspection. Are there grounds for supposing that the Septuagint just changed hands, that it moved, like a residential property, from one ownership to another? In the very long run, the translations would indeed come within a hair's breadth of disappearing from much of Jewish consciousness.[5] That is another matter. But the Greek-speaking Jewish diaspora did not just disappear when Christianity appeared, and we have to ask whether the Septuagint could just have disappeared out of it. We shall find grounds for concluding the opposite. Deconstruction, however, must come first.

The Christian Church embraced and preserved not only the Greek Bible but a large part of the substantial Jewish literary heritage in Greek, ranging from the earliest Alexandrian authors, now surviving as fragments,[6] to the large-scale works of Philo and Josephus. Rabbinic Jewish literature, by contrast, does not refer to those authors (though the Rabbis were quite aware of the Greek Bible translation, as we shall see) and it took centuries before Jewish memory reincorporated them. So the takeover has a bearing not only on the history of the Septuagint, but also on the broader agenda which underlies this study, that of 'rescuing' the submerged world of Hellenistic Judaism, that entire tradition of Jewish writing, thinking, and living in ancient Greek which evolved around the Septuagint, the tradition which I attempted to describe in Chapters 6 and 7. Jewish–Greek literature was so crucial to the identity of the early Christians that it was even understood as a Christian literature.[7] Notably, Philo became, as David Runia put it, 'a Christian *honoris causa*': in the fourth century CE, Eusebius already asserted that the philosopher had been an admiring witness of the Christian way of life as lived by the

---

[5] With the notable and much neglected exception of the Byzantine Jewish communities, an area under investigation in a major AHRC project directed at Cambridge by Nicholas de Lange.

[6] On these authors, see Chap. 6, pp. 217–27.

[7] The careful scholarly study of Hengel (2002) is fully aware of the problems, while written from a generally conservative standpoint.

ascetics of Lake Mareotis (in reference to the ascetics he called *therapeutai*, who, whatever they were, were not Christians at all), and he even maintained that Philo had met Saint Peter in Rome. Later, Christian *catenae*, strings of useful passages, often have the heading 'of Philo the Bishop' above excerpts taken from Philo.[8] It will be evident that by these means the debt to the Jews could be circumvented.

A puzzling feature of the current picture of the Septuagint takeover is the conception of things suddenly stopping short in the Jewish world in reaction to this single act of appropriation. The idea is that the old Greek versions of the Bible, after serving as a fundamental resource for a large part of the Jewish world for several centuries, stopped doing so within a very few years, with a speed altogether unusual in the slow-moving sphere of cultural history. Terms such as 'elimination' and 'abandonment' are deployed.[9] Either (on a theological reading) the translations were held to have been simply removed from their unworthy caretakers by a higher power—be it the Almighty, the Holy Spirit, or just manifest destiny—or else, in a modern, more rational, and more benign interpretation, the old Greek versions were deliberately dropped by their Jewish users. Sometimes both things are thought to have happened together. This reconstruction has its origins in the writings of the Church Fathers, as we shall see. In one way or another, it has been adopted as part of Church history, and also of Septuagint scholarship, ever since. Jewish scholars too have been inclined to go along with it, tied in as they were to the same scholarly framework.[10]

The ideology that emerges is a counterpart to the notion entrenched in the older readings of Jewish–Christian relations, which

---

[8] Eusebius *HE*, 2.16–17. Runia 1993: 3–33 outlines the process of Philo's Christianization, as prelude to his comprehensive study of the philosopher's Christian reception.

[9] See, for example, Dorival in *BGS*, 122–4, for whom things move rapidly from a stage where 'la méfiance s'installe' to a stage of 'l'élimination de la Septante dans les années 90–130'. It is, however, conceded here that this did not happen in one fell swoop, but took just as long as it took Aquila's translation to appear.

[10] For example, Seeligmann 1948; Orlinsky 1975; Wasserstein and Wasserstein 2006. A notable exception to the consensus on all sides is to be found in Treu 1973, a strikingly independent study.

have it that Judaism itself became fossilized after the destruction of the Temple, concurrently with the spread of Christianity. The new religion arrived providentially at the right moment to replace its predecessor. The consensus on the fortunes of the Septuagint may itself indeed be described as a kind of supersession doctrine, a spin-off from the overarching supersessionism entrenched in much of the older writing. The supersessionist claim, quite simply, is that Christianity had made its parent obsolete. This comes often with the added implication that the parent had been inadequate, so that, as Origen wrote, God's invitation to blessedness had been transferred to others (*Contra Celsum*, 2.8; 4.22). Different theologians took different lines as to how early this happened: for Barnabas, it came as early as the sin of the making of the golden calf. Since, however, Judaism patently continued to be physically still there, was hard to ignore, and was often rather successful, it had to be sidelined. That could effectively be done by deeming Jewish attitudes and practices ossified and legalistic, as already suggested in some parts of the New Testament: they were thus destroyed by their own malign scrupulousness and rigidity, and were ripe for dismissal.[11] That is familiar territory in theological discussion nowadays, but it is important to grasp that those far-reaching ideas have been also the context for the way the Greek Bible's trajectory is understood.

The foundations were laid for a construction of the Septuagint takeover as a quick and decisive development by way of ingenious embellishments and comments in the rewritings by the Church Fathers of the story of Ptolemy's commissioning of the translation.[12] To follow this up is to come upon some remarkable twists to the story. It is not just that the event—well on its way to being miraculous in Philo[13]—becomes ever more miraculous in the retelling, but that the miracle is of a particularly meaningful kind, closely connected to the nature and source of the translators' inspiration. In the ascription of their achievement to divine intervention, the scholars,

---

[11] For a good description and history of this wide–ranging idea and various revisions of it, see Jacobs 2003: 96–105. Simon 1997 is concerned with this large topic.

[12] On the account and its tradition, see Chap. 1. For the patristic tradition, see Hengel 1994; Müller 1996: 68–97.

[13] As Seidman points out (2006: 55), 'Philo had already put in place most of the elements necessary for a Christian appropriation of the legend'.

and thus the Jewish people as a whole, become no more than the unwilling medium for the transmission of truth. We recall that in these Christian versions Ptolemy put the translators in separate booths but they still came up with exactly the same translation. What is interesting is the explanation offered for why he did this. The good King knew his customers, and his intent was to prevent the cunning translators from conspiring together in order to suppress the prophetic messages of the prophets which were obscurely present in the Hebrew scriptures. The key element in this explanation emerges in Irenaeus' attack on heresies, as quoted by Eusebius. The emphasis there, in a brief retelling of the translation story, is on the vital role of the Holy Spirit in bringing about the perfect unanimity between the Seventy, a unanimity which in its turn guarantees the independence of the translation from its human agents, and thus its sanctity. Ptolemy put them in separate cells partly as a test of their skill, but more importantly to make it impossible for them to contrive to conceal their deceit.[14] Another third-century author gives us a fuller version of the story and puts his own, Hellenocentric, stamp on the doctrine. Although these Jewish scholars, says Clement of Alexandria, were the instrument, God had in advance so arranged things to ensure that the biblical prophecy should reach Greek ears.[15] Among their other defects it may be noted that these accounts ignore what the original Aristeas story had made perfectly clear: that the Pentateuch translation alone belonged to Ptolemy's reign or had anything to do with his intervention. The rest of scripture was not in that story.

In relation to the Hebrew original, it was not essential, and perhaps not even desirable, to detach its original creators from their handiwork in quite the same way. Rather, a wedge could be driven between past and present. Those among whom the patriarchs had done their virtuous deeds and among whom the prophets had walked, it was explained by Tertullian, had been the Hebrews, a people special to God. They were quite different from the Jews of his own day

---

[14] So Irenaeus, *Adv. Haer.*, 3.21.2 and 4; in Eusebius, *HE*, 5.8.11–15. A fragment of Irenaeus also alleges that had the Jews had a chance, they would have burned their translation: see Veltri 2006: 48 and n. 73.

[15] Clement, *Strom.*, 1.148, See Eusebius, *PE*, 8.1.

(Tertullian, *Apologet*, 18). It was these successor-Jews who were bent upon hiding the truth away. Thus, the gold letters of that Hebrew Torah brought from Jerusalem to Alexandria were 'a fountain sealed', requiring to be unlocked. At one level this referred to the unknown language of the scrolls and the need to send for translators. But the double sense is clear. The craftsmanship of a new agency was necessary for the nations to be brought to the faith, as Epiphanius wrote, in the most developed and extended version of the Aristeas story.[16]

For Augustine, too, these old sacred texts survived so as to be able one day to offer salvation to the Gentiles. So it was, he concluded, that Divine Providence arranged for the knowledge which the Jews, either through over-scrupulousness, jealousy, or sheer malevolence, withheld from the world, to be given to all the peoples. It was partly because the Jews hid the texts that they lost them.[17] By contrast, another major figure of the late fourth-century CE, John Chrysostom, accorded a measure of credit to Ptolemy's translators because they were at least not like their successors. Rather, it was those Jews who came after Jesus but still chose to remain Jews and became consumed by hatred, who were responsible for distorting their own holy scriptures and veiling their content by deliberate new mistranslations.[18]

Thus the doctrine enunciated in these twists and flourishes of the Septuagint's divine revelation is expressed in terms which serve not only to elevate the Greek scriptures[19] but also neatly to detach them from their Jewish origins and ownership. The second purpose is articulated at least as prominently as the first, yet it has been far less noticed. The benefit of such a theology was that it could retain the Jewish substructure of Christianity without the unease of obligation to the Jews. Alison Salvesen puts it clearly: 'reliance on Jewish learning rarely went hand in hand with a respect for Jews and Judaism.'[20]

However, as is well known, matters took yet another turn. Jerome came to appreciate and to assert that the Hebrew text and not the

---

[16] So Epiphanius, *de Mens. et Pond.* III, in *PG*, 43.24.2.
[17] Augustine, *Civ. Dei*, 18.42 and 15.11–13; *de Doctrina Christiana*, 2.15.22.
[18] John Chrysostom, *Hom. Matth*, 5.2 = *PG*, 57.57. He refers to Aquila, Theodotion, and Symmachus.
[19] On this purpose, see Veltri 2006: 72.
[20] Salvesen 2003: 256.

Greek was the 'true' text, a point stressed in his various supporting communications for the Vulgate translations of individual books from the 390s CE onwards. He was harshly criticized by Rufinus and others for taking this position.[21] We also know that Jerome was dependent upon learned Jews—like Origen before him –for guidance in language and interpretation. The result was ambivalence. While Jerome did retain a considerable respect for the Septuagint, he came to be unable unequivocally to describe it as divinely inspired.[22] In his exegetical writing he pointed out that neither the *Letter of Aristeas* nor Josephus, as adapter of the *Letter*, had spoken of the translators as prophets, merely as scholars working together.[23] He also clarified the point that the translation of the Torah alone had been in question in the days of Ptolemy.[24] At the same time, Jerome did not always and altogether deny that the Holy Spirit had a share in the translation, at least of the Torah.[25] Robert Hayward shows that the doctrine of inspiration still had some importance for Jerome, in that it accorded due recognition to the apostles' understanding of the Septuagint as a holy book, and also for the simple reason that he did not want to set himself up as the shatterer of the Septuagint's prestige.[26] But the stakes were different for Jerome. And so the doctrine of the secrets of the Jews could now be put to work in a different way, serving to put the Septuagint in its proper place. The translation was in certain ways deficient, Jerome wrote, for a very particular reason: the translators, while not themselves subject to error, had nevertheless not wanted to make all the mysteries locked in scripture available to Ptolemy, lest they themselves be regarded as worshipping false gods by this monarch who was (supposedly) a

---

[21] On the prefaces to the translations *iuxta hebraeos* and Jerome's understanding of *hebraica veritas*, see Williams 2006: 85–95. For Jerome's defence against Rufinus in *Against Rufinus*, see Adler 1990.

[22] As he had done a few times earlier in his career: see Müller 1996: 84, n. 25. For a sensitive account of Jerome's positions, see Hayward 1995: 29–34 and 49–72. Useful also is Kamesar 1993. On the rejection of the theology of inspiration in the *Contra Rufinum*, see Rebenich 2002: 103.

[23] Jerome, *Praef. in Pent.* (*PL*, 28), 150–2.

[24] Jerome, *Quaest. in Gen.*, 23. 985; and in commentaries on Micah and Ezekiel.

[25] For example, Jerome, *Praef. in Libra Paralip. iuxta LXX Interpretes* in *PL*, 29, 402; 404.

[26] Hayward 1995: 59 and n. 72. See also Müller 1996: 85.

Platonizing monotheist. For this reason, the translators passed over certain dubious passages in silence. This curious interpretation emerges as less derogatory of the translators but still as diminishing their work.[27]

For other Church Fathers at this point the picture was more straightforward. In spite of the many textual uncertainties which had necessitated, in the third century, the great and very influential collations in Origen's Hexapla, they were able, without too much hesitation, to elevate 'their' Septuagint to the supreme position, satisfied that it had been rescued from those who had never deserved it. Jerome notwithstanding, Augustine, who corresponded with him on the subject, was still able to accord primacy to the Septuagint, though in the wake of Jerome he was less insistent than earlier scholars on the subject of alleged Jewish tampering.[28]

A glance forward over the centuries will show what a very long life has been granted to that line of interpretation that ascribes the Greek Bible to a very particular divine dispensation. In 1850, this is what the Revd Dr Edward Grinfield, founder of the surviving Septuagint lectureship in the University of Oxford, had to say, in his passionate *Apology for the Septuagint*:

If the Hebrew language had always maintained its original power and prerogative, it may be questioned how far the gracious design of making the Gentiles fellow heirs of the promise given to the Patriarchs could have been carried into effect. The ancient Hebrew was strictly suited to a theocracy, to the privileges of a separate and exclusive people set apart from the nations of the earth ... The decline and fall of the Hebrew tongue in the Jewish and Christian Church is tacitly assumed in the reasoning of the Apostle concerning the grafting of the Gentiles on the stock of Israel. The pride of the Jew, as the lineal descendant of Abraham, could never have been broken down if he had retained the language and speech of Abraham ... It is the glory alike of the Hebrew and of the Septuagint to have found their consummation in the New Testament.[29]

---

[27] In the introduction to his *Quaestiones Hebraicae in Gen.*, 14 = CCL, 79.61–3.
[28] On the Hexapla, see below, pp. 295–6. For Augustine's reservations about Jerome's unseating of the Septuagint from its position of primacy, see Augustine, Letter 28 2.2 and 71.2.4, with the exposition in Veltri 2006: 65–70. For his moderation on Jewish tampering, see Adler 1990: 23–7.
[29] Grinfield 1850: 29.

For Grinfield, who equipped his prose with more than the occasional purple passage, the Septuagint was the 'viaduct' between the Old and New Testaments, the 'bond of union' between Jews (whom he aspired to convert) and Gentiles, the 'morning star before the sun of righteousness, the key of the sacred treasury, the light of the Alexandrian Pharos, the sacred amalgam'. Studying the Septuagint was a hedge against falling into new-fangled error. Thus, there was even an educational programme to be promoted:

> It still remains a desideratum to behold the Greek version raised to its proper rank as a prominent object of academic study... The late eminent Dr Arnold introduced the reading of the Septuagint among the seniors at Rugby and it is earnestly to be desired that his example should be followed in all our public schools... There are numbers who can read off Lycophron and Pindar, construe the most difficult passages of Thucydides, unthread the maze of Greek choruses and compose elegant Latin and Greek verse, who have never once looked into that version of the ancient Scriptures.[30]

Grinfield was an enthusiast, and something of an eccentric, even in his own day. He sought to prove that Greek and only Greek had been the language of Jesus—hence his devotion to the Septuagint.[31] He was also a vociferous anti-Catholic and an active proponent of the mission to the Jews. But countless more sober statements of the sentiments in the first quoted paragraph (if not in the second) can easily be found in the scholarship of the succeeding years. Some half a century later than Grinfield, Thackeray's well-regarded grammar of the Septuagint[32] spoke baldly of a *praeparatio evangelica*, a preparation for the Gospel. So, again, Adolf Deissmann, a great scholar and still a major influence, adopted a different metaphor for the same idea and announced that: 'Greek Judaism with the Septuagint had ploughed the furrows for the Gospel seed in the Western world'.[33]

Fortunately, few scholars write in quite this vein today. But the mindset has left its mark, and one of its legacies is the picture that has

---

[30] Ibid., 130.
[31] On this aspect of Grinfield's thought, and on his precursor in the advocacy of a Greek-speaking Jesus, the Neapolitan Domenico Diodati, see Momigliano 1992: 554.
[32] Thackeray 1909.
[33] Deissmann, quoted by Meecham 1932: 344.

crystallized of the Jewish side of the takeover. The malevolent and secretive Jews seem to have vanished, but they have been replaced by a different cast of characters—pious practitioners of a faith-in-the-building, relentless rabbinists to whom it fell to abandon a large slice of their past in the interests of a narrowly conceived future. One might wonder whether, among well-disposed commentators, the anxieties of takeover have perhaps had something to do with the success of the theory of Jewish abandonment. It is easier to feel comfortable about removing something from someone if the appropriator fully believes that the owner did not want it any more. Neither law nor morality forbids the acquisition of *res derelicta*.

THE ABANDONMENT THEORY

When the Philonic scholar David Runia[34] describes the Christianization of Philo in terms of Jewish abandonment, he invokes the model of the Septuagint as a back-up to his explanation of what happened to the writings of Philo. It is interesting to see how Runia's argument is constructed: 'In the absence of any direct evidence', he writes, 'it is worth considering whether the Rabbis were encouraged to reject Philo as an exegetical predecessor precisely because his thought had been exploited by prominent Christian thinkers such as Clement, Origen, and Eusebius. The process of rejection would then run parallel to the rejection of the Septuagint as an acceptable translation of the Hebrew Bible'. In other words, the supposed fate of the Septuagint is found in the Jews' assumed instantaneous and reactive rejection of the old Greek as an acceptable translation of the Hebrew Bible, once Christians had associated themselves with it, and it serves as the key to the loss within Judaism of the rest of Jewish–Greek writing. The Jewish abandonment of the Septuagint is confidently relied upon as a basic fact.

The case for the voluntary rejection of their heritage by the Jews centres on what has now turned out to be an item of invented

---

[34] Runia 1993: 15.

history—the supposition that in 90 CE (more or less precisely) an event took place, sometimes rather curiously described as the 'synod of Jamnia', which made far-reaching decisions about the future of Judaism in the wake of the disaster of 70 CE and the destruction of the Temple. The conception of a formal council of Jewish leaders seems to be extrapolated from mention in the Mishnah of seventy-two elders of the academy of Yavneh (in Greek, Jamnia).[35] To this are added perfectly reasonable suppositions about what might be needed to set about building a new order in the Jewish world. And we can indeed find the elements of remodelling in rulings on essential matters ascribed by tradition to rabbis associated with Yavneh, especially the all-important fixing of the calendar. But the model of Church councils is then rather crudely mapped on to this minimal information. The spectre of Yavneh has only recently halted its relentless advance, in the face of arguments first made some years ago that no lasting decisions can confidently be ascribed to that setting, and it may be doubted whether anything like a council—let alone a synod—even took place.[36]

Among other things, the assembled rabbis of Yavneh, asserting their claim to pre-eminent religious authority in Jewry, are credited with fixing the biblical canon for Jews.[37] And, in the same vein, it was believed that this gathering also addressed other questions concerning the authority of scripture. It is maintained that Jews everywhere were now told to stop using the old Greek, the version produced and cherished during the preceding centuries. This reversal was largely driven, it is supposed, by reaction to the Christian appropriation and new circumstances brought about by it. The Jesus movement was at that time busy composing the books which became the New Testament (as well as many that did not), and its intensive engagement with them rendered the old Greek Bible translations unserviceable and unappealing, non-kosher as it were, for Jews. Moreover, as we shall see, there were problems over tampering with the text. Divorce from them was an act of self-demarcation. This reaction

[35] Simon ben Azzai in M.Yad. 3.5.
[36] Barr 1983: 56; Lewis 1964; Schäfer 1975; Leiman 1976; Stemberger 1977. And now see Hezser 2001 and Stern 2003.
[37] On the question of canon formation, see Chap. 6, p. 212–16.

on the Jewish side expressed itself specifically, the theory runs, by producing alternative translations which were backed as more correct and were designed as more 'rabbinic'.

AQUILA OF PONTUS

First and foremost among the substitutes was the famous rendition attributed to Aquila the proselyte, which in terms of word-for-word equivalence was a considerably more exact version than the Septuagint. Aquila is very helpful to that narrative, into which he can be slotted all too neatly. He does indeed earn special praise in rabbinic literature for his achievement and the fineness of his rendering. In a discussion in the Jerusalem Talmud of Rabban Shimon ben Gamaliel's ruling that the Torah was not to be translated except into Greek, Rabbi Eliezer and R. Joshua, to whom Aquila's translation was imagined as having been presented, bring praise of his achievement. They acclaim Aquila, saying 'you are more beautiful than the children of men', quoting Psalm 45: 3, and playing on the verbal resemblance of the Hebrew word for 'beauty' and the name of Japhet, progenitor of the Greeks.[38] Since Noah's blessing to his son Japhet, 'may God beautify Japhet and may he dwell in the tents of Shem' (Genesis 9: 27) was interpreted by Bar Kappara as meaning 'may the words of the Torah be spoken in the language of Japheth [Greek] in the tent of Shem [the Jewish people]',[39] there is an understood context for this neat eulogy.

It is hard to know what to make of the apparent conflation in Talmudic tradition on the basis of phonetic similarity in their names, of the identity of the scarcely known Aquila, with the even less-known Onkelos, author of the standard Aramaic Targum to the Torah that goes under his name. But, again, an embrace of Aquila is suggested.[40]

---

[38] J. Meg 1.11.71c.
[39] Gen. Rabbah 36. 26–7.
[40] This led Veltri 2006: 163–89 to suggest that the name was transferred by the Rabbis from a Greek translation to an Aramaic one as a 'canonical substitution'.

In the mid-sixth century CE, the Emperor Justinian's well-known ruling about the languages permitted for synagogue use demanded general recourse to the Septuagint, but still allowed Aquila as an alternative, presumably, as we shall see, responding to a body of current practice among Jews.[41]

Aquila's rendering has to be painstakingly reconstituted in minute droplets from the vestiges of Origen's Hexapla, Cairo Geniza fragments, papyri, and occasional quotations.[42] It is evident that this was a translation which reproduced with a particular kind of neatness the lexicon and constructions of the Hebrew; that is to say, it tended to opt for an extreme adherence to the source as against the target language. In Aquila, Greek words very often function as calques, or stand-ins for Hebrew ones. He coined, for example, as a new form of *horaō*, 'to see', the verb *horamatizesthai*, where Hebrew has the unusual *ḥazah* in place of *ra'ah*. This verb does not appear in any other Jewish–Greek writer, let alone in standard Greek, but for Aquila it served the purpose of preserving the variation in the Hebrew. It is well-known that in Genesis 1: 1 Aquila has the semantically close *kephalaion* for *r'eshit*, 'in the beginning', instead of *archē*, the expected word for 'beginning', used in the older Greek translation. A typical example of the extreme word-for-word technique in Aquila is the rendering of *le-meraḥoq*, 'from afar' or 'from of old', in 2 Kings 19: 25, with a nonsensical juxtaposition of Greek prepositions, as *eis apo makrothen*. Here we can see how such a technique could produce downright gobbledygook. Famously, Aquila represents the Hebrew accusative particle when it is followed by the definite article with the Greek preposition *sun*, 'with', incorrectly governing a noun in the accusative case.

A sustained attempt to systematize Aquila's translation style on the basis of his extremely fragmentary remnants as achieving the maximum exact matching between Hebrew and Greek, such that each Hebrew term could be shown to get its Greek counterpart, was not able to achieve its goal.[43] Indeed, in reviewing the results, James Barr was able to demonstrate that there were 'aspects in which the trans-

---

[41] Justinian, *Novella*, 146, discussed below, pp. 302–3.
[42] For the documentation on these sources, see Fernández-Marcos 2000: 113–15.
[43] Hyvärinen 1977.

lator could without great difficulty have been more strictly regular than he seems to have been'.⁴⁴ Examples of such cases are the systematic lack of correspondence in the various renderings of 'stick' or 'staff'; and, again, perhaps more significantly, the interchangeability of the range of words representing the semantic field of 'joy' across the two languages. So, even for Aquila's procedure, a more nuanced view is necessary. This should be borne in mind when we examine the role that scholars have ascribed to Aquila.

The temptation was great to accommodate Aquila to the abandonment theory. Both his methods and his warm reception by certain rabbis seemed so well to suit the image of a hardening, pedantic, self-contained, inward-looking Judaism. The word-for-word rendering could have operated almost like a secret code. Aquila's translation style has readily lent itself to hostile criticism and his bad press goes right back to Origen's description of him as a 'slave of the Hebrew'. Jerome denigrates Aquila as a translator who, though he may be accurate, is 'enslaved to every word', describing him as 'deceived by the perverse interpretation of the Pharisees'. Enslavement to the word, that is to say, being bound by the letter of the text, is an obvious counterpart to that enslavement to the letter of Law of which Paul had spoken in Galatians (5: 1–5).⁴⁵

No less a scholar than Alfred Rahlfs, in the historical survey which introduces his standard one-volume Septuagint, first published in 1935 and regularly reprinted since then, breaks out into scathing criticism, and then goes on to damn Aquila with faint praise:⁴⁶

> Aquila... rendered every detail of the sacred text as precisely as possible into Greek, and he did not shrink from perpetrating the most appalling outrages to the whole essence of the Greek language... The extraordinary consistency with which he made these distinctions deserves our genuine admiration. Aquila must have possessed not only a will of iron, but also an incredible memory, as is demonstrated by the way in which he regularly provided a uniform rendering for each Hebrew word as it occurs.

---

[44] So Barr 1967.
[45] Origen, *Letter to Africanus*, 2, and on this letter see further pp. 297–8 below. Jerome, *Ep.*, 57 (*ad Pammachium*); *Comm. Isaiah*, 13. The Pauline and patristic slavery rhetoric is brilliantly teased out in Seidman 2006: 94–101.
[46] Rahlfs, Editor's Preface (pp. xxxiii and xxxv).

The persistent stereotype of the clever and obstinate Jew surely lurks behind this imaginative sketch of Aquila. The spectre of Jewish legalism walks here.[47]

The negative slur of 'literalism' has also affected scholarly analyses of the language of the Septuagint itself.[48] At other times, however, in the interests of a very negative portrayal of Aquila, the elsewhere maligned Greek of the Septuagint could become impliedly a masterpiece of Hellenic prose. Such a contrast is also drawn in Rahlfs' editorial remarks:[49]

Owing to the influence of Akiba, in the first thirty years or so of the second century AD, there became prominent a school of rabbinic interpretation which laid emphasis upon every detail of the sacred text, and which drew the most far-fetched and also the most singular conclusions from the most unimportant of details... It is quite evident that this type of interpretation, adhering firmly, as it does, to every single letter, *could not rest satisfied with such a manifestly free translation as the Septuagint* [my italics].

Aquila was one of a trio of translators, the so-called 'Three', who occupied the middle columns of Origen's Hexapla. Some kind of Jewish identity was ascribed to all three, as we shall see. And all three have fallen foul of the same kind of ambivalent judgement. What stands out is the eagerness of the interpreters to fix literalism as the hallmark of the Jewish approach. Yet it has long been clear that Symmachus, another of the 'Three', replaced many of the Septuagint's paratactic (juxtaposed) constructions with Greek subordinate clauses and did away with juxtaposed verbs and other Hebraisms. And Alison Salvesen's fundamental study of the remnants of his work has revealed a translator of distinct character and sophistication, with a visibly good control of Greek syntax, alongside what may perhaps have been a somewhat standardized vocabulary.[50]

---

[47] For other modern critiques of Aquila's literalism in similar vein, if not as harsh, see Seidman 2006: 76–7.
[48] Yet detailed study of Greek biblical language-units, especially in the masterly hands of Marguerite Harl, continually yields evidence of subtlety and skill.
[49] Rahlfs, Editor's Preface (p. xxxiii).
[50] Salvesen 1991. For further material on the style of Symmachus, see Fernández-Marcos 2000: 128–33.

Life is breathed into the hostile portrait of Aquila by the linkage regularly made between Aquila and rabbinic exegesis, especially with the interpretative techniques of Rabbi Akiva (who was implicated, significantly enough, with Bar Kokhba's revolt against Hadrian in 132–5 CE, and the consequent decisive expulsion of the Jews from Jerusalem). This link was a surprisingly important part of Barthélemy's enormously influential reconstruction of the history of revisions to the Greek text in *Les Dévanciers d'Aquila*,[51] and it goes right back to Jerome.[52] It is unlikely that Jerome knew any more about Aquila than we do. Just once in rabbinic literature Aquila is described as interpreting a halakhic problem in front of Rabbi Akiva.[53]

The Akiva connection is made by way of the rabbinic hermeneutical rules (*middot*). In particular, a midrashic statement that Akiva ascribed to the Hebrew particle *et* an 'inclusive' meaning has been identified with Aquila's rendering of *et* by the Greek *sun*.[54] Yet the system of fundamental hermeneutical principles of the Tannaitic Rabbis is not exclusive to Akiva. Indeed, Lester Grabbe has found there to be no marked similarity between Aquilan renderings and any one identifiable school of exegesis.[55] Here we need to explore the Aquila–Akiva associations no further. Our main concern is with the kind of use to which they have been put.

COMPETING TEXTS

Early Christian–Jewish argument often took the form of one side dismissing the authority of the other side's texts and interpretations. A particular kind of challenge was to contest textual readings and produce others, claimed as more authentic, in defence of a particular

---

[51] Barthélemy 1963: 85–8; 246.
[52] Jerome commenting on Isa. 7: 14 says that Akiva was Aquila's teacher.
[53] J. Kiddushin 1.1.59a, ascribed to R.Yossi in the name of R.Yohanan.
[54] This Akivan methodology is spelled out in Gen. Rabbah 1.14; B. Hagigah 12a.
[55] Grabbe 1982. See also, for reservations on the linkage, Greenspoon 1990; Tov 2005: 392–3.

exegesis. In particular, the Jews were accused of extensive tampering.[56] Contested passages came especially from the prophetic books of the Bible, which were so crucial to Christian theology. This activity has permitted an extra twist to the abandonment theory. Not only are the Jews supposed, in modern scholarship, to have abandoned the Septuagint version because it had become the lynchpin of Christianity with which they wanted to have nothing to do; but also, it is claimed, they were in urgent need of versions of their own, which they could now regard as more faithful to the Hebrew, for the urgent purpose of argument with Christians (and Jewish Christians). The formidable enterprise of collating textual variants which constituted Origen's Hexapla[57] has been described as 'one of the greatest single monuments of Roman scholarship', and also as deeply dependent upon the 'centuries-old tradition... of Hellenistic biblical learning'.[58] Its author, ironically enough, in arguing against Africanus (and against appearances) that the Septuagint story of Susannah came from an original Hebrew book of Daniel, explicitly described his enterprise as a tool in argument against the Jews.[59] But if it were true that the Jews forgot the labour that had gone into the Old Greek and replaced it with Aquila out of a desire for exclusivity and a sense that the original Greek translation was no longer theirs, then they would have scored an own goal. The sequel, in terms of Jewish–Christian relations, would have been a paradoxical one. Jewish scholars looking to sequester their privileged and private version, would then have achieved the opposite, opening the door to an intensification of the battle of texts, in which that private version was given a very open and regular exposure, displayed even to the public at large in debates such as those that took place between Jews and Christians in Origen's

---

[56] For a study of this charge, see Adler 1990.
[57] For a review of what Origen's scholarly methods and objectives appear to have been in the Hexapla, see Ulrich 1999b; Clements 1999: 321–9. Grafton and Williams (2006: 86–129), locate the Hexapla within a wider set of textual efforts undertaken by Origen to provide a 'suite of tools' for future work.
[58] The quotations are from Grafton and Williams 2006: 130 and 132.
[59] Origen, *Letter to Africanus*, 9 (5), is interpreted by Clements 1999: 324–7 as revealing why Origen needed to fold the Hebrew tradition into the Christian sphere. Further discussion in Brock 1974: 563 and also Veltri 2006: 53. For an edition and commentary, see de Lange and Harl 1983.

Caesarea. Their opponents, the scholars of the early Church, would have had to delve into Aquila almost as much as they ransacked the Septuagint, if they were to compare and refute. And that indeed is precisely what Origen did, as Ruth Clements has neatly demonstrated.[60] Having depended upon rabbinic teachers almost throughout his time in Palestine, now Origen drew above all on Aquila for his attempts to 'heal' the Septuagint text. Furthermore, to suggest that this proselyte (if that is indeed what Aquila was) retranslated the Hebrew Bible for the express purpose of forging a weapon for arguments with Christians, is to have the new movement call the whole tune, turning response to external pressure into the primary influence on the evolution of Jewish tradition.[61] Rabbis were indeed sometimes hard put to it to meet Christian arguments: in one case, Rabbi Abbahu of Caesarea had to rescue a Babylonian sage from a dialogic near-disaster.[62] But these occasions of encounter were scarcely at the centre of the Rabbis' interests. They actually mattered more to Christians than to Jews.

REINTERPRETING THE EVIDENCE

Another consequence of Christianization in the scholarly agenda is that the spotlight has fallen specifically on the Septuagint, which was the first Bible of the Church and is still canonical for some denominations, while all other material has played an ancillary role in reconstructing the main line of historical development. Yet an equally significant part of the history of the Greek Bible is the emergence of that range of different translations by Jews, or at least by those somewhere on the margins of Jewry—we shall see shortly that this is how Christian tradition described not only Aquila but also Theodotion and Symmachus. These new versions stood in a complicated relationship to the fate of the Septuagint. We should not forget too that other such enterprises may have been undertaken which, not

---

[60] Clements 1999: 316–29.
[61] Veltri 1994 has useful remarks on this kind of fallacy.
[62] For this story, see Clements 1999: 315, n. 43.

salvaged by Origen, will simply have been lost to the record. The contribution of all of them has been largely obscured by the dominance of the Septuagint, now understood as Christian, into whose triumphal progress their story was subsumed.

We shall have the opportunity to return to the question of needs and motivations. But we need first to go to the supposed Jewish abandonment of the basic text, the old Greek itself, as represented in the Septuagint. We have seen the ideological roots of this reading and we have become suspicious. How solid is the evidence invoked in support of such a theory? In seeking to restore the balance, it is important to grasp that the Jewish reception-history is not at all the same thing as the rabbinic reception history of the various Greek versions. In this enquiry, how the Rabbis reacted must be considered secondary to the thinking of primary users of the corpus, that is to say Jewish users of Greek rather than those within a Hebrew-Aramaic milieu. Of course, the former, reflected in a huge surviving literature, is by far the more accessible to us and it tends, therefore, to call the tune.

The abandonment theory is largely constructed on the platform of a handful of specific statements taken out of a patristic or a rabbinic context, often detached from their context, and pressed rather hard. Those on the Christian side come from polemical contexts in works of disputation, a point easily forgotten when they are cited in isolation. They must be taken separately, before we consider whether there is any more than an illusory convergence with anything in rabbinic texts. Most influential, though not earliest, is the statement of Origen in his *Letter to Africanus* that Jews trusted Aquila, a slave to the Hebrew, for his accuracy in rendering scripture and that his was the version most commonly read by readers ignorant of Hebrew.[63] Origen himself, no doubt on the assurance of his Jewish instructors, here seems to admit that he too relied on Aquila. His testimony is not to be ignored. The question is what it tells us. First, we may accept that Aquila was well known in the third century CE, at least in circles with which Origen had contact. These circles were most likely to be found in Caesarea in Palestine, the city above all others where Jewish

---

[63] Origen, *Letter to Africanus*, 2; Simon 1986: 444, n. 150.

and Christian scholars met. Second, what Origen's formulation suggests is that when the call was for a rendition of the Hebrew with a particular stamp, above all for the reassurance of a close rendering, it was Aquila who scored. But, at the same time, Origen's wording implies that other versions—unspecified—were also still in use in Jewish circles. Indeed he goes on after this passage in the *Letter to Africanus* (6) to say that in order to be able to resist charges of ignorance from Jewish disputants it is necessary to compare the different versions with thoroughness and care, just as he has done. Thus Jews were seen as in control of the versions, and choices were still there to be made in Origen's day, well over a century after the destruction of the Temple and well into the the new order in the Jewish world. We do not know exactly what those versions were, but there is every reason to include among them the old Greek as well as the other texts included in the Hexapla.[64] In other words, Origen's remark is much more interesting as evidence of diversity than as proof of the supremacy of Aquila among Jews.[65]

It was three-quarters of a century or so before Origen that Justin Martyr constructed in the *Dialogue with Trypho the Jew* a complex and influential definition of Christian theology on the basis, largely, of a succession of proof texts from the Old Testament, all of which he naturally cites in Greek. He is a leading culprit. He talks disparagingly of Jews who had no respect for the Septuagint and who had blithely deleted prophetic material or altered wordings in order not to be disadvantaged in engaging with Christians.

> But I do not trust your teachers who refuse to admit that the interpretation made by the seventy elders who were at the court of Ptolemy king of Egypt is well done and attempt to translate for themselves. I also want you to know that they have entirely deleted many passages from the version composed by

---

[64] To these texts we might add exemplars of the text types described by textual scholars as proto-Lucianic texts, such as the text Josephus seems to have used in his paraphrase of 1 Sam.

[65] Origen also figures in a speculation offered by Barthélemy, and cautiously reported by David Runia, that a clutch of non-Septuagintal biblical quotations found in certain Philo manuscripts actually derive from Jewish alterations carried out in Origen's *scriptorium* in Caesarea, and that these might be ascribed to Rabbi Hoshaya, a Caesarean scholar whom Origen is known to have consulted. See Runia 1993: 25, referring to Barthélemy 1963: 66–76.

the elders who were at the court of Ptolemy, from which it is clearly shown that the crucified one was proclaimed as both God and man, and as dying on the cross. But since I know that people of your race reject these passages, I will not engage in discussions of this kind...[66]

Justin then moves on to issue a challenge over the Greek translation of one crucial word in Isaiah 7: 14, probably the best known of all the points of difference. The Hebrew, in Orlinsky's careful translation,[67] reads:

> See the young woman is with child
> and about to bear a son.
> She shall call him 'Immanu 'El.

Justin expounds the Jewish–Christian difference as follows:

Thus far you have admitted the authenticity of all my quotations except this: 'behold the virgin [*parthenos*] shall conceive' which you say ought to be read 'behold the young woman [*neanis*] shall conceive'. I promised to show you that this prophecy referred not to Hezekiah, as you were taught, but to this my Christ. This I now intend to prove.[68]

Trypho is not even allowed by his creator, Justin, to enter into discussion of the prophetic reading of this passage, nor even of the rival Greek translations, still less of the real meaning of the original Hebrew word, '*almah* (which normally does not connote virginity).[69] Instead, he

---

[66] Justin, *Dialogue with Trypho*, 71.1–2 (my translation). Cf. *Trypho*, 137.3, where Justin claims that the Septuagint (Isa. 3.9) had 'let us take away the just one for he is hateful to us', but the Jews had it as 'let us bind the just one for he is hateful to us' (which is indeed the Septuagint reading). For further specific cases of such polemic, see Hengel 2002: esp. 31–4; BGS, 185. For a critical edition of the *Trypho* see Marcovitch 1997. Translation with brief commentary in *St Justin Martyr. Dialogue with Trypho* 2003 (re-edition of the Falls translation).

[67] See Orlinsky 1990: 128 for this translation with discussion.

[68] *Trypho*, 71.3, followed up in 84.1–4.

[69] *Trypho*, 71.4. Subsequently, Irenaeus criticized Aquila and Theodotion's rendering, which is *neanis* like Trypho's, as part of a critique of the Jewish–Christian Ebionites: see *Adv. Haer.*, 3.21.1–4. Veltri 2006: 164–5 regards Irenaeus' critique as the first Christian reference to Aquila. The remarkable history and ramifications of the textual, translational, and interpretative arguments set in motion by Justin's challenge over Isa. 7.14, and their role in separating Jews from Christians down to the mid-twentieth century are explored by Seidman: 39–46. Seidman's subsequent interpretation of the history of this fissure largely accepts, however, the Christian paradigm of Jewish rejection of the Septuagint and seems to subscribe to a reading of

moves on: 'We ask you first to quote to us some of the passages which you allege have been completely omitted [by Jewish teachers].' This gives Justin an opening to bring out several further passages with great conviction. In reality, this is slippery ground: none of the passages can be found in the main manuscripts of the Greek Bible, while verses which he ascribes to Jeremiah and to Ezra appear in no known version of scripture at all. In other words, when Justin claims to be quoting authentic Septuagint, he is doing the opposite. So, when he asserts that the Jews had removed the phrase '[the Lord has reigned] from the wood', *apo xulou*, which might be taken to refer to the cross from the text of (LXX) Psalm 95, there is every reason to take those two Greek words not as a Jewish deletion but as a Christian addition.[70]

Evidently, it was to Justin's purpose to depict his Jewish opponents, rather than himself, as refusing to use the common text and as stubbornly adhering to an incomplete and falsified one designed to deny the prophetic truths and to do damage to their opponents.[71] What is entirely clear is that the mutual allegations of licentious tampering have little to do with any serious correction of the Greek by anyone. Oskar Skarsaune made out a good case for ascribing aberrations in the Christian citations not to defective memory nor to Justin's personal tampering but to his source, a collection of proof texts assembled and adapted, perhaps specifically, for the purposes of anti-Jewish polemic.[72] Skarsaune reaches the remarkable conclusion that 'the readings which Justin brands as "non-LXX", and "Jewish", seem to be precisely those found in the biblical manuscripts from which he himself copies other long LXX quotations'. So 'what Justin calls the "LXX" text is actually the text of his testimony source(s)

Hellenistic Judaism as Judaism universalized, which is not entirely free of the *praeparatio evangelica* tradition.

[70] LXX Ps 95.10 = Hebr. Ps. 96.10. Remarkably, Justin appears later to cite Ps. 96 without the crucial words. But they do appear in the Old Latin, certain Greek manuscripts, and the main Coptic tradition: see Adler 1990: 4, n. 9 and Falls 1948: 113, n. 7. For the Jeremiah and Ezra passages, see Adler 1990: 4–6.

[71] As demonstrated by Simon 1997. Simon had earlier offered a pioneering analysis of Justin's strategies set beside those of his successors (1986: 151–6). Significantly, his book was published in its first French edition in 1948, in the wake of the Holocaust.

[72] Skarsaune 1987: 26–138 examines the texts in detail.

while the "Jewish" text is the text of Justin's Greek biblical MS'.[73] If Skarsaune is right, there will have been little need for Jews to distrust the Septuagint. In most cases—admittedly with the notable exception of the *parthenos* of Isaiah 7: 14—the readings found there still served them well.[74]

Justin is a lynchpin of the abandonment theory. His observation is made by modern scholars to serve as evidence of much more even than he asserts: not only of the Jews' lack of respect for the available texts of the old Greek, but of their rigid adherence to their own special and divergent version in the shape of Aquila, to whose text Justin's examples of Jewish variant readings in fact emerge as equally distant.[75] As for Aquila, the traditional dating ascribed to him, in the reign of Hadrian, does make him a contemporary of Justin Martyr— as well as of Akiva. But we can say no more than that about any connection or opposition. Whether Justin was even aware of Aquila's existence we do not know.

Again, when Augustine in his *City of God* protests that the Jews hold Jerome's Vulgate to be a more faithful rendering of the Greek than the Septuagint,[76] this reveals how Augustine disliked Jerome's radical enterprise of going back to the Hebrew, taking the Septuagint off its pedestal. But it also suggests that Augustine had to recognize the Jews with whom he was in contact as ready to appreciate a valid translation, however unappealing its origins. Controversy between Jews and Christians is thus by no means the governing principle behind the line-up. Nor does the evidence prove Jews to be wholly dissociating themselves for purposes of scholarship from the old Greek, even as late as 410 CE. After all, according to Augustine, they felt themselves able to make an informed comparison.

---

[73] Skarsaune 1987: 43.

[74] Cf. Hengel 2002: 30: 'Justin's argument assumes that, on the whole, his Jewish partners still recognize the authority of the Alexandrian translation of the LXX.'

[75] Barthélemy (1963), on the basis of his close study of the XII Prophets Scroll, discovered in 1952 at Nahal Hever in the Judaean Desert, judged some of the 'Jewish' readings to have belonged to a Jewish revision back toward the Hebrew, in his view a precursor of the later version of another of the later Hexaplaric translators, Theodotion. This shares many features with Thackeray's *kaige* tradition. However, our samples may be too small for a secure conclusion. Authoritative publication by Tov et al. (1990); and see there the dating by P. Parsons (pp. 19–26).

[76] For a helpful discussion, see Hayward 1995: 49–72.

Looking forward another century-and-a-half we can see how matters developed. Now the context is liturgical, and the text legal. The emperor Justinian, in his *Novella* 146, issued in Constantinople in the year 553 CE a ruling on the permitted languages for synagogue readings in the broader context of the correction of Jewish error—'part of a theological war', as Mordechai Rabello calls it.[77] The intervention is explained as occasioned by an alleged Jewish disputation on the language issue, and most immediately by petitions (from one or both warring parties?) to the emperor. There was no trouble, it would seem, on the language of prayer, but it is alleged that some Jews objected to the use of Greek scripture as an addition to the Hebrew, suggesting, perhaps, that rabbinic influence which favoured Hebraization had made considerable advances by this late date.[78] The background to Justinian's ruling is not clearly conveyed, and perhaps his preamble should not be taken at face value. But the resulting instruction is plain: translation into Greek, Latin, or other languages is permitted. Furthermore the Emperor shows a curious concern over which Greek translation may be used. The Septuagint is brought forward as the most accurate and only approved text, because the story of its origins, with the miraculous concordance of versions between the seventy translators (by now seventy, not seventy-two) indicates divine provenance (a point denied, as it happens, by Jerome). But Aquila will do, Justinian says—'although he was a Gentile'. In a surprise move, Justinian also forbids altogether the *deuterōsis* (second text, or repetition), a term which seems to refer specifically to the Mishnah, but may rather mean the Oral Law in its entirety, since this could be described as a sort of second Torah.[79] It

---

[77] Rabello 1987: ii. 814–28: 'il motivo per cui gli Ebrei non sono arrivati alla vera fede consiste, secondo giustiniano, nel fato che hanno delle interpretazioni insensate (p. 815).'

[78] So de Lange 1999: 151.

[79] For the text of the Novella, with commentary, Linder 1987: 409. 'Mishnah' means 'to teach' or 'to repeat', for which *deuterōsis* would be an apt translation. For discussion of the linguistic implications of the ruling, including the revival of Hebrew implied by it, see Colorni 1964. For a fresh interpretation of the *novella* as a whole, see Veltri in Hengel and Schwemer 1994: 116–30. The ingenious and sceptical interpretation by Rutgers 2006, in terms of Justinian's 'hidden agenda', the shoring up of Christian identity and the undermining of Judaism by the banning of the Hebrew language is insufficiently supported by the evidence.

would seem to emerge from these rulings that Aquila was indeed in widespread use among Jews and associated by outsiders with Jewish use. Of the 'Three', no other translator even rates a mention by name. But other important points are also suggested. First, even if we suppose that Justinian exaggerated the dissension in the Jewish ranks, it appears that Judaism was still multiform and by no means monolithic. It is hard to see how the dissension could be wholly fabricated. Second, it is more plausible that some Jews or groups of Jews were, already before this ruling, in the habit of reading in the synagogue from the text transmitted under the name of the Septuagint, rather than that Justinian was imposing on them something by then wholly alien to all parties. Even if the Emperor's aim was their Christianization, it would have been unproductive for him to ram down their throats something with which they were known no longer to have any truck at all. Indeed, Justinian may even seem to be allowing the Septuagint as a Jewish text through that peculiar insistence that it was Aquila who was a Gentile.[80]

JEWISH ATTITUDES TO TRANSLATION IN THE SECOND CENTURY

Certainly, Jews, or rather, some learned Jews, did appreciate Aquila. There are admiring remarks about his version embedded in the Jerusalem Talmud. His translation, it has been suggested in modern times, even went through two of its own recensions. All sorts of reasons might be suggested for this rabbinic respect, apart from the obvious, that the version was an achievement of ingenuity and consistency. We must ask, however, whether these occasional praises imply condemnation of every other version. In reality, we find ample interest in the old Greek still reflected in a number of midrashim, going on into late antiquity. Such interest emerges graphically in the discussions of more than a dozen changes wrought by the translators

---

[80] Justinian's parenthetical remark about Aquila being 'a Gentile' contradicts the usual Christian view and is hard to explain.

'for King Talmai' which we have already had occasion to touch upon more than once.[81] These served for Giuseppe Veltri as support for a convincing claim that there simply was no rejection of the Old Greek by the Rabbis of the classical rabbinic period.[82] In Emanuel Tov's more nuanced view this accepting attitude should be ascribed more specifically to the earlier phases of rabbinic literature.[83]

Only when we get to a pair of interrelated minor tractates concerned with scribal activity, *masekhet sefer torah* (1: 8-9), and *masekhet soferim* (1: 7-8), of late and uncertain date and generally printed now as Talmudic addenda, do we find a version of the list of changes made for King Ptolemy prefaced with the grim statement that the day of the initiation of the Septuagint was as hard for Israel as the day of the making of the golden calf 'for the Torah could not be properly translated'.[84] Both tractates doubtless contain early material among their regulations, but the attitudes they evince are likely to belong to the seventh or eighth century CE. *Ta'anit* (Fasting), a text from gaonic (late rabbinic) Babylonia, declares a fast in remembrance of the misfortune of the translation and reports that three days of darkness came upon the world 'when the Torah was written in Greek'.[85] Jewish–Christian relations had entered a new phase by the time these various passages were written.

In any event, in the period of the new translators, which coincided, in Palestine, with the era of the early teachers known as Tannaim, rabbinic influence had severe social and geographical limits. For all the intensity of the Rabbis' teachings, the breadth of their knowledge

---

[81] pp. 36–7 and 89.

[82] This is the central argument in Veltri's close study (1994).

[83] Tov 1999: 75–82. Against Veltri's problematic conclusion that the rabbinic discussion refers to interpretative changes inside the Hebrew rather than to Greek renderings, we may add the objection that, in Greek as in Hebrew, the vocabulary for 'translation', 'interpretation', and related concepts is not stable enough to permit systematic analysis. Veltri seems also to take *Aristeas* as straight history. Tov 1999 disputed Veltri's understanding of the history of the alterations, but subsequently (Tov 2005: 398–9) he has conceded the point.

[84] For a recent summary of these traditions, see Wasserstein and Wasserstein 2006: 69–73.

[85] On the eighth day of the month Tevet. *Ta'anit* was apparently added as a final chapter to a much earlier text, *Megillat Ta'anit*, which itself concerns dates on which fasting was forbidden. For a full edition of the versions and scholia, see Noam 2003.

and their unhesitating claims to authority, their writ may not have run very far at all.[86] Thus, all we can safely say is that Aquila was endorsed as one kind of acceptable written translation from Hebrew to Greek, for particular circles. For other purposes, we may suppose, other versions. Some of the divergences may have been due simply to geography, to varying local practice, to the isolated circumstances of scribal activity and to the complications of transporting texts around. To compare texts and translations, assuming this were desirable, and then to acquire the best for a community, will have required an altogether special effort and much labour, all of it dependent upon the presence of scholars and resources. More fundamentally, the absence of a centralized Jewish authority means the lack of that political impulse towards the public creation of a standardized text to serve as a cultural asset and an appurtenance of power—something which, ironically enough, had been amply supplied by Ptolemy at the start of the Septuagint's history. The textual history of the Homeric poems is suggestive. Thus, the scholia (commentators) often refer to the existence of city texts—the Chian, the Argive, the Massaliot, the Sinopic.[87] And then, in the Hellenistic period, to explain the somewhat puzzling evolution of the Homeric text consequent upon the labours of Aristarchus of Alexandria, Margalit Finkelberg looks to the stamp put upon it by centres of power outside Alexandria: Pergamum, Antioch in Syria, and Macedon, and possibly others too.[88] In the Jewish world, we may compare the absence until deep into the rabbinic period of unification of the calendar: with regard, for example, to observations of the new moon and intercalation, independent local activity persisted.[89] For the Greek Bible of the Jews, too, variety rather than standardization (around Aquila or anyone else) were the hallmarks of the period.

Evidence of the survival of a range of translations in play, in this case in the same city though not necessarily at exactly the same time, is provided by the wording of two epitaphs from two different Jewish

---

[86] See esp. important discussions by Levine 1989; Kalmin 1999; and Goodman 2000.
[87] For these local Homeric texts, see Fraser 1972: 320.
[88] In an unpublished paper given in Jerusalem, 2005. I am indebted to Finkelberg's clarity in conceptualizing the connection between texts and power.
[89] Detailed demonstration in S. Stern 2001. Cf. S. Stern 2003.

catacombs in the city of Rome, to be dated perhaps to the third century CE. One quotes the familiar text of Proverbs 10: 7, 'the memory of a just man is for a blessing', according to Aquila, reading *mnia* [= *mnēmē*] *dikaiou eis eulogian*,[90] while the other has a version closer to the Septuagint text, using the same noun, and reading 'the memory of a just man is with praise', *mnēmē dikaio[u] s[un] enkōmio* [*sic*].[91] Long after 90 CE, then, there are traces of diversity.

This is not to say that within the Jewish world all was sweetness and light. We have met with hints of underlying tension about the acceptability of the Septuagint in the rabbinic assertions, and in the much later statements of Justinian we have seen indications of internal divisions attached to differences over choice of text so serious as to allow the Emperor to step in.

What, then, lay behind the drift in the second century towards making new renderings? Why all this activity? The straightforward need to reduce textual corruption in the Greek, and of bringing it closer to the Hebrew, may be admitted. Such activity seems to go back quite a way in Judaism, even if its consistency and sophistication have sometimes been overvalued. No doubt in places the old Greek tradition, or parts of it, had indeed been damaged by scribal error to an extent where it had become troublesome to use. So, Jerome in the Preface to his translation of Chronicles speaks of the mistakes made by the copyists in Hebrew names.[92] Another problem would have been that the original Greek terminology, which breathed the milieu of its creation, was now visibly obsolete, even unintelligible, especially items of Hellenistic political and administrative vocabulary and topographical allusions.

There was, though, much more to it than this. There were evidently powerful forces at work. For we can discern a truly remarkable level of commitment in Jewish–Greek circles at this time to a process of retranslating and updating. In a nutshell, the Jewish world was generating new Greek translations of different kinds, of which

---

[90] *CIJ*, i. 370 = *JIWE*, ii. 112 (from the Monteverde catacomb). Cf. also the mixed version in *CIJ*, i. 80 = *JIWE*, ii. 276.

[91] *CIJ*, i. 201 = *JIWE*, ii. 307 (from the Vigna Randanini catacomb); the precise wording of LXX is *met' enkōmiōn*, 'with praises'. Cf. van der Horst 1991: 37.

[92] Jerome in *PL*, 29, cols. 402; 404.

Origen's 'Three' are no doubt a selection.[93] This diversity has a number of explanations: regional preference and geographical limitation were surely factors, as already suggested. We should also envisage a comparable range of needs and demands as had occasioned the first translation, emanating from an overlapping list of institutions and activities—synagogue, *bet midrash* (or equivalent), and education of the young, both formal or informal. Although the concrete evidence is limited, it has been persuasively argued that the period saw the beginnings of a process of re-Hebraization emanating primarily from Palestine. For the late antique Latin West, and above all Italy and Spain, unmistakable if limited evidence comes to us by way of the appearance of quite extensive Hebrew texts in surviving inscriptions.[94] For the Greek East, some surmise is involved. Aquila, a version in much closer touch with the original, was particularly appropriate for such times. His translation served, in de Lange's words, as 'a bridge from Greek to Hebrew... an invaluable tool for the Jew who recognized the primacy of the Hebrew Bible'.[95] It has been rightly said that 'Aquila is virtually unintelligible without at least some knowledge of the Hebrew'.[96] If the translation language of the Old Greek was designed precisely to maintain an ineradicable link with the Hebrew, as I have argued,[97] then Aquila has travelled a good distance further along the same road. An interesting interpretation of the rabbinic politics involved in the promotion of the Hebrew language has been put forward by Philip Alexander,[98] who argues that the Palestinian Rabbis needed to establish and spread abroad the

---

[93] On the 'semi-canonical' status conferred by Origen on the 'Three', see Grafton and Williams 2006: 129.
[94] See de Lange 1996 and de Lange 1996a: 122–37. On the changing position of rabbinic Hebrew, cf. Paul 1986 and S. Schwartz 1995. Williams' observation (1999: 50–1) on the (possibly temporary) increase over the generations in the Hebrew expressions appearing in the late catacomb inscriptions from Venosa in Apulia, southern Italy, deserves investigation. For the status of the Hebrew language in the Second Temple period, see Chap. 4, pp. 146–52.
[95] de Lange 1996b: 352.
[96] Brock 1974: 562. See Chap. 4, p. 143 on the application of a similar judgement to the original Alexandrian Torah translation by proponents of the 'interlinear theory'.
[97] See Chap. 4, pp. 152–61.
[98] P. Alexander, 1999a, and in oral discussion.

authority of their interpretations and that those interpretations were expressed in the first place in Hebrew, the language of Mishnah and Tosefta. Alexander suggests that the praise of some rabbis for Aquila, the version whose ideological justification lay specifically in its ties to the Hebrew language, was part and parcel of their promotion of this medium, which they had made their own.

Aquila's enterprise is very readily connected with Hebraizing tendencies. But this same development may have had the opposite outcome elsewhere. A suggestion by Sebastian Brock explains economically the concurrence of contrasting types of translation, the free and the literal.[99] Brock reasons that in milieux where the Bible in Hebrew still counted as the principal reference point and where the Hebrew alone was deemed to be imbued with sanctity, any Greek version would have a subordinate function. There the primary role of the Greek in the synagogue would have been to be read after the Hebrew original. In that situation, what was required of the Greek was intelligibility and fluency, and so a door was opened to a more flexible rendering, a phenomenon indeed exemplified in a different language-medium in the Aramaic Targum, which regularly adds interpretation to translation. The purpose in those circumstances, Brock suggests, was to make theological and other kinds of sense of the words, and, through the translation, to expound the text at more than one level. But this development coexisted with the flourishing and indeed strengthening of a different Jewish tradition, that of respect for the text *per se*, leading to the search for exact equivalence. That tradition perhaps embodied a different kind of learning; at any rate, it reflected a different kind of relationship with the original. Aquila was an offshoot of this second tradition.

There is also much to be gained by considering the Greek linguistic dimension alongside the Hebrew. This was an era when the cultural and political emphasis on the best usage of the Greek language and literature flourished throughout the Roman Empire, and this went together with a strong Hellenic consciousness, personified and promoted by the philhellenism of the Emperor Hadrian himself.[100]

---

[99] Brock 1992.
[100] See esp. the important studies of Bowie 1970; Swain 1996; Goldhill 2001; and Whitmarsh 2001.

In the Jewish world, all elements were increasingly at home with the language and often with quite a lot more of Greek culture too, as testified by R. Jose's well-known approval of the *shema* being recited in Caesarea in Greek by those who could not do it in Hebrew.[101] The prevailing style of the original Greek translation, which fell between so many stools, could have felt inappropriate for those more refined times, and a sense that something which is not proper Greek should not seem to posture as such could well lead to a preference among Greek speakers (assuming they also had an awareness of Hebrew) for a version like Aquila's that made absolutely no pretence to be other than what it was, a replication of the original. It is interesting that Origen in his polemic against Celsus testifies to pagan Greek contempt for the poverty, *euteleia*, of the Bible.[102]

Christians, by contrast, would not have reacted in the same way. As we saw, when they took over that past, claiming the identity of the true Israel, they acquired the translation. Their early commitment to the Old Greek, or to a version something very like it, is demonstrated by its far-reaching integration into the New Testament, which we observed in Chapter 6. That integration in turn strengthened the symbiosis with those scriptures.

Translation continued to be the primary mode of contact with their central text also for Greek-speaking diaspora Jews in the high Roman Empire. It is tempting to compare German Jewry's extraordinary productivity in this same sphere. The era starts with Moses Mendelssohn's landmark rendering (1780–3) into a German striving for correctness but spelt out in Hebrew lettering, which came to symbolize the start of the Jewish enlightenment. It reached its climax in 1929 with the conclusion of the Buber-Rosenzweig version in a deliberately Hebraizing German intended to affirm loyalty to the original, and, even, some would have it, cultural defiance. These manifestations of what Naomi Seidman has called 'a translator culture' represented a complex negotiation

---

[101] In J. Sotah 7.1.
[102] See p. 128 on this motif.

between two traditions as well as two languages.[103] The parallel is highly suggestive, in spite of one major difference, that the Bible, deeply embedded as it was in German life, and also, ever since Martin Luther's translation, in German literature, was in principle a possession treasured by both groups; the same could not be said of the Bible among the Greeks. German–Jewish Bibles deepened immeasurably the conception nurtured by German–Jewish writers, translators, and theorists of translation as cultural conversation. None the less, for ancient Hellenistic Jews, like their modern German–Jewish counterparts, translation was, as we have come to understand, a highroad to cultural maintenance and to self-expression, if not directly to integration. Abandonment of their first translation would have meant the loss of a large portion of their own past, doing violence to a well-formed identity. Now that historians have taken on board the evidence for a vigorous, multi-faceted, Greek-speaking (or worshipping) Jewry in the cities of the eastern Roman Empire, flourishing down to Constantine and not negligible for many years afterwards, it is time to work those insights into the history of the Septuagint.[104]

These cities, we should remember, are the very world to which at least two of the three revisers in the Hexapla are ascribed in consistent Christian tradition: Pontus was supposedly the home of Aquila,[105] and Ephesus in the later second century CE that of Theodotion. Symmachus has now been plausibly associated by Alison Salvesen with the multicultural world of Caesarea in Palestine, in the second and third centuries—home equally to the Roman governors, to the library of Origen, and to the school of Rabbi Hoshaya. This was as much a Greek city as any in the Jewish diaspora. It is striking that to each of the 'Three' is assigned a role on the margins of Jewry. In *On Weights and Measures* (14–17), Epiphanius relates that

---

[103] On this line of German–Jewish biblical translators, which also included Leopold Zuntz, Lewis Philippson, and Samson Raphael Hirsch, as well as a Bible commissioned by the Berlin Jewish community from Harry Torczyner as late as 1934, see Seidman 2006: 153–98, and the bibliography cited there.

[104] For this paradigm shift, see Chap. 3, pp. 114–19.

[105] It has been argued with some plausibility, however, that this ascription arises out of a conflation with the Aquila of Acts 18.2 who was a native of Pontus. See Veltri 2006: 168–70.

Aquila, who had worked for Hadrian on the building of Aelia Capitolina, after becoming a Christian, converted to Judaism out of pique when he was told to stop doing astrology; he then resolved, apparently, to produce a rival version to the Septuagint. Rabbinic tradition describes how he studied Torah and then went and told the Emperor Hadrian, sometimes fancifully described as his uncle, that it would not be proper to do so any more without converting, which meant being circumcised.[106] Irenaeus makes Theodotion a former Marcionite (which implies total rejection of the Old Testament) who converted to Judaism.[107] Symmachus was for Eusebius, referring back to Origen, and also for Jerome, an Ebionite, that is to say a Jewish Christian; though for Epiphanius he is a Samaritan convert, a story cautiously preferred by Salvesen.[108] Palladius calls him 'the translator of the Jews'. The historicity of the specific traditions is unverifiable, and their diversity as well as their apparently emblematic character make them suspect. To emphasize the Jewish associations of the newer translators was to discredit them as against the Septuagint. Still, the accumulation of claims suggests there is more here than pure invention, and the climate they evoke is telling. While linking the translators with Judaism, they suggest a world of religious interpenetration.

Interestingly, the new Jewish translators were no longer believed to have produced anonymous versions, but translations to which authorial names of some kind, or at least assumed names, became attached, just as the Targum-makers did.[109] This in itself betokens a living and changing approach to the Hebrew Bible. Arguably, this work was, for the non-rabbinized Jewish diaspora, the counterpart of the prolific generation of halakhic Midrash in the rabbinic world, a route to renewal through the Bible appropriate to Jews whose

---

[106] Exod. Rabbah 30.12. Also in the later Midrash Tanḥuma Mishpatim 5.5. The latter passage is subjected to intensive analysis in Seidman 2006: 101–3.

[107] Irenaeus *Adv. Haer.*, 3.2.1.

[108] Eusebius, *Hist. Eccl.*, 6.17; Jerome *de Vir. Ill.*, 54; Palladius, *Historia Lausiaca*, 64; Salvesen 1991: 287–9.

[109] The identification between Aquila and the Targumist Onkelos goes back to a confusion found already in talmudic and midrashic literature. See Rabinowitz 1971. Curiously, the identification is described as widely accepted in Schürer iii: 496, following Silverstone 1931.

business was living a shared life in Greek cities with Greeks—and with Christians. In the case of Aquila as much as the others, the rabbinic context need not be the crucial one.

Finally, as stated at the opening of this chapter, it may well be right to ascribe to this same context the last additions to the corpus of the Septuagint itself. No one now disputes that the process of translation of the prophetic books and the 'writings' went on for several centuries, whether privately or in communal initiatives.[110] The commonly accepted date for the Greek Qohelet, Ecclesiastes, and for the book of Ruth, is the remarkably late one of the first quarter of the second century CE, based on the total lack of earlier attestation to the existence of these works in Greek, and to a perceived affinity with Aquila's technique.[111] To these Lamentations is often added, but a date nearer to the destruction of 70 CE might make more sense. For the other two books, that is the best guess we can make, and such a dating makes Alexandria an unlikely provenance, since the Alexandrian community was decimated by the failure of the Jewish revolt under Trajan, and signs of life are hard to find for a long time after that. A fair number of diaspora locations present good possibilities, and a Greek-speaking environment in Palestine should also come into the picture.

Marguerite Harl has described the 'old' Greek translation of the Bible as continuous 'work in progress' (the English term appears inside her elegant French exposition), and some work is in progress for a very long time. How, at a late date, a version could achieve sufficient status to be added to the venerable corpus requires discussion. In the case of two of the more dubious books of the Bible, Song of Songs and Ecclesiastes, the Rabbis appear to have had doubts even

---

[110] See Dorival in *BGS*, 109–10 for a good discussion of categorizations of the Greek Torah as a 'private' translation (Bickerman) and of renderings of some prophetic passages as 'semi-official' translations (Thackeray). Dorival's reservations are consonant with his view that study in the milieu of the synagogue was the primary context for the proliferation of translations. On a broader front, Hezser 2001: 452–63 argues for the overwhelming dominance of public over private reading in antiquity, maintaining that the Jewish milieu was no exception. The evidence is, however, inconclusive and in relation to the early Christian movement it has been vigorously debated.

[111] The identification, again, derives from Barthélemy 1963.

about the authority of the Hebrew. But in any event we should remember that when it came to the translation only the Greek versions of the pentateuchal books were ever promoted as in some sense divinely inspired through the legend of their origins; and that even for those books, not everyone followed Philo's understanding of the translation process as a prophetic unveiling of mysteries (*Life of Moses*, 2.37–40).[112]

What I have suggested amounts to saying that the creative production of different types of Bible translation is a central element in that small corpus of Jewish–Greek literature which has survived the transition to Christianity and the ravages of time. For us, the important consequence is greatly to extend that period of the constructive relationship between Greek-speaking Jews and their Bible which began with the original Jewish translation enterprise, and to appreciate that this period did not bring about a divorce from their most treasured possession, the Old Greek versions. Their bond continued well into the Christian era, evidently in a complex relationship with the Christian attachment to the text, which mirrored their own. The Septuagint was willy-nilly a common possession of Jews and Christians for several centuries after Justin's challenge to Trypho. The Jewish involvement with their first translated Bible was too deep for any simple act of abandonment. The takeover was a more untidy and more protracted business than scholars like to think—as was the parting of the ways itself and the division of the two religions. We still have not done with their consequences.

---

[112] Josephus, for example, did not speak in terms of divine inspiration. See Chap. 1, pp. 35–6.

Bibliography

Abusch, R.(2003), 'Negotiating Difference: Genital Mutilation in Roman Slave Law and the History of the Bar Kokhba Revolt', in P. Schäfer (ed.), *The Bar Kokhba War Reconsidered: New Perspectives on the Second Jewish Revolt against Rome* (Tübingen: Mohr Siebeck), 71–91.

Ackroyd, P. R. and C. F. Evans (eds.) (1970), *The Cambridge History of the Bible*, i. *From the Beginnings to Jerome* (Cambridge: Cambridge University Press).

Acosta-Hughes, B., M. Baumbach, and E. Kosmetatou (2003), *Labored in Papyrus Leaves: Perspectives on an Epigram Collection Attributed to Posidippus (P. Mil. Vogl. VIII 309)*, Hellenic Studies, 2 (Washington, DC: Center for Hellenic Studies Trustees for Harvard University).

Adams, J. N. (2003), *Bilingualism and the Latin Language* (Cambridge: Cambridge University Press).

——M. Janse, and S. Swain (eds.) (2002), *Bilingualism in Ancient Society: Language Contact and the Written Word* (Oxford: Oxford University Press).

Adler, W. (1990), 'The Jews as Falsifiers: Charges of Tendentious Emendation in Anti-Jewish Christian Polemic', in '*Translation of Scripture*', Proceedings of a conference at the Annenberg Research Institute, 15–16 May 1989 (Philadelphia: Annenberg Research Institute), 1–27.

Aejmelaeus, A. (1982), *Parataxis in the Septuagint: A Study of the Renderings of the Hebrew Coordinate Clauses in the Greek Pentateuch*, Annales Academiae Scientiarum Fennicae, Dissertationes humanarum litterarum, 31 (Helsinki: Suomalainen Tiedeakatemia).

——(1987), 'The Significance of Clause Connectors in the Syntactical and Translation-Technical Study of the Septuagint', in *VI Congress of the International Organization for Septuagint and Cognate Studies, Jerusalem, 1986*, ed. C. E. Cox (Atlanta, Ga.: Scholars Press), 361–81.

——(1993), On the Trail of the Septuagint Translators: Collected Essays (Kampen: Kok Pharos).

——(2001), 'Characterizing Criteria for the Characterization of the Septuagint Translators: Experimenting on the Greek Psalter', in R. J. V. Hiebert, C. E. Cox, and P. J. Gentry (eds.), *The Old Greek Psalter: Studies in Honour of Albert Pietersma* (Sheffield: Sheffield Academic Press), 54–73.

Ager, S. L. (2003), 'An Uneasy Balance: From the Death of Seleukos to the Battle of Raphia', in A. Erskine (ed.), *A Companion to the Hellenistic World* (Oxford: Blackwell), 35–50.

Aitken, J. (2007), 'Poet and Critic: Royal Ideology and the Greek Translator of Proverbs', in T. Rajak, S. Pearce, et al. (eds.), *Jewish Perspectives on Hellenistic Rulers* (Berkeley, Calif.: University of California Press), 190–204.

Aland, K. (ed.) (1976), *Repertorium der griechischen christlichen Papyri*, i. Biblische Papyri (Berlin: de Gruyter).

Alexander, L. C. A. (2002), 'Foolishness to the Greeks: Jews and Christians in the Public Life of the Empire', in G. Clark and T. Rajak (eds.), *Philosophy and Power in the Graeco-Roman World: Essays in Honour of Miriam Griffin* (Oxford: Oxford University Press), 229–49.

——(2004), '"This is That": The Authority of Scripture in the Acts of the Apostles', *Princeton Seminary Bulletin* (July).

——(2006), 'Septuaginta, Fachprosa, Imitatio: Albert Wifstrand, and the Language of Luke–Acts', in *Acts in its Literary Context: A Classicist Looks at the Acts of the Apostles* (London: T. and T. Clark), 231–52.

Alexander, P. S. (1984), 'Epistolary Literature', in M. E. Stone (ed.), *Jewish Writings of the Second Temple Period* (Assen: Van Gorcum), 579–96.

——(1985), 'The Targumim, and Rabbinic Rules for the Delivery of Targum', in *Congress Volume Salamanca, 1983*, Supplements to *Vetus Testamentum*, 36 (Leiden: Brill), 14–28.

——(1986), 'Incantations, and Books of Magic', in E. Schürer, *The History of the Jewish People in the Age of Jesus Christ (175 BC-AD 135)*, ed. F. Millar, G. Vermes, and M. Goodman (Edinburgh: T. and T. Clark), 342–79.

——(1988), 'Retelling the Old Testament', in D. A. Carson and H. G. M. Williamson (eds.), '*It is Written*': *Scripture Citing Scripture, Essays in Honour of Barnabas Lindars SSF* (Cambridge: Cambridge University Press), 99–121.

——(1998), '"Homer the Prophet of All" and "Moses Our Teacher": Late Antique Exegesis of the Homeric Epics and of the Torah of Moses', in L. V. Rutgers and P. W. van der Horst, et al. (eds.), *The Use of Sacred Books in the Ancient World*, Contributions to Biblical Exegesis and Theology, 22 (Leuven: Peeters), 127–42.

——(1999a), 'How Did the Rabbis Learn Hebrew?', in W. Horbury (ed.), *Hebrew Study from Ezra to Ben-Yehuda* (Edinburgh: T. and T. Clark), 71–89.

——(1999b), 'Jewish Elements in Gnosticism and Magic CE 70–CE 270', in W. Horbury, W. D. Davies, and J. Sturdy (eds.), *The Cambridge History of Judaism*, iii. *The Early Roman Period* (Cambridge: Cambridge University Press), 1052–78.

Alexander, P. S. (2003), 'Literacy Among Jews in Second Temple Palestine: Reflections on the Evidence from Qumran', in M. F. J. Baasten and W. T. van Peursen (eds.), *Hamlet on a Hill: Semitic and Greek Studies Presented to Professor T. Muraoka on the Occasion of His Sixty-Fifth Birthday* (Leuven: Peeters), 3–24.

——and L. Alexander (2007), 'The Image of the Oriental Monarch in the Third Book of Maccabees', in T. Rajak, S. Pearce, et al. (eds.), *Jewish Perspectives on Hellenistic Rulers* (Berkeley, Calif.: University of California Press), 129–63.

Alter, R. (2000), *Canon and Creativity: Modern Writing and the Authority of Scripture* (New Haven, Conn.: Yale Unversity Press).

Aly, Z., and L. Koenen (eds.) (1980), *Three Rolls of the Early Septuagint: Genesis and Deuteronomy. A Photographic Edition Prepared in Collaboration with the International Photographic Archive of the Association internationale de papyrologues* (Bonn: Habelt).

Amaru, B. H. (1994), *Rewriting the Bible: Land and Covenant in Post-biblical Literature* (Valley Forge, Pa.: Trinity Press International).

Amichai, Y. (2000), *Open Closed Open*: Poems Translated from the Hebrew by Chana Bloch and Chana Kronfeld (New York: Harcourt).

Amir, Y. (1988), 'Authority and Interpretation of Scripture in the Writings of Philo', in M. J. Mulder and H. Sysling (eds.), *Mikra: Text, Translation, Reading and Interpretation of the Hebrew Bible in Ancient Judaism and Early Christianity* (Assen and Philadelphia, Pa.: Van Gorcum/Fortress Press), 421–53.

Anderson, G. W. (1970), 'Canonical and Non-Canonical', in P. R. Ackroyd and C. F. Evans (eds.), *The Cambridge History of the Bible. i. From the Beginnings to Jerome* (Cambridge: Cambridge University Press), 113–58.

Applebaum, S. (1971), 'Jews and Service in the Roman Army', in *Roman Frontier Studies*, Proceedings of the Seventh International Congress, Tel Aviv, 1967 (Tel Aviv: Students' Organization of Tel Aviv), 181–4.

——(1979) *Jews and Greeks in Ancient Cyrene* (Leiden: Brill).

Arnaldez, R., R. Kuntzmann, and J. Schlosser (1983) [1984], *Études sur le judaïsme hellénistique*, Congrès de Strasbourg, Lectio Divina, 119 (Paris: Éditions du Cerf, 1984).

Ashton, S. A. (2004), 'Ptolemaic Alexandria and the Egyptian Tradition', in A. Hirst and M. S. Silk (eds.), *Alexandria, Real and Imagined* (Aldershot: Ashgate), 15–40.

Asper, M. (2001), 'Gruppen und Dichter. Zu Progammatik und Adressatenbezug bei Kallimachos', *Antike und Abendland*, 47: 84–116.

Assmann, J. (1997), *Moses the Egyptian: The Memory of Egypt in Western Monotheism* (Cambridge, Mass.: Harvard University Press).

Attridge, H. W. (1976), *The Interpretation of Biblical History in the Antiquitates Judaicae of Flavius Josephus*, Harvard Dissertations in Religion, 7 (Missoula, Mont.: Scholars Press for Harvard Theological Review).
——(1984), 'Historiography', in M. E. Stone (ed.), *Jewish Writings of the Second Temple Period* (Assen: Van Gorcum), 157–84.
——(1989), *A Commentary on the Epistle to the Hebrews* (Philadelphia, Pa.: Hermeneia: A Critical and Historical Commentary on the Bible, Fortress Press).
Audollent, A. (1904), 'Defixionum tabellae quotquot innotuerunt tam in Graecis orientis quam in totius occidentis partibus praeter Atticas in Corpore inscriptionum Atticarum editas' (Diss. Paris University; Albert Fontemoing).
Austin, C., and G. Bastianini (eds.) (2002), *Posidippi Pellaei quae supersunt omnia* (Milan: LED).
Baasten, M. F. J., and W. T. van Peursen (eds.) (2003), *Hamlet on a Hill: Semitic and Greek Studies Presented to Professor T. Muraoka on the Occasion of His Sixty-Fifth Birthday* (Leuven: Peeters).
Bagnall, R. S. (1976), *The Administration of the Ptolemaic Possessions Outside Egypt* (Leiden: Brill).
——(2002), 'Alexandria, Library of Dreams', *Proceedings of the American Philosophical Society*, 146: 348–62.
——and P. Derow (2004), *The Hellenistic Period: Historical Sources in Translation* (Oxford: Blackwell).
Bar-Kochva, B. (1996), *Pseudo-Hecataeus, 'On the Jews': Legitimizing the Jewish Diaspora*, Hellenistic Culture and Society, 21 (Berkeley, Calif.: University of California Press).
Bar Asher, M. (1998), *Studies in Mishnaic Hebrew* (Jerusalem: Magnes Press).
Barclay, J. M. G. (1996), *Jews in the Mediterranean Diaspora: From Alexander to Trajan (323 BCE-117 CE)* (Edinburgh: T. & T. Clark).
——(ed.) (2004), *Negotiating Diaspora: Jewish Strategies in the Roman Empire* (London and New York: T. & T. Clark International).
——(2007), *Against Apion: Flavius Josephus Translation and Commentary*, ed. S. Mason, x. (Leiden: Brill).
Barnes, R. (2000), 'Cloistered Bookworms in the Chicken Coop of the Muses: The Ancient Library of Alexandria', in R. M. MacLeod (ed.), *The Library of Alexandria: Centre of Learning in the Ancient World* (London: I. B. Tauris), 61–77.
Barnes, T. D. (1971), *Tertullian: A Historical and Literary Study* (Oxford: Clarendon Press).
Barnstone, W. (1993), *The Poetics of Translation: History, Theory, Practice* (New Haven, Conn.: Yale University Press).

Barr, J. (1961), *The Semantics of Biblical Language* (Oxford: Oxford University Press).

——(1967), Review of Reider-Turner, *Index to Aquila, Journal of Semitic Studies*, 12: 296–304.

——(1979), 'The Typology of Literalism in Ancient Biblical Translations', *Mitteilungen des Septuaginta-Unternehmens*, 15 (Göttingen: Vandenhoeck and Ruprecht), 279–325.

——(1983), *Holy Scripture: Canon, Authority, Criticism*, Sprunt Lectures Delivered at Union Theological Seminary, Richmond, Va., Feb. 1982 (Oxford: Clarendon Press).

——(1985), 'Doubts about Homophony in the Septuagint', *Textus: Annual of the Hebrew University Bible Project*, 12: 1–77.

——(2003), 'Did the Greek Pentateuch Really Serve as a Dictionary for the Translation of the Later Books?', in M. F. J. Baasten and W. T. van Peursen (eds.), *Hamlet on a Hill: Semitic and Greek Studies Presented to Professor T. Muraoka on the Occasion of His Sixty-Fifth Birthday* (Leuven: Peeters), 523–44.

Barthélemy, D. (1963), Les Devanciers d'Aquila: première publication intégrale du texte des fragments du dodécaprophéton, Supplements to Vetus Testamentum, 10 (Leiden: Brill).

Bartlett, J. R. (2002), *Jews in the Hellenistic and Roman Cities* (London: Routledge).

Barton, J. (1986), *Oracles of God: Perceptions of Ancient Prophecy in Israel after the Exile* (London: Darton, Longman, and Todd).

——and J. Muddiman (2001), *The Oxford Bible Commentary* (Oxford: Oxford University Press).

Bastianini, G., and C. Gallazzi (eds.) (2001), *Posidippus of Pella: Epigrammi: P. Mil. Vogl. VIII. 309* (Milan: LED).

Bauer, W., W. Arndt, and F. W. Danker (2000), *A Greek-English Lexicon of the New Testament and Other Early Christian Literature* (3rd edn., Chicago, Ill.: University of Chicago Press).

Baumgarten, A. L. (2002), 'Bilingual Jews and the Greek Bible', in J. L. Kugel (ed.), *Shem in the Tents of Japhet: Essays on the Encounter of Judaism and Hellenism* (Leiden: Brill), 14–30.

Becker, A. H., and A. Y. Reed (eds.) (2003), *The Ways That Never Parted: Jews and Christians in Late Antiquity and the Early Middle Ages* (Tübingen: Mohr Siebeck).

Beckwith, R. T. (1985), The Old Testament Canon of the New Testament Church and Its Background in Early Judaism (London: SPCK).

Benjamin, W. (1968), *Illuminations*, trans. H. Zohn (New York: Shocken Books).

Benner, A. R., and F. H. Fobes (1949), *The Letters of Alciphron, Aelian and Philostratus*, Loeb Classical Library (Cambridge, Mass.: Harvard University Press).

Bentley, R. J. H. (1699), *A Dissertation upon the Epistles of Phalaris: With an Answer to the Objections of the Honourable Charles Boyle, Esquire* (London: Henry Mortlock at the Phoenix in St Paul's Church-Yard and John Hartley Over-Against Gray's Inn in Holborn).

Ben Ze'ev, M. P. (1996), 'Jewish Rights in the Roman World: New Perspectives', studies on the Jewish Diaspora in the Hellemstic and Roman Renods, *Te'uda*, 12: 39–53.

——(1998), *Jewish Rights in the Roman World: The Greek and Roman Documents Quoted by Josephus Flavius* (Tübingen: Mohr Siebeck).

——(2005), *Diaspora Judaism in Turmoil: 116/117 CE: Ancient Sources and Modern Insights* (Leuven: Peeters).

Bergmann, C. (2006), 'Idol Worship in Bel and the Dragon and other Jewish Literature from the Second Temple Period', in *Septuagint Research: Issues and Challenges in the Study of the Greek Scriptures. Septuagint and Cognate Studies*, ed. W. Kraus and G. Wooden (Atlanta: Society of Biblical Literature), 207–24.

Bernstein, M. J. (1998), 'Pentateuchal Interpretation at Qumran', in P. W. Flint and J. C. VanderKam (eds.), *The Dead Sea Scrolls after Fifty Years* (Leiden: Brill), 128–59.

——(2003), 'The Contribution of the Qumran Discoveries to the History of Early Biblical Interpretation', in H. Najman and J. H. Newman (eds.), *The Idea of Biblical Interpretation: Essays in Honor of James L. Kugel* (Leiden: Brill), 215–38.

Betz, H. D. (1986), *The Greek Magical Papyri in Translation Including the Demotic Spells* (Chicago, Ill.: University of Chicago Press).

——(1997), 'Jewish Magic in the Greek Magical Papyri', in P. Schäfer and H. G. Kippenberg (eds.), *Envisioning Magic: A Princeton Seminar and Symposium* (Leiden: Brill), 45–63.

Bickerman, E. J. (1944), 'The Colophon of the Greek Book of Esther', *Journal of Biblical Literature*, 63: 339–62.

——(1950a), 'Notes on the Greek Book of Esther', *Proceedings of the American Academy of Jewish Research*, 20: 101–33.

——(1950b), 'Some Notes on the Transmission of the Septuagint', in S. Lieberman (ed.), *Alexander Marx: Jubilee Volume on the Occasion of His Seventieth Birthday* (New York: Jewish Theological Seminary of America), 149–78.

——(1952), 'Origines Gentium', *Classical Philology*, 47: 65–81.

Bickerman, E. J. (1959), 'The Septuagint as a Translation', *Proceedings of the American Academy of Jewish Research*, 28: 1–39.
——(1976), Studies in Jewish and Christian History, i. Arbeiten zur Geschichte des antiken Judentums und des Urchristentums, 9 (Leiden: Brill).
——(1988), *The Jews in the Greek Age* (Cambridge, Mass.: Harvard University Press).
Bing, P. (2005), 'The Politics and Poetics of Geography in the Milan Posidippus, Section One: In Stones', in K. J. Gutzwiller (ed.), *The New Posidippus: A Hellenistic Poetry Book* (Oxford: Oxford University Press), 119–40.
Bingen, J. (2007), *Hellenistic Egypt: Monarchy, Society, Economy, Culture*, ed. with an introduction by R. S. Bagnall (Edinburgh: Edinburgh University Press).
Birnbaum, E. (1996), *The Place of Judaism in Philo's Thought: Israel, Jews, and Proselytes*, Brown Judaic Studies, 290 (Atlanta, Ga.: Scholars Press).
——(2001), 'Philo on the Greeks: A Jewish Perspective on Culture, and Society in First-Century Alexandria', *Studia Philonica Annual*,13: 37–58.
——(2004), 'Portrayals of the Wise and Virtuous in Alexandrian Jewish Works: Jews' Perceptions of Themselves and Others', in W. V. Harris and G. Ruffini (eds.), *Ancient Alexandria between Egypt and Greece* (Leiden: Brill), 125–60.
Blair, J. (1785), *Lectures on the Canon of the Scriptures. Comprehending a Dissertation on the Septuagint Version Delivered in the Cathedral Church of Westminster* (London: T. Cadell).
Bloom, H. (1994), *The Western Canon: The Books and School of the Ages* (New York and London: Harcourt Brace).
Blowers, P. M. (1997) [1984], *The Bible in Greek Christian Antiquity*, The Bible Through the Ages, i (Notre Dame, Ind.: University of Notre Dame Press); orig. edn.: C. Mondésert (ed.), *Le Monde grec ancien et la bible* (Paris: Beauchesne, 1984).
Blum, R. (1991), *Kallimachos: The Alexandrian Library and the Origins of Bibliography*, trans. H. H. Wellisch (Madison, Wis.: University of Wisconsin Press).
Bohak, G. (1996), *Joseph and Aseneth and the Jewish Temple in Heliopolis*, Early Judaism and its Literature, 10 (Atlanta, Ga.: Scholars Press).
——(2002), 'Ethnic Continuity in the Jewish Diaspora in Antiquity', in J. R. Bartlett (ed.), *Jews in the Hellenistic and Roman Cities* (London: Routledge), 175–92.
Borgeaud, P. (2004), *Aux origines de l'histoire des religions* (Paris: Seuil).
Borgen, P. (1997), *Philo of Alexandria: An Exegete for His Time*, Supplements to *Novum Testamentum*, 86 (Leiden: Brill).

—— (1999), 'Application of and Commitment to the Laws of Moses: Observations on Philo's Treatise *On the Embassy to Gaius*', in D. T. Runia and G. E. Sterling (eds.), *The Studia Philonica Annual: Studies in Hellenistic Judaism*, 11 (1999), Brown Judaic Studies, 332 (Atlanta, Ga.: Scholars Press), 86–101.

Bowersock, G. W. (1994), *Fiction as History: Nero to Julian*, Sather Classical Lectures, 58 (Berkeley, Calif.: University of California Press).

—— (1995), *Martyrdom and Rome* (Cambridge: Cambridge University Press).

—— (1996), 'Late Antique Alexandria', in *Alexandria and Alexandrianism* (Malibu, Calif.: J. Paul Getty Museum), 263–72.

Bowie, E. L. (1970), 'Greeks and Their Past in the Second Sophistic', *Past and Present*, 46: 3–41.

Bowman, A. K., and G. Woolf (eds.) (1994), *Literacy and Power in the Ancient World* (Cambridge: Cambridge University Press).

Boyarin, D. (1999), *Dying for God: Martyrdom and the Making of Christianity and Judaism* (Stanford, Calif.: Stanford University Press).

Boyarin, J., and D. Boyarin (2002), *Powers of Diaspora: Two Essays on the Relevance of Jewish Culture* (Minneapolis, Minn.: University of Minnesota Press).

Boyd-Taylor, C. (1998), 'A Place in the Sun: The Interpretative Significance of LXX-Psalm 18:5c', *Bulletin of the International Organization for Septuagint and Cognate Studies*, 5.

Boyle, A. J., and W. Dominik (eds.) (2003), *Flavian Rome: Culture, Image, Text* (Leiden: Brill).

Brague, R. (2007) [2005], *Law of God: The Philosophical History of an Idea*, trans. L. G. Cochrane (Chicago, Ill.: Chicago University Press); orig. edn.: *La Loi de Dieu: histoire philosophique d'une alliance* (Paris: Gallimard, 2005).

Bremmer, J. N., and F. G. Martinez (eds.) (1992), *Sacred History and Sacred Texts in Early Judaism* (Kampen: Kok Pharos).

Brenton, L. C. L. (1844), The Septuagint Version of the Old Testament according to the Vatican text translated into English with the principal various readings of the Alexandrine copy, and a table of comparative chronology (London: S. Bagster and Sons).

Brock, S. P. (1974) [1969], 'The Phenomenon of Biblical Translation in Antiquity', in S. Jellicoe (ed.), *Studies in the Septuagint: Origins, Recensions, and Interpretations*, Library of Biblical Studies (New York: Ktav); orig. edn.: *Alta: University of Birmingham Review*, 2 (1969), 96–102.

Brock, S. P. (1972), 'The Phenomenon of the Septuagint', *Old Testament Studies*, 17: 11–36.

——(1979), 'Aspects of Translation Technique in Antiquity', *Greek, Roman and Byzantine Studies*, 20: 69–87.

——(1992), 'To Revise or Not to Revise: Attitudes to Jewish Biblical Translation', in G. J. Brooke and B. Lindars (eds.), *Septuagint, Scrolls and Cognate Writings, Papers Presented to the International Symposium on the Septuagint and its Relations to the Dead Sea Scrolls and Other Writings*, Manchester, 1990, Septuagint and Cognate Studies Series, 33 (Atlanta, Ga.: Scholars Press), 301–8.

Brooke, G. J. (1997), 'The Canon Within the Canon at Qumran and in the New Testament', in S. E. Porter and C. A. Evans (eds.), *The Scrolls and the Scriptures: Qumran Fifty Years After* (Sheffield: Sheffield Academic Press), 242–66.

——and B. Lindars (eds.) (1992), *Septuagint, Scrolls and Cognate Writings, Papers Presented to the International Symposium on the Septuagint and its Relations to the Dead Sea Scrolls and Other Writings*, Manchester, 1990, Septuagint and Cognate Studies Series, 33 (Atlanta, Ga.: Scholars Press).

Brooten, B. J. (1982), *Women Leaders in the Ancient Synagogue: Inscriptional Evidence and Background Issues*, Brown Judaic Studies, 36 (Atlanta, Ga.: Scholars Press).

Buell, D. K. (2005), *Why This New Race: Ethnic Reasoning in Early Christianity* (New York: Columbia University Press).

Bungarten, J. J. (1967), *Menander und Glykeras Brief bei Alkiphron* (Bonn: Bonn University).

Burnyeat, M. F. (2005), 'Platonism in the Bible: Numenius of Apamea on Exodus and Eternity', in R. Salles (ed.), *Metaphysics, Soul and Ethics in Ancient Thought* (Oxford: Clarendon Press), 143–69.

Calabi, F. (1998), The Language and the Law of God: Interpretation and Politics in Philo of Alexandria (Atlanta, Ga.: Scholars Press).

Campbell, J. G. (1999), 'Hebrew and its Study at Qumran', in W. Horbury (ed.), *Hebrew Study from Ezra to Ben-Yehuda* (Edinburgh: T. & T. Clark), 38–52.

——(2000), '4QMMTd and the Tripartite Canon', *Journal of Jewish Studies*, 51: 181–90.

Cancik, H. (2003), 'Standardization and Ranking of Texts in Greek and Roman Institutions', in M. Finkelberg and G. A. G. Stroumsa (eds.), *Homer, the Bible, and Beyond: Literary and Religious Canons in the Ancient World* (Leiden: Brill), 117–30.

Canfora, L. (1989) [1986], *The Vanished Library*, trans. M. H. Ryle (London: Hutchinson Radius); orig. edn.: *La biblioteca scomparsa* (Palermo: Sellerio Editore, 1986).

Carlebach, E., J. M. Efron, and D. N. Myers (eds.) (1998), *Jewish History and Jewish Memory: Essays in Honor of Yosef Hayim Yerushalmi*, Tauber Institute for the Study of European Jewry Series, 29 (Hanover, NH and London: University Press of New England for Brandeis University Press).

Carr, D. M. (2005), *Writing on the Tablet of the Heart: Origins of Scripture and Literature* (Oxford and New York: Oxford University Press).

Carson, D. A., and H. G. M. Williamson (eds.) (1988), *It is Written. Scripture Citing Scripture: Essays in Honour of Barnabas Lindars, SSF* (Cambridge: Cambridge University Press).

Cartledge, P., P. Garnsey, and E. S. Gruen (eds.) (1997), *Hellenistic Constructs: Essays in Culture, History, and Historiography*, Hellenistic Culture and Society, 26 (Berkeley, Calif.: University of California Press).

Casson, L. (2001), *Libraries in the Ancient World* (New Haven, Conn. and London: Yale University Press).

Castelli, E. (2004), *Martyrdom and Memory: Early Christian Culture Making* (New York: Columbia University Press).

Chadwick, H. (1965), *Origen: Contra Celsum*, trans. with an introduction and notes (2nd edn., Cambridge: Cambridge University Press).

Chaniotis, A. (2002), 'The Jews of Aphrodisias', *Scripta Classica Israelica*, 21: 209–42.

——(2003), 'The Divinity of Hellenistic Rulers', in A. Erskine (ed.), *A Companion to the Hellenistic World* (Oxford: Blackwell), 431–45.

——(2005), *War in the Hellenistic World: A Social and Cultural History* (Malden, Mass.: Blackwell Publishing).

Chapman, S. (2003), 'How the Biblical Canon Began: Working Models and Open Questions', in M. Finkelberg and G. A. G. Stroumsa (eds.), *Homer, the Bible, and Beyond: Literary and Religious Canons in the Ancient World* (Leiden: Brill), 29–51.

Charlesworth, J. H. (1983), *The Old Testament Pseudepigrapha*, 2 vols. (Garden City, NY: Doubleday).

Chazon, E. G. (2000a), 'The Function of the Qumran Prayer Texts: An Analysis of the Daily Prayers (4Q503)', in Lawrence H. Schiffman, E. Tov, and J. C. VanderKam (eds.), *The Dead Sea Scrolls: Fifty Years after Their Discovery*, Proceedings of the Jerusalem Congress, 20–5 July 1997 (Jerusalem: Israel Exploration Society in cooperation with the Shrine of the Book, Israel Museum), 217–25.

——(2000b), 'When Did They Pray? Times for Prayer in the Dead Sea Scrolls and Associated Literature', in R. A. Argall, B. A. Bow, and

R. A. Werline (eds.), *For A Later Generation: The Transformation of Tradition in Israel, Early Judaism and Early Christianity* (Harrisburg, Pa.: Trinity Press International), 42–51.

——(2003a), 'Human and Angelic Prayer in Light of the Dead Sea Scrolls', in R.A. Clements and A. Pinnick (eds.), *Liturgical Perspectives: Prayer and Poetry in Light of the Dead Sea Scrolls*, Proceedings of the Fifth International Symposium of the Orion Center for the Study of the Dead Sea Scrolls and Associated Literature, 19–23 Jan. 2000 (Leiden: Brill), 35–47.

——(2003b), 'The Use of the Bible as a Key to Meaning in Psalms from Qumran', in M. P. Shalom, R. A. Kraft, et al. (eds.), *Emanuel: Studies in Hebrew Bible, Septuagint and Dead Sea Scrolls in Honor of Emanuel Tov* (Leiden: Brill), 85–96.

Clark, G., and T. Rajak (2002), *Philosophy and Power in the Graeco–Roman World: Essays in Honour of Miriam Griffin* (Oxford: Oxford University Press).

Clements, R. (1999), 'Origen's Hexapla and the Christian–Jewish Encounter in the Second and Third Centuries', in T. L. Donaldson (ed.), *Religious Rivalries and the Struggle for Success in Caesarea Maritima* (Waterloo, Ont.: Canadian Corporation for Studies in Religion/Wilfrid Laurier University Press), 303–29.

Clines, D. J. A. (1984), 'The Esther Scroll: The Story of the Story', *Journal for the Study of the Old Testament, Suppl. Ser.*, 30.

Coggins, R. J., and J. L. Houlden (eds.) (1990), *A Dictionary of Biblical Interpretation* (London: SCM Press).

Cohen, N. G. (1984), 'The Names of the Translators in the Letter of Aristeas. A Study in the Dynamics of Cultural Transition', *Journal for the Study of Judaism*, 15: 32–64.

——(1995), *Philo Judaeus: His Universe of Discourse* (Frankfurt: Peter Lang).

——(1997), 'The Names of the Separate Books of the Pentateuch in Philo's Writings', in D. T. Runia and G. E. Sterling (eds.), *Studia Philonica Annual, Studies in Hellenistic Judaism*, ix. *Wisdom and Logos: Studies in Jewish Thought in Honor of David Winston*, Brown Judaic Studies, 312 (Atlanta Ga.: Scholars Press), 54–78.

——(2002), 'Context and Connotation: Greek Words for Jewish Concepts in Philo', in J. L. Kugel (ed.), *Shem in the Tents of Japhet: Essays on the Encounter of Judaism and Hellenism* (Leiden: Brill), 31–61.

——(2007), *Philo's Scriptures: Citations from the Prophets and Writings: Evidence for a Haftarah Cycle in Second Temple Judaism*, Supplements to the Journal for the Study of Judaism 123 (Leiden: Brill).

Cohen, S. J. D. (1981), 'Epigraphical Rabbis', *Jewish Quarterly Review*, 72: 1–17.

——(1987), *From the Maccabees to the Mishnah* (Philadelphia, Pa.: Westminster Press).
——(1999), *The Beginnings of Jewishness: Boundaries, Varieties, Uncertainties*, Hellenistic Culture and Society, 31 (Berkeley, Calif. and London: University of California Press).
——and E. S. Frerichs (eds.) (1993), *Diasporas in Antiquity*, Brown Judaic Studies, 288 (Atlanta, Ga.: Scholars Press).
Collins, J. J. (1992), 'The King has Become a Jew: The Perspective on the Gentile World in Bel and the Snake', in *Diaspora Jews and Judaism: Essays in Honour of and in Dialogue with A. Thomas Kraabel*, ed. J. Overman and R. S. McLennan (Atlanta: Scholars Press), 335–45.
——(1993), *A Commentary on the Book of Daniel. Hermeneia: A Critical and Historical Commentary on the Bible* (Minneapolis: Fortress Press).
——(1997), *Jewish Wisdom in the Hellenistic Age* (Edinburgh: T. and T. Clark).
——(2000) [1983], *Between Athens and Jerusalem: Jewish Identity in the Hellenistic Diaspora* (2nd edn., Grand Rapids, Mich.: Eerdmans; orig. edn., 1983).
——(2002), 'The Literature of the Second Temple Period', in M. Goodman, J. Cohen, and D. J. Sorkin (eds.), *The Oxford Handbook of Jewish Studies* (Oxford: Oxford University Press), 53–78.
Collins, N. L. (2000), *The Library in Alexandria and the Bible in Greek*, Supplements to *Vetus Testamentum*, 82 (Leiden: Brill).
Colorni, V. (1964), 'L'uso del greco nella liturgia del giudaismo ellenistico e la novella 146 di Giustiniano', *Annali di storia del diritto*, 8, 19–80.
Connerton, P. (1989), *How Societies Remember* (Cambridge: Cambridge University Press).
Conybeare, F. C., and S. G. Stock (1988) [1905], *Grammar of Septuagint Greek with Selected Readings from the Septuagint According to the Text of Swete* (Peabody, Mass.: Hendricksen; orig. edn. 1905).
Cowey, J. M. S. (2004), 'Das ägyptische Judentum in hellenistischer Zeit-neue Erkentnisse aus jüngst veröffentlichten Papyri', in S. Kreuzer and J. P. Lesch (eds.), *Im Brennpunkt: Die Septuaginta. Studien zur Entstehung und Bedeutung der griechischen Bibel*, ii. (Stuttgart: Kohlhammer).
——and K. Maresch (eds.) (2001), *Urkunden des politeuma der Juden von Herakleopolis (144/3–133/2 v. Chr.) (P. Polit. Iud.): Papyri aus den Sammlungen von Heidelberg, Köln, München und Wien*, Papyrologica Coloniensia, 29 (Wiesbaden: Westdeutscher).
Cox, C. E., (ed.) (1987), *Sixth Congress of the International Organization for Septuagint and Cognate Studies, Jerusalem, 1986*, Septuagint and Cognate Studies Series, 23 (Atlanta, Ga.: Scholars Press).

Cribiore, R. (1996), *Writing, Teachers, and Students in Graeco-Roman Egypt*, American Studies in Papyrology, 36 (Atlanta, Ga.: Scholars Press).

Cross, F. M. (2002), 'The Hebrew Inscriptions from the Sardis Synagogue', *Harvard Theological Review*, 95: 3–19.

Daniel, S. (1966), *Recherches sur le vocabulaire du culte dans la Septante*, Études et Commentaires, 61 (Paris: C. Klincksieck).

Daube, D. (1963), *The Exodus Pattern in the Bible* (London: Faber and Faber).

Davies, P. R. (1991), 'Daniel in the Lions' Den', in L. Alexander (ed.), *Images of Empire*, Journal for the study of the old Testament Supplement Series, 122, 160–78.

Davies, W. D., and L. Finkelstein (eds.) (1989), *The Cambridge History of Judaism*, ii. *The Hellenistic Age* (Cambridge: Cambridge University Press).

Davila, J. R. (2005), '(How) Can We Tell if a Greek Apocryphon or Pseudepigraphon Has Been Translated from Hebrew or Aramaic?', *Journal for the Study of the Pseudepigrapha*, 15: 3–61.

Dawson, D. (1992), *Allegorical Readers and Cultural Revision in Ancient Alexandria* (Berkeley, Calif.: University of California Press).

De Troyer, K. (2000), *The End of the Alpha Text of Esther: Translation and Narrative Technique in MT 8:1–17, LXX 8:1–17, and AT 7:14–41*, Septuagint and Cognate Studies Series, 48 (Atlanta, Ga.: Society of Biblical Literature).

——(2003), *Rewriting the Sacred Text: What the Old Greek Texts Tell Us about the Literary Growth of the Bible* (Leiden: Brill).

Deissmann, A. (1903), *Bible Studies: Contributions, Chiefly from Papyri and Inscriptions, to the History of the Language, the Literature, and the Religion of Hellenistic Judaism and Primitive Christianity*, trans. A. Grieve (2nd edn., Edinburgh: T. and T. Clark).

——(1927) [1923], *Light from the Ancient East: The New Testament Illustrated from Recently Discovered Texts of the Graeco-Roman World*, trans. L. R. M. Strachan (new and rev. edn., London: Hodder and Stoughton; orig. edn. Tübingen: Licht vom Osten, 1923).

Delia, D. (1992), 'From Romance to Rhetoric: The Alexandrian Library in Classical and Islamic Traditions', *American Historical Review*, 97: 1449–67.

Denny, F. M., and R. L. Taylor (eds.) (1985), *The Holy Book in Comparative Perspective* (Columbia, SC: University of South Carolina Press).

Dimant, D. (1987), 'The Problem of Non-Translated Biblical Greek', in C. E. Cox (ed.), *Sixth Congress of the International Organization for Septuagint and Cognate Studies, Jerusalem, 1986* (Atlanta, Ga.: Scholars Press), 1–19.

——(1988), 'Use and Interpretation of Mikra in the Apocrypha and Pseudepigrapha', in M. J. Mulder and H. Sysling (eds.), *Mikra: Text,*

Translation, Reading and Interpretation of the Hebrew Bible in Ancient Judaism and Early Christianity (Assen: Van Gorcum), 379–419.

Dines, J. M. (2004), *The Septuagint: Understanding the Bible and its World* (London: T. and T. Clark).

——(2007), 'The King's Good Servant? Loyalty, Subversion and Greek Daniel', in T. Rajak, S. Pearce, et al. (eds.), *Jewish Perspectives on Hellenistic Rulers*, Hellenistic Culture and Society, 50 (Berkeley, Calif.: University of California Press), 205–24.

Dionisotti, C. (2005), 'Translator's Latin', in J. N. Adams (ed.), *Aspects of the Language of Latin Prose* (Oxford: British Academy/Oxford University Press), 357–75.

Dodd, C. H. (1935), *The Bible and the Greeks* (London: Hodder and Stoughton).

Dogniez, C. (1995), *Bibliography of the Septuagint*, Supplements to *Vetus Testamentum*, 60 (Leiden and New York: Brill).

Doran, R. (1981), *Temple Propaganda: The Purpose and Character of 2 Maccabees.* (Washington, DC: Catholic Biblical Association of America).

——(1986), 'The Jewish Hellenistic Historians before Josephus', in *Aufstieg und Niedergang der Römischen Welt* ii. 20.1 (Berlin: de Gruyter), 246–97.

Dorival, G. (1989), 'À propos de la Septante', in D. Tollet (ed.), *Politique et religion dans le judaïsme ancien et médiéval: interventions au colloque des 8 et 9 décembre 1987* (Paris: Desclée), 21–8.

——(1988), M. Harl and O. Munnich, *La Bible grecque des Septante: du Judaïsme hellenistique au Christianisme ancien.* Initiations au christianisme ancien (Paris: Éditions du Cerf/éditions du CNRS).

Droge, A. J. and J. D. Tabor (1992), *A Noble Death: Suicide and Martyrdom among Christians and Jews in Antiquity* (San Francisco, Calif.: Harper).

Dunand, F. (1966), *Papyrus grecs bibliques (Papyrus F, inv.266: volumina de la Genèse et du Deuteronome* (Cairo: Imprimerie de l'institut français et d'archeologie orientale).

——(1981), 'Fête et propagande à Alexandrie sous les Lagides', in *La fête, pratique et discours: d'Alexandrie hellénistique à la mission de Besançon* (Paris: Les Belles Lettres), 13–40.

Edmonds, J. M. (1957), *The Fragments of Attic Comedy after Meineke, Bergk and Kock.* iiiB: Menander (Leiden: Brill).

Edmondson, J. C., S. Mason, and J. B. Rives (eds.) (2005), *Flavius Josephus and Flavian Rome* (Oxford: Oxford University Press).

Ego, B., A. Lange, et al. (1999), *Gemeinde ohne Tempel: Zur Substituierung und Transformation des Jerusalemer Tempels und seines Kults im Alten*

Testament, antiken Judentum und frühen Christentum, Wissenschaftliche Untersuchungen zum Neuen Testament, 118 (Tübingen: Mohr Siebeck).

Ellis, E. E. (1988), 'Biblical Interpretation in the New Testament Church', in M. J. Mulder and H. Sysling (eds.), *Mikra: Text, Translation, Reading and Interpretation of the Hebrew Bible in Ancient Judaism and Early Christianity* (Assen: Van Gorcum), 691–725.

——(1991), *The Old Testament in Early Christianity: Canon and Interpretation in the Light of Modern Research*, Wissenschaftliche Untersuchungen zum Neuen Testament, 54 (Tübingen: Mohr Siebeck).

Ellison, H. L. (1983), 'Torah', in *Torah and Other Essays: A Symposium in Honour of the 80th Birthday of H. L. Ellison* (Ramsgate: International Hebrew Christian Alliance).

Engberg-Pedersen, T. (2001), *Paul beyond the Judaism/Hellenism Divide* (Louisville, Kt.: Westminster/John Knox Press).

Erskine, A. (1995), 'Culture and Power in Ptolemaic Egypt: The Museum and Library of Alexandria', *Greece and Rome*, 42: 38–48.

——(ed.) (2003), *A Companion to the Hellenistic World* (Oxford: Blackwell).

Evans, T. V. (2001), *Verbal Syntax in the Greek Pentateuch: Natural Greek Usage and Hebrew Interference* (Oxford: Oxford University Press).

——(2005), 'Approaches to the Language of the Septuagint', *Journal of Jewish Studies*, 56, 25–33.

——(2007), 'The Court Function of the Interpreter in Genesis 42.23 and Early Greek Papyri', in T. Rajak, S. Pearce, J. Aitken, and J. Dines (eds.), *Jewish Perspectives on Hellenistic Rulers* (Berkeley, Calif.: University of California Press), 238–52.

Fabry, H.-J., and U. Offerhaus (2001), *Im Brennpunkt: die Septuaginta. Studien zur Entstehung und Bedeutung der griechischen Bibel* (Stuttgart: Kohlhammer).

Falls, T. B. (1948), *Justin Martyr, First Apology*, in *Writings of Saint Justin Martyr*, Fathers of the Church (New York: Christian Heritage, Inc.)

Feldman, L. H. (1993), *Jew and Gentile in the Ancient World: Attitudes and Interactions from Alexander to Justinian* (Princeton, NJ: Princeton University Press).

——(1996), *Studies in Hellenistic Judaism*, Arbeiten zur Geschichte des antiken Judentums und des Urchristentums, 30 (Leiden: Brill).

——(1998a), *Josephus' Interpretation of the Bible*, Hellenistic Culture and Society, 27 (Berkeley, Calif.: University of California Press).

——(1998b), *Studies in Josephus' Rewritten Bible*, Supplements to the Journal for the Study of Judaism, 58 (Leiden: Brill).

——(2002), Review of M. Niehoff, *Philo on Jewish Identity and Culture* (2001), *Scripta Classica Israelica*, 21: 314–18.

——(2006), *Judaism and Hellenism Reconsidered* (Leiden: Brill).
Feldman, L. H., and M. Reinhold (eds.) (1996), *Jewish Life and Thought among Greeks and Romans: Primary Readings* (Minneapolis, Minn.: Fortress Press).
Fernández-Marcos, N. (2000), *The Septuagint in Context: Introduction to the Greek Version of the Bible* (Leiden: Brill).
——(2001), 'David the Adolescent: On Psalm 151', in R. J. V. Hiebert, C. E. Cox, and P. J. Gentry (eds.), *The Old Greek Psalter: Studies in Honour of Albert Pietersma*. Journal for the Study of the Old Testament, Suppl. Ser., 332 (Sheffield: Sheffield Academic Press), 205–17.
——(2002), 'The Other Septuagint: From the Letter of Aristeas to the Letter of Jeremiah', *Journal of North-Western Semitic Languages*, 28: 27–41.
Fewster, P. (2002), 'Bilingualism in Roman Egypt', in J. N. Adams, M. Janse, and S. Swain (eds.), *Bilingualism in Ancient Society: Language Contact and the Written Word* (Oxford: Oxford University Press), 220–45.
Fine, S. (1996), *Sacred Realm: The Emergence of the Synagogue in the Ancient World* (New York and Oxford: Oxford University Press/Yeshiva University Museum).
——(ed.) (1999), *Jews, Christians, and Polytheists in the Ancient Synagogue: Cultural Interaction during the Greco-Roman Period* (London: Routledge).
——(2005), *Art and Judaism in the Greco–Roman World: Toward a New Jewish Archaeology* (Cambridge: Cambridge University Press).
Finkelberg, M. (2003), 'Homer as a Foundation Text', in M. Finkelberg and G. A. G. Stroumsa (eds.), *Homer, the Bible, and Beyond: Literary and Religious Canons in the Ancient World* (Leiden: Brill), 75–96.
Finkelberg, M. and G. A. G. Stroumsa (eds.) (2003), *Homer, the Bible, and Beyond: Literary and Religious Canons in the Ancient World*, Jerusalem Studies in Religion and Culture, 2 (Leiden: Brill).
Finkelstein, L. (1936), *Akiba: Scholar, Saint and Martyr* (New York: Corvici Friede).
Fishbane, M. A. (1985), *Biblical Interpretation in Ancient Israel* (Oxford: Clarendon Press).
——(1988), 'Use, Authority and Interpretation of Mikra at Qumran', in M. J. Mulder and H. Sysling (eds.), *Mikra: Text, Translation, Reading and Interpretation of the Hebrew Bible in Ancient Judaism and Early Christianity* (Assen: Van Gorcum), 339–77.
Fishman, J. A. (ed.) (1985), *Readings in the Sociology of Jewish Languages* (Leiden: Brill).
Forbes, C. (1995), *Prophecy and Inspired Speech in Early Christianity and its Hellenistic Environment*, Wissenschaftliche Untersuchungen zum Neuen Testament, 2/75 (Tübingen: Mohr Siebeck).

Fortenbaugh, W. W., and E. Schütrumpf (2000), *Demetrius of Phalerum: Text, Translation and Discussion*, Rutgers University Studies in Classical Humanities, 9 (New Brunswick, NJ: Transaction Publishers).
Fraade, S. (1992), 'Rabbinic Views on the Practice of Targum and Multilingualism in Jewish Galilee in the Third–Sixth Centuries', in L. I. Levine (ed.), *The Galilee in Late Antiquity* (New York and Jerusalem: Jewish Theological Seminary of America), 253–86.
—— (1993) 'Interpretive Authority in the Studying Community at Qumran', *Journal of Jewish Studies*, 44: 46–69.
—— (1999), 'Literary Composition and Oral Performance in Early Midrashim', *Oral Tradition*, 41: 33–51.
—— (2006a), 'Locating Targum in the Textual Polysystem of Rabbinic Pedagogy', *Bulletin of the International Organization for Septuagint and Cognate Studies*, 39: 69–91.
—— (2006b), 'Rewritten Bible and Rabbinic Midrash as Commentary', in C. Bakhos (ed.), *Current Trends in the Study of Midrash*, Supplements to the Journal for the Study of Judaism, 106 (Leiden: Brill), 61–70.
Frankel, Z. (1851), *Ueber den Einfluss der Palästinischen Exegese. Auf die alexandrinische Hermeneutik* (Leipzig).
Fraser, P. M. (1972), *Ptolemaic Alexandria*, 3 vols. (Oxford: Clarendon Press).
—— (1994), 'The World of Theophrastus', in S. Hornblower (ed.), *Greek Historiography* (Oxford: Clarendon Press), 166–92.
Frend, W. H. C. (1965), *Martyrdom and Persecution in the Early Church: A Study of a Conflict from the Maccabees to Donatus* (Oxford: Blackwell).
Freudenthal, J. (1874), *Alexander Polyhistor und die von ihm erhaltenen Reste jüdischer und samaritanischer* Geschichtswerke (Breslau: Grass).
Frey, J. (1999), 'Temple and Rival Temple—the Cases of Elephantine, Mt Gerizim and Leontopolis', in *Gemeinde ohne Tempel*, ed. B. Ego, A. Lange, and P. Pilhofer (Tübingen: Mohr Siebeck), 171–204.
Freyne, S. (2002), 'Studying the Jewish Diaspora in Antiquity', in J. R. Bartlett (ed.), *Jews in the Hellenistic and Roman Cities* (London: Routledge), 1–9.
Funkenstein, A. (1993), *Perceptions of Jewish History* (Berkeley, Calif.: University of California Press).
Gafni, I. M. (1997), *Land, Centre and Diaspora: Jewish Constructs in Late Antiquity*, Journal for the Study of the Pseudepigrapha, Suppl. Series 21 (Sheffield: Sheffield Academic Press).
Gager, J. G. (1972), *Moses in Greco-Roman Paganism*, Society of Biblical Literature Monograph Series, 16 (Nashville, Tenn.: Abingdon Press).
—— (ed.) (1992), *Curse Tablets and Binding Spells from the Ancient World* (New York and Oxford: Oxford University Press).

——(1994), 'Moses the Magician: The Hero of an Ancient Counter-Culture', *Helios*, 21: 179–88.
Gamble, H. Y. (1995), *Books and Readers in the Early Church: A History of Early Christian Texts* (New Haven, Conn.: Yale University Press).
Gammie, J. G. (1987), 'The Septuagint of Job: Its Poetic Style and Relationship to the Septuagint of Proverbs', *Catholic Biblical Quarterly*, 49 (1): 14–31.
Gehman, H. S. (1951), 'The Hebraic Character of Septuagint Greek', *Vetus Testamentum*, 1: 81–90.
——(1954), "Ἅγιος in the Septuagint and its Relation to the Hebrew Original', *Vetus Testamentum*, 4: 337–48.
George, A. R. (2003), The Babylonian Gilgamesh Epic: Introduction, Critical Edition and Cuneiform Texts (Oxford: Oxford University Press).
Gera, D. (1998), *Judaea and Mediterranean Politics, 219 to 161 BCE* (Leiden: Brill).
Gibson, E. L. (1999), *The Jewish Manumission Inscriptions of the Bosporan Kingdom* (Tübingen: Mohr Siebeck).
Gilbert, M. (1973), *La Critique des dieux dans le livre de la sagesse (Sg 13–15)* (Rome: Biblical Institute Press).
Gilman, S. L. (1986), *Jewish Self-Hatred: Anti–Semitism and the Hidden Language of the Jews* (Baltimore, Md. and London: Johns Hopkins University Press).
Goldhill, S. (2001), *Being Greek under Rome: Cultural Identity, the Second Sophistic, and the Development of Empire* (Cambridge: Cambridge University Press).
Goldstein, J. A. (1991), 'The Message of Aristeas to Philocrates in the Second Century BCE: Obey the Torah, Venerate the Temple of Jerusalem, but Speak Greek and Put your Hopes in the Ptolemaic Dynasty', in M. Mor (ed.), *Eretz Israel, Israel, and the Jewish Diaspora: Mutual Relations*, Proceedings of the First Annual Symposium of the Philip M. and Ethel Klutznick Chair in Jewish Civilization, Held on 9–10 Oct. 1988 (Lanham, Md.: University Press of America), 1–23.
Goodblatt, D. M. (2006), *Elements of Ancient Jewish Nationalism* (Cambridge: Cambridge University Press).
Goodenough, E. R. (1953–68), *Jewish Symbols in the Greco-Roman Period*, Bollingen Series, 37, 13 vols. (New York / Princeton, NJ: Pantheon Books and Princeton University Press).
——(1988), *Jewish Symbols in the Greco–Roman Period*, ed. Jacob Neusner (abridged edn., Princeton, NJ: Princeton University Press).
——and V. Nikiprowetzky (1983), 'Philo's Bible in the De Gigantibus and Quod Deus', in D. Winston and J. M. Dillon (eds.), *Two Treatises of Philo*

of Alexandria: A Commentary on De gigantibus and Quod Deus sit immutabilis (Chico, Calif.: Scholars Press), 89–125.
Gooding, D. W. (1963), 'Aristeas and Septuagint Origins: A Review of Recent Studies', *Vetus Testamentum*, 13: 357–79.
Goodman, M. (1989), 'Nerva, the fiscus iudaicus and Jewish Identity', *Journal of Roman Studies*, 79: 40–4.
——(1990), 'Sacred Scripture and "Defiling the Hands"', *Journal of Theological Studies*, 41: 99–107.
——(1991), 'Babatha's Story', *Journal of Roman Studies*, 81: 169–75.
——(1992), 'Jewish Proselytizing in the First Century', in J. Lieu, J. North, and T. Rajak (eds.), *The Jews among Pagans and Christians in the Roman Empire* (London: Routledge), 53–78.
——(1994a), *Mission and Conversion: Proselytizing in the Religious History of the Roman Empire* (Oxford: Clarendon Press).
——(1994b), 'Texts, Scribes, and Power in Roman Judaea', in A. K. Bowman and G. Woolf (eds.), *Literacy and Power in the Ancient World* (Cambridge: Cambridge University Press), 99–108.
——(ed.) (1998), *Jews in a Graeco–Roman World* (Oxford: Clarendon Press).
——(2000), *State and Society in Roman Galilee, AD 132–212*, Parkes–Wiener Series on Jewish Studies (2nd edn., London: Vallentine Mitchell).
——(2001), 'The Apocrypha', in J. Barton and J. Muddiman (eds.), *The Oxford Bible Commentary* (Oxford: Oxford University Press), 617–26.
——(2004), 'Trajan and the Origins of Roman Hostility to the Jews', *Past and Present*, 182: 3–49.
——(2007), *Rome and Jerusalem: The Clash of Ancient Civilizations* (London: Allen Lane).
Gordon, R. (1997), 'Reporting the Marvellous: Private Divination in the Greek Magical Papyri', in P. Schäfer and H. G. Kippenberg (eds.), *Envisioning Magic: A Princeton Seminar and Symposium* (Leiden: Brill), 66–92.
Goulet, R. (1987), *La philosophie de Moïse: essai de reconstitution d'un commentaire philosophique préphilonien du Pentateuque*, Histoire des doctrines de l'antiquité classique, 11 (Paris: J. Vrin).
Gow, A. S. F. (1950), *Theocritus*, 2 vols. (Cambridge: Cambridge University Press).
Grabbe, L. L. (1982), 'Aquila's Translation and Rabbinic Exegesis', *Journal of Jewish Studies*, 33: 527–36.
——(1997), *Wisdom of Solomon* (Sheffield: Sheffield Academic Press).
Graf, F. (1991), 'Prayer in Magic and Religious Ritual', in C. A. Faraone and D. Obbink (eds.), *Magika Hiera: Ancient Greek Magic and Religion* (New York and Oxford: Oxford University Press), 188–213.

——(1997), 'How to Cope With a Difficult Life: A View of Ancient Magic', in P. Schäfer and H. G. Kippenberg (eds.), *Envisioning Magic: A Princeton Seminar and Symposium* (Leiden: Brill), 93–114.
Grafton, A. (1983–93), *Joseph Scaliger: A Study in the History of Classical Scholarship*, Oxford–Warburg Studies, 2 vols. (Oxford and New York: Oxford University Press).
——(1990), *Forgers and Critics: Creativity and Duplicity in Western Scholarship* (London: Juliet Gardiner Books/Collins and Brown).
——(1998), 'Jacob Bernays, Joseph Scaliger and Others', in D. N. Myers and D. B. Ruderman (eds.), *The Jewish Past Revisited: Reflections on Modern Jewish Historians* (New Haven, Conn. and London: Yale University Press), 16–38.
——and M. Williams (2006), *Christianity and the Transformation of the Book: Origen, Eusebius and the Library of Caesarea* (Cambridge, Mass.: Harvard University Press).
Grainger, J. D. (1991), *Hellenistic Phoenicia* (Oxford: Clarendon Press).
Granata, G. (ed.) (2006), *L'archivio Arnaldo Momigliano. Inventario analitico* (Rome: Edizioni di storia e letteratura).
Green, P. (1990), *Alexander to Actium: The Historical Evolution of the Hellenistic Age* (Berkeley, Calif.: University of California Press).
Greenspoon, L. J. (1990), 'Recensions, Revisions, Rabbinics: Dominique Barthélemy and Early Developments in the Greek Tradition', *Textus: Annual of the Hebrew University Bible Project*, 15: 153–63.
Griffin, M. T. (2005), '"Lifting the Mask": Syme on Fictional History', in Griffin and R. Tomlin (eds.), *History and Fiction: Six Essays Celebrating the Centenary of Sir Ronald Syme* (London: Grime and Selwood).
Griffith, T. M. (2002), 'ΕΙΔΩΛΟΝ as "Idol" in Non-Jewish and Non-Christian Greek', *Journal of Theological Studies*, 53: 95–101.
Grimm, G. (1996), 'City Planning?', in *Alexandria and Alexandrian* (Malibu, Calif.: J. Paul Getty Museum), 55–74.
Grinfield, E. W. (1850), *An Apology for the Septuagint, in Which its Claims to Biblical and Canonical Authority are Stated and Vindicated* (London: William Pickering).
Gruen, E. S. (1997), 'Fact and Fiction: Jewish Legends in a Hellenistic Context', in P. Cartledge, P. Garnsey, and Gruen (eds.), *Hellenistic Constructs: Essays in Culture, History, and Historiography* (Berkeley, Calif.: University of California Press), 72–88.
Gruen, E. S. (1998), *Heritage and Hellenism: The Reinvention of Jewish Tradition*, Hellenistic Culture and Society, 30 (Berkeley, Calif.: University of California Press).
——(2002), *Diaspora: Jews amidst Greeks and Romans* (Cambridge, Mass. and London: Harvard University Press).

——(2003), 'Jews and Greeks', in A. Erskine (ed.), *A Companion to the Hellenistic World* (Oxford: Blackwell), 264–79.

——(2007), 'Persia through the Jewish Looking-Glass', in T. Rajak, S. Pearce, et al. (eds.), *Jewish Perspectives on Hellenistic Rulers* (Berkeley, Calif.: University of California Press), 58–98.

Gutzwiller, K. J. (ed.) (2005), *The New Posidippus: A Hellenistic Poetry Book* (Oxford: Oxford University Press).

Haas, C. (1997), *Alexandria in Late Antiquity: Topography and Social Conflict* (Baltimore, Md. and London: Johns Hopkins University Press).

Habicht, C. (1970) [1956], *Gottmenschentum und Griechische Städte* (2nd edn., Munich: Beck; orig. edn.: 1956).

Hacham, N. (2005), 'The Letter of Aristeas: A New Exodus Story?', *Journal for the Study of Judaism*, 36: 1–20.

Hachlili, R. (1998), *Ancient Jewish Art and Archaeology in the Diaspora* (Leiden: Brill).

Hadas, M. (1951), *Aristeas, to Philocrates: The Letter of Aristeas*, trans. M. Hadas (New York: Harper and Bros. (for the Dropsie College).

——(1953), *The Third and Fourth Books of Maccabees* (New York: Dropsie College/Harper).

Hadas-Lebel, M. (1973), *De Providentia I et II, Philo d'Alexandrie, Introduction, Traduction et Notes* (Paris: Editions du Cerf).

Halbertal, M. (1997), *People of the Book: Canon, Meaning, and Authority* (Cambridge, Mass.: Harvard University Press).

——and A. Margalit (1992), *Idolatry*, trans. N. Goldblum (Cambridge, Mass. and London: Harvard University Press).

Halbwachs, M. (1925), *Les cadres sociaux de la mémoire* (Paris: F. Alcan).

——(1950), *La Mémoire collective* (Paris: Presses Universitaires de France).

——(1980), *The Collective Memory* (New York: Harper and Row).

——(1992), *On Collective Memory*, trans. L. A. Coser (Chicago, Ill.: University of Chicago Press, 1992; orig. edn.: *Les Cadres sociaux de la mémoire* (1925).

Hall, J. M. (2002), *Hellenicity: Between Ethnicity and Culture* (Chicago: University of Chicago Press).

Hallo, W. W. (1996), *Origins: The Ancient Near Eastern Background of Some Modern Western Institutions* (Leiden: Brill).

Haran, M. (1983), 'Book Scrolls at the Beginning of the Second Temple Period: The Transition from Papyrus to Skins', *Hebrew Union College Annual*, 54: 111–22.

——(1985), 'Bible Scrolls in Eastern and Western Jewish Communities from Qumran to the Middle Ages', *Hebrew Union College Annual*, 56: 21–62.

——(1996), *Ha-asufah Ha–mikr'ait* (*The Biblical Collection: Its Consolidation to the End of the Second Temple Times and Changes of Form to the End of the Middle Ages*), 2 vols. (Jerusalem: Mosad Bialik and Magnes Press, Hebrew University).
Harl, M. (1992), *La langue de Japhet: quinze études sur la Septante et le grec des Chrétiens* (Paris: Éditions du Cerf).
——and M. Alexandre (1986), *Bible d'Alexandrie*, i. *La Genèse* (Paris: Éditions du Cerf).
Harland, P. A. (2003), *Associations, Synagogues, and Congregations: Claiming a Place in Ancient Mediterranean Society* (Philadelphia, Pa.: Fortress).
——(2006), 'Acculturation and Identity in the Diaspora: A Jewish Family and "Pagan" Guilds at Hierapolis', *Journal of Jewish Studies*, 57: 222–44.
Harris, W. V. (1989), *Ancient Literacy* (Cambridge, Mass.: Harvard University Press).
——and G. Ruffini (eds.) (2004), *Ancient Alexandria between Egypt and Greece*, Columbia Studies in the Classical Tradition, 26 (Leiden: Brill).
Hatch, E., H. A. Redpath, et al. (1897), *A Concordance to the Septuagint and the Other Greek Versions of the Old Testament (Including the Apocryphal Books)* (Oxford: Clarendon Press).
Hayward, C. T. R. (1982), 'The Jewish Temple at Leontopolis: A Reconsideration', *Journal of Jewish Studies*, 33: 429–43.
——(1990), 'Rewritten Bible', in R. J. Coggins and J. L. Houlden (eds.), *A Dictionary of Biblical Interpretation* (London: SCM Press), 595–8.
——(1995), *Saint Jerome's Hebrew Questions on Genesis*, trans. with introduction and commentary (Oxford: Clarendon Press).
Hazzard, R. A. (2000), *Imagination of a Monarchy: Studies in Ptolemaic Propaganda*, Phoenix Supplement, 37 (Toronto: University of Toronto Press).
Hegerman, H. (1989), in W. D. Davies and L. Finkelstein (eds.), *The Cambridge History of Judaism*, ii. *The Hellenistic Age* (Cambridge: Cambridge University Press), 115–66.
Heller-Roazen, D. (2005), *Echolalias: On the Forgetting of Language* (New York: Zone).
Hengel, M. (1974) [1969], *Judaism and Hellenism: Studies in their Encounter in Palestine during the Early Hellenistic Period*, trans. J. Bowden, 2 vols. (London: SCM Press; orig. edn.: Judentum und Hellenismus, Studien zu ihrer Begegnung unter besonderer Berücksichtigung Palästinas bis zur Mitte des 2. Jh.v.Chr., Wissenschaftliche Untersuchungen zum Neuen Testament, 10 (Tübingen: Mohr Siebeck, 1969).

——(1989), *The Zealots: Investigations into the Jewish Freedom Movement in the Period from Herod I until 70 AD*, trans. D. Smith (Edinburgh: T. and T. Clark).

——(1994), 'Die Septuaginta als "christliche Schriftensammlung": ihre Vorgeschichte und das Problem ihres Kanons', in Hengel and A. M. Schwemer (eds.), *Die Septuaginta zwischen Judentum und Christentum* (Tübingen: Mohr Siebeck), 182–284.

——(2002), *The Septuagint as Christian Scripture: Its Prehistory and the Problem of its Canon*, trans. M. E. Biddle (Edinburgh: T. and T. Clark).

Hercher, R. (1873), *Epistolographoi Hellenikoi (Epistolographi Graeci)* (Paris: Didot).

Herman, G. (1997), 'The Court Society of the Hellenistic Age', in P. Cartledge, P. Garnsey, and E. S. Gruen (eds.), *Hellenistic Constructs: Essays in Culture, History, and Historiography* (Berkeley, Calif. and London: University of California Press), 199–224.

Hezser, C. (2001), *Jewish Literacy in Roman Palestine* (Tübingen: Mohr Siebeck).

Hiebert, R. J. V., C. E. Cox, and P. J. Gentry (2001), *The Old Greek Psalter. Studies in Honour of Albert Pietersma, Journal for the Study of the Old Testament*, Suppl. Ser., 332 (Sheffield: Sheffield Academic Press).

Higger, M. (1937), *Massekhet Soferim (Talmud Minor Tractates)* (New York: Hotsa'at D'vei Rabbanan).

——(1937), *Sheva Massekhot Ketanot (Talmud Minor Tractates)* (New York: Blokh).

Hirst, A., and M. S. Silk (2004), *Alexandria, Real and Imagined* (Aldershot: Ashgate).

Hody, H. (1684–5), *Contra historiam Aristeæ de lxx interpretibus dissertatio, in qua probatur illam a Judæo aliquo confictam fuisse ad conciliandam authoritatem versioni Græcæ* (Oxford).

——(1705), *De bibliorum textibus originalibus, versionibus Græcis et Latina vulgata* (Oxford).

Hoepfner, W. (2002), *Antike Bibliotheken* (Mainz am Rhein: Philip von Zabern).

Hölbl, G. (2001) [1994], *A History of the Ptolemaic Empire*, trans. T. Saavedra (London: Routledge; orig. edn.: Geschichte des Ptolemäerreiches: Politik, Ideologie und religiose Kultur von Alexander dem grossen bis zur römischen Eroberung (Darmstadt: Wissenschaftliche Buschgesellschaft, 1994).

Holladay, C. R. (1983–96), *Fragments from Hellenistic Jewish Authors*, i, *Historians*, ii, *Poets*, iii, *Aristobulus*, iv. *Orphica* (Chico, Calif.: Scholars Press).

―― (2002), 'Hellenism in the Fragmentary Hellenistic Jewish Authors: Resonance and Resistance', in J. L. Kugel (ed.), *Shem in the Tents of Japhet: Essays on the Encounter of Judaism and Hellenism* (Leiden: Brill), 66–91.

Hölscher, G., 'Josephus' (1916), in Pauly–Wissowa (*Realencyclopädie der Classischen Altertumswissenschaft* (Stuttgart, 1890–).

Honigman, S. (2002), 'The Jewish "Politeuma" at Heracleopolis': Review of M. S. Cowey and K. Maresch, *Urkunden des Politeuma der Juden von Herakleopolis (144/3–133/2 v. Chr.) (P. Polit. Iud.)*' (2001), *Scripta Classica Israelica*, 21: 251–66.

―― (2003), *The Septuagint and Homeric Scholarship in Alexandria: A Study in the Narrative of the Letter of Aristeas* (London: Routledge).

―― (2007), 'The Narrative Function of the King and the Library in the Letter of Aristeas', in T. Rajak, S. Pearce, et al. (eds.), *Jewish Perspectives on Hellenistic Rulers* (Berkeley, Calif.: University of California Press), 196–232.

Horbury, W. (1994), 'Jewish Inscriptions and Jewish Literature in Egypt, with Special Reference to Ecclesiasticus', in J. W. van Henten and P. W. van der Horst (eds.), *Studies in Early Jewish Epigraphy* (Leiden: Brill), 9–43.

Horbury, W. (ed.) (1999), *Hebrew Study from Ezra to Ben-Yehuda* (Edinburgh: T. and T. Clark).

―― W. D. Davies, and J. Sturdy (eds.) (1999), *The Cambridge History of Judaism*, iii. *The Early Roman Period* (Cambridge: Cambridge University Press).

Horrocks, G. C. (1997), *Greek: A History of the Language and its Speakers*, Longman Linguistics Library (London: Longman).

Horsley, G. H. R. (1989), *New Documents Illustrating Early Christianity*, v. *Linguistic Essays* (North Ryde, NSW: Ancient History Documentary Research Centre, Macquarie University).

Humphreys, W. L. (1973). 'A Lifestyle for the Diaspora: A Study of the Tales of Esther and Daniel', *Journal of Biblical Literature* 92, 211–23.

Hurtado, L. W. (2006), The Earliest Christian Artifacts: Manuscripts and Christian Origins (Grand Rapids, Mich.: Eerdmans).

Huss, W. (2001), *Ägypten in hellenistischer Zeit: 332–30 v.Chr* (Munich: Beck).

Hyvärinen, K. (1977), *Die Übersetzung von Aquila* (Lund: LiberLäromedel-Gleerup).

Inowlocki, S. (2005), 'Neither Adding nor Omitting Anything: Josephus' Promise not to Modify the Scriptures in Greek and Latin Context', *Journal of Jewish Studies*, 56: 48–65.

Isaac, B. (1992), 'The Babatha Archive: A Review Article', *Israel Exploration Journal*, 42: 62–75.

——(2003), 'Roman Religious Policy and the Bar Kokhba War', in P. Schäfer (ed.), *The Bar Kokhba War Reconsidered: New Perspectives on the Second Jewish Revolt against Rome* (Tübingen: Mohr Siebeck), 37–54.

——(2004), *The Invention of Racism in Classical Antiquity* (Princeton, NJ: Princeton University Press).

——and A. Oppenheimer (1996), *Studies on the Jewish Diaspora in the Hellenistic and Roman Periods*, Te'uda, 12 (Tel Aviv: Tel Aviv University).

Jackson, C. N. (1912), 'An Ancient Letter-Writer–Alciphron', in H. W. Smyth (ed.), *Harvard Essays on Classical Subjects* (Boston and New York: Houghton Mifflin Company), 67–96.

Jacob, C., and F. de Polignac (2000) [1992], *Alexandria, Third Century BC: The Knowledge of the World in a Single City*, trans. C. Clement (Alexandria: Harpocrates Publishing; orig. edn.: *Alexandrie, IIIe siècle av. J.-C. Tous les savoirs du monde ou le rêve d'universalité des Ptolémées* (Paris: Éditions Autrement, 1992).

Jacobs, A. (2003), 'The Lion and the Lamb: Reconsidering "Jewish–Christian Relations" in Antiquity', in A. H. Becker and A. Y. Reed (eds.), *The Ways That Never Parted: Jews and Christians in Late Antiquity and the Early Middle Ages* (Tübingen: Mohr Siebeck), 95–118.

Jacobson, H. (1983), *The Exagoge of Ezekiel* (Cambridge: Cambridge University Press).

——(1996), *A Commentary on Pseudo-Philo's Liber Antiquitatum Biblicarum, with Latin Text and English Translation*, Arbeiten zur Geschichte des antiken Judentums und des Urchristentums, 31, 2 vols. (Leiden: Brill).

——(2006), 'Artapanus Judaeus', *Journal of Jewish Studies*, 57: 210–21.

Jaffee, M. S. (2001), *Torah in the Mouth: Writing and Oral Tradition in Palestinian Judaism, 200 BCE–400 CE* (Oxford: Oxford University Press).

Janowitz, N. (1991), 'The Rhetoric of Translation: Three Early Perspectives on Translating Torah', *Harvard Theological Review*, 84: 129–40.

Janse, M. (2002), 'Aspects of Bilingualism in the History of the Greek Language', in J. N. Adams, M. Janse, and S. Swain (eds.), *Bilingualism in Ancient Society: Language Contact and the Written Word* (Oxford: Oxford University Press), 332–90.

Jellicoe, S. (1968), *The Septuagint and Modern Study* (Oxford: Clarendon Press).

——(1974), *Studies in the Septuagint: Origins, Recensions, and Interpretations*, (New York: Ktav).

Jobes, K. H., and M. Silva (2000), *Invitation to the Septuagint* (Grand Rapids, Mich.: Baker Academic).

Johnson, S. R. (2004), *Historical Fictions and Hellenistic Jewish Identity: Third Maccabees in its Cultural Context*, Hellenistic Culture and Society, 43 (Berkeley, Calif., and London: University of California Press).

Jones, S., and S. Pearce (1998), *Jewish Local Patriotism and Self-Identification in the Graeco-Roman Period*, Journal for the Study of the Pseudepigrapha, Suppl. Ser., 31 (Sheffield: Sheffield Academic Press).

Joosten, J. (2003), 'On Aramaicizing Renderings in the Septuagint', in M. F. J. Baasten and W. T. van Peursen (eds.), *Hamlet on a Hill: Semitic and Greek Studies Presented to Professor T. Muraoka on the Occasion of His Sixty-Fifth Birthday* (Leuven: Peeters), 587–600.

Kahana, A. (1956), *Ha-Sefarim Ha-Hitzoniim*, 2 vols. (Tel Aviv: Masada).

Kalmin, R. L. (1999), *The Sage in Jewish Society of Late Antiquity* (London: Routledge).

——, and S. Schwartz (2003), *Jewish Culture and Society under the Christian Roman Empire*, Interdisciplinary Studies in Ancient Culture and Religion, 3 (Leuven: Peeters).

Kamesar, A. (1993), *Jerome, Greek Scholarship and the Hebrew Bible: A Study of the Quaestiones Hebraicae in Genesim*, Oxford Classical Monographs (Oxford: Clarendon Press).

Karrer, M. (2006), 'The Epistle to the Hebrews and the Septuagint', in *Septuagint Research: Issues and Challenges in the Study of Greek Scriptures. Septuagint and Cognate Studies*, ed. W. Kraus and G. Wooden (Atlanta: Society of Biblical Literature), 335–54.

Kasher, A. (1985), *The Jews in Hellenistic and Roman Egypt: The Struggle for Equal Rights*, Texte und Studien zum antiken Judentum, 7 (Tübingen: Mohr Siebeck).

Kerkeslager, A. (1998), 'Jewish Pilgrimage and Jewish Identity in Hellenistic and Early Roman Egypt', in D. Frankfurter (ed.), *Pilgrimage and Holy Space in Late Antique Egypt* (Leiden: Brill), 99–225.

Kiefer, J. (2005), *Exil und Diaspora: Begrifflichkeit und Deutungen im antiken Judentum und in der hebräischen Bibel*, Arbeiten zur Bibel und ihrer Geschichte, 19 (Leipzig: Evangelische Verlagsanstalt).

Kippenberg, H. G. (1997), 'Magic in Roman Civil Discourse: Why Rituals Could Be Illegal', in P. Schäfer and H. G. Kippenberg (eds.), *Envisioning Magic: A Princeton Seminar and Symposium* (Leiden: Brill), 137–63.

Kister, M. (1998), 'A Common Heritage: Biblical Interpretation at Qumran and its Implications', in M. E. Stone and E. G. Chazon (eds.), *Biblical Perspectives: Early Use and Interpretation of the Bible in Light of the Dead*

Sea Scrolls, Proceedings of the First International Symposium of the Orion Center for the Study of the Dead Sea Scrolls and Associated Literature, 12–14 May 1996 (Leiden: Brill), 101–11.

Kittel, G., and G. Friedrich (1932–79), *Theologisches Wörterbuch zum Neuen Testament*, 11 vols. (Stuttgart: W. Kohlhammer).

——G. Friedrich, and G. W. Bromiley (1964), *Theological Dictionary of the New Testament*, 10 vols. (Grand Rapids, Mich.: Eerdmans).

Klawans, J. (2006), *Purity, Sacrifice, and the Temple: Symbolism and Supersessionism in the Study of Ancient Judaism* (Oxford and New York: Oxford University Press).

Kloppenborg, J. S. (2000), 'Dating Theodotos (*CIJ* II 1404)', *Journal of Jewish Studies*, 51: 243–80.

Kock, T. (1880–8), *Comicorum atticorum fragmenta*, 3 vols. (Leipzig: Teubner).

Kraabel, A. T.(1992a), 'Impact of the Discovery of the Sardis Synagogue', in J. A. Overman and R. S. MacLennan (eds.), *Diaspora Jews and Judaism* (Atlanta, Ga.: Scholars Press), 269–91.

——(1992b), 'Paganism and Judaism: the Sardis Evidence', in J. A. Overman and R. S. MacLennan (eds.), *Diaspora Jews and Judaism* (Atlanta, Ga.: Scholars Press), 237–56.

Kraeling, C. H. (1956), *The Synagogue: The Excavations at Dura Europus. Final Report 8.1* (New Haven, Conn.: Yale University Press).

Kraemer, R. S. (1989), 'On the Meaning of the Term "Jew" in Greco-Roman Inscriptions', *Harvard Theological Review*, 82: 35–53.

——(1998), When Asenath Met Joseph: A Late Antique Tale of the Biblical Patriarch and his Egyptian Wife Reconsidered (New York and Oxford: Oxford University Press).

Kraft, R. A. (1975), *Septuagintal Lexicography* (rev. edn., Missoula, Mont.: Scholars Press).

——(2003), 'The "Textual Mechanics" of Early Jewish LXX/OG Papyri and Fragments', in S. McKendrick and O. O'Sullivan (eds.), *The Bible as Book: The Transmission of the Greek Text* (London: British Library), 51–72.

Kreuzer, S. (2007), 'Die Septuagint im Kontext alexandrinischer Kultur und Bildung', in *Im Brennpunkt: Die Septuaginta. Band 3. Studien zur Theologie, Anthropologie, Ekklesiologie, Eschatologie und Liturgie der Griechischen Bibel*, ed. H.-J. Fabry and D. Bohler (Stuttgart: W. Kohlhammer), 28–55.

——and J. P. Lesch (2004), *Im Brennpunkt: die Septuaginta. ii. Studien zur Entstehung und Bedeutung der Griechischen Bibel*, Beiträge zur Wissenschaft vom Alten und Neuen Testament, 161 (Stuttgart: W. Kohlhammer).

Kroll, J. H. (2001), 'The Greek Inscriptions of the Sardis Synagogue', *Harvard Theological Review*, 94: 5–127.

Kugel, J. L. (1998), *Traditions of the Bible: A Guide to the Bible as it was at the Start of the Common Era* (Cambridge, Mass.: Harvard University Press).

——(ed.) (2002), *Shem in the Tents of Japhet: Essays on the Encounter of Judaism and Hellenism*, Supplements to the Journal for the Study of Judaism, 74 (Leiden: Brill).

Kuttner, A. (2005), 'Cabinet Fit for a Queen: The "Lithika" as Posidippus' Gem Museum', in K. J. Gutzwiller (ed.), *The New Posidippus: A Hellenistic Poetry Book* (Oxford: Oxford University Press), 141–65.

La'da, C. A. (2002), *Foreign Ethnics in Hellenistic Egypt*, Prosopographica Ptolemaica, 10/ Studia Hellenistica, 38 (Leuven: Peeters).

Lamberton, R. (1986), *Homer the Theologian: Neoplatonist Allegorical Reading and the Growth of the Epic Tradition*, Transformation of the Classical Heritage, 9 (Berkeley, Calif.: University of California Press).

Lampe, G. W. H. (1961), *A Patristic Greek Lexicon* (Oxford: Clarendon Press).

de Lange, N. R. M. (1976), *Origen and the Jews: Studies in Jewish–Christian Relations in Third-Century Palestine*, University of Cambridge Oriental Publications, 25 (Cambridge: Cambridge University Press).

——(1996a), 'The Hebrew Language in the Jewish Diaspora', *Te'uda*, 12: 111–37.

——(1996b), 'The Revival of the Hebrew Language in the Third Century CE', *Jewish Studies Quarterly*, 3: 342–58.

——(1999), 'A Thousand Years of Hebrew in Byzantium', in W. Horbury (ed.), *Hebrew Study from Ezra to Ben-Yehuda* (Edinburgh: T. and T. Clark), 147–61.

——and M. Harl (1983), *Origène, sur les écritures et la lettre à Africanus sur l'histoire de Suzanne. Introduction, texte, traduction et notes* (Paris: Éditions du Cerf).

Langslow, D. (2002), 'Approaching Bilingualism in Corpus Languages', in J. N. Adams, M. Janse, and S. Swain (eds.), *Bilingualism in Ancient Society: Language Contact and the Written Word* (Oxford: Oxford University Press), 23–51.

Le Boulluec, A. (2000), 'Alien Wisdom', in C. Jacob and F. de Polignac (eds.), *Alexandria, Third Century BC: The Knowledge of the World in a Single City* (Alexandria: Harpocrates Publishing), 56–72.

Le Déaut, R. (1984), 'La Septante: un Targum', in R. Kuntzmann, J. Schlosser, and R. Arnaldez (eds.), *Études sur le judaïsme hellénistique. Congrès de Strasbourg, 1983* (Paris: Éditions du Cerf), 147–95.

Lebram, J. C. H. (1975), 'Ein Streit um die Hebräische Bibel und die Septuaginta', in T. H. Lunsingh Scheurleer and G. H. M. Posthumus

Meyjes (eds.), *Leiden University in the Seventeenth Century: An Exchange of Learning* (Leiden: Universitaire Pers Leiden/Brill), 21–63.

Lee, J. A. L. (1983), *A Lexical Study of the Septuagint Version of the Pentateuch*, Septuagint and Cognate Studies Series, 14 (Chico, Calif.: Scholars Press).

——(2003), ' "A Lexical Study" Thirty Years On, with Observations on "Order" Words in the LXX Pentateuch', in S. M. Paul, R. A. Kraft et al. (eds.), *Emanuel: Studies in Hebrew Bible, Septuagint and Dead Sea Scrolls in Honor of Emanuel Tov* (Leiden: Brill), 513–24.

Lefkowitz, M. R. (1981), *The Lives of the Greek Poets* (London: Duckworth).

Lehnardt, A. (1999), *Bibliographie zu den Jüdischen Schriften aus hellenistisch-römischer Zeit* (Gütersloh: Gütersloher Verlagshaus).

Leiman, S. Z. (1976), *The Canonization of Hebrew Scripture: The Talmudic and Midrashic Evidence* (Hamden, Conn.: Archon Books).

Leon, H. J. (1995), *The Jews of Ancient Rome* (rev. edn., Peabody, Mass.: Hendrickson Publishers).

Leonhardt, J. (2001). *Jewish Worship in Philo of Alexandria*, Texts and Studies in Ancient Judaism 84 (Tübingen: Mohr Siebeck).

Levine, L. I. (1989), *The Rabbinic Class of Roman Palestine in Late Antiquity* (Jerusalem and New York: Yad Izhak Ben-Zvi/Jewish Theological Seminary of America).

——(2005), *The Ancient Synagogue: The First Thousand Years* (2nd edn., New Haven, Conn. and London: Yale University Press).

Levinskaya, I. (1997), *The Book of Acts in its First Century Setting*, v. *Diaspora Setting* (Grand Rapids, Mich.: Eerdmans).

Lewis, B. (2004), *From Babel to Dragomans: Interpreting the Middle East* (London: Weidenfeld and Nicolson).

Lewis, J. P. (1964), 'What Do We Mean by Jabneh?', *Journal of Bible and Religion*, 32: 125–32.

Lewis, N. (1989), *The Documents from the Bar Kokba Period in the Cave of Letters: Greek Papyri* (Jerusalem: Israel Exploration Society).

Lieu, J. (2002), 'Not Hellenes but Philistines? The Maccabees and Josephus Defining the "Other"', *Journal of Jewish Studies*, 53: 246–63.

——(2004), *Christian Identity in the Jewish and Graeco-Roman World* (Oxford: Oxford University Press).

——J. North, and T. Rajak (eds.) (1992), *The Jews among Pagans and Christians in the Roman Empire* (London: Routledge).

Lim, T. H. (1997), *Holy Scripture in the Qumran Commentaries and Pauline Letters* (Oxford: Clarendon Press).

——(2000), *The Dead Sea Scrolls in their Historical Context* (Edinburgh: T. and T. Clark).

Linder, A. (1987), *The Jews in Roman Imperial Legislation* (Detroit: Wayne State University Press).
Littré, E. (1861), *Œuvres complètes d'Hippocrate*, ix. (Paris: Baillière).
Long, L. (2001), *Translating the Bible from the Seventh to the Seventeenth Century* (Aldershot: Ashgate).
Lynch, J. P. (1972), *Aristotle's School: A Study of a Greek Educational Institution* (Berkeley, Calif.: University of California Press).
Ma, J. T. (1999), *Antiochos III and the Cities of Western Asia Minor* (Oxford: Oxford University Press).
——(2003), 'Kings', in A. Erskine (ed.), *A Companion to the Hellenistic World* (Oxford: Blackwell), 177–95.
Magness, J. (2005), 'The Date of the Sardis Synagogue in Light of the Numismatic Evidence', *American Journal of Archaeology* 109(3), 443–75.
McGing, B. (2002), 'Population and Proselytism. How Many Jews were there in the Ancient World?', in J. R. Bartlett (ed.), *Jews in the Hellenistic and Roman Cities* (London: Routledge), 88–106.
McKay, H. A. (1994), *Sabbath and Synagogue: The Question of Sabbath in Ancient Judaism*, Religions in the Graeco-Roman World, 122 (Leiden: Brill).
McKendrick, S., and O. A. O'Sullivan (eds.) (2003), *The Bible as Book: The Transmission of the Greek Text* (London: British Library).
McKenzie, J. S. (2003), 'Glimpsing Alexandria from Archaeological Evidence', *Journal of Roman Archaeology*, 16: 35–63.
——S. Gibson, and A. Reyes (2004), 'Reconstructing the Serapeum in Alexandria from the Archaeological Evidence', *Journal of Roman Archaeology*, 94: 73–121.
McLay, T. (2003), *The Use of the Septuagint in New Testament Research* (Grand Rapids, Mich.: Eerdmans).
MacLeod, R. M. (2000), *The Library of Alexandria: Centre of Learning in the Ancient World* (London: I. B. Tauris).
Maddox, G. (1998), 'Prophetic Religion and the Roots of Political Opposition', in T. Hillard, R. Kearsley, et al. (eds.), *Ancient History in a Modern University* (Grand Rapids, Mich.: Eerdmans), 459–67.
Maehler, H. (2004), 'Alexandria, the Mouseion, and Cultural Identity', in A. Hirst and M. S. Silk (eds.), *Alexandria, Real and Imagined* (Aldershot: Ashgate), 1–14.
Marcovich, M. (2006), *Iustini Martyris Dialogus cum Tryphone*, Patristische Texte und Studien, 47 (Berlin: de Gruyter).
Maresch, K., and J. S. Cowey (2003), 'A Recurrent Inclination to Isolate the Jews from their Ptolemaic Environment? Eine Antwort auf Sylvie Honigman', *Scripta Classica Israelica*, 22: 307–10.

Mason, S. (ed.) (2000), *Flavius Josephus, Translation and Commentary* (Leiden: Brill).

Meecham, H. G. (1935), *The Letter of Aristeas,: A Linguistic Study with Special Reference to the Greek Bible*, Publications of the University of Manchester, 241 (Manchester: Manchester University Press).

Meeks, W. A. (2003), 'A Nazi New Testament Professor Reads His Bible: The Strange Case of Gerhard Kittel', in H. Naijman and J. H. Newman (eds.), *The Idea of Biblical Interpretation: Essays in Honor of James L. Kugel* (Leiden: Brill), 513–44.

Mélèze Modrzejewski, J. (1988), 'Philiscos de Milet et le jugement de Salomon: la première référence grecque à la bible', *Bullettino dell'Istituto di diritto romano*, 30: 571–97.

——(1993), 'How to be a Jew in Hellenistic Egypt?', in S. J. D. Cohen and E. S. Frerichs (eds.), *Diasporas in Antiquity* (Atlanta, Ga.: Scholars Press), 65–92.

——(1995), *The Jews of Egypt: From Rameses II to Emperor Hadrian*, trans. R. Cornman (Edinburgh: T. & T. Clark).

——(1996), 'Jewish Law and Hellenistic Legal Practice in the Light of Greek Papyri from Egypt', in N. Hecht et al. (eds.), *An Introduction to the History and Sources of Jewish Law* (Oxford: Clarendon Press), 75–99.

——(1997), 'La Septante comme nomos. Comment la Torah est devenue une "loi civique" pour les Juifs d'Egypte', *Annali di Science Religiose*, 2: 143–58.

Mendels, D. (1987), *The Land of Israel as a Political Concept in Hasmonean Literature* (Tübingen: Mohr Siebeck).

Mendelson, A. (1982), *Secular Education in Philo of Alexandria*, Monographs of the Hebrew Union College, 7 (Cincinnati, Ohio: Hebrew Union College Press).

——(1988), *Philo's Jewish Identity*, Brown Judaic Studies, 161 (Atlanta, Ga.: Scholars Press).

Mez, A. (1895), *Die Bibel des Josephus Untersucht fur Buch V-VII der Archäologie* (Basle).

Millar, F. (1992), 'The Jews of the Graeco-Roman Diaspora between Paganism and Christianity, AD 312–438', in J. Lieu, J. North, and T. Rajak (eds.), *The Jews among Pagans and Christians in the Roman Empire* (London: Routledge), 97–123.

——(1997), 'Hellenistic History in a Near Eastern Perspective: The Book of Daniel', in P. Cartledge, P. Garnsey, and E. S. Gruen (eds.), *Hellenistic Constructs: Essays in Culture, History, and Historiography* (Berkeley, Calif. and London: University of California Press), 89–104.

——(2004), 'Christian Emperors, Christian Church and the Jews of the Diaspora in the Greek East, CE 379–450', *Journal of Jewish Studies*, 55: 1–24.

——(2006), *The Greek World, the Jews and the East*, iii. ed. H. M. Cotton and G. M. Rogers (Chapel Hill, NC: University of North Carolina Press).
Mitchell, S. (1999), 'The Cult of Theos Hypsistos', in P. Athanassiadi and M. Frede (eds.), *Pagan Monotheism in Late Antiquity* (Oxford: Clarendon Press), 81–148.
Momigliano, A. (1975), *Alien Wisdom: The Limits of Hellenization* (Cambridge: Cambridge University Press).
——(1990), *The Classical Foundations of Modern Historiography*, Sather Classical Lectures, 54 (Berkeley, Calif.: University of California Press).
——(1992), *Nono contributo alla storia degli studi classici e del mondo antico* (Rome: Edizioni di storia e letteratura).
Mondésert, C. (ed.) (1984), *Le Monde grec ancien et la bible, bible de tous les temps*, i. (Paris: Beauchesne).
Montevecchi, O. (1956), 'Pantokrator', in *Studi in onore di Aristide Calderini e Roberto Paribeni* (Milan: Ceschina), 401–30.
——(1999), *Bibbia e papyri* (Barcelona: Institut de Teologia Fonamental).
Moore, C. A. (ed.) (1977), *Daniel, Esther, and Jeremiah: The Additions, Anchor Bible* (Garden City, NY: Doubleday).
Mooren, L. (1975), The Aulic Titulature in Ptolemaic Egypt: Introduction and Prosopography (Brussels: Paleis der Academiën).
Morgan, T. (1998), *Literate Education in the Hellenistic and Roman Worlds* (Cambridge: Cambridge University Press).
Morris, J. (1987), 'The Jewish Philosopher Philo', in E. Schürer, *The History of the Jewish People in the Age of Jesus Christ (175 BC–AD 135), A New English Edition*, ed. F. Millar, G. Vermes, and M. Goodman (Edinburgh: T. and T. Clark), 809–89.
Mossé, C. (2000), 'Demetrius of Phaleron: A Philosopher in Power?', in C. Jacob and F. de Polignac, *Alexandria, Third Century BC: The Knowledge of the World in a Single City*, trans. C. Clement (Alexandria: Harpocrates Publishing), 74–82.
Moulton, J. H., and G. D. D. Milligan (1914), *The Vocabulary of the Greek Testament Illustrated from the Papyri and Other Non-Literary Sources* (London: Hodder and Stoughton).
Mulder, M. J., and H. Sysling (eds.) (1988), *Mikra: Text, Translation, Reading and Interpretation of the Hebrew Bible in Ancient Judaism and Early Christianity*, Compendia Rerum Iudaicarum ad Novum Testamentum, Section 2, i. (Assen: Van Gorcum).
Müller, M. (1996), *The First Bible of the Church: A Plea for the Septuagint*, Copenhagen International Seminar, 1 (Sheffield: Sheffield Academic Press).
Murphy, F. J. (1988), 'Idolatry in Pseudo-Philo', *Journal of Biblical Literature*, 107: 275–87.

Murray, O. (1967), 'Aristeas and Ptolemaic Kingship', *Journal of Theological Studies*, 18: 337–71.

——(1975), 'Aristeas and His Sources', *Studia Patristica*, 12: 123–8.

——(1986), 'Aristeasbrief', *Reallexikon für Antike und Christentum*, Suppl. 1: 537–87.

Myers, D. N. (1998), 'Between Diaspora and Zion: History, Memory and the Jerusalem Scholars', in D. N. Myers and D. B. Ruderman (eds.), *The Jewish Past Revisited: Reflections on Modern Jewish Historians* (New Haven, Conn. and London: Yale University Press), 88–103.

——and D. B. Ruderman (1998), *The Jewish Past Revisited: Reflections on Modern Jewish Historians*, Studies in Jewish Culture and Society (New Haven, Conn. and London: Yale University Press).

Naveh, J. and S. Shaked (1993), *Magic Spells and Formulae: Aramaic Incantations of Late Antiquity* (Jerusalem: Magnes Press).

Neusner, J. (1965–70), *A History of the Jews in Babylonia*, 5 vols. (Leiden: Brill).

——and W. S. Green (1989), *Writing with Scripture: The Authority and Uses of the Hebrew Bible in the Torah of Formative Judaism* (Minneapolis, Minn.: Fortress Press).

Newman, J. H. (1999), *Praying by the Book: The Scripturalization of Prayer in Second Temple Judaism*, Early Judaism and its Literature, 14 (Atlanta, Ga.: Scholars Press).

Nickelsburg, G. W. E. (1984), 'The Bible Rewritten and Expanded', in M. E. Stone (ed.), *Jewish Writings of the Second Temple Period* (Assen: Van Gorcum), 89–156.

Niditch, S. (1996), *Oral World and Written Word: Ancient Israelite Literature* (Louisville, Ken.: Westminster John Knox Press).

Niehoff, M. (2001), *Philo on Jewish Identity and Culture*, Texte und Studien zum antiken Judentum, 86 (Tübingen: Mohr Siebeck).

Nikiprowetzky, V. (1977), *Le Commentaire de l'écriture chez Philon d'Alexandrie, son caractère et sa portée: observations philologiques*, Arbeiten zur Literatur und Geschichte des Hellenistischen Judentums, 11 (Leiden: Brill).

Noam, V. (2003), *Megillat Ta'anit: ha–nusahim, pesharim, toldotehem: betseruf mahadurah bikortit. Versions, Interpretation, History, with a Critical Edition* (Jerusalem: Yad Yitzhak ben Zvi).

Olofsson, S. (1990a), *God is My Rock: A Study of Translation Technique and Theological Exegesis in the Septuagint*, Coniectanea biblica, Old Testament Series, 31 (Stockholm: Almqvist and Wiksell).

——(1990b), *The LXX Version: A Guide to the Translation Technique of the Septuagint*, Coniectanea biblica, Old Testament Series, 30 (Stockholm: Almqvist and Wiksell).

Olsson, B., and M. Zetterholm (eds.) (2003), *The Ancient Synagogue from its Origins until 200 CE, Papers presented at an International Conference at Lund University, 14–17 Oct. 2001*, Coniectanea Biblica, New Testament Series, 39 (Stockholm: Almqvist and Wiksell).

Omanson, R. L., and P. A. Noss (eds.) (1997), *A Handbook on the Book of Esther: The Hebrew and Greek Texts*, United Bible Societies Handbook Series (New York: United Bible Societies).

Oppenheimer, A. (2003), 'The Ban on Circumcision as a Cause of the Revolt: A Reconsideration', in P. Schäfer (ed.), *The Bar Kokhba War Reconsidered: New Perspectives on the Second Jewish Revolt against Rome* (Tübingen: Mohr Siebeck), 55–69.

Orlinsky, H. M. (1975), 'The Septuagint as Holy Writ and the Philosophy of the Translators', *Hebrew Union College Annual*, 46: 89–114.

Orru, C. (2002), 'Ein Raub der Flammen? Die königliche Bibliothek von Alexandria', in W. Hoepfner (ed.), *Antike Bibliotheken* (Mainz am Rhein: Philip von Zabern), 31–8.

Orth, W. (2001), 'Ptolemaios II und die Septuaginta-Übersetzung', in H.-J. Fabry and U. Offerhaus (eds.), *Im Brennpunkt: Die Septuaginta. Studien zur Entstehung und Bedeutung der griechischen Bibel* (Stuttgart: W. Kohlhammer), 97–41.

Overman, J. A., and R. S. MacLennan (1992), *Diaspora Jews and Judaism: Essays in Honor of and in Dialogue with A. Thomas Kraabel*, South Florida Studies in the History of Judaism, 41 (Atlanta, Ga.: Scholars Press).

Paget, J. C. (1994), *The Epistle of Barnabas: Outlook and Background*, Wissenschaftliche Untersuchungen zum Neuen Testament, 2 (Tübingen: Mohr Siebeck).

Paget, J. C. (2004), 'Jews and Christians in Ancient Alexandria from the Ptolemies to Caracalla', in A. Hirst and M. S. Silk (eds.), *Alexandria, Real and Imagined* (Aldershot: Ashgate), 143–66.

Parente, F. (1972), 'La Lettera di Aristea come fonte per la storia del giudaismo alessandrino durante la prima metà del I secolo a.C.', *Annali della Scuola normale superiore di Pisa*, 2: 177–237.

Parsons, E. A. (1952), *The Alexandrian Library, Glory of the Hellenic World: Its Rise, Antiquities, and Destructions* (London: Cleaver-Hume Press).

Paul, A. (1986), 'La Bible grecque d'Aquila et l'idéologie du judaïsme ancien', *Aufstieg und Niedergang der Römischen Welt*, II, xx, 1 (Berlin: de Gruyter), 221–45.

——(1987a), 'La Torah sapienziale a confronto con il mondo culturale ellenistico. La Lettre d'Aristée, Sapienza e Torah', in *Atti della XXIX Settimana Biblica* (Bologna), 88–97.

——(1987b), *Le Judaïsme ancien et la Bible* (Paris: Desclée).

—— (1988), 'Traductions grecques de la Bible avant la Septante?', in M. M. Mactoux and E. Geny (eds.), *Mélanges P. Lévêque* (Paris: Belles Lettres), 315–28.

Paul, S. M., R. A. Kraft, et al. (eds.) (2003), *Emanuel: Studies in Hebrew Bible, Septuagint, and Dead Sea Scrolls in Honor of Emanuel Tov*, Supplements to *Vetus Testamentum*, 94 (Leiden: Brill).

Pearce, S. J. K. (2004a), 'Jerusalem as Mother City in the Writings of Philo of Alexandria', in J. M. G. Barclay (ed.), *Negotiating Diaspora: Jewish Strategies in the Roman Empire* (London: T. and T. Clark), 19–37.

—— (2004b), 'King Moses: Notes on Philo's Portrait of Moses as an Ideal Leader in the Life of Moses', in E. Gannagé, P. Crone, et al. (eds.), *The Greek Strand in Islamic Political Thought*, Proceedings of the Conference held at the Institute for Advanced Study, Princeton, 16–27 June 2003, Mélanges de l'Université Saint-Joseph, 57 (Beirut), 37–74.

—— (2007a), *The Land of the Body. Studies in Philo's Representation of Egypt*, Wissenschaftliche Untersuchungen zum Neuen Testament, 208 (Tübingen: Mohr Siebeck).

—— (2007b), 'Translating for Ptolemy. Patriotism and Politics in the Greek Pentateuch?', in T. Rajak, S. Pearce, et al. (eds.), *Jewish Perspectives on Hellenistic Rulers* (Berkeley, Calif.: University of California Press), 165–89.

Pelletier, A. (1962), *La Lettre d'Aristée à Philocrate*, Sources Chrétiennes, 89 (Paris: Éditions du Cerf).

Peremans, W. (1985), 'Notes sur les traductions de textes non littéraires sous les Lagides', *Chronique d'Égypte*, 60: 248–62.

Perrot, C. (1988), 'The Reading of the Bible in the Ancient Synagogue', in M. J. Mulder and H. Sysling (eds.), *Mikra: Text, Translation, Reading and Interpretation of the Hebrew Bible in Ancient Judaism and Early Christianity* (Assen and Philadelphia, Pa.: Van Gorcum/Fortress Press), 137–59.

Pestman, P. W. (1981), *A Guide to the Zenon Archive*, Papyrologica Lugduno-Batava 21A (Leiden: Brill).

Pfeiffer, R. (1968), *History of Classical Scholarship: i, From the Beginnings to the End of the Hellenistic Age* (Oxford: Clarendon Press).

Pietersma, A. (1985), 'Septuagint Research, A Plea for a Return to Basic Issues', *Vetus Testamentum*, 35: 296–311.

—— (2002), 'A New Paradigm for Addressing Old Questions: The Relevance of the Interlinear Model for the Study of the Septuagint', in J. Cook (ed.), *Bible and Computer, Stellenbosch AIBI 6 Conference, Proceedings* of the *Association Internationale Bible et Informatique, 'From Alpha to Byte', University of Stellenbosch, 17–21 July 2000* (Leiden: Brill), 337–64.

——and B. G. Wright (eds.) (2007), *A New English Translation of the Septuagint and other Greek Translations Traditionally Included under that Title, The Psalms* (New York and Oxford: Oxford University Press).
Pinault, J. R. (1992), *Hippocratic Lives and Legends, Studies in Ancient Medicine*, iv. (Leiden: Brill).
Poorthuis, M. and C. Safrai (eds.) (1996), *The Centrality of Jerusalem* (Kampen: Kok Pharos).
Porten, B. (1968), *Archives from Elephantine: The Life of an Ancient Jewish Military Colony* (Berkeley, Calif.: University of California Press).
Preisendanz, K., and A. Henrichs (1973), *Papyri Graecae Magicae*, 2 vols. (2nd edn., Stuttgart: Teubner).
Rabello, A. M. (1987), *Giustiniano, Ebrei e Samaritani alla luce delle fonti storico-letterarie, ecclesiastiche e giuridiche*, Monografie del Vocabolario di Giustiniano, 2 vols. (Milan: A. Giuffrè).
Rabin, C. (1968), 'The Translation Process and the Character of the Septuagint', *Textus*, 6: 1–26.
Rabinowitz, L. J. (1971), 'Onkelos and Aquila', in *Encyclopaedia Judaica*, 12: 1405–6.
Rahlfs, A., and Hauhart, R. (2006), *Septuaginta* (Stuttgart: Deutsche Bibelgesellschaft).
Rajak, T. (1975), 'Flavius Josephus: Jewish History and the Greek World', Diss. University of Oxford, http://pace.mcmaster.ca/York/york/dissert.htm?id=13.
——(1983), 'Josephus and the "Archaeology" of the Jews', in *The Jewish Dialogue with Greece and Rome: Studies in Cultural and Social Interaction* (Leiden: Brill, 2000; orig. edn.: G. Vermes and J. Neusner (eds.), *Essays in Honour of Yigael Yadin* (Totowa, NJ: Allanheld Osmun), 465–77, 11–37.
Rajak, T. (1992), 'The Jewish Community and its Boundaries', in J. Lieu, J. North, and T. Rajak (eds.), *The Jews among Pagans and Christians in the Roman Empire* (London: Routledge), 9–28.
——(2000), *The Jewish Dialogue with Greece and Rome: Studies in Cultural and Social Interaction*, Arbeiten zur Geschichte des antiken Judentums und des Urchristentums, 48 (Leiden: Brill).
——(2002a), *Josephus: The Historian and His Society* (2nd edn., London: Duckworth).
——(2002b), 'Synagogue and Community in the Graeco-Roman Diaspora', in J. R. Bartlett (ed.), *Jews in the Hellenistic and Roman Cities* (London: Routledge), 22–38.
——(2003), 'The Ancient Synagogue', *The Studia Philonica Annual*, 15, 100–8.

——(2005a), 'An Invitation from Ptolemy: Aristeas, Alciphron and Collective Memory', in M. Mor and J. Pastor (eds.), *For Uriel: Studies in the History of Israel in Antiquity Presented to Professor Uriel Rapaport* (Jerusalem: Zalman Shazar Centre), 145–64.

——(2005b), 'Josephus in the Diaspora', in J. C. Edmondson, S. Mason, and J. B. Rives (eds.), *Flavius Josephus and Flavian Rome* (Oxford: Oxford University Press), 79–100.

——(2007), 'Document and Rhetoric in Josephus: Revisiting the Charter for the Jews', in S. D. Cohen and J. D. Schwartz (eds.), *Studies in the Varieties of Ancient Judaism. Louis H. Feldman Jubilee Volume* (Leiden: Brill), 177–89.

——and D. Noy (2000), 'Archisynagogoi: Office, Title and Social Status in the Greco-Jewish Synagogue', in *The Jewish Dialogue with Greece and Rome: Studies in Cultural and Social Interaction* (Leiden: Brill), 393–429.

——S. Pearce, J. Aitken, and J. Dines (eds.) (2007), *Jewish Perspectives on Hellenistic Rulers*, Hellenistic Culture and Society, 50 (Berkeley, Calif.: University of California Press).

Ramelli, I., G. A. Lucchetta, and R. Radice (2004), *Allegoria* (Milan: V. & P. Università).

Rebenich, S. (2002), *Jerome. Early Church Fathers* (London: Routledge).

Reeg, G. (1985), *Die Geschichte von den zehn Martyren*, Texte und Studien zum antiken Judentum, 10 (Tübingen: Mohr Siebeck).

Reider, J. (1966), 'Completed and revised by Nigel Turner, *An Index to Aquila: Greek–Hebrew, Hebrew–Greek, Latin–Hebrew. With the Syrian and Armenian Evidence*. Vetus Testamentum Supplements, 12 (Leiden: Briu).

Reinhartz, A. (1992), 'Philo on Infanticide', in D. T. Runia (ed.), *Studia Philonica Annual*, 4, Brown Judaic Studies, 264 (Atlanta, Ga.: Scholars Press), 42–58.

Reiser, M. (2005), 'Die Quellen des neutestamentlichen Griechisch und die Frage des Judengriechischen in der Forschungsgeschichte von 1689–1989', *Biblische Zeitschrift*, 49: 46–56.

Reynolds, J. M., and R. Tannenbaum (1987), *Jews and Godfearers at Aphrodisias* (Cambridge: Cambridge Philological Society).

Reynolds, L. D., and N. G. Wilson (1991), *Scribes and Scholars: A Guide to the Transmission of Greek and Latin Literature* (3rd edn., Oxford: Clarendon Press).

Rice, E. E. (1983), *The Grand Procession of Ptolemy Philadelphus*, Oxford Classical and Philosophical Monographs (Oxford: Oxford University Press).

Richardson, P., and S. Westerholm (1991), *Law in Religious Communities in the Roman Period: The Debate Over Torah and Nomos in Post-biblical Judaism and Early Christianity*, Studies in Christianity and Judaism, 4 (Waterloo, Ont.: Canadian Corporation for Studies in Religion).
Ritschl, F. W. (1838), *Die Alexandrinischen Bibliotheken unter den ersten Ptolemäern und die Sammlung Gedichte durch Pisistratus nach Anleitung eines Plautinischen Scholions* (Breslau: G. P. Aderholz).
Roberts, C. H., and T. C. Skeat (1983), *The Birth of the Codex* (London: British Academy/Oxford University Press).
Rokeah, D. (1968), 'A New Onomastikon Fragment from Oxyrhynchus and Philo's Etymologies', *Journal of Theological Studies*, 19: 70–82.
Rokeah, D. (2001), *Justin Martyr and the Jews*, Jewish and Christian Perspectives, 5.
Rösel, M. (2007), 'The Reading and Translation of the Divine Name in the Masoretic Tradition and the Greek Pentateuch', *Journal for the Study of the Old Testament* 31.4, 411–28.
Rosenmeyer, P. A. (2001), *Ancient Epistolary Fictions: The Letter in Greek Literature* (Cambridge: Cambridge University Press).
Rowlandson, J. (2003), 'Town and Country in Ptolemaic Egypt', in A. Erskine (ed.), *A Companion to the Hellenistic World* (Oxford: Blackwell), 249–63.
Runesson, A. (2001), *The Origins of the Synagogue: A Socio-Historical Study*, Coniectanea Biblica, New Testament Series, 37 (Stockholm: Almqvist and Wiksell).
Runia, D. T. (1993), *Philo in Early Christian Literature: A Survey*, Compendia Rerum Iudaicarum ad Novum Testamentum, Section 3, iii (Assen and Philadelphia, Pa.: Van Gorcum/Fortress Press).
——(2001a), *On the Creation of the Cosmos According to Moses*, Philo of Alexandria Commentary Series, 1 (Leiden: Brill).
——(2001b), 'Philo's Reading of the Psalms', in D. T. Runia and G. E. Sterling (eds.), *In the Spirit of Faith: Studies on Philo and Early Christianity in Honor of David Hay*, Studia Philonica Annual (Atlanta Ga.: Scholar's Press), 102–21.
Rutgers, L. V. (1995), *The Jews in Late Ancient Rome: Evidence of Cultural Interaction in the Roman Diaspora*, Religions in the Graeco–Roman World, 126 (Leiden: Brill).
——(1998), *The Hidden Heritage of Diaspora Judaism*, Contributions to Biblical Exegesis and Theology, 20 (Leuven: Peeters).
——(2003), 'Justinian's Novella 146 between Jews and Christians', in R. K. Kalmin and S. Schwartz (eds.), *Jewish Culture and Society under the Christian Roman Empire* (Leuven: Peeters), 385–407.

——P. W. van der Horst, et al. (eds.) (1998), *The Use of Sacred Books in the Ancient World*, Contributions to Biblical Exegesis and Theology, 22 (Leuven: Peeters).

Rydbeck, L., and S. E. Porter (eds.) (2005), *Epochs and Styles: Selected Writings on the New Testament, Greek Language and Greek Culture in the Post–Classical Era*, Wissenschaftliche Untersuchungen zum Neuen Testament, 179 (Tübingen: Mohr Siebeck).

Sáenz-Badillos, A. (1993), *A History of the Hebrew Language*, trans. J. Elwolde (Cambridge: Cambridge University Press).

Safrai, S. (1974), 'Relations between the Diaspora and the Land of Israel', in S. Safrai and M. Stern (eds.), Compendia Rerum Iudaicarum ad Novum Testamentum, Section I, i: *The Jewish People in the First Century*, i. (Assen: van Gorcum), 184–215.

Salvesen, A. (1991), *Symmachus in the Pentateuch*, Journal of Semitic Studies Monographs, 15 (Manchester: University of Manchester).

——(1998), *Origen's Hexapla and Fragments, Papers presented at the Rich Seminar on the Hexapla, Oxford Centre for Hebrew and Jewish Studies, 25 July–3 Aug. 1994*, Texte und Studien zum antiken Judentum, 58 (Tübingen: Mohr Siebeck).

——(2003), 'The Judaizing of Christian Scripture by Origen and Jerome', in A. H. Becker and A. Y. Reed (eds.), *The Ways That Never Parted: Jews and Christians in Late Antiquity and the Early Middle Ages* (Tübingen: Mohr Siebeck), 233–58.

Samuel, A. E. (1993), 'The Ptolemies and the Ideology of Kingship', in P. Green (ed.), *Hellenistic History and Culture* (Berkeley, Calif. and Oxford: University of California Press), 168–211.

Sanders, E. P. (1990), *Jewish Law from Jesus to the Mishnah: Five Studies* (London and Philadelphia: SCM/Trinity Press International).

——(1994), *Judaism: Practice and Belief, 63 BCE–66 CE* (2nd edn., London: SCM Press).

Sandmel, S. (1978), 'Philo's Knowledge of Hebrew: The Present State of the Problem', *Studia Philonica Annual*, 5: 107–12.

Sawyer, J. F. A. (1999), *Sacred Languages and Sacred Texts. Religion in the First Christian Centuries* (London: Routledge).

Scarpat, G. (2006), *Quarto Libro dei Maccabei*, Biblica 9 (Brescia: Paideia).

Schäfer, P. (1975), 'Die sogenannte Synode von Jabne 1: Zur Trennung von Juden und Christen im 1.–2. Jh. n. Chr. 2: Der Abschluss des Kanons', *Judaica*, 31: 54–64, 116–24.

——(1992), *The Hidden and Manifest God: Some Major Themes in Early Jewish Mysticism* (Albany, NY: State University of New York Press).

——(1997), *Judeophobia: Attitudes toward the Jews in the Ancient World* (Cambridge, Mass. and London: Harvard University Press).

——(ed.) (2003), *The Bar Kokhba War Reconsidered: New Perspectives on the Second Jewish Revolt against Rome*, Texte und Studien zum antiken Judentum, 100 (Tübingen: Mohr Siebeck).

——and H. G. Kippenberg (eds.) (1997), *Envisioning Magic: A Princeton Seminar and Symposium*, Studies in the History of Religions, 75 (Leiden: Brill).

Schaper, J. (1995), *Eschatology in the Greek Psalter*, Wissenschaftliche Untersuchungen zum Neuen Testament, 76 (Tübingen: Mohr Siebeck).

——(1999), 'Hebrew and its Study in the Persian Period', in W. Horbury (ed.), *Hebrew Study from Ezra to Ben Yehuda* (Edinburgh: T. and T. Clark), 15–26.

Scharfenberg, J. G. (1780), *Prolusio de Iosephi in the Antiquitates Judaicae et versionis Alexandrinae consensu* (Leipzig).

Schechter, S. (1909), *Some Aspects of Rabbinic Theology* (London: A. and C. Black).

Scheidel, W. (2004), 'Creating a Metropolis: A Comparative Demographic Perspective', in W. V. Harris and G. Ruffini (eds.), *Ancient Alexandria between Egypt and Greece* (Leiden: Brill), 1–32.

Schepers, M. A. (1905), *Alciphronis rhetoris epistularum libri IV* (Leipzig: Teubner).

Schmidt, F. (1922), *Die Pinakes des Kallimachos*, Klassisch-philologische Studien, 1 (Berlin: Ebering).

Schmidt, W. (1986), *Untersuchungen zur Fälschung historischer Dokumente bei Pseudo-Aristaios*, Habelts Dissertationsdrucke, Reihe klassische Philologie, 37 (Bonn: Rudolf Habelt).

Schröder, B. (1996), *Die 'väterlichen Gesetze': Flavius Josephus als Vermittler von Halachah an Griechischen und Römer* (Tübingen: Mohr Siebeck).

Schürer, E. (1901–9), *Geschichte des jüdischen Volkes im Zeitalter Jesu Christi*, 3 vols. (4th edn., Leipzig: J. C. Hinrichs).

——(1973–87), *The History of the Jewish People in the Age of Jesus Christ (175 BC–AD 135), A New English Version*, ed. F. Millar, G. Vermes, and M. Goodman, 3 vols. (Edinburgh: T. & T. Clark).

Schwartz, D. R. (1992), *Studies in the Jewish Background of Christianity*, Wissenschaftliche Untersuchungen zum Neuen Testament, 60 (Tübingen: Mohr Siebeck).

——(1996), 'Temple or City? What Did Hellenistic Jews See in Jerusalem?', in M. Poorthuis and C. Safrai (eds.), *The Centrality of Jerusalem: Historical Perspectives* (Kampen: Kok Pharos), 114–27.

——(1999), 'From the Maccabees to Masada: On Diasporan Historiography of the Second Temple Period', in A. Oppenheimer (ed.),

Jüdische Geschichte in hellenistisch-römischer Zeit: Wege der Forschung: vom alten zum neuen Schürer (Munich: R. Oldenbourg), 29–40.

——(2000), 'How at Home Were the Jews of the Hellenistic Diaspora?' *Classical Philology*, 95: 349–57.

——(2004), *The Second Book of Maccabees: Introduction, Hebrew Translation and Commentary* (Jerusalem: Yad Ben-Zvi Press).

——(2005), 'From Punishment to Program, From Program to Punishment: Josephus and the Rabbis on Exile', in M. Mor and J. Pastor (eds.), *For Uriel. Studies in the History of Israel in Antiquity Presented to Professor Uriel Rappaport* (Jerusalem: Zalman Shazar Center for Jewish History), 205–26.

——(2007), '"Judaean" or "Jew"? How Should we Translate "Ioudaios" in Josephus?', in J. Frey, D. R. Schwartz, and S. Gripentrog (eds.), *Jewish Identity in the Greco–Roman World* (Leiden: Brill), 3–27.

Schwartz, S. (1995), 'Language, Power and Identity in Ancient Palestine', *Past and Present*, 148, 3–47.

——(2001), *Imperialism and Jewish Society, 200 BCE to 640 CE, Jews, Christians and Muslims from the Ancient to the Modern World* (Princeton, NJ: Princeton University Press).

Seeligmann, I. L. (1948), *The Septuagint Version of Isaiah: A Discussion of its Problems* (Leiden: Brill).

Segal, A. F. (1987), *The Other Judaisms of Late Antiquity*, Brown Judaic Studies, 127 (Atlanta, Ga.: Scholars Press).

Seidman, N. (2006), *Faithful Renderings: Jewish–Christian Difference and the Politics of Translation* (Chicago, Ill.: University of Chicago Press).

Shain, M. (1998), *Antisemitism* (London: Bowerdean).

Shavit, J. (1997), *Athens in Jerusalem: Classical Antiquity and Hellenism in the Making of the Modern Secular Jew*, trans. C. Naor and N. Werner, Littman Library of Jewish Civilization (London: Littman Library of Jewish Civilization).

Siegert, F. (2001), *Zwischen Hebräischer Bibel und Altem Testament: Eine Einführung in die Septuaginta* (Münster: LIT Verlag).

——(2003), *Register zur 'Einführung in die Septuaginta'. Mit einem Kapitel zur Wirkungsgeschichte*, Münsteraner Judaistische Studien, 13 (Münster: LIT Verlag).

Silva, D. A. de (2006), *4 Maccabees. Introduction and Commentary on the Greek Text In Codex Sinaiticus*. Septuagint Commentary Series (Leiden: Brill).

Silva, M. (1980), 'Bilingualism and the Character of Septuagint Greek', *Biblica*, 61: 198–221.

Silverstone, A. E. (1931), *Aquila and Onkelos* (Manchester: Manchester University Press).

Simon, M. (1986) [1948; 1964], *Verus Israel: A Study of the Relations between Christians and Jews in the Roman Empire (135–425)*, trans. H. McKeating, Littman Library of Jewish Civilization (Oxford: Oxford University Press (for the Littman Library); orig. edn. *Verus Israel. Étude sur les relations entre chretiens et juifs dans l'empire romain* (Paris: Boccard, 1948).

——(1997)[1984], 'The Bible in the Earliest Controversies between Jews and Christians', in P. M. Blowers (ed.), *The Bible in Greek Christian Antiquity* (Notre Dame, Ind.: University of Notre Dame Press, 1997); orig. edn.: C. Mondésert (ed.), *Le monde grec ancien et la Bible* (Paris: Beauchesne, 1984).

Skarsaune, O. (1987), *The Proof from Prophecy: A Study in Justin Martyr's Proof-Text Tradition: Text-Type, Provenance, Theological Profile*, Supplements to Novum Testamentum, 56 (Leiden: Brill).

Slusser, M. (ed.) (2003), *St Justin Martyr. Dialogue with Trypho*, trans. Thomas B. Falls and Thomas P. Halton (Washington, DC: Catholic University of America).

Soffer, A. (1957), 'The Treatment of Anthropomorphisms and Anti-Anthropomorphisms in the Septuagint of Psalms', *Hebrew Union College Annual* 28, 85–107.

Smallwood, E. M. (1976), *The Jews under Roman Rule: From Pompey to Diocletian. A Study in Political Relations* (Leiden: Brill).

——(1999), 'The Diaspora in the Roman Period before CE 70', in W. Horbury, W. D. Davies, and J. Sturdy, *The Cambridge History of Judaism*, iii. *The Early Roman Period* (Cambridge: Cambridge University Press), 168–91.

Smith, J. Z. (1978), *Map is Not Territory: Studies in the History of Religions*, Studies in Judaism in Late Antiquity, 23 (Leiden: Brill).

——(1990), *Drudgery Divine: On the Comparison of Early Christianities and the Religions of Late Antiquity*, Jordan Lectures in Comparative Religion, 14 (London: School of Oriental and African Studies, University of London).

Smith, R. R. R. (1988), *Hellenistic Royal Portraits*, Oxford Monographs on Classical Archaeology (Oxford: Clarendon Press).

——(1996), 'Ptolemaic Portraits: Alexandrian Types, Egyptian Versions', in *Alexandria and Alexandrianism* (Malibu, Calif.: J. Paul Getty Museum), 203–13.

Smith, W. D. (1979), *The Hippocratic Tradition*, Cornell Publications in the History of Science (Ithaca, NY: Cornell University Press).

——(1990), *Hippocrates: Pseudepigraphic Writings*, Studies in Ancient Medicine, 2 (Leiden: Brill).

Sorkin, D. (1997), '1783: The Final Volume of Moses Mendelssohn's Edition of the Pentateuch Appears', in S. L. Gilman and J. D. Zipes (eds.), *Yale*

Companion to Jewish Writing and Thought in German Culture, 1096–1996 (New Haven, Conn.: Yale University Press), 93–100.

Spilsbury, P. (1998), *The Image of the Jew in Flavius Josephus' Paraphrase of the Bible*, Texte und Studien zum antiken Judentum, 69 (Tübingen: Mohr Siebeck).

—— (2005), 'Reading the Bible in Rome: Josephus and the Constraints of Empire', in G. Lembi and J. Sievers (eds.), *Josephus and Jewish History in Flavian Rome and Beyond* (Leiden: Brill), 209–27.

Stambaugh, J. E. (1972), *Sarapis Under the Early Ptolemies*, Études préliminaires aux religions orientales dans l'empire romain, 25 (Leiden: Brill).

Steiner, G. (1975), *After Babel: Aspects of Language and Translation* (Oxford: Oxford University Press).

Stemberger, G. (1977), 'Die sogenannte Synode von Jabne und das früe Christentum', *Kairos*, 19: 14–21.

—— (1988), 'Jabne und der Kanon', *Jahrbuch für Biblische Theologie*, 3: 163–74.

—— (1995), 'Rabbinic Sources for Historical Studies', in J. Neusner and A. J. Avery-Peck (eds.), *Judaism in Late Antiquity* (Leiden: Brill), 169–86.

—— (1996), M. N. A. Bockmuehl, and H. L. Strack (ed.), *Introduction to the Talmud and Midrash* (2nd edn., Edinburgh: T. and T. Clark).

Stendahl, K. (1954), *The School of St. Matthew and its Use of the Old Testament* (2nd edn., Philadelphia, Pa.: Fortress Press, 1968; orig. edn.: Uppsala).

Stephens, S. (2004), 'Posidippus' Poetry Book: Where Macedon Meets Egypt', in W. V. Harris and G. Ruffini (eds.), *Ancient Alexandria between Egypt and Greece* (Leiden: Brill), 63–86.

Sterling, G. E. (1992), *Historiography and Self-Definition: Josephos, Luke-Acts and Apologetic Historiography*, Supplements to Novum Testamentum, 64 (Leiden: Brill).

—— (1999), 'Recherché or Representative? What is the Relationship between Philo's Treatises and Greek-Speaking Judaism?', in D. T. Runia and G. E. Sterling (eds.), *Studia Philonica Annual*, 11, Brown Judaic Studies, 323 (Atlanta, Ga.: Scholars Press), 1–30.

Stern, D. (2003), 'On Canonization in Rabbinic Judaism', in M. Finkelberg and G. A. G. Stroumsa (eds.), *Homer, the Bible, and Beyond: Literary and Religious Canons in the Ancient World* (Leiden: Brill), 227–52.

Stern, M. (1973), 'Hecataeus of Abdera and Theophrastus on Jews and Egyptians', *Journal of Egyptian Archaeology*, 59: 159–68.

——(1974), 'The Jewish Diaspora', in S. Safrai and M. Stern (eds.), *The Jewish People in the First Century*, Compendia Rerum Iudaicarum ad Novum Testamentum, Section 1, i. (Assen: Van Gorcum), 117–83.
——(1974–84), *Greek and Latin Authors on Jews and Judaism*, i-iii. (Jerusalem: Israel Academy of Sciences and Humanities).
Stern, S. (1994), *Jewish Identity in Early Rabbinic Writings*, Arbeiten zur Geschichte des Antiken Judentums und des Urchristentums, 23 (Leiden: Brill).
Stern, S. (2001), *Calendar and Community: A History of the Jewish Calendar, Second Century BCE to Second Century CE* (Oxford: Oxford University Press).
——(2003), *Time and Process in Ancient Judaism* (Oxford: Littman Library of Jewish Civilization).
Stewart, A. F. (1993), *Faces of Power: Alexander's Image and Hellenistic Politics*, Hellenistic Culture and Society, 11 (Berkeley, Calif.: University of California Press).
Stock, B. (1983), *The Implications of Literacy: Written Language and Models of Interpretation in the Eleventh and Twelfth Centuries* (Princeton, NJ: Princeton University Press).
Stone, M. E. (1984), *Jewish Writings of the Second Temple Period: Apocrypha, Pseudepigrapha, Qumran Sectarian Writings, Philo, Josephus*, Compendia Rerum Iudaicarum ad Novum Testamentum, Section 2, ii. (Assen: Van Gorcum).
——and E. G. Chazon (1998), *Biblical Perspectives: Early Use and Interpretation of the Bible in Light of the Dead Sea Scrolls, Proceedings of the First International Symposium of the Orion Center for the Study of the Dead Sea Scrolls and Associated Literature, 12–14 May 1996*, Studies on the Texts of the Desert of Judah, 28 (Leiden: Brill).
Stroumsa, G. A. G. (1998), 'The Christian Hermeneutical Revolution and its Double Helix', in L. V. Rutgers, P. W. van der Horst, et al. (eds.), *The Use of Sacred Books in the Ancient World*, Contributions to Biblical Exegesis and Theology, 22 (Leuven: Peeters), 9–28.
——(2003), 'Early Christianity–A Religion of the Book?', in M. Finkelberg and G. Stroumsa (eds), *Homer, the Bible, and Beyond: Literary and Religious Canons in the Ancient World* (Leiden: Brill), 153–73.
Sundberg, A. C. (1964), *The Old Testament of the Early Church*, Harvard Theological Studies, 20 (Cambridge, Mass.: Harvard University Press).
Swain, S. (1996), *Hellenism and Empire: Language, Classicism, and Power in the Greek World, AD 50–250* (Oxford: Clarendon Press).

Swete, H. B. (1914) [1900], *An Introduction to the Old Testament in Greek*, rev. R. R. Otley (Cambridge: Cambridge University Press; orig. edn.: 1900).

Talmon, S. (1989), *The World of Qumran from Within: Collected Studies* (Jerusalem and Leiden: Magnes Press and Brill).

Talshir, Z. (1999), *I Esdras: From Origin to Translation* (Atlanta, Ga.: Society of Biblical Literature).

Tanner, R. G. (2000), 'Aristotle's Works: The Possible Origins of the Alexandrian Collection', in R. M. MacLeod (ed.), *The Library of Alexandria: Centre of Learning in the Ancient World* (London: I. B. Tauris), 79–91.

Taylor, J. (1998), 'A Second Temple in Egypt: The Evidence for the Zadokite Temple of Onias in Egypt', *Journal for the Study of Judaism*, 29: 297–321.

——(2003), *Jewish Women Philosophers of First-Century Alexandria: Philo's 'Therapeutae' Reconsidered* (Oxford: Oxford University Press).

Tcherikover, V. A. (1957), 'Jewish Apologetic Literature Reconsidered', *Eos*, 48: 169–93.

——(1958), 'The Ideology of the Letter of Aristeas', *Harvard Theological Review*, 51: 59–85.

——(1959), *Hellenistic Civilization and the Jews* (Philadelphia, Pa. and Jerusalem: Magnes Press, Hebrew University).

Thackeray, H. S. J. (1908), 'Renderings of the Infinitive Absolute in the Septuagint', *Journal of Theological Studies*, 9: 597–601.

——(1909), *A Grammar of the Old Testament in Greek according to the Septuagint* (Cambridge: Cambridge University Press).

——(1923), *The Septuagint and Jewish Worship: A Study in Origins* (2nd edn., London: British Academy).

Thompson, D. J. (1988), *Memphis under the Ptolemies* (Princeton, NJ: Princeton University Press).

——(1994), 'Literacy and Power in Ptolemaic Egypt', in A. K. Bowman and G. Woolf (eds.), *Literacy and Power in the Ancient World* (Cambridge: Cambridge University Press), 67–83.

——(2000), 'Philadelphus' Procession: Dynastic Power in a Mediterranean Context', in L. Mooren (ed.), *Politics, Administration and Society in the Hellenistic and Roman World*, Proceedings of the International Colloquium, Bertinoro, 19–24 July 1997 (Leuven: Peeters), 365–88.

——(2003), 'The Ptolemies and Egypt', in A. Erskine (ed.), *A Companion to the Hellenistic World* (Oxford: Blackwell), 105–20.

Thumb, A. (1901), *Die griechische Sprache im Zeitalter des Hellenismus. Beitrag zur Geschichte und Beurteilung der KOINH* (Strasbourg: Trubner).

Tollet, D. (ed.) (1989), *Politique et religion dans le judaïsme ancien et médiéval: interventions au colloque des 8 et 9 décembre 1987* (Paris: Desclée).

Torijano, P. A. (2002), *Solomon, the Esoteric King: From King to Magus, Development of a Tradition*, Supplements to the Journal for the Study of Judaism, 73 (Leiden: Brill).

Toury, G. (1995), *Descriptive Translation Studies and Beyond* (Amsterdam: Benjamins).

Tov, E. (1986), 'Die griechischen Bibelübersetzungen', *Aufstieg und Niedergang der Römischen Welt* (Berlin: de Gruyter), 121–89.

Tov, E. (1988), 'The Septuagint', in *Mikra: Text, Translation, Reading and Interpretation of the Hebrew Bible in Ancient Judaism and Early Christianity*, ed. M. J. Mulder and H. Sysling (Assen: Van Gorcum), 161–88.

——(1997), The Text–Critical Use of the Septuagint in Biblical Research, 2nd rev. edn., Jerusalem Biblical Studies, 8 (Jerusalem: Simor).

——(1999), *The Greek and Hebrew Bible: Collected Essays on the Septuagint*, Supplements to *Vetus Testamentum*, 72 (Leiden: Brill).

——(2003), 'The Greek Biblical Texts from the Judaean Desert', in S. McKendrick and O. O'Sullivan (eds.), *The Bible as Book: The Transmission of the Greek Text* (London: British Library), 97–122.

——(2005), 'The Evaluation of the Greek Scripture Translations in Rabbinic Sources', in F. García-Martínez and M. Vervenne (eds.), *Interpreting Translation. Studies on the LXX and Ezekiel in Honour of J. Lust* (Leuven: Peeters).

——R. A. Kraft, and P. J. Parsons (1990), *The Greek Minor Prophets Scroll from Nahal Hever (8HeXIIgr)*, Discoveries in the Judaean Desert, 8 (Oxford: Clarendon Press).

Trapp, M. B. (2004), 'Images of Alexandria in the Writings of the Second Sophistic', in A. Hirst and M. S. Silk (eds.), *Alexandria, Real and Imagined* (Aldershot: Ashgate), 113–32.

Treu, K. (1973), 'Die Bedeutung des Griechischen für die Juden im römischen Reich', *Kairos*, 15: 123–44.

Troiani, L. (1987), 'Il libro di Aristea ed il guidaismo ellenistico (Premesse per un'interpretazione)', in B. Virgilio (ed.), *Studi ellenistici* (Pisa: Giardini), 31–61.

Troxel, R. L. (2008), *LXX–Isaiah as Translation and Interpretation: The Strategies of the Translator of the Septuagint of Isaiah* (Leiden: Brill).

Turner, E. (1984), 'Ptolemaic Egypt', in F. Walbank and A. E. Austin (eds.), *The Cambridge Ancient History* (Cambridge: Cambridge University Press), 118–74.

Tyacke, N. (1997), *The History of the University of Oxford*, iv. *Seventeenth-Century Oxford* (Oxford: Oxford University Press).

Ulrich, E. C. (1978), *The Qumran Text of Samuel and Josephus*, Harvard Semitic Monographs, 19 (Missoula, Mont.: Scholars Press).

——(1999a), *The Dead Sea Scrolls and the Origins of the Bible*, Studies in the Dead Sea Scrolls and Related Literature (Grand Rapids, Mich. and Leiden: Eerdmans/Brill).

——(1999b), 'Origen's Old Testament Text and the Transmission History of the Septuagint to the Third Century CE', in *The Dead Sea Scrolls and the Origins of the Bible* (Grand Rapids, Mich. and Leiden: Eerdmans/Brill), 202–23.

Van der Berg, R. M. (2006), 'Does it Matter to Call God Zeus?' in *The Revelation of the Name YHWH to Moses*, ed. G. H. Koopten (Leiden: Brill), 169–83.

van der Horst, P. W. (1978), *The Sentences of Pseudo-Phocylides*, Studia in Veteris Testamenti Pseudepigrapha, 4 (Leiden: Brill).

——(1988), 'The Interpretation of the Bible by the Minor Hellenistic Jewish Writers', in M. J. Mulder and H. Sysling (eds.), *Mikra: Text, Translation, Reading and Interpretation of the Hebrew Bible in Ancient Judaism and Early Christianity* (Assen: Van Gorcum), 519–46.

——(1990), *Essays on the Jewish World of Early Christianity*, Novum Testamentum et Orbis Antiquus, 14 (Freiburg and Göttingen: Universitätsverlag/Vandenhoeck and Ruprecht).

——(1991), *Ancient Jewish Epitaphs: An Introductory Survey of a Millennium of Jewish Funerary Epigraphy (300 BCE–700 CE)*, Contributions to Biblical Exegesis and Theology, 2 (Kampen: Kok Pharos).

——(1994), *Hellenism, Judaism, Christianity: Essays on Their Interaction* (Kampen: Kok Pharos).

——(1999), 'Was the Synagogue a Place of Sabbath Worship Before 70 CE?', in S. Fine (ed.), *Jews, Christians, and Polytheists in the Ancient Synagogue: Cultural Interaction during the Greco–Roman Period* (London: Routledge), 18–43.

——(2006), *Jews and Christians in their Graeco–Roman Context*, Wissenschaftliche Untersuchungen zum Neuen Testament, 196 (Tübingen: Mohr Siebeck).

van der Kooij, A. (1998), 'Perspectives on the Septuagint: Who Are the Translators?', in F. G. Martínez and E. Noort (eds.), *Perspectives in the Study of the Old Testament and Early Judaism* (Leiden: Brill), 214–29.

——(1999), 'The Origin and Purpose of Bible Translation in Ancient Judaism: Some Comments', *Archiv für Religionsgeschichte*, 1: 204–14.

—— (2001), 'The Septuagint of Psalms and the First Book of Maccabees', in R. J. V. Hiebert, C. E. Cox, and P. J. Gentry (eds.), *The Old Greek Psalter: Studies in Honour of Albert Pietersma* (Sheffield: Sheffield Academic Press), 229–47.

—— (2003), 'On the Use of "Bomos" in the Septuagint', in M. F. J. Baasten and W. T. van Peursen (eds.), *Hamlet on a Hill: Semitic and Greek Studies Presented to Professor T. Muraoka on the Occasion of His Sixty-Fifth Birthday* (Leuven: Peeters), 601–7.

—— and K. van der Toorn (1998), *Canonization and Decanonization*, Studies in the History of Religions, 82 (Leiden: Brill).

van Henten, J. W. (1994), 'A Jewish Epitaph in a Literary Text: 4 Macc.17: 8–10', in J. W. van Henten and P. W. van der Horst (eds.), *Studies in Early Jewish Epigraphy* (Leiden: Brill), 44–69.

—— (1995), 'The Martyrs as Heroes of the Christian People. Some Remarks on the Continuity of Jewish and Christian Martyrology, with Pagan Analogy', in M. Lamberigts and P. van Deun (eds.), *Martyrium in Multidisciplinary Perspective: Memorial Louis Reekmans* (Leuven: University Press / Peeters), 304–22.

—— (1997), *The Maccabean Martyrs as Saviours of the Jewish People: A Study of 2 and 4 Maccabees*, Supplements to the Journal for the Study of Judaism, 57 (Leiden: Brill).

—— (1999), 'The Ancestral Language of the Jews in 2 Maccabees', in W. Horbury (ed.), *Hebrew Study from Ezra to Ben-Yehuda* (Edinburgh: T. and T. Clark), 53–68.

—— and F. Avemarie (2002), *Martyrdom and Noble Death: Selected Texts from Graeco-Roman, Jewish and Christian Antiquity*, Context of Early Christianity (London: Routledge).

—— and P. W. van der Horst (eds.) (1994), *Studies in Early Jewish Epigraphy*, Arbeiten zur Geschichte des antiken Judentums und des Urchristentums, 21 (Leiden: Brill).

van Unnik, W. C. (1993), *Das Selbstverständnis der jüdischen Diaspora in der hellenistisch-römischen Zeit* (Leiden: Brill).

VanderKam, J. C., and P. W. Flint (eds.) (2002), *The Meaning of the Dead Sea Scrolls: Their Significance for Understanding the Bible, Judaism, Jesus and Christianity* (San Francisco, Calif.: Harper).

Veltri, G. (1994), *Eine Tora für den König Talmai: Untersuchungen zum Übersetzungsverständnis in der jüdisch–hellenistischen und rabbinischen Literatur*, Texte und Studien zum antiken Judentum, 41 (Tübingen: Mohr Siebeck).

—— (2006), *Libraries, Translations, and 'Canonic' Texts. The Septuagint, Aquila, Ben Sira and Christian Traditions*, Supplements to the Journal for the Study of Judaism, 109 (Leiden: Brill).

Venuti, L. (1995), *The Translator's Invisibility: A History of Translation* (London: Routledge).
Vergote, J. (1938), 'Grecque biblique', in *Dictionnaire de la Bible*, Suppl. 3: 1321–96.
Vermes, G. (1966), Review of Barthélemy, *Les devanciers d'Aquila*, *Journal of Semitic Studies*, 11: 261–4.
——(1973), *Scripture and Tradition in Judaism: Haggadic Studies*, 2nd rev. edn., Studia Post-Biblica, 4 (Leiden: Brill).
——(2004), *The Complete Dead Sea Scrolls in English* (rev. edn., London: Penguin).
——and M. Goodman (1984), 'La Littérature juive intertestamentaire à la lumière d'un siècle de recherches et de découvertes', in R. Arnaldez, R. Kuntzmann, and J. Schlosser (eds.), *Études sur le judaïsme hellénistique: Congrès de Strasbourg (1983)* (Paris: Éditions du Cerf), 19–39.
Wacholder, B. Z. (1974), *Eupolemus: A Study of Judaeo–Greek Literature* (Cincinnati: Hebrew Union College, Jewish Institute of Religion).
Wagner, J. R. (2002), *Heralds of the Good News: Isaiah and Paul 'in Concert' in the Letter to the Romans*, Supplements to *Novum Testamentum*, 101 (Leiden: Brill).
Walbank, F. W. (1991–2), 'The Hellenistic World: New Trends and Directions', *Scripta Classica Israelica*, 11: 90–113.
Walser, G. (2001), *The Greek of the Ancient Synagogue: An Investigation on the Greek of the Septuagint, Pseudepigrapha and the New Testament*, Studia Graeca et Latina Lundensia, 8 (Stockholm: Almquist and Wiksell).
Walter, N. (1964), *Der Thoraausleger Aristobulos: Untersuchungen zu seinen Fragmenten und zu pseudepigraphischen Resten der jüdisch–hellenistischen Literatur*, Texte und Untersuchungen zur Geschichte der altchristlichen Literatur, 86 (Berlin: Akademie-Verlag).
Walzer, R. (1949), *Galen on Jews and Christians* (Oxford: Oxford University Press).
Wasserstein, A. and D. J. Wasserstein (2006), *The Legend of the Septuagint: From Classical Antiquity to Today* (Cambridge: Cambridge University Press).
Wasserstein, D. J. (2002), Review of L. Casson, *Libraries in the Ancient World*, *Scripta Classica Israelica*, 21: 278–82.
Weinberg, J. (2001), *The Light of the Eyes: Azariah de' Rossi (me'or 'enayim*, translated from the Hebrew, with an introduction and annotations, Yale Judaica Series, 31 (New Haven, Conn. and London: Yale University Press).
Weitzman, S. (2005), *Surviving Sacrilege: Cultural Persistence in Jewish Antiquity* (Cambridge, Mass.: Harvard University Press).

Wendland, J. T. P., and L. Mendelssohn (1900), *Aristeae ad Philocratem epistula* (Leipzig: Teubner).
Wevers, J. W. (1990), *Notes on the Greek Text of Exodus*, Septuagint and Cognate Studies Series, 30 (Atlanta, Ga.: Scholars Press).
Whiston, W. (1722), *Essay Towards Restoring the True Text of the Old Testament* (London: Printed for J. Senex and W. Taylor).
White, L. M. (1997), 'Synagogue and Society in Imperial Ostia: Archaeological and Epigraphic Evidence', *Harvard Theological Review*, 90: 23–58.
Whitmarsh, T. (2001), *Greek Literature and the Roman Empire: The Politics of Imitation* (Oxford: Oxford University Press).
Wifstrand, A. (1940), 'Lukas och den gresiska klassicismen', *Svensk Exegetisk Årsbok*, 5: 139–51.
——(2005), *Epochs and Styles. Selected Writings on the New Testament, Greek Language and Greek Culture in the Post–Classical Era*, ed. L. Rydbeck and S. E Porter, Wissenschaftliche Untersuchungen zum Neuen Testament, 179, trans. D. Searby (Tübingen: Mohr Siebeck).
Wilken, R. L. (1983), *John Chrysostom and the Jews: Rhetoric and Reality in the Late Fourth Century*, Transformation of the Classical Heritage, 4 (Berkeley, Calif. and London: University of California Press).
Williams, M. H. (1997), 'The Meaning and Function of *Ioudaios* in Graeco-Roman Inscriptions', *Zeitschrift für Papyrologie und Epigraphik*, 116: 249–62.
——(1998a) *The Jews among the Greeks and Romans: A Diasporan Sourcebook* (London: Duckworth).
——(1998b) 'The Structure of the Jewish Community in Rome', in M. Goodman (ed.), *Jews in a Graeco–Roman World* (Oxford: Clarendon Press), 215–28.
——(1999), 'The Jews of Early Byzantine Venusia: The Family of Faustinus the Elder', *Journal of Jewish Studies*, 50: 38–52.
——(2004), 'Being a Jew: Sabbath Fasting as an Expression of Romano-Jewish Identity', in J. M. G. Barclay (ed.), *Negotiating Diasporas* (London and New York: T. and T. Clark), 8–18.
——(2006), *The Monk and the Book. Jerome and the Making of Christian Scholarship* (Chicago, Ill.: University of Chicago Press).
Wills, L. M. (1990), *The Jew in the Court of the Foreign King: Ancient Jewish Court Legends* (Minneapolis, Minn.: Fortress Press).
——(1995), *The Jewish Novel in the Ancient World* (Ithaca, NY: Cornell University Press).
Wilson, N. G. (1983), *Scholars of Byzantium* (London: Duckworth).

Wilson, W. T. (2005), *The Sentences of Pseudo-Phocylides* (Berlin: de Gruyter).

Winston, D. (ed.) (1979), *The Wisdom of Solomon: A New Translation*, Anchor Bible (Garden City, NY: Doubleday).

——and J. M. Dillon (1983), *Two Treatises of Philo of Alexandria: A Commentary on De Gigantibus and Quod Deus Sit Immutabilis*, Brown Judaic Studies, 25 (Chico, Calif.: Scholars Press).

Wittstruck, T. (1976), 'The So-Called Anti-Anthropomorphisms in the Greek Text of Deuteronomy', *Catholic Bible Quarterly* 38, 29–34.

Wolfson, H. A. (1947), *Philo: Foundations of Religious Philosophy in Judaism, Christianity, and Islam*, 2 vols. (Cambridge, Mass.: Harvard University Press).

Wright, B. G. (2002), 'The Jewish Scriptures in Greek: The Septuagint in the Context of Ancient Translation Activity', in F. W. Knobloch (ed.), *Biblical Translation in Context*, Studies and Texts in Jewish History and Culture, 10 (Bethesda, Md.: University Press of Maryland), 3–18.

——(2003a), 'Access to the Source: Cicero, Ben Sira, the Septuagint and Their Audiences', *Journal for the Study of Judaism*, 34: 1–27.

——(2003b), 'Why a Prologue? Ben Sira's Grandson and His Greek Translation', in S. M. Paul, R. A. Kraft, et al. (eds.), *Emanuel: Studies in Hebrew Bible, Septuagint, and Dead Sea Scrolls in Honor of Emanuel Tov*, Supplements to *Vetus Testamentum*, 94 (Leiden: Brill), 633–44.

——(2006), 'Translation as Scripture: The Septuagint in Aristeas and Philo', in R. G. Wooden and W. Kraus (ed.), *The Septuagint: Issues and Challenges in the Study and Translation of the Greek Bible* (Atlanta, Ga.: Society of Biblical Literature).

Wyrick, J. (2004), *The Ascension of Authorship: Attribution and Canon Formation in Jewish, Hellenistic, and Christian Traditions* (Cambridge, Mass. and London: Harvard University Press).

Yerushalmi, Y. H. (1982), *Zakhor, Jewish History and Jewish Memory. The Samuel and Althea Stroum Lectures in Jewish Studies* (Seattle, Wash.: University of Washington Press).

——(1995), *Diener von Königen und nicht Diener von Dienern: einige Aspekte der politischen Geschichte der Juden* (Munich: Carl Friedrich von Siemens Stiftung).

Young, F. M. (1997), *Biblical Exegesis and the Formation of Christian Culture* (Cambridge: Cambridge University Press).

Zeitlin, F. (2001), 'Visions and Revisions of Homer', in S. Goldhill (ed.), *Being Greek under Rome: Cultural Identity, the Second Sophistic and the Development of Empire* (Cambridge: Cambridge University Press), 195–264.

Zellentin, H. (2008), 'The End of Jewish Egypt: Artapanus and the Second Exodus', in G. Gardner and K. Osterloh (eds.), *Antiquity in Antiquity: Jewish and Christian Pasts in the Graeco–Roman World* (Tübingen: Mohr Siebeck).

Zuntz, G. (1959), 'Aristeas Studies: 1. The Seven Banquets, 2. Aristeas on the Translation of the Torah', *Journal of Semitic Studies*, 4: 21–36, 109–26.

——(1972), *Opuscula Selecta. Classica, Hellenistica, Christiana* (Manchester and Totowa, NJ: University Press/Rowman and Littlefield).

Index

abandonment theory, 6, 13–14, 279–81, 288–90, 292, 295, 297, 299 n. 69, 301, 304, 313
Abraham, 13, 167, 219, 220, 229, 272, 286
acculturation, 7, 10, 114, 116 n. 75, 120, 126, 153, 204
Acmonia, 117
Acts, book of, 105, 118, 172, 235, 246–7, 249. *See also* New Testament
Adiabene, royal dynasty of, 119
Aelia Capitolina, 94, 100, 123, 278, 310–11
Agatharchides of Cnidus, 76, 264
aggada, *see* Haggadah
Agrippa I, 105
Akiba, Rabbi, *see* Akiva, Rabbi
Akiva, Rabbi, 123, 293, 294, 301
Alciphron, 56–60, 62, 70
Alexander Polyhistor, 218, 265–6
Alexander the Great, 9, 42, 58, 66, 67, 71–3, 77, 96–7
Alexandria, 3, 9, 13, 30, 102 n. 26, 120, 185, 259, 312
  Hellenized, 68, 70
  intellectual life, 70, 74–5
  library, 9, 15, 32, 40, 41, 42, 45 n. 52, 46, 64–5, 70, 71, 73, 75
'Alexandrian paradigm', 55–6
allegorizers, 111, 149, 229, 241–2
allegory, 35, 109, 149, 195, 220, 223, 232, 241–2, 251–2
altar, 100, 166, 185, 197
Amichai, Yehuda, 1, 36, 215–16
Ammon, 71, 74
Amos, book of, 144
angels, 271–2, 275
anger
  divine, 11, 191–3
  human, 11, 192–3
Anglo-Saxon texts, 143–4
animal worship, 201
anthropomorphism, 189

anti-Judaism, 10, 13–14, 120–2, 281–5, 298–301. *See also* antisemitism
  polemic, *see* polemic, Jewish-Christian
Antioch, 16–17, 112, 118, 121, 235, 305
Antiochus III, 120, 147
Antiochus IV, 97, 174, 175 n. 158, 192–3, 197, 207, 226
antisemitism, 38–40, 83, 135–6, 164, 208. *See also* anti-Judaism
Antoninus Pius, 123
Apamea, 121
Aphrodisias, 117, 124
Aphthonius, 45
Apion, 263
apocalyptic texts, 176
Apocrypha, 5, 15, 21, 114, 170, 182, 187
Apollonius, 81, 87
Aquila, 13–14, 19, 89, 153, 168, 188, 259 n. 3, 279, 281 n. 9, 284 n. 18, 290–4, 295–6, 297–8, 299 n. 69, 301, 302–3, 305–6, 307–9, 310–12
  vocabulary of, 291–3
Aramaic, language, 12, 52, 84, 96, 112, 145, 146, 147, 148, 151, 152, 172–3, 176, 198, 211, 217, 224, 272, 290, 308
Aristarchus of Alexandria, 305
Aristeas, author, 31–2, 220, 259–60
Aristobulus the philosopher, 34, 35 n. 20, 78, 98 n. 14, 115, 220–1, 222–3, 241
Aristotle, 9, 74–8, 142
army, Ptolemaic, 79–80, 85
Arsinoe III, 44
Artapanus, 49 n. 69, 229, 266
Artaxerxes, 61–2, 183–5
ascetics, 110, 229, 280–1
assimilation, 6, 145–6, 206
Athenaeus, 75 n. 30, 265 n. 16
Athens, 9, 56–60, 61, 62, 70, 72, 75 n. 30, 76 n. 39, 77, 86

Augustine, 15, 284, 286, 301
Augustus, emperor, 108, 120

Babatha, 123
Babylon, 96, 122, 179, 187–8, 198–200, 212, 230, 304
  exile to, 94, 193, 200, 205
banquets, 33, 35, 52, 61–2, 178
Bar Kappara, 290
Bar Kokhba revolt, 100, 122, 147, 278–9, 294
barbarians, 75, 76
Barnabas, 282
Baruch, book of, 193, 199–200
Bel and the Dragon, 5, 11, 48, 176, 198–9
Ben Sira, Hebrew book of, 134–5, 169, 174, 178. *See also* Ecclesiasticus, book of
benefactors, *see* gentiles, as benefactors
Benjamin, Walter, 155–6, 161, 162
Berenice, 113, 116
bet midrash, 173, 307
Bialik, Hayyim Nachman, 216
bilingualism, 145, 151–2, 273–4
Buber, Martin, 6, 309
burial practices
  Christian, 116
  Jewish, 115–116

Caecilius, 268
Caesarea, 81, 102, 121, 228, 295–6, 297–8, 309, 310
Cairo Geniza, 291
Caligula, emperor, 105, 120–1, 180 n. 13, 200–1
Callanus, 72
Callimachus, 75, 264–5
calques, 11, 22, 128, 291. *See also* Hebraisms
canon, 8, 12, 15, 21, 212–14, 216, 289, 296, 305, 307 n. 93
  canonicity, 212–14, 215, 216
  canonization, 140, 212–14, 257, 305
Canopus decree, 26
catacombs, Roman Jewish, 22 n. 36, 104, 116, 228, 234, 305–6, 307 n. 94. *See also* epitaphs, Jewish; inscriptions

Celsus, 128
charter myth, *see* myth
Christian
  appropriation of Jewish literature, 4–5, 6, 13–14, 15, 278–90, 294–7, 309, 313
  art, 198
  communities, 217, 243–5
  teachers and philosophers, 173 n. 151
  theology, vocabulary of, 164
  writings, 14, 15–16, 36, 46, 78, 89, 111, 120, 127–8, 132 n. 24, 151, 187, 189, 218, 221, 244–5, 261, 265–6, 279–86, 289, 297–300. *See also* Church, fathers
Christianity, 1, 4–5, 9, 13–16, 21, 44, 91, 99, 119, 120, 164, 165 n. 130, 207 n. 59, 208, 213–14, 257, 258–9, 278–87, 295–7, 309, 312 n. 110, 313
  and Jewish magic, 13, 271 n. 32
Chronicles, books of, 170 n. 142, 182, 224, 306
Church, 111
  councils, 289
  fathers, 15–16, 127–8, 218, 261, 279, 281–6, 297–300. *See also* Christian, writings
Cicero, 72, 127, 140 n. 47, 268 n. 26
circumcision, 81, 108, 122–3, 167, 232, 260, 311
citations, biblical, 13, 226–7, 230, 246–50, 251, 264–5, 268–9, 291
  in magical papyri, 270–6
citizenship, 95, 104
city, Greek, 95, 99, 113, 116–24
  councillors, 117, 124
  foundation, 52
Claudius, emperor, 121, 207
Clearchus of Soli, 72, 75–6
Clement of Alexandria, 35 n. 20, 42, 78, 98 n. 14, 115, 218, 223, 265 n. 17, 269, 283, 288
Cleodemus Malchas, 219
Cleopatra II, 98
cleruchic land, 80, 85
Codex Alexandrinus, 16
Codex Sinaiticus, 16

Codex Vaticanus, 16
codices, medieval Jewish, 158
coins, 121–2, 147
colonization terminology, 102
commandments, 21, 22 n. 36, 191
Community Rule, 245
conversion, 118–19, 121, 197–9, 203, 224, 287, 310–11
converts, 3, 140
Corinthians, *see* Paul, Epistles
Cos, island of, 61–2
'counter-culture', 272
'counter-history', 262–4
courts
  Jewish, 233
  procedures, 52
covenant, 167–8
cruelty, 178–9
cults
  of Attica, 58
  imperial, 11, 117, 200–1, 202
  Jewish, 166
  pagan, 43–4, 73, 95, 97, 102, 117, 122, 165, 186, 187, 190, 194–205
  ruler cult, 11, 95, 200–1, 202, 203
  sacrificial, 101
  Temple, *see* Temple, cult
culture
  cultural survival, 7–9, 13–14, 92, 124, 126, 145–6, 148, 156, 180, 205–6, 208
  Egyptian, 68
  Jewish-Greek, 12, 13–14, 103, 211, 216–17, 255–7, 258–9
curse, *see also* magic
  formulae, 13, 230–1
  texts, 118
Cyprus, 122
Cyrenaica, 111, 116–17, 122
Cyrus, king of Persia, 96

Damascus, 118
Daniel, 62–3
Daniel, book of, 11, 72, 101, 170, 175, 176, 177–8, 188, 190, 197–9, 205–6, 295
Darius, king, 84
David, king, 190, 195, 219, 224, 272

Day of Atonement, *see* festivals, Jewish, Yom Kippur
de' Rossi, Azariah, 30–1
Dead Sea, 80–1, 123, 225, 244
  sect, 110, 214, 236. *See also* Qumran, community
Dead Sea Scrolls, *see* Qumran, scrolls
Decapolis, 102
decrees, 4, 84, 120, 184. *See also* Canopus decree; Rosetta Stone
Deissmann, Adolf, 287
Delphic oracle, 57
Demetrius of Phaleron, 30, 31, 32, 34–5, 42, 64, 70, 76–7
Demetrius the Chronographer, 115, 220, 266 n. 19
democracy, 58
Demotic, 84, 87, 136, 138
Demotic Chronicle, 84
Deuteronomy, book of, 2, 17, 53, 90–1, 100, 130 n. 16, 189, 190, 194, 226–7, 232, 249, 250, 266–7, 273 n. 40
diaspora, Jewish, *passim*
  term, 11, 93, 100, 101, 162, 193–4
dietary laws, 108, 232, 241, 275
Diodati, Domenico, 287 n. 31
Diodorus, 264
Dionysus, god, 70, 72, 203
Dis, god, *see* Zeus, god
divine
  inspiration, 36
  omnipotence, 177
Divine Name, 2, 13, 131–2, 141–2, 186–7, 236, 271–2
divorce, 233–4
Domitian, emperor, 122
dragomans, 40, 137–9
Dura Europus, 111–12, 199

Ebionites, 311
Ecclesiastes, book of, 188, 247, 264, 278, 312–13
Ecclesiasticus, book of, 114, 134–5, 136, 162, 174, 177–8, 231 n. 76. *See also* Ben Sira, Hebrew book of
Edicts, Roman
  on Jewish privileges, 99, 105, 120–1, 180–1, 207

education, 10, 54, 61, 70 n. 18, 91, 95, 114, 143, 144, 145, 150, 151, 169, 172–3, 214, 240, 256, 307, 312 n. 110. *See also* bet midrash; synagogue
Egypt, 17
ekklesia, 180–1
Eleazar, 2 Maccabees, 97
Eleazar, 3 Maccabees, 53–4, 226
Eleazar, High Priest, 60–1, 77
Elephantine, 80, 103, 148–9
enlightenment, Jewish, 309–10
Ephesus, 112, 310
Epicurus, 57
epigraphy, *see* inscriptions
Epiphanius, 45, 46, 284, 310–11
epistolography, 31, 56–8
epitaphs, Jewish, 22 n. 36, 104, 115, 230, 234, 237, 305–6. *See also* catacombs, Roman Jewish; inscriptions
Esdras
  first book, 166, 170, 175, 182–3
  second book, 100, 175
Essenes, 110
Esther
  book of, 111, 112, 170, 174–5, 183–5, 205, 231 n. 76, 235
  story, 250, 254
ethical mean, theory of, 77
etymologies in Philo, *see* Philo of Alexandria
Eupolemus, 218–19, 221, 224, 266 n. 19
Eusebius of Caesarea, 4, 35 n. 20, 78, 98 n. 14, 115, 218, 219, 223, 265 n. 17, 269, 280–1, 283, 288, 311
exegesis, 11, 19 n. 28, 21, 22, 140, 148–9, 210–11, 234, 241–2, 244–8, 249–50, 251–3, 294–5, 308
exile, 52, 94, 100, 101 n. 22, 102 n. 25, 107, 146, 179, 193, 205, 294
Exodus, 83, 201, 203, 250, 275
  archetype, 53–4
  book of, 21, 22 n. 38, 54, 90, 112, 131–3, 140, 144, 159, 170, 231 n. 76, 233, 262–3
  story of the, 115, 229, 242, 262–4
Ezekiel, book of, 111, 226

Ezekiel the tragedian, 115, 170, 220, 229, 251, 263
Ezra-Nehemiah, book of, 25, 52, 100, 146, 170 n. 142, 173, 175, 182, 247, 300

fasts, 108
Fayyum, 86, 103–4, 138
festivals, Jewish, 49, 172
  Hanukkah, 49
  of the kalends, 116
  Passover, 53 n. 85, 108, 116, 182, 262
  Purim, 49
  Shavuot (Pentecost), 108, 116, 116–17
  Simchat Torah, 215
  Sukkot (Tabernacles), 53, 108, 111, 133
  Yom Kippur, 173 n. 148, 231
Flavian dynasty, 121–2
'foreignizing', *see* translation, 'foreignizing'
freedom, 58, 61, 194

Galatians, *see* Paul, Epistles
Galen, 55–6
Galilee, 95, 102, 147
garrisons, Jewish, 79–80, 148–9. *See also* army, Ptolemaic
Genesis, book of, 17 n. 22, 22, 91, 138, 144, 163, 167, 188, 191, 220, 224, 267–8
gentiles, 13, 73, 100, 108–9, 195–6, 196, 258, 284, 286–7, 302–3
  as benefactors, 9, 10, 33, 116–18, 230
Gerasa, 121
Gilgamesh, book of, 25
glossary (onomastikon), 149–50, 174, 254
Glycera, 56–8, 60, 70
God, 33–4, 237 n. 95, 283
  Jewish, 2, 8, 51, 62–3, 66, 73, 77, 100–1, 109 n. 53, 118, 131, 140–2, 160, 167–8, 177–9, 181–6, 186–8, 189–204, 220, 228–9, 230, 231, 235–6, 245, 269, 271–2, 274, 275
god-fearers, 105, 117, 118–19, 124

gods
    Egyptian, 69–70, 73–4
    Greek, 191, 241, 243
    pagan, 73–4
Gospels, 143–4, 187, 188 n. 31, 246, 287. *See also* New Testament
grammarians, Alexandrian, 240
Greek, language, 2, 10, 86, 104, 124, 127–9, 132, 133, 139–40, 143, 148–9, 152, 159, 163, 166–7, 217, 222, 230, 287, 291, 304 n. 83, 307–9
    knowledge of, 65, 95, 130
    koine, 4, 6, 9–10, 95, 125–6, 130–1, 133 n. 26, 167 n. 137, 170–1, 207
Grinfield, Edward, 6 n. 10, 286–7

Habakkuk, prophet, 199, 203
Hadrian, emperor, 94, 122, 278, 294, 308, 310–11
haftarot, 172–3
Haggadah, 150, 224, 273–5
Halakhah, 96, 150, 201, 243, 250, 294, 311
Halbwachs, 47–8
Hallel, liturgical sequence, 133. *See also* prayers
Haman, 111, 112, 184–5
Hannah, prophetess, 251
Hasmoneans, 97, 98, 99, 101, 106 n. 41, 147, 197, 221
Hebraisms, 11, 128, 133, 136, 293. *See also* calques
Hebraization, 302, 307–8, 309
Hebrew, language, 2, 6, 7, 8, 12, 19, 22–3, 89, 126, 127, 128–9, 130, 131–2, 134, 139–40, 141–2, 143, 145–52, 153, 156–7, 159–61, 163, 166–7, 171, 173, 175, 176–7, 184, 186–7, 189, 195, 211, 216–17, 221, 222, 224–5, 230, 250, 252, 271–2, 286, 291, 302 n. 79, 304 n. 83, 307–9
    alphabet, 146–7, 151, 187
    corpus, 212–14
    as a holy language, 3, 11, 114, 141, 145–7, 147, 214–15
Hebrew people, 283–4
Hebrews, epistle to the, 166, 247
Hecataeus of Abdera, 83, 219–20
hekhalot literature, 272–3

Heliopolis, 80, 83, 98, 203, 224
Hellenism, Jewish, 3, 5, 6, 8, 216–17
Hellenization, 66, 86–7, 97, 115, 125, 153, 197, 255–6
Hengel, Martin, 5
Heracleopolis, 80, 85–6, 104, 113 n. 65, 233–4
Herakles, 117
Hermippus of Smyrna, 26, 42
Hermopolis, 84
Herod, king, 279
Herodian dynasty, 120
Herodotus, 73–4, 182, 201, 260
Hierapolis, Phyrgia, necropolis of, 115–16
Hieronymus of Cardia, 80
High Priest, 9, 30, 32, 33, 51, 54, 60, 72, 77, 82, 108, 126, 224, 229, 235–6, 241
Hillel and Shammai, Houses of, 109
Hippocrates, 61–2
historiography, Egyptian, 262
history
    Egyptian, 83
    Jewish sense of, 229–30
    and memory, 47–8
Hody, Humphry, 38–40, 42
holiness, of scripture, 214–15
Hollander, John, 158–9
Holocaust, 162
Holy of Holies, 166
homeland, 12, 93, 94, 96, 100, 101–2, 194, 197
Homer, 12, 86, 154–5, 164, 239–43, 251, 268, 305
    Iliad, 154–5, 266
homophony, 160
Hoshaya, Rabbi, 298 n. 65, 310
Hyrcanus, son of Joseph, 82

identity, 58–9, 119, 125, 148, 154, 240–1, 245
    Christian, 280, 302 n. 302
    cultural, 62, 114
    Jewish, 6–7, 8, 12, 13–14, 48–50, 51, 91, 92–3, 106–7, 114, 116, 124, 133, 146–7, 152–3, 156, 175, 179–80, 191, 195, 205–6, 208–9, 216–17, 222–3, 225, 229–30, 255–7, 281–2, 309–10

idolatry, 6, 11, 177, 179, 184, 194–205, 232, 285–6
idols, 162, 190, 194–205. *See also* idolatry
Idumaea, 81
images, 190, 227–8
  biblical illustrations, 111–12
  worship, *see* idolatry
imperialism, *see* Ptolemies, imperialism of
impurity, 200
India, 72
infanticide, 233
infinitive-absolute construction, *see* qatol qatal
inscriptions, 4, 8, 22 n. 36, 93 n. 2, 104, 105 n. 37, 109, 112, 115–17, 118, 123–4, 130, 227–8, 230–1, 234, 237, 307
interlinear text, 156
interlinear theory, 143–52, 307 n. 96
intermarriage, 185. *See also* marriage
interpretation, *see* exegesis
interpreters, 26, 137–8, 139, 219, 228, 234
intertextuality, 161, 207, 224–5, 250
Ioudaioi, 8, 79, 80, 102, 106, 120
Irenaeus, 283, 299 n. 69, 311
Isaiah, book of, 100, 130 n. 16, 144, 161, 173 n. 148, 174, 188, 196, 201–2, 203, 226, 265, 299
Islamic writings, 37, 210
Isocrates, 77
Israel, land of, 94, 100, 101, 167, 168 n. 140

Jason of Cyrene, 97, 114, 158, 193, 218, 221
Jeremiah, 223, 275
  book of, 101, 160, 199–200, 300
Jericho, 81
Jerome, 15–16, 140 n. 47, 149, 152 n. 88, 284–6, 292, 294, 301, 302, 306, 311
Jerusalem, 9, 54–5, 59, 60–1, 66, 72, 81, 82, 83, 87 n. 67, 94, 95, 97, 98, 99–100, 100, 101–2, 109, 119, 121–2, 123, 126, 146–7, 147, 149, 173–4, 178, 179, 194, 199, 201, 217, 219, 221, 228 n. 60, 230, 235, 275, 278
Jesus, 85, 111, 275, 279, 298–9
  movement, 244–5, 256, 289, 312 n. 110
Jews, *see also* Judaism
  of Alexandria, 3, 9, 15, 20–1, 32, 35, 41, 51, 52–4, 63, 76 n. 35, 79, 86–7, 88, 92, 97–8, 103, 112–13, 121, 126, 135–6, 140, 148–9, 150, 152, 156, 163, 207, 211, 216, 222, 229, 240, 242, 256, 278, 312
  of Asia Minor, 99, 103, 117
  of Babylonia, 122
  beliefs of, 33
  Byzantine communities, 280 n. 5
  in the city of Rome, 104, 116, 121
  communities, 7, 8, 10, 104–5, 112, 121, 227, 243–4
  of the Egyptian countryside, 103
  expulsion of, 121
  German, 6, 309–10
  Greek-speaking, 1, 3, 7, 12–13, 50, 172, 175, 211–12, 216, 230, 232, 237, 255–7, 309, 313
  of Judaea, 7, 99, 101, 115
  of medieval Spain, 146
  of Palestine, 95, 110, 123
  population size, 106
  practices of, 107–8, 232
  of Provence, 146
  in the Roman army, 108
  of Rome, 116
  as a subject people, 193
  of Syria, 72
Job, 220, 223
  book of, 144, 161, 178, 186, 192, 231 n. 76
John, Gospel of, 188, 246. *See also* Gospels
John Chrysostom, 284
John Hyrcanus, 99
John Tzetzes, 45
Joppa (Jaffa), 95
Jordan River, 81, 102, 149
Joseph, 272
Joseph, son of Tobias, 82
Joseph and Asenath, 48, 108–9, 203, 224, 237

Josephus, 116, 255, 280, 298 n. 64
 on Alexander's visit to Jerusalem, 66, 72
 on anti-Judaism, 208 n. 61, 263–4
 Against Apion, 35–6, 49 n. 69, 75–6, 97 n. 11, 98 n. 14, 116, 119, 172, 208 n. 61, 218, 229–30, 236–7, 240, 243, 260, 263–4, 266
 closeness to scripture, 13, 141, 168, 183, 229–30, 252–4
 on Daniel, 198
 on Greekness, 75–6
 Jewish Antiquities, 35–6, 49 n. 69, 72 n. 22, 98, 101–2, 105, 120, 141, 168, 183, 198, 207, 220–1, 229–30, 234, 237 n. 94, 252–4, 269
 on Jewish authors, 218–20
 on Jewish diaspora, 101–2, 105–6, 113 n. 64
 on the Jewish homeland, 101–2
 on Jewish military settlements, 80
 on the Jewish revolt, 110–11, 121, 228–30
 on the Jewish temple in Leontopolis, 98–9 n. 16, 110–11
 Jewish War, 80, 98 n. 16, 101, 110–11, 118, 121, 188, 220–1, 230, 237 n. 94
 on Judaism, 75–6, 172, 218–23, 234–5, 236–7, 243, 260
 on Judaizers, 118, 119, 121
 and language, 147, 166–8, 188, 190, 251–4
 on the *Letter of Aristeas*, 31, 38 n. 30, 141, 222–3, 285, 313 n. 112
 on the Maccabees, 49 n. 69, 97 n. 11, 220–1
 on Manetho, 83
 on Moses, 229, 269
 on Moses' Ethiopian expedition, 49 n. 69
 on the Oniad family, 98
 in other authors, 4, 15, 285
 on other authors, 260, 266
 on plot reversal tales, 112 n. 62
 as a Roman author, 101, 230 n. 73
 on Roman decrees on Jewish privileges, 99, 105–6, 108, 120, 207
 on the Tobiad family, 82, 98
 on the translation of the Torah, 15
Josiah, king, 91
Judaea, 9, 17, 30, 33, 52, 54, 79, 80–1, 88, 94–5, 97, 99–100, 102, 106, 115, 123, 192, 212, 217, 218, 221, 256–7, 278
Judaean desert, 94
Judah Hanasi, Rabbi, 109
Judaism, 2–3, 8, 12–14, 21, 72, 73, 74, 76, 79, 88, 94, 99, 105, 107–8, 109, 110–11, 111, 115, 118, 120, 164–5, 172, 208, 215, 218, 251, 255, 281–2, 288–90, 295–6, 299 n. 69, 302–3, 305
 practices, 2, 10, 20 n. 29, 21–2, 33, 251. *See also* Temple, cult
Judaizers, 105, 118–19, 121, 230–1, 233
Judges, book of, 192
Judith, book of, 5, 170, 235
Julius Caesar, 45 n. 52, 120
Justin Martyr, 43 n. 47, 278, 298–301, 313
Justinian, emperor, 291, 302–3, 306

Karaites, 142
King James Bible, 6, 90, 158
Kingdoms
 first book, 198–9
 second book, 128, 188
 third book, 188
kings, *see* Ptolemies; rulers; Seleucids
Kings, books of, 91, 224, 250, 267, 291. *See also* Kingdoms
Kittel, Gerhard, 164, 165 n. 130

Lagid dynasty, 37, 68, 89
Lamentations, book of, 278, 312
Latin, 104, 267
law
 codes, 28–9, 84, 88
 Egyptian, 84
 Greek, 85–6
 Jewish, 13, 15, 21–3, 30, 35–6, 50, 52, 53, 73, 77, 78, 84–6, 90, 111, 139, 142, 228, 236, 237, 243
 lawgivers, 75, 228–9, 232, 268, 269
 Roman, 104, 123

legal and bureaucratic writings, 171, 302–3
Leontopolis, temple of, 98–9, 110, 224 n. 48
Letter of Aristeas, 9, 15, 27, 28, 30–2, 51, 125–6, 130, 140–1, 149, 178, 191, 222–3, 232, 241, 250, 259–60, 261, 279, 282–5, 304 n. 83, 313
  as a 'charter myth', 3, 50
  dating of, 34–5, 41, 50
Letter of Jeremiah, 11, 196 n. 45, 199–200
Leviticus, book of, 21, 90, 91, 231, 232
lexicography, 164–5
literacy, 157–8
literalism, 7, 8. *See also* translation, word for word translation
literature, 218, 241
  'foreign', 43, 46
  genres, 243, 246, 249, 250–1, 261
  Hellenistic-Jewish, 4, 10–13, 21, 23, 114–15, 171, 222–4, 249, 260, 265–70, 280–1, 288, 313
  knowledge of, 250–1
  pagan, 268–70 *See also* Wisdom Literature
liturgy, 133, 172, 214
Livius Andronicus, 25
Livy, 29
Longinus, 188, 268–9
Lucian the Presbyter, 16–17
Luke, Gospel of, 246–7, 247 n. 28. *See also* Acts, book of; Gospels
Lyceum, 75–6
Lycian curse texts, 118
Lycophron, 287
Lysimachus of Jerusalem, 185

Maccabees, 82, 97, 99, 146, 174, 175, 176, 195, 197, 221, 235–6, 249
  books of, 48, 186, 214, 218
  first book, 96, 170, 175, 190, 197, 221, 250
  fourth book, 99, 114, 166, 170, 178, 192–3, 218 n. 29, 226–7, 249
  second book, 78, 97, 99, 100, 114, 147, 158, 170, 192–3, 218, 221
  third book, 49, 53–4, 97 n. 11, 114, 170, 178, 203, 226, 231 n. 76, 235–6, 250
Macedon, 305
magic, 13, 118, 270–6. *See also* curse bowls, 272
  Hadrumentum love charm, 273–4
  hebraikos logos, 275–6
  and Judaism, 272–6
  magical papyri, *see* papyri, magical
  Prayer of Jacob, 274
Manetho of Sebennytus, 83, 262–3
manumission, 118
Marcionites, 311
Marcus Antonius, 120
Mareotis, lake, 110, 229, 280–1
Mark, Gospel of, 85, 246. *See also* Gospels
marriage, 85, 108
Martial, 108
Martin Luther, 6, 310
martyrdom, 97, 99, 147, 192–3, 226–7, 236, 237 n. 94
  Christian, 48
masekhet sefer torah, 304
masekhet soferim, 304
Masoretic text, 11, 19, 132 n. 22, 133, 179, 183, 189, 231 n. 75
Matthew, Gospel of, 85, 246. *See also* Gospels
Megasthenes, 72
megillah, *see* scrolls
Megillat Ta'anit, 304 n. 85. *See also* Ta'anit
memorization, 157–8, 173
memory, collective Jewish, 8, 9, 29, 35, 47–9, 51, 53 n. 84, 58, 64, 95–6, 205–6, 222–3, 229, 255, 273–4, 280
Memphis, 71
Menander, 56–60, 63, 70, 77 n. 39
Mendelssohn, Moses, 6, 309
menorah, 111
Midrash, 91, 172, 178, 182, 210, 220, 224, 253, 294, 303, 311
mikra, 157
mines of Arabia, 80–1
Minor Prophets Scroll, 17, 158 n. 103, 225, 247, 248, 301 n. 75

Index

Mishnah, 94, 109, 147, 210, 241, 289, 302, 308
missions, Christian, 119
modern scholarship, 38–42
Momigliano, Arnaldo, 217, 258, 261, 287 n. 31
monarchies, Hellenistic, 11, 67–8, 178–80
monarchs, *see* Ptolemies; rulers; Seleucids
monotheism, 186–7, 214
Mordecai, 111, 112, 184, 235
Moses, 29, 49 n. 69, 52, 83, 108, 131, 139, 178, 190, 220, 228–9, 231 n. 75, 243, 262–3, 268, 269–70, 271–2
multilingual texts, 25–6, 84, 272–4
mysteries, 245–6, 271–2
mysticism, Jewish, 272–3
myth
 charter myth, 3, 49–50, 222–3
 historical, 9, 42, 47–50
 historicity of, 27, 28

Nahal Hever, 17, 225, 301 n. 75
names, Jewish, 117 n. 79
Nebuchadnezzar, 197–9
Nehemiah, book of, *see* Ezra-Nehemiah, book of
neologisms, 11, 166, 168, 171, 225
Nero, emperor, 117
Nerva, emperor, 122
Nestle, Eberhard, 5
New Testament, 4, 5, 12, 127, 130, 161, 166, 188, 217, 246–8, 257, 278–9, 282, 286–7, 289, 309
Nike, goddess, 72
Noah's blessing, 258, 290
nomos, 13, 22–3, 75, 84, 90, 120, 165, 181–2, 228 n. 60, 233, 236–7, 255. *See also* Torah
Numbers, book of, 231 n. 76
Numenius of Apamea, 269–70

Ocellus Lucanus, 267
Odyssey, 25
'old Greek' translation, 14, 18, 288–9, 295, 297–8, 301

Old Testament, 13, 127, 165, 246, 287, 298, 311
Oniad family, 82, 98–9, 110
Onias, 80, 98, 98 n. 16
Onkelos, 290, 311 n. 109. *See also* Aquila
Oracle of the Potter, 136
oral tradition, 21–2, 47, 49, 142, 157, 210, 237, 240, 302
orientalizing, 185
Origen, 16, 18, 19 n. 28, 128, 269, 282, 286, 288, 291, 292, 293, 295–8, 306–7, 309, 310–11
ossuaries, 116
Ostia, 104, 123
Oxyrhynchus, 84, 267

pagans, 91
Palestinian Patriarch, 109
Palladius, 311
papyri, 2, 4, 17, 84–5, 103–4, 113 n. 65, 122, 130, 131 n. 18, 137, 141–2, 148–9, 158, 187, 207 n. 58, 233–4, 254, 266–7, 291
 magical, 13, 109, 270–6
parataxis, 159
Passover, *see* festivals
Pastoral Epistles, 247
Patriarch, in Palestine, 109
Patriarchs, biblical, 107, 109 n. 53, 132, 223, 272, 283, 286
patronage, 87, 88–9, 95, 125, 171, 193
Paul, 105, 108, 128, 158, 200, 201–2, 235, 292
 Epistles, 246–8
Pausanias, 42
Pentateuch, *see* Torah
'people of the book', 210–11
Pergamum, 99, 105–6, 242, 305
peripatetics, 74–5, 76, 78, 220
Persian empire, 84, 205
pesher, 249. *See also* exegesis
Peter, saint, 281
Petronius, 267
P.Fouad Inv. 266, 2, 17, 187 n. 27
Pharaoh, 53–4
Pharisees, 8, 110, 241, 292
Pharos island of, 30, 35, 49, 52, 69
Philemon, 56, 59

Philiscus of Miletus, 267
Philo of Alexandria, 103, 173 n. 148, 221–2, 298 n. 65
 de Abrahamo, 229 n. 69
 allegory in, 109–10, 111, 220, 227 n. 58, 241–2
 on ascetics, 110
 Christianization of, 280–2, 282, 288
 on conversion, 119
 on education, 255–6
 Embassy to Gaius, 228
 etymologies in, 149–50, 254 n. 48
 exegesis, 132 n. 24, 149–50
 on God, 191
 and Greek, 171 n. 146
 on Greek and Hebrew, 139–40
 and Greek literature, 114
 his knowledge of Hebrew, 149–50
 idolatry in, 203 n. 52
 on infanticide, 233
 on Jewish diaspora, 101–2, 104–5
 on the Jewish homeland, 101–2
 on Jewish population size, 106
 on Jewish practices, 232, 237
 on the Jewish temple in Leontopolis, 110
 and language, 166, 190
 Legatio ad Gaium., 105, 108, 158, 232
 on the *Letter of Aristeas*, 35–6, 221–2, 222–3, 313
 Life of Moses, 35, 139, 228–9, 233 n. 81, 313
 de Migratione Abrahami, 111, 229 n. 69, 232, 242
 on Moses, 139, 178, 228–9
 de Mutatione Nominum, 132 n. 24
 in other authors, 13
 de Providentia, 110
 on Ptolemy II Philadelphus, 68–9
 Quod Deus Immutabilis Sit, 191
 reception of, 217–18, 280–1
 on Roman decrees on Jewish privileges, 108
 on scripture, 228
 de Specialibus Legibus, 119 n. 84, 229 n. 64
 and teaching, 172–3
 on the Torah, 22
 on the translation of the Torah, 35–6, 139–40, 251–2
 de Virtutibus, 119 n. 84, 227 n. 58
 de Vita Contemplativa, 110, 229 n. 68, 251–2
 vocabulary in, 23, 190
Philo the elder, 219, 266 n. 19
Philo the epic poet, 115
Philocrates, 62, 83
Phocylides (Pseudo-Phocylides), 232–3
Phoenicia, 80, 102
Phrygia, 230–1
pilgrimage, 110
Pisistratus, 77, 239–40
Pithom stele, 26
Plato, 74, 243, 251–2, 269–70
 Middle Platonism, 242
Pliny, 207 n. 59
Pliny the Elder, 26–7, 45–6
Plutarch, 268
polemic, Jewish-Christian, 13–14, 294–301
politeuma, 80, 85–6, 103–4, 113, 116, 233–4
Polybius, 171, 188
Pontus, 310
Posidippus, 67–8, 69, 70–1
post holders, 113, 117
post-colonialism, 7
power, 192–3, 196–7, 204, 208, 236
 display of, 67–70, 88
 vocabulary for, 177–90
prayers, 76, 100, 108, 133, 147, 184–5, 226, 235–6
priests, 199, 200
 Egyptian, 55, 83, 84, 136
 of imperial cult, 117
 Jewish, 97, 98, 107, 110. *See also* High Priest
prisoners of war, 30, 32, 33, 41, 51, 53, 54, 65, 73, 74 n. 28, 79, 88
Prophets, Hebrew Bible division, 22, 45, 100–1, 151, 168, 170, 172–3, 175, 186, 188, 203, 213, 214, 215, 226–7, 233, 235, 295, 298, 312
proselytes, 117, 119, 121, 162, 290, 296
Proverbs, book of, 144, 169, 177–9, 182, 186, 226, 230, 305–6

Psalms, book of, 22, 100, 133, 161, 166, 168, 174, 181, 185–6, 187, 188, 188–90, 195, 214, 224–5, 226, 244, 247, 251, 275, 290, 300
Pseudo-Eupolemus, 219
Pseudo-Hecateus, 115, 166 n. 136, 219–20
Pseudo-Longinus, *see* Longinus
Ptolemies, 2, 88, 37, 68, 89, 179–83, 182–3. *See also* rulers
  cultural policies of, 7, 9, 43–4, 55–62, 66, 70, 79, 86, 88–9, 154, 261 n. 8
  imperialism of, 67–8
  wars, 67
Ptolemy I Soter, 42, 58–9, 67–9, 71, 77, 79, 80, 83, 219
Ptolemy II Philadelphus, 9, 15, 27, 30, 31–3, 36–7, 40, 42, 46 n. 58, 51, 53–4, 61, 62, 64, 66, 67–9, 72–3, 77, 79, 81–2, 88–9, 92, 97, 120, 125, 150, 282–3, 285–6, 303–4, 305
  procession of, 69–70, 72, 265
  wars of, 67
Ptolemy III Euergetes I, 26, 44, 46 n. 58, 55, 82
Ptolemy IV Philopator, 26, 53–4, 71, 79, 97 n. 11, 226
Ptolemy V Epiphanes, 26
Ptolemy VI Philomotor, 35 n. 20, 76, 78, 97–8
Ptolemy VIII Euergetes II (Physkon), 97 n. 11, 174
purification, 197
purity, 120, 200, 201
  regulations, 91, 108
Pythagoras, 260

qatol qatal formation, 128–9, 159–60
Qohelet, book of *see* Ecclesiastes, book of
Qumran, 177 n. 4, 195, 199, 213–14, 244–6, 248, 256
  community, 12, 173
  scrolls, 6, 12, 17, 19, 142, 146–7, 227 n. 57, 236, 245–6, 249, 250
  site, 17
Quran, 210

Rabbinic
  Judaism, 94, 241
  literature, 96, 142, 151, 178, 272–3, 279, 290, 294, 297
  tradition, 6, 11, 21, 36–7, 91, 107, 108, 109, 123, 145, 147, 151, 153, 157, 210, 215, 220, 234, 280, 288–90, 292, 293, 294, 296, 297, 302, 303, 304–5, 306, 307–8, 311–13
Rahlfs, Alfred, 292–3
Rashi, 29
reading aloud, 157, 173. *See also* sound, of the biblical language; Torah, reading
'rejection paradigm', 61
religion
  Graeco-Egyptian, 43–4, 69–70
  Jewish, *see* Judaism
  Roman, 29
religious 'marketplace', 119, 270
resistance, cultural, 156
Revelation
  book of, 105–6, 247
  seven churches of, 105–6
revolts, 197
  Egyptian, 82
  Jewish, 6, 82, 94, 97, 99, 100, 103, 110–11, 119, 121, 122, 123, 147, 174, 176, 204, 209, 221, 228, 230 n. 73, 278, 312
'rewritten Bible', 223–4
Rheneia, tablets from, 231
rituals, *see* Judaism, practices
Romans, *see* Paul, Epistles
Rome, 6, 27, 29, 44, 50 n. 76, 94, 99–100, 102, 103–4, 105–6, 111, 113, 119, 120, 121–3, 202, 206–7, 218, 228, 230, 277, 278, 308, 310–11
  administrative vocabulary, 175
  city of Rome, 22 n. 36, 25, 75 n. 30, 101, 104, 116, 121, 180 n. 13, 221, 228, 230, 234, 281, 305–6
  edicts on Jewish privileges, *see* edicts
  tria nomina, 117
Rosenzweig, Franz, 24, 309
Rosetta Stone, 26
Rufinus, 285

rulers, 7, 9, 11, 25–6, 51–2, 55–60, 67–8, 80, 81–2, 84, 87, 88, 91, 92, 95–9, 112–13, 119–20, 175, 176, 177–98, 200–8, 218, 226, 228–9. *See also* cults, ruler cult; Ptolemies; Seleucids
Ruth, book of, 278, 312

Sabbath, 2, 172, 232, 235, 237
  observance, 108
sacred text, 3, 18, 20, 139–42, 214–15, 227, 285
sacrifice, 167
Sadducees, 241
Samaritans, 219, 266, 311
Samuel, books of, 111, 132 n. 23, 192, 198. *See also* Kingdoms
sanctity of scripture, *see* holiness
Sardis, 112, 123–4, 234
Saul of Tarsus, 110
Scaliger, Joseph Justus, 38–9, 42
Schlegel, Friedrich von, 154
Schürer, Emil, 211
scribes, 2, 17 n. 21, 18, 142, 150 n. 77, 157, 225, 234, 237, 304, 305, 306
scrolls, 15, 17 n. 21, 18, 73, 87, 90, 91, 111, 142, 147, 158, 173, 210, 228, 266–7
Scythopolis, 95
second sophistic, 56, 59 n. 102, 226
Second Temple period, 94
sefer, *see* scrolls
Sefer Yosippon, 37
Seleucia, 112
Seleucids, 79, 82, 120, 174, 197, 205, 230. *See also* rulers
Semitisms, 184, 247
Septimius Severus, emperor, 121
Septuagint, *passim*
  Christian appropriation, *see* Christian, appropriation of Jewish Literature
  divine origin of, 51, 139–40, 282–6, 302, 313
  Jewish reception of, 6, 13–14, 52
  language of, 4, 6, 131–6, 139–42, 145, 152–3, 156, 159–61, 162–3, 169–72, 175, 177–81, 207, 224–5, 231

  techniques, 162–3
  term, 14–16
  textual transmission and criticism, 16–20
  translators, *see* translators, of the Septuagint
  vocabulary of, 11, 131–3, 161, 163–72, 174, 175, 177–81, 186–91, 201, 207–8, 224–6, 231, 293, 306
Serapeum, 55
  library of, 43–6, 261
Serapis, 43–4, 55, 61, 265 n. 15
shema prayer, 147, 309
sicarii, 111
Sidon, 121
Sirach, book of, *see* Ecclesiasticus, book of
Siwah oasis, 71
soldiers, Jewish, 85, 103, 108
Solomon, 219, 224, 272, 275
  judgment of, 267
Song of Songs, book of, 265 n. 15, 312–13
sound, of the biblical language, 10, 157–61
stereotypes, 107–8, 165, 166, 177
Stobi, 109, 112
Stoicism, 252
  allegory, 149
Strabo, 71, 75, 106, 112–13
Suetonius, 122
supersessionism, 282
Susannah and the Elders, 5, 176, 198, 295
Symmachus, 168, 284 n. 18, 293, 296, 310–11
synagogue, 7, 10, 41, 98, 103, 104, 105, 109, 111, 113, 117–18, 119, 120, 123–4, 133, 150–1, 172–3, 199, 201, 228, 234–5, 291, 302–3, 307, 308, 312 n. 110
  house synagogues, 112
'synod of Jamnia', 288–9
Syria, 3, 79, 80, 82, 102, 118, 121

Ta'anit, 304
Tacitus, 55–6, 61, 233, 264
Talmud, 36, 89, 96, 103, 210, 290, 303–4

Index

tannaim, 94, 304–5
Targum, 150–1, 152 n. 88, 172–3, 253, 290, 308, 311
Teacher of Righteousness, 245
Temple, the, 8, 12, 33, 54, 69, 72, 91, 97, 108, 119, 120, 121, 123, 166, 176, 197, 219, 221, 223, 224, 231–2. *See also* Holy of Holies
  cult, 8 n. 14, 111, 232, 251
  destruction, 94, 99, 101, 110, 111, 121, 278, 281–2, 288–9, 312
  furniture, 51, 54
Temple tax, 110, 122, 232
Tertullian, 43, 44–6, 120, 261, 283–4
tetragrammaton, 2, 17 n. 21, 146–7, 187. *See also* Divine Name
text-centredness, 7–8, 12, 12–13, 210, 227, 234, 237–8, 239, 244–5, 247–8, 249–50, 255–7
Thackeray, Henry St John, 287
Theocritus, 67, 265 n. 15
Theodectes the tragedian, 77, 260–1
Theodoret, 128 n. 8, 151
Theodosius II, emperor, 46
Theodotion, 198, 199, 284 n. 18, 296, 299 n. 69, 301 n. 75, 310–11. *See also* Bel and the Dragon
Theodotus, 219, 251
  inscription, 235
Theological Dictionary of the New Testament (TDNT), 164
Theophrastus, 57, 59, 67, 76–7, 78
Theopompus of Chios, 77
Theopompus the historian, 260–1
Third Reich, 164
Tiberius, emperor, 121
titles, honorific, 113
Titus, emperor, 121, 228 n. 60
Tobiad family, 81–2, 98
Tobit, book of, 5, 170
Torah, 3, 8, 15, 20–3, 29, 34, 50, 59, 64, 75, 83, 84–5, 87, 90, 91, 107, 111, 123, 151, 165, 168, 186, 210–11, 213, 215, 223, 226, 227 n. 58, 228, 232, 233–6, 243, 245, 251, 253, 255–6, 258, 283–4, 285, 290, 304, 307 n. 96, 311, 313
  reading, 2, 10, 172–3, 215 n. 21, 234–5, 302–3, 312 n. 110

teaching, 172
Torah shrines, 111–12, 235
Tosefta, 94, 308
Toubias the Ammonite, 81–2
Tractate megillah, 36
tragedy, 86
Trajan, emperor, 103, 122, 204, 207 n. 59, 209 n. 63, 278, 312
translation, *see also* dragomans; interpreters
  ancient precedents, 24–5, 136
  as enterprise, 1–2, 4, 88, 114, 125, 136, 144, 163, 175, 309–10
  'foreignizing', 153–5
  later versions, 13–14, 87
  techniques, 7, 10, 19 n. 28, 127, 128–30, 153–5, 156–7, 159–61, 173 n. 152, 189, 240, 253, 291–3, 306. *See also* word for word translation
  word for word translation, 2, 6, 7, 10, 127, 132, 133–4, 137, 140, 143–4, 145, 290–3, 297–8, 307–9, 312
translators, of the Septuagint, 90, 138, 234
  foundation story, 119–20
  as men of culture, 54
  tradition of the seventy-two, 9, 15, 20, 30, 32–3, 35–7, 43, 52, 54, 59, 60–2, 64–5, 87, 234, 282–3, 298–9, 302
translocation, 56–1
trilingualism, 152, 163
Trojan War, 240
Trypho, 298–300
typology, 250
tyrants, 11, 61, 77, 178, 192, 202, 203, 206, 226, 236

versification, 146
Vespasian, emperor, 99, 110, 253
vocabulary
  of Christian theology, *see* Christian theology
  Roman administrative, 175
  of the Septuagint, *see* Septuagint
Vossius, Isaac, 39
Vulgate, 162, 183, 285, 301

wars
    first Syrian War, 67 n. 10
    fourth Syrian War, 79
Wisdom Literature, 22, 169, 178, 182, 203, 233
Wisdom of Solomon, 11, 114, 181–2, 186, 200–2, 204, 207–8, 209
women, 117, 123, 145, 182–3, 227 n. 58
    post holders, 113
word for word translation, *see* translation
writing, importance of, 157

Writings, Hebrew Bible division, 214, 215, 312

Yavneh, 289. *See also* 'synod of Jamnia'
Yom Kippur, *see* festivals, Jewish, Yom Kippur

Zechariah, book of, 231
Zenodotus of Ephesus, 42
Zenon archive, 26, 81–2, 87
Zeus, god, 32, 73–4, 118, 187
Zoroaster, 26–7, 45–6